THE ROUTLEDGE COMPANION TO DECOLONIZATION

'Packed with factual information, this book ranges across individual colonies and empires with considerable assurance'

Martin Thomas, University of Exeter

The decolonization of the European colonies in Africa and Asia was perhaps the most important historical process of the twentieth century. Within less than two decades from 1947 to the mid-1960s several colonial empires disappeared and scores of new nations became independent. Altogether it had taken more than three centuries to expand and consolidate these empires, yet it took less than twenty years for colonialism to become an anachronism.

This essential companion to the process of decolonization includes thematic chapters as well as a detailed chronology, a thorough glossary, biographies of key figures, suggestions for further reading, maps and a guide to sources. Examining decolonization in Africa, Asia, the Caribbean and the Pacific, this guide explores:

- The global context for decolonization
- Nationalism and the rise of resistance movements
- Resistance by white settlers to moves towards independence
- Hong Kong and Macau and decolonization in the late twentieth century
- Debates surrounding neocolonialism, and the rise of 'development' projects and aid
- The legacy of colonialism in law, education, administration and the military.

An invaluable resource for students and scholars of the colonial and post-colonial eras, this volume is an indispensable guide to the reshaping of the world in the twentieth century.

Dietmar Rothermund is Professor Emeritus of South Asian History at the University of Heidelberg. He is chairman of the European Association of South Asian Studies. His publications include *The Global Impact of the Great Depression* (1996), and (with Hermann Kulke) *A History of India* (2004).

Routledge Companions to History
Series Advisors: Chris Cook and John Stevenson

Routledge Companions to History offer perfect reference guides to key historical
events and eras, providing everything that the student or general reader needs to
know. These comprehensive guides include essential apparatus for navigating
through specific topics in a clear and straightforward manner – including
introductory articles, biographies and chronologies – to provide accessible and
indispensable surveys crammed with vital information valuable for beginner and
expert alike.

The Routledge Companion to Medieval Europe
Baerbel Brodt

The Routledge Companion to Twentieth Century Britain
Mark Clapson

The Routledge Companion to Britain in the Nineteenth Century, 1815–1914
Chris Cook

The Routledge Companion to European History since 1763
Chris Cook and John Stevenson

The Routledge Companion to World History since 1914
Chris Cook and John Stevenson

The Routledge Companion to Fascism and the Far Right
Peter Davies and Derek Lynch

The Routledge Companion to the Crusades
Peter Lock

The Routledge Companion to Historiography
Alun Munslow

The Routledge Companion to Britain in the Eighteenth Century, 1688–1820
John Stevenson and Jeremy Gregory

The Routledge Companion to the American Civil War Era
Hugh Tulloch

The Routledge Companion to the Stuart Age, 1603–1714
John Wroughton

THE ROUTLEDGE COMPANION
TO DECOLONIZATION

Dietmar Rothermund

Routledge
Taylor & Francis Group

LONDON AND NEW YORK

First published 2006
by Routledge
2 Park Square, Milton Park, Abingdon, Oxon OX14 4RN

Simultaneously published in the USA and Canada
by Routledge
711 Third Ave, New York, NY 10017

Routledge is an imprint of the Taylor & Francis Group

© 2006 Dietmar Rothermund

Typeset in Times by
Keystroke, Jacaranda Lodge, Wolverhampton

British Library Cataloguing in Publication Data
A catalogue record for this book is available from the British Library

Library of Congress Cataloging in Publication Data
Rothermund, Dietmar, 1933–
The Routledge companion to decolonization / Dietmar Rothermund.
p. cm. — (Routledge companions to history)
Includes bibliographical references and index.
1. History, Modern—1945–1989—Handbooks, manuals, etc.
2. Decolonization—Handbooks, manuals, etc. I. Title. II. Series.
D840.R59 2006
325′.309045—dc22
2005025550

ISBN10: 0–415–35632–6 (hbk)
ISBN10: 0–415–35633–4 (pbk)

ISBN13: 9–78–0–415–35632–9 (hbk)
ISBN13: 9–78–0–415–35633–6 (pbk)

CONTENTS

MAPS

Cartography: Nils Harm, South Asia Institute, University of Heidelberg.

PREFACE

The preparations for this book began about fifty years ago. Of course, I did not know this at that time. I wrote my Ph.D. thesis on the colonial history of Pennsylvania on the eve of the American Revolution. I thus studied a very early incident of 'decolonization'. My main interest was in the interaction of various denominational and political groups and the contribution of this process to the development of democratic institutions. After finishing this work I went to India where I spent three years doing archival work on the history of the Indian freedom movement. I also had a chance to interview Jawaharlal Nehru and many other Indian politicians who had participated in the freedom movement. The main focus of my work was the alternating current of nationalist campaigns and British constitutional reforms. I subsequently continued my research work at the India Office Library in London. On one of my trips to India I also visited East Africa in 1964 and had a long interview with Julius Nyerere. Some of his reactions to my questions reminded me of my interview with Nehru. Seeing Tanganyika, Kenya and Uganda soon after the attainment of independence was a great experience.

My studies of nationalism and decolonization led me to a deeper interest in the economic history of the interwar period. I worked on the agrarian distress caused by the Great Depression and after doing a book on India in the Great Depression, I expanded my research interests to the global impact of the Great Depression. The sufferings of the peasants in this period attracted my attention. They had hardly been taken note of by historians up to that point. In doing all this work I somehow acquired the qualifications for undertaking the present work. Nevertheless, I approached the task of writing this *Companion* with some trepidation. Dealing with the whole world single-handedly seemed to be a frightening challenge. An edited volume with contributions by several area specialists would perhaps have been a better idea. But it would have been impossible to produce a reference work with a unified perspective in this way. Fortunately I could rely on the help of generous colleagues who read my chapters and commented on them in detail. Basudeb Chaudhuri, Caen, read the chapter on neocolonialism; Bernhard Dahm, Passau, read the sections on Southeast Asia; Andreas Eckert, Hamburg, had a quick glance at the Africa chapters; Mark Figueroa, University of the West Indies, had a close look at the chapters on the Caribbean and on the sugar colonies; Bernd Hausberger, Berlin, also read the chapter on the Caribbean; Dane Kennedy, Washington, examined the chapter on the white settlers in Africa; Malyn Newitt, London, commented on the chapter on the Portuguese empire and

Walter Schicho, Vienna, looked in great detail at the chapter on the 'Wind of Change' in Africa. To all of them I owe a debt of gratitude. I also wish to thank my wife, Chitra, for reading the text, correcting mistakes and pointing out some errors of judgement. I am, of course, entirely responsible for all errors which may have remained in the text.

Dietmar Rothermund
Heidelberg, July 2005

INTRODUCTION

The decolonization of the European colonies in Africa and Asia was perhaps the most important historical process of the twentieth century. Within less than two decades, from 1947 to the mid-1960s, several colonial empires disappeared and scores of new nations became independent. Altogether it had taken more than three centuries to expand and consolidate these empires. Compared to this long span of time, the short period of decolonization appears to be only a fleeting moment in the course of history, and yet it is of utmost significance.

The focus of this *Companion* is on this brief period. But further developments up to the return of Hong Kong and Macao to China in 1997 and 1999 respectively will also be taken into consideration. Colonies in Europe, like Cyprus and Malta, will not be discussed in this book, which is exclusively devoted to the emancipation of the colonies in Africa, Asia, the Caribbean and the Pacific. The Union of South Africa is also not covered by the present text. No doubt the regime of white supremacy, which prevailed until 1994, was a quasi-colonial one, but Great Britain had 'decolonized' South Africa long ago. It had become a dominion like Canada in 1910. As far as all other countries are concerned, the phenomenon of 'decolonization' will be seen in a broad perspective. Current usage of this term as reflected in dictionaries is a rather narrow one. 'Decolonize' means 'to release from being a colony, to grant independence'. This attributes the action exclusively to the metropolitan government. Accordingly the student of decolonization would have to find out how, when and why this action was taken. Actually, most studies of decolonization have followed this line. Moritz Julius Bonn (1873–1965), the scholar who coined the term 'decolonization' in the 1930s, however, had something else in mind. Bonn was a German economist who taught at the London School of Economics. In 1932 he had contributed the article on 'Imperialism' to the *Encyclopedia of the Social Sciences* in which he referred to 'decolonization'. He explained the meaning of this term in greater detail in a book which he published in 1938 under the prophetic title *The Crumbling of Empire. The Disintegration of World Economy*.[1] In this book he frequently used the term 'counter-colonization' as a synonym for decolonization. With this new term he wanted to characterize the movements of subject peoples who wished to put an end to colonial rule as well as the trend of global developments, which led to the demise of colonial empires. The subtitle of his book refers to this trend. He witnessed the years of the Great Depression and criticized the practice of exchange manipulations and protectionism. 'Vertical colonialism', as he called the penetration of subject societies,

1

could not be extended any longer. It had passed its zenith and was on the decline. At the most, hungry powers could indulge in wars of conquest like the Japanese did in Manchuria, but this was also bound to fail. Such belated efforts at empire building would only strengthen the forces of counter-colonization. For Europe he predicted an imminent civil war but also a future federation of Europe. Colonial empires, however, were bound to crumble as the epoch in which they could flourish was drawing to an end. Bonn would have agreed with Karl Hack's recent suggestion of a 'broader conception, in which imperialism and globalization are themselves the taproots of decolonization'.[2]

In studying decolonization along the lines suggested by Bonn, one would have to trace the currents of 'counter-colonization' in social, political and economic terms. The acts of metropolitan governments which relinquish crumbling empires would only be one aspect of this study. The movements of colonial subjects as well as the social and economic context of colonial rule would also have to be taken into consideration. Furthermore, the study of decolonization should not stop with the formal transfer of power. There is a complex legacy of colonial rule, which would escape our attention if we stopped at that point. In most cases the national elites that replaced the colonial rulers took over the state as a going concern with all its instruments of governance. They also accepted the boundaries of the colonial states as if they were 'natural' ones. Programmes drafted by national movements before the 'transfer of power' were often shelved in the interest of consolidating the new states. Lifestyles adopted in colonial times often persisted for a long time. Leopold Sédar **Senghor**, the famous poet and statesman of Senegal, had once made a comment on the French policy of assimilation. He had said that the Africans wanted to assimilate and not be assimilated. This distinction sounded convincing, but in the daily lives of colonial 'subjects' it could not be made as easily. Education and language were very pervasive. **Senghor** himself, who was a specialist in West African linguistics, could hardly address his immediate neighbours, the Woloff, in their language and had to resort to French when talking to their leaders.[3]

In recent years the problem of 'decolonizing the mind' has attracted the attention of many scholars. The term 'post-colonialism' has been introduced in this context. There have been lively debates on 'hybrid culture' and on the relation between power and knowledge as exemplified by 'Orientalism'. Unfortunately many of these studies have ended up in the rarified atmosphere of 'discourse analysis'. The *Companion* will not follow this path, but some of the insights of its votaries will be noted. Another contentious subject, which has given rise to heated debates, is 'neocolonialism'. This term has often been used as a slogan by those who have been disappointed with the results of decolonization. The 'promised land', which they had hoped to enter at the attainment of independence, eluded them. Therefore, they argued that formal political independence only masked the harsh reality of continued economic dependence. Actually, the influence which the colonial rulers had hoped to gain by handing over power more or less gracefully receded very soon. But global relations of creditors and debtors emerged, which often proved to be burdensome. This will be discussed at the end of section II.

ORGANIZATION OF THE BOOK

Like all Companions in this series, this book is divided into three key reference sections. The first one begins with a chronology of events, taking the end of the First World War as a point of departure, when the Ottoman Empire was dismantled and the German colonies were entrusted to other colonial powers under mandates of the **League of Nations**. The chronology ends with the return of Hong Kong and Macao to China in 1997 and 1999 respectively. The second part of the first section is devoted to the colonial background without which the process of decolonization cannot be understood. This is followed by a part on historiography which contains a critical evaluation of the major trends of analysis of the process of decolonization. The maps appended to the first reference section show the regions discussed subsequently in the second reference section.

The second section contains eleven thematic chapters. The first chapter outlines the global political and economic context of the process of decolonization. It also contains an analysis of the emergence of nationalism in the colonies and the mobilization of the people into various movements of resistance to colonial rule. The third section of this first chapter deals with Afro-Asian solidarity and non-alignment and the fourth section is devoted to the system of mandates of the League of Nations followed by the organization of trusteeship by the **United Nations**. The subsequent chapters deal with the regional processes of decolonization in Asia, Africa, the Caribbean and the Pacific. Two major problems have been highlighted in specific chapters: the impediments to decolonization, which existed in those colonies where white settlers played an important political role and the peculiar situation of the sugar colonies in which Indian immigrant labour more or less balanced the indigenous population. Another special chapter deals with the Portuguese empire, which was of a rather different kind to the other ones. Portugal was ruled for a long time by an authoritarian government which held that all Portuguese colonies were integral parts of the Portuguese state. 'Decolonization' in this context meant the dissolution of that state and this required a revolution, which took place in 1974. By that time the 'Cold War' was in full swing and this affected the belated decolonization of this diehard empire. The last two chapters of the second reference section are devoted to general themes concerning the fate of the new nations after the attainment of independence. The legacy of colonialism is studied in its various aspects. Finally an attempt has been made to deal with 'neocolonialism'. Some of the economic issues touched upon in earlier chapters will again be taken up in this last chapter.

The third reference section begins with a survey of the sources related to the process of decolonization and recommendations for secondary reading. Metropolitan powers have published selections of archival sources, often amounting to many volumes. Spurred by the publication of such sources, some of the decolonized countries have turned to a documentation of their freedom movements. Such publications will also be included in this survey.

A further part of the third section contains biographies of African, Asian and

Caribbean leaders. The inclusion of European politicians who were in one way or another involved in the process of decolonization would have taken up too much space, the more so as the respective biographical information would have to be amplified by detailing the role which they had played in this context. Most of them held their respective offices only for a short time. The glossary, which follows this biographical section, is aimed at explaining terms contained in the text of the first and the second reference sections. The final bibliography lists only those books that have been used for the preparation of the text. The copious index is the main tool for locating cross-references. For ready reference, all names and terms in the text, which have been also mentioned in the biographies and in the glossary, are printed in bold. This will also help the reader to retrieve information in the text at a quick glance.

I
CHRONOLOGY, BACKGROUND, HISTORIOGRAPHY

CHRONOLOGY

Abbreviations: Com. = Member of the (British) Commonwealth of Nations; Conf. = conference; indep. = independent; occ. = occupy, occupied; Pres. = president; PM = prime minister; Rep. = republic

1914

(Aug. 1) First World War begins

1916

(May) **Sykes-Picot Agreement**. Secret British–French deal concerning Syria, Palestine, etc.

1917

(April 6) USA joins war
British declaration: **responsible govern-ment** is the aim of future constitutional reforms in India
(Nov. 2) **Balfour Declaration**. Jewish national home in Palestine
(Nov.) Bolshevik revolution in Russia. Soviets publish **Sykes-Picot Agreement** and other secret deals

1918

(Jan. 8) Pres. Wilson's speech outlining 14 points, among them plea for the autonomy of the provinces of the Ottoman Empire, international control of colonies, establishment of **League of Nations**

1919

(April 24) Constitution of **League of Nations** adopted

1920

League of Nations sanctions distribution of **mandate territories** among colonial powers
Non-cooperation campaign led by M. K. **Gandhi** (British India)

1922

(Feb. 28) Egypt indep., Head of State: King Fuad, PM S. **Zaghlul**

1927

Congress of Oppressed Nations convened in Brussels by German communist H. Münzenberg, attended by many African and Asian nationalists, including J. **Nehru**

1930

(March–April) Civil Disobedience campaign (Salt March) led by M. K. **Gandhi** in India
(July) Wheat price drops by about 50 per cent, impact of Great Depression noted in Africa and Asia; decline of prices of raw materials reduces value of colonies

1931

(Jan.) Rice price drops by more than 50 per cent. Peasant unrest increases
(March) **Gandhi**–Irwin Pact, suspension of civil disobedience
(Sept.) Second Round Table Conf., London, M. K. **Gandhi** participates

Ceylon (Sri Lanka): Donoughmore Constitution introduces adult suffrage and **responsible government**, following the model of the London County Council rather than the **Westminster model**

1932

(Oct. 3) Iraq indep., becomes member of **League of Nations**, Head of State: King Faisal

1935

(Aug.) Government of India Act passed by British Parliament
(Oct.) Italian troops invade Ethiopia

1936

(March 7) Hitler occ. Rhineland, violates Treaty of Versailles
(May) Mussolini declares annexation of Ethiopia, British and French diplomatic recognition of this fact, Emperor Haile Selassi in exile in Palestine

1937

Indian National Congress forms governments in seven provinces (Hindu majority provinces), Bengal and Punjab (Muslim majority provinces) are governed by regional parties

1939

(Aug. 23) Hitler–Stalin Pact
(Sept. 1–3) Second World War begins
(Oct.) Congress ministries resign in seven provinces of British India

1940

(March 24) Session of the **Muslim League** in Lahore passes 'Pakistan' resolution, M.A. **Jinnah** expounds 'Two Nations Theory' (Hindus and Muslims)

1941

(March 11) American Lend-lease Act passed (supporting Allied war effort) (May) Brit. troops enter Ethiopia, Emperor Haile Selassi reinstated
(June 22) Hitler launches surprise attack against Soviet Union
(Aug. 14) **Atlantic Charter** signed by Churchill and Roosevelt (specifying Allied war aims)
(Dec. 7) Japanese attack American fleet at Pearl Harbour (Hawaii), USA at war. Germany and Italy also declare war on USA

1942

(Feb. 15) Japanese occ. Singapore
(March 7) Japanese occ. Rangoon, Burma, also Indonesia, Philippines, Vietnam
(April) Stafford Cripps, member of British war cabinet, flies to India, offers indep. after the war if **Indian National Congress** and **Muslim League** join a national government and support the war effort; the offer is rejected
(May 29) S. C. **Bose** meets Hitler in Berlin; Hitler sends him to Japan
(June 4) Americans defeat Japanese fleet near Midway Islands (Pacific)
(July 9) **Indian National Congress** passes 'Quit India' Resolution, **Gandhi**, **Nehru** and other leaders are arrested before any action can be taken
(Aug.) 'August Revolution' of Indian nationalists

1943

(Jan. 14–26) Casablanca Conf., Roosevelt and Churchill; demand of 'unconditional surrender' of the enemies
(Jan. 22) Roosevelt visits Sultan of Morocco, encourages Moroccan nationalism
(Feb.) German army corps surrenders at Stalingrad

(Nov. 22–26) Cairo Conf., Roosevelt, Churchill, Chiang Kai-shek
(Nov. 28) Teheran Conf., Roosevelt, Churchill, Stalin

1945

(Feb. 4) Yalta Conf.: Churchill, Roosevelt and Stalin agree on post-war distribution of territories
(April 4) (Brit.) Commonwealth Conference
(April 12) Death of Pres. Roosevelt
(April 25) First Conf. **United Nations** in San Francisco
(May 8) Germany surrenders
(July) Churchill defeated in post-war election by Labour Party, PM C. Attlee forms government, no declaration concerning Indian indep.
(July 17–Aug. 2) Potsdam Conf. of victorious Allies; Brit. requested to occ. South of Indo-China, Chinese North of Indo-China (border: 16th parallel)
(Aug. 6 and 9) USA drops atom bombs on Hiroshima and Nagasaki; (Aug. 15) Japan surrenders
(Aug. 17) **Sukarno** proclaims indep. Rep. of Indonesia; end of Japanese occ. of Malaya, Philippines, Vietnam; also end of Japanese colonial rule in Korea and Taiwan
(Sept. 2) **Ho Chi Minh** proclaims indep. Rep. of Vietnam

1946

(March 22) Transjordania (later: Jordania) indep., Head of State: King **Abdullah**
(April 17) Syria indep.
(Aug. 16) 'Direct Action Day' announced by M. A. **Jinnah**; 'Great Calcutta Killing'
(Aug. 24) J. **Nehru** interim PM of British India

1947

(Aug. 14) Pakistan indep. (Dominion), Com., Governor General: M.A. **Jinnah**, PM Liaquat Ali Khan
(Aug. 15) India indep. (Dominion), Com., Governor General: L. Mountbatten, PM J. **Nehru**

1948

(Jan.) Burma (Myanmar) indep. Rep., Pres. U **Nu**
(Feb.) British inauguration of **Federation of Malaya** against wishes of Malays
(Feb.) Ceylon (Sri Lanka) indep. (Dominion), Com., PM D. S. **Senanayake**
(May) British relinquish **mandate** in Palestine, D. **Ben Gurion** proclaims Rep. of Israel, Jordanian troops occ. remaining part of Palestine

1949

(Feb.) Ceasefire agreement: Arab states and Israel
(Sept.) Division of Vietnam: North Vietnam (Hanoi), Pres. **Ho Chi Minh**, South Vietnam (Saigon), Pres. (ex-Emperor of Annam) Bao Dai
(Dec.) United States of Indonesia indep., Pres. **Sukarno**, PM M. **Hatta**

1950

(June 27) Korean War begins. Global rise of raw material prices enhances value of colonies

1951

Oman indep., Head of State: Sultan Said bin Taimur
(Dec.) Libya indep., Head of State: King Idris

1952

(March) K. **Nkrumah** de facto PM of Gold Coast (Ghana)

1953

(July 27) Korean War ends. Ceasefire agreement at Panmunjon
(Sept.) Central African Federation (Northern and Southern Rhodesia, Nyasaland) established, PM G. Huggins

1954

(April) G. A. **Nasser** seizes power in Egypt
(May) Vietminh forces under General **Vo Nguyen Giap** defeat French at Dien Bien Phu
(June) **Geneva Conference** on Indo-China

1955

(Feb. 24) Iraq and Turkey sign Bagdad Pact (CENTO), subsequently joined by Great Britain, Pakistan and Iran
(April) **Bandung Conf.** (Afro-Asian Solidarity)
(Oct.) South Vietnam indep. Rep. Pres. Ngo Dinh Diem

1956

(Jan.) Sudan indep. Rep.
(March) Morocco indep., Head of State: Sultan **Mohammed V.**
(March) Tunisia indep., PM H. **Bourguiba**
(June 23) **Loi cadre**, French constitutional law for African colonies
(Aug.) French army fights against Algerian **Front de Libération Nationale (FLN)**
(July) G. A. **Nasser**, J. **Nehru** and J. Tito meet on the Yugoslavian island of Brioni and initiate the **Non-aligned Movement**
(Oct. 23) Revolt in Hungary suppressed by Soviet troops
(Oct. 30–Nov. 5) British, French and Israeli troops attack Egypt after **Nasser**'s seizure of Suez Canal in July 1956

1957

(March 6) Ghana indep., PM K. **Nkrumah**
(March 25) Treaty of Rome: Belgium, France, Germany, Italy, Luxemburg, the Netherlands form European Community, the colonial powers secure status of associated membership for the African, Caribbean and Pacific colonies (Art. 131–6)
(July 25) Tunisia Rep., Pres. H. **Bourguiba**

1958

(Jan. 8) Inauguration of the Federation of the West Indies based on the Federation of the West Indies Act, 1956, passed by the British Parliament and a subsequent Order-in-Council of 1957
(March 25) Federal elections, Federation of the British West Indies, PM Grantley **Adams**
(Feb.) United Arab Rep. formed by Egypt and Syria, Pres. G. A. **Nasser**
(July) Military coup in Iraq, General Qasim seizes power
(September) Referendum in French African colonies on the new constitution of the Communauté Française (former **Union Française**)
(September) Guinea indep., Pres. Sekou **Touré**

1959

(Dec.) De Gaulle declares in Dakar, Senegal, that he is now prepared to accept French colonies which opt for indep. as members of **French Community**
Madagascar indep. Pres. Philibert **Tsiranance**

1960

(Jan. 1) Federal Rep. of Cameroon indep., Pres. A. **Ahidjo**
(Jan. 10) PM Macmillan's 'Wind of Change' speech, Accra, Ghana
(Jan.) Congo Conf. in Brussels, Belgium
(April) Rep. of Togo indep., Pres. S. **Olympio**
(June) The following African states

attained indep.: Democratic Rep. of Congo, Pres. J. **Kasavubu**, PM P. **Lumumba**; Mali (incl. Senegal), Pres. M. **Keita**; Mauritania, Pres. M. O. **Daddah**

(July) Somali Democratic Republic (British plus Italian Somalia), Pres. A. Osman Daar

(July) Katanga (Congo) under M. **Tshombe** declares indep.

(Aug.) Gabon, Rep., Pres. L. **M'Ba**; Rep. of the Congo (Brazzaville), Pres. F. **Youlou**, Rep. of Upper Volta (later: Burkina Faso), Pres. M. **Yameogo**, Rep. of Niger, Pres. H. **Diori**

(Sept.) Central African Rep. (Ubanghi-Shari), Pres. D. **Dacko**; Rep. of Chad, Pres. F. **Tombalbaye**. Dahomey, Pres. Hubert **Maga**

(Sept.) P. **Lumumba** (Congo) murdered in Katanga

(Sept. 14) Organization of Petroleum Exporting Countries (OPEC) founded

(Oct.) Nigeria indep. (Dominion), Governor General N. **Azikiwe**, PM T. **Balewa**

(Nov.) Rep. of Ivory Coast, Pres. F. **Houphouet-Boigny**

Ghana Rep., Pres. K. **Nkrumah**

South-West African People's Organization (SWAPO) founded by S. **Nujoma**

1961

(Jan.) De Gaulle authorized by referendum to negotiate with Algerian nationalists

(Aug. 14) J. **Kenyatta** released from prison (Kenya)

Northern part of Cameroon joins Nigeria, southern part joins Rep. of Cameroon

Jamaica votes in a referendum against Federation of the West Indies

(April) Failed revolt of French army in Algeria, formation of Organisation Armée Secrète (OAS) by those opposed to De Gaulle

(April) Sierra Leone indep., Com., PM M. **Margai**

Kuwait indep., Head of State: Emir al-Sabah al Sabah

British Guyana gets internal self-government under People's Progressive Party led by C. **Jagan**

(Sept.) **Belgrade Conf.** of **Non-aligned Movement**

(Dec. 9) Tanganyika indep., Com., PM J. **Nyerere**

(Dec. 18) Indian troops occ. Portuguese colony of Goa

1962

(May) Federation of British West Indies dissolved

(July 3) Algeria indep., Pres. M. A. **Ben Bella**

(Aug. 6) Jamaica indep., Com., PM A. **Bustamante**

(Aug. 13) Trinidad and Tobago indep., Com., PM E. **Williams**

(Aug. 15) Transfer of Dutch New Guinea (West Irian) to Indonesia

(Oct. 9) Uganda indep., PM M. **Obote**

(Oct. 20) China attacks Indian border in Kashmir and Assam

(Oct. 22) Cuban Missile Crisis, Pres. Kennedy's ultimatum

Frente de Libertacao de Mocambique (FRELIMO) established in Dar-es-Salaam, Tanganyika

Western Samoa, indep. (since 1995: Independent State of Samoa)

Rwanda indep., Pres. G. Kayibanda. Burundi indep., Head of State: King Mwami Mambusta IV

1963

(Jan.) S. **Olympio** (Togo) assassinated, successor: N. **Grunitzky**

(Feb. and March) Military coups by members of **Baath Party** in Iraq and Syria

(July 20) Treaty of Jaunde: European Community extends associate membership to 18 African states (according to Art. 131–6, Treaty of Rome)

(Sept.) Singapore indep., PM **Lee Kuan Yew**; Federation of Malaysia inaugurated (Malaya, Sabah, Sarawak, Singapore)

Emergency in British Guyana, British troops sent in

(Oct.) Nigeria Rep., Pres. N. **Azikiwe**, PM T. **Balewa**

(Nov.) Ngo Dinh Diem (Pres. South Vietnam) assassinated, military coup

(Dec.) Kenya indep., PM J. **Kenyatta**

(Dec.) Zanzibar indep., Head of State: Sultan of Zanzibar

Katanga secession ends, M. **Tshombe** in exile

(Dec.) Dissolution of the Central African Federation

(Dec.) Uganda Rep., Pres. **Mutesa II**, PM M. **Obote**

1964

(Jan.) Sultan of Zanzibar overthrown by revolutionaries

(Jan.) Black soldiers start mutinies in several African states, forcing governments to ask for British troops to restore law and order

(Jan.) Palestine Liberation Organization (PLO) founded in Cairo, sponsored by G. A. **Nasser**

(April) Tanganyika and Zanzibar merge: Rep. of Tanzania, Pres. J. **Nyerere**

(May 22) Death of J. **Nehru**

(July) Nyasaland indep., Rep. Malawi, Pres. H. **Banda**

(Aug.) Vietminh patrol boats allegedly attack US destroyer in Gulf of Tonkin, beginning of Vietnam War

(Sept.) **FRELIMO** attacks Portuguese in Mozambique

(Oct.) Second conf. of the **Non-aligned Movement** in Cairo

(Oct. 24) Northern Rhodesia indep., Rep. of Zambia, Pres. K. **Kaunda**

British Honduras (later: Belize) attains internal self-government

1965

(Feb.) The Gambia, indep., Com., PM D. Jawara

Botswana indep., PM Seretse **Khama**

(July 26) Maldives indep.

(Nov.) 'Unilateral Declaration of Independence' of Southern Rhodesia, PM I. Smith

1966

(Jan.) Military coup in Nigeria, Pres. **Azikiwe** overthrown, PM T. **Balewa** and other leading politicians (A. Bello, S. Akintola) assassinated; Pres. General Ironsi

(Feb.) Military coup in Ghana, Pres. K. **Nkrumah** overthrown

(May) British Guyana indep., Com., PM F. **Burnham**

(May) Uganda: PM M. **Obote** overthrows Pres. **Mutesa II**; Pres. M. **Obote**, **Mutesa II** in exile in London

(July) Nigeria: Pres. General Ironsi assassinated, successor: Pres. General Gowon

(Sept.) Bechuanaland (Botswana) Rep., Pres.: Seretse **Khama**

(Oct.) Basutholand (Lesotho) indep., Head of State: King Moshoeshoe II, PM Leabua Jonathan

Swaziland indep., absolute monarchy, King Sobuzha II

(Oct.) United Nations (General Assembly) terminates **mandate** of South Africa in Southwest Africa (Namibia)

(Nov.) Barbados indep., PM Errol Walton **Barrows**

1967

(May) Nigeria: Col. Ojukwu, military commander, Eastern Region, declares indep. of Biafra, Nigerian civil war begins

(June 5–10) Israel occ. East Jerusalem and West Bank (of River Jordan): 'Six Days War' against Egypt, Jordania and Syria

People's Rep. of Yemen (South Yemen and Aden) indep., leaves Com.

1968

(Jan. 31) Nauru indep., Com.
(March 12) Mauritius indep. PM Seewoosagur **Ramgoolam**
(Dec.) Spanish colonies Rio Muni, Fernando Po and other islands indep., (former Equatorial Guinea)

1969

(Dec.) Libya: Military coup, Colonel M. Ghaddafi; King Idris overthrown

1970

(Sept. 28) Death of G. A. **Nasser**
(Oct. 10) Fiji indep., Com., PM Kamisese Mara
Nigeria: Biafran army surrenders, end of civil war

1971

Uganda: Military coup: M. **Obote** overthrown, Pres. General Idi Amin
Sierra Leone Rep., Pres. S. Stevens
(Dec.) United Arab Emirates indep., head of federation of seven emirates: Sheikh Zayed of Abu Dhabi. Bahrain and Qatar, which were supposed to join the federation, attained independence separately

1972

Ceylon Rep., adopts name Sri Lanka, Pres. Sirimavo Bandaranaike

1973

Bahamas indep., Com., PM Lynden **Pindling**

1974

Grenada indep., PM Eric **Gairy**
Guinea-Bissau indep., Pres. Luis **Cabral**

1975

(April) Vietminh occ. Saigon (Ho Chi Minh City); end of Vietnam War
(June) Mozambique indep. Rep., Pres. S. **Machel**
(July) Comores declared indep. by Pres. A. Abdallah
(Nov) Suriname (Dutch Guyana) indep., Pres. Johan **Ferrier**
(Nov.) Angola indep. Rep., Pres. A. **Neto**
(Dec.) Papua New Guinea indep., PM Michael **Somare**

1976

Seychelles indep., PM James Mancham
(July) Indonesia occ. East Timor, which was left by the Portuguese. Tonga indep. kingdom

1977

Djibouti indep. Pres. H. G. **Aptidon**

1978

(July 7) Solomon Islands indep., Com.
(Oct. 1) Ellice Islands (Tuvalu) indep., Com.
Dominica, indep., PM Patrick John
Southern Rhodesia: A. **Muzorewa** forms government tolerated by I. Smith but not recognized by other nations

1979

(July 12) Gilbert Islands (Kiribati) indep. Rep., Com.
St Vincent and the Grenadines, indep., PM Milton Cato
St Lucia, indep. PM John **Compton**
Uganda: M. **Obote** supported by Tanzania overthrows Idi Amin

1980

Zimbabwe (Southern Rhodesia), indep., Pres. R. **Mugabe**

Vanuatu (New Hebrides), indep., PM Walter **Lini**

1981

Belize (Brit. Honduras) indep., PM George **Price**
Antigua and Barbuda indep., PM Vere **Bird**

1983

St Kitts and Nevis indep., PM Kennedy **Simmonds**

1984

Brunei indep., Head of State: Sultan Hassanal Bolkiah

1986

Federated States of Micronesia indep., Compact of Free Association with USA
Marshall Islands indep., Compact of Free Association with USA

1987

(May 14) Military coup in Fiji headed by Colonel S. Rabuka

(Oct. 7) Fiji Rep., leaves Com., Pres. S. Rabuka

1990

(March 21) Namibia indep., Pres. Sam **Nujoma**

1994

Palau indep., Compact of Free Association with USA

1997

Hong Kong transferred to Chinese Sovereignty

1999

Macao transferred to Chinese Sovereignty

2000

(June 13) Treaty of Cotonou (Benin): European Community extends associate membership to 77 African, Caribbean and Pacific states

2002

East Timor indep., Pres. Xanana **Gusmao**

BACKGROUND: THE PHASES OF
EUROPEAN IMPERIALISM

The empires which experienced rapid decolonization after 1945 had been built up over a long period of more than four centuries. During those centuries European imperialism had frequently changed its character. Different powers took the lead in the quest for European expansion. The thrust of this expansion shifted from continent to continent and the economic conditions changed dramatically over time. In the mid-eighteenth century Europe's standard of living was probably somewhat lower than that of most other parts of the world.[1] By 1830 Western Europe had moved far ahead of the rest of the world in this respect. Throughout the nineteenth century the European imperial powers led by Great Britain forged ahead at a fast pace. The fatal sequence of First World War–Great Depression–Second World War then broke the back of European imperialism and prepared the ground for decolonization. Periodizations have at the most a didactic value as they invariably reflect simplifications which scholars may rightly criticize. Nevertheless, an attempt will be made to sketch five phases of European imperialism: 1) From early maritime expansion to the Seven Years War which ended in 1763; 2) The consolidation of colonial rule until the 1870s; 3) The high tide of imperialism until 1914; 4) The sequence war–depression–war; 5) Post-war imperialism as a rearguard action against inevitable decolonization.

The protagonists of the first phase were the Portuguese, the Spanish and the Dutch who established impressive seaborne empires. Advances in shipbuilding and nautical knowledge, the skill of installing guns on ships, the control of trade in precious metals, spices and finally cotton textiles helped to establish European rule overseas. Most European outposts were merely bridgeheads at that time; only in a few places did the Europeans aim at more extensive territorial rule as the Dutch did in the Netherlands Indies (Indonesia) and the Spanish in Latin America. The Dutch also found out about the profits of intra-Asian maritime trade, mostly in textiles, and the British followed them, tapping the enormous wealth of textile production in India. The method of auctioning Asian goods in Amsterdam and London permitted the testing of the European demand for new items and this is how Indian cotton textiles entered the European market in a big way. The growth of trade also gave rise to a financial revolution which was institutionalized in banks such as the Bank of England and the Bank of Amsterdam or in joint stock companies like the English and Dutch East India companies. These institutional innovations which set the pace for future economic development were made around 1600.[2] All this happened when, in terms of per capita incomes and living standards, Europe was not yet ahead of the rest of the world. It was a time of intense European rivalries which often culminated in terrible internecine wars. These wars also produced institutional innovations which then became important for warfare overseas. Well-financed standing armies replaced the rather irregular troops of earlier times. The strategy of combining a powerful field artillery with a well-drilled infantry put an end to cavalry warfare. The 'man on horseback' might still direct the battle, but the cavalry would be mowed down by the superior firepower of artillery and infantry.

The new achievements of international finance and of military strategy culminated in the Seven Years War which was in fact the first 'world' war, raging on three continents and ending with a triumph for Great Britain.[3] The British fought their battles mostly in Canada and India; in Europe they financed allies such as Frederick the Great of Prussia. The French lost this war and with it their Spanish allies. The Spanish had joined the French for political reasons which conflicted with Spanish commercial interests. Both French and Spanish imperialism suffered a setback due to the war. Much of the Spanish empire was decolonized in the second phase of European imperialism. French imperialism was revived once more in the third phase, while in the meantime British hegemony enveloped the globe.

The second phase of European imperialism was dominated by the British, although they suffered a setback in its early years due to the secession of the American colonies. Imperial overstretch forced the British to tax the American settlers who protested against this with the famous slogan: 'No taxation without representation'. At the same time the British were more successful in India which they conquered at the expense of the Indian taxpayer who had no idea of representation as yet. After capturing the rich revenue of Bengal, the British could recover the silver which they had earlier brought to India in order to buy Indian textiles. This financed the war efforts as well as the booming trade in Chinese tea. It has sometimes been argued that 'the plunder of Bengal' financed the Industrial Revolution. There was no such direct connection. The early decades of the Industrial Revolution were marked by the invention of simple labour-saving devices such as spinning jennies and looms driven by waterpower. The entrepreneurs concerned could easily finance these means of production from their earnings, but, of course, the increasing commercial wealth of Great Britain helped them to sell their products. Indirectly, therefore, 'the plunder of Bengal' did contribute to financing the Industrial Revolution.

This 'revolution' was not a sudden event, but rather a slow process. Advances in metal work and mechanical engineering were required before powerlooms could replace handlooms in the 1830s. Finally the steam engine would drive such powerlooms as well as railways and ships, among them the new gunboats which helped the British to win the Opium War against the Chinese. The Industrial Revolution not only added to military power, but also created new outlets for British investments. Railways were built and financed by the British in America and in India at a very rapid rate in the mid-nineteenth century. Steamers crossing the oceans independent of adverse winds brought down freight rates and contributed to the growth of international trade. The telegraph speeded up intercontinental communications. Commercial intelligence was available within a short time and instructions from imperial centres to the colonial periphery could be transmitted with lightning speed. Further progress in the control of international financial markets backed up all these developments. The British were far ahead of their rivals, the French, in this respect. French financial institutions lagged behind the British ones by about 100 years.[4] There had also been a surprising demographic development: in c. 1750 the British Isles were inhabited by about 5 million people whereas France had 27 million; by 1850 the respective figures were 20 and 35 million. Initially the Industrial Revolution came about due to the lack of manpower which necessitated the invention of labour-saving machinery, but as industrialization progressed it offered employment and thus bred an expanding proletariat.

Throughout the second phase of imperialism Great Britain consolidated its rule overseas and produced more and more industrial goods. The years from 1850 to 1875 were a period of rapid economic growth both in Great Britain and in France. Towards the end of this phase, however, industrial growth slowed down while the service sector expanded by leaps and bounds. Much of this was due to the role of the City of London as the centre of international finance. Walter Bagehot, the editor of *The Economist*, remarked at that time that the British Isles would soon be inhabited only by moneylenders and their servants. Invisible earnings from capital investment abroad rivalled industrial exports. The lion's share of British overseas investment from 1865 to 1914 was attracted by North America (34 per cent); India and Ceylon received only a minor share (10 per cent), about the same as Australia.[5]

The third phase of imperialism was characterized by conflicting trends. The Great Depression of the late nineteenth century – a long period of decline of commodity prices in terms of gold – affected the metropolitan countries, but this did not impede their imperialist vigour. Many parts of the globe which had so far not been 'colonized' were now subjected to foreign rule. The European powers competed for territories, very often establishing their claims mainly in order to prevent others from getting there first. The British annexed Upper Burma in 1885 while the French penetrated Indo-China at the same time. Siam (Thailand) was left as a buffer state between them. The **Scramble for Africa** was the most notorious of these imperial endeavours. The British and the French were the main con-testants, but they were now joined by the Germans who had so far not shown much interest in colonial pursuits because they had been busy consolidating their own nation. Chancellor Bismarck, the architect of the German 'Reich', was initially not interested in colonies but he was pushed by German pressure groups to join the fray. Finally he volunteered to act as the 'honest broker' at the Berlin Conference of 1884–1885 where Africa was divided up into suitable pieces. The straight lines on the map show, even today, that the borders of African territories were drawn at a conference table without regard for local realities. It is interesting to note that the **Organization of African Unity (OAU)** endorsed these borders in the 1960s so as to discourage all revisionist claims.

At the time when the imperial powers met in Berlin, they did not yet control these African territorities. Very often they had only bridgeheads on the coast and a rather vague idea of the hinterland. In making actual occupation the criterion for the recognition of territorial rule, the Berlin Conference speeded up the **Scramble for Africa** on the ground. Most imperial powers built railways for this purpose which went straight from the bridgeheads into the hinterland. Wherever this hinterland was suitable for cash crop production for export, the new railways helped to open it up, linking it to the world market. The home markets of the colonies in Africa and Asia were thus subjected to the world market before they actually emerged 'at home'. The decade before the First World War witnessed a boom in all commodity markets. The gains from this trade accrued only to a limited extent to the producers; they benefited the traders, most of all the great metropolitan firms which controlled the export markets.

The glory of European imperialism was terminated by the First World War which disrupted maritime trade and ruined the international gold standard. Both Great Britain and France emerged from this war with a much reduced political and economic power. The zest for empire which had earlier inspired the educated middle class was waning. When prime minister Lloyd George made his famous speech in 1922 in which he compared the Indian Civil Service to a 'steel frame', this was no imperial bravado but a desparate attempt to recruit young men for this service. The future of the empire appeared to be dim, thus the thought of a lifetime service in India seemed to be less attractive. Prospects seemed to be better in the mid-1920s after Great Britain had once more joined the gold standard at the pre-war parity. This proved to be a wrong decision only a few years later, but while the going was good it revived imperial optimism. However, this was soon dampened by the sudden blow of the Great Depression which started in the USA in 1929 and subsequently engulfed the whole world. The consequences of the disintegration of the world economy will be discussed in a subsequent chapter. Here it may suffice to point out that the slump in commodity prices caused by the Great Depression reduced the value of colonial possessions, but since most colonies were indebted to their European masters, imperial control was tightened so as to save the creditors from bankruptcy. Great Britain was forced off the gold standard in 1931, but the flow of gold from the indebted periphery to the centre then supported the newly created Sterling Area. It was backed up by 'Imperial Preference', a tariff wall protecting the British empire. This greatly annoyed the USA which had always pursued an 'Open Door' policy. American anti-colonialism, which became more assertive under President Roosevelt, owed much to this development.

The economic policy of the imperial powers changed under the impact of the new challenges which they had to meet. Economic liberalism was abandoned step by step, while protectionism emerged as a reaction to the depression. State intervention was introduced to meet the need of managing the economy during the Second World War. While the apparatus of colonial rule had been of modest dimensions before the war, it was far more formidable by the end of the conflict. The concept of economic planning had emerged during the war and then became a characteristic feature of post-war imperialism.

The last phase of imperialism was riddled with contradictions. Great Britain was practically bankrupt at the end of the war and depended on the credit of the USA and of some of its own colonies, which had turned from debtors into creditors as India had done during the war. France and the Netherlands had, as a result of Nazi occupation, practically ceased to exist during the course of the war and had to restore their sovereignty both at home and in their colonies. The French and the Dutch governments conceived of these tasks as interrelated. The **French Union** whose constitution was introduced in 1946 encompassed France as well as its 'overseas territories'; the Dutch envisioned a Union headed by the Queen of the Netherlands and including the colonies. While the French and the Dutch launched great campaigns to recover their colonies, the British set the pace for decolonization by granting independence to India in 1947. Since India was now a creditor of Great Britain it was easier to let it go, particularly as the Indian interim government had to sign a moratorium on the eve of independence. A strong motive for the rapid decolonization of India was the demobilization of the huge British-Indian army which was a potentially dangerous task. But whereas Great Britain withdrew quickly from South Asia, it clung to its African possessions and produced plans for their economic development just as the French did. By the mid-1950s both the French and the British governments realized that they could not make financial ends meet in their colonies. Even before Harold Macmillan noted the 'Wind of Change' blowing across Africa he had felt it in Whitehall where he had conducted a cost/benefit analysis of colonial rule, showing that the costs far outweighed the benefits. At about the same time a French minister had made similar calculations. If France was really serious about raising the standard of living throughout the **French Union** to the same level, the French in France would have to reduce their standard of living by at least 25 per cent. If imperialism no longer paid, or even demanded economic sacrifices, it was time to give it up.

Admittedly, this outline of the phases of imperialism is rather Eurocentric. It does not account for activities at the periphery of empires. Some scholars have advocated an 'excentric' theory of imperialism in order to correct this perspective. They argue that the 'agency' of people at the periphery was sometimes more important for imperial growth than the political will of the imperialists. In a way Mahatma **Gandhi** was an early representative of this 'excentric' theory when he asserted that the Indians had given India to the British by cooperating with them. Of course, for **Gandhi** this was a polemical argument meant to convince the Indians of the need for non-cooperation. The European 'excentrics' have also stressed the role of 'collaborating elites' in supporting the empires. They tend to forget the importance of systematic coercion which radiated from imperial authority. This coercion sometimes appeared in the form of outright military intervention, but it usually expressed itself in institutional arrangements with the threat of force as a residual element. The 'native authorities' on which the European imperialists relied in Africa could be characterized as 'collaborating elites'. The imperialist discourse on preserving traditions and respecting the 'natural leaders' of the people would tend to give credence to 'excentric' views. But these 'natural leaders' were often appointed chiefs and even if they had the dignity of some ancient lineage, they knew very well that they were at the mercy of the colonial rulers. It was only at the time of the initial imperial encounter when the colonial rulers had to look for military allies in order to consolidate their power that 'collaborators' could make a difference. But even then, the superior organization of the imperial power and the collective memory embodied in its civil and military staff was more important than the intentions of the individual 'collaborator' who could be easily replaced if he was no longer useful. Colonial rule was not a rule of warlords, but was managed by bureaucrats controlled by the respective imperial centre.

The arguments against 'excentrism' should not distract from the need to correct the Eurocentric perspective. Perhaps one should suggest an interactive and contextual theory of imperialism which would portray imperialism as an open system which could adapt to new challenges. Similarly we shall have to think of decolonization as an interactive process which encompassed the intiatives of the colonial rulers as well as those of anti-colonial movements. The rulers tried to set the agenda and to define the arena of political activity, but those who defied them had their own agenda and mobilized their supporters so as to shift the arena of political action.

HISTORIOGRAPHY

Decolonization has given rise to a voluminous historiography which could be the subject of a special comparative study. It includes the accounts written by historians of the countries of the former colonial rulers as well as those of the decolonized nations. The former range from apologetic studies to proud proclamations of a successful transfer of power, while the latter include the work of nationalist myth-makers as well as the critical analyses of trained historians. In addition to the work of historians of nations directly involved in the process of decolonization, there have also been important contributions by historians of other nations who had a more detached view. The brief historiographical survey provided here is restricted to a few examples of the major approaches to the subject. Since there is also a Guide to Sources and Secondary Reading in this book (see pp. 272–92), the present chapter concentrates on the work of a few authors. They are discussed here because their work illustrates the variety of perspectives.

THE METROPOLITAN AGENDA OF DECOLONIZATION

Many scholars writing on decolonization viewed it first and foremost as an initiative taken by the metropolitan powers and tried to reconstruct the agenda of these powers with regard to colonial administration, constitutional reform and the final 'transfer of power'. Those who explored European archives were naturally influenced by the type of sources available to them. Colonial proconsuls and the staff of colonial ministries as well as European politicians discussing colonial affairs were the actors in the drama which they portrayed. The views of colonial nationalists were at the most reflected through the prism of official reactions to them. The metropolitan approach was also attractive because it provided a panorama seen from the commanding heights of imperial power. Metropolitan policies rarely applied to single colonies only, as there were always larger issues to be taken into consideration. The scholar who looked at decolonization from the metropolitan perspective could therefore claim to base his analysis on a wide range of information. In general such scholars would not openly assert that the colonial 'subjects' were at the receiving end and that their actions hardly mattered, but their work often reflected this attitude. Of course, there were also scholars in this field who modestly stated that they saw their work as a part of European history and were unable to spend years in Africa or Asia to do their research there.

The most comprehensive study of the metropolitan agenda was undertaken at an early stage by a Swiss scholar, Rudolf von Albertini, whose book on decolonization has the subtitle 'The Discussion on the Administration and the Future of the Colonies, 1919–1960'.[1] This accurately reflects his main aim in writing this book. He concentrated his work on comparing the British and the French colonial administrations and their plans for decolonization. The Dutch and the Portuguese empires are only discussed very briefly at the end of the book. There are also two brief sections on the Americans in the Philippines and the Belgians in the Congo. The book is not based on archival research, but there are frequent references to official publications, parliamentary papers, newspaper reports, etc. As a comprehensive study of this particular subject, von Albertini's work has not yet been superseded by any subsequent publication.

Almost at the same time, a French scholar, Henri Grimal, published his book on *Decolonization: the British, French, Dutch and Belgian Empires, 1919–1963*.[2] Since he taught colonial history in France, he was very well informed about the French colonial empire and its decolonization, but he examined the French record from a critical perspective and tended to give more credit to the British approach. He also showed a sympathetic interest in the nationalists of the colonies to whose movements he gave due importance without covering them in detail. In general he devoted more attention to the metropolitan agenda, but he was also aware of the influence of outside forces on the process of decolonization to which he devoted an essential chapter of his book. The work of von Albertini and Grimal reflects the state of the debate in the early 1960s.

A much shorter book on European decolonization with a similar scope was published by Roy Fraser Holland at a later stage.[3] He also takes the end of the First World War as his point of departure but takes 1981 as his cut-off point. He thus includes the decolonization of the Portuguese empire. His treatment of this subject, however, is fairly short. Just like von Albertini, Holland also deals mainly with British and French colonial policy. Holland is an avowed advocate of the metropolitan approach to decolonization and asserts that it arose more directly from changes within the metropoles than from a metamorphosis of the periphery.

John Darwin also belongs to the metropolitan historians. He has restricted his study of decolonization to the British empire.[4] Unlike other historians he pays much attention to economic aspects, particularly to currency affairs. The devaluation of sterling and its impact on the Sterling Area are discussed by him in detail. Nevertheless he asserts that political rather than economic reasons have been the main cause of decolonization.

A French metropolitan historian, Jacques Marseille, has come to a different conclusion in this respect.[5] In dealing with the relations between French imperialism and capitalism he argues that economic growth in the 1950s and the attractions of the European market weakened the colonial lobby and strengthened those who wished to invest in Europe rather than waste money on colonial development. When he started his research he wanted to find evidence for the hypothesis that the export of capital to the colonies was the driving force of imperialism, but his findings disproved it. He found that the Great Depression was the turning point in imperial relations. It compelled the French to restructure their industries as well as the relations with their empire. In many ways Marseille's findings correspond to Bonn's *The Crumbling of Empire*, but it seems that he did not know of Bonn's work. In its subtitle Marseille calls his book the 'History of a Divorce'. He shows that this divorce was not a sudden event but took place over a long time during which capitalism lost its intimate relationship with imperialism. The tragic irony of this divorce was that before the marriage broke up bloody wars were fought in Indo-China and Algeria in order to retain political control over colonies which were no longer useful from an economic point of view.

THE DIMINISHING RETURNS TO COLLABORATION

Whereas metropolitan historians tend to attribute 'agency' exclusively to the colonial rulers, there are others who adopt an 'excentric' view and stress the 'agency' of collaborators among the colonized people. These collaborators were used by the colonialists but also made use of their rulers to serve their own interests. The advocates of the excentric view hold that the periphery did not accept passively what the centre imposed on it but shaped the imperial impact to a large extent. Ronald Robinson, the pioneer of 'excentrism', even claims that this theory can explain the rise and fall of colonialism through the reversal of a single model.[6] Colonialism thrives on recruiting collaborators and when it can no longer do so, decolonization becomes inevitable. It seems that diminishing returns to collaboration lead to the reversal of the model. Robinson has not used these terms, but they help to elucidate the process which he has tried to explain.

The original type of collaborator was the 'comprador'. This Portuguese word meant 'buyer' but referred more generally to an intermediary agent who helped foreign traders to transact their business with his countrymen. When commercial relations receded and territorial rule was established, other types of collaborators were required: chiefs, military entrepreneurs, revenue accountants, etc. In general, the colonial rulers were more exacting revenue collectors but also more reliable paymasters than their indigenous predecessors. Therefore they could reward their collaborators on a regular basis. The main function of colonial pro-consuls was that of arbiters of the fate of various types of collaborators. As colonial rule progressed and developed into a bureaucratic machine, the importance of the collaborators diminished. Robinson argues that the demise of colonial rule began when it ran out of collaborators. But in some instances the real problem was that there were more potential collaborators than the colonial machine could absorb. The diminishing returns to collaboration could thus refer both to restrictions on collaborators and to the lack of opportunities for those who wanted to collaborate but did not get a chance to do so.

Research on collaborating elites proved to be particularly attractive to British scholars influenced by the ideas of the great historian, Lord Namier. He had fashioned his unique methodology in the study of eighteenth-century British parliamentary politics.[7] Parties of the modern type did not yet exist at that time; politics was based on 'interests'. The aggregation of such interests could be studied by minute biographical research on individual Members of Parliament. Namier impressed more than a generation of scholars with his methodology. It had a special affinity for British scepticism with regard to ideologies or deterministic social theories. 'Interests' were real and down to earth and could be identified by using Namier's method. The drawback of this very rational method was that it could not account for movements such as nationalism or socialist revolution, etc. Why would people be prepared to risk their lives or go to prison instead of looking after their individual 'interests'? But even though 'Namierism' did not provide answers to such questions, it had made an important contribution to historical research as long as it did not claim that only 'interests' mattered and everything else could be safely neglected.

Similarly, the excentric model proposed by Robinson had a heuristic value for the study of decolonization. It served as a corrective of metropolitanism and drew attention to the 'agency' of the periphery, indicating that colonial rule was to some extent the product of 'negotiation'.

Critics have pointed out that the fascination with the periphery has tended to let the excentrics forget about the prime movers in the imperial centre.[8] Obviously one has to keep both sides in mind.

THE EMANCIPATION FROM COLONIAL RULE

The historians who studied national freedom movements and various forms of anti-colonial protest tended to disagree with the metropolitan historians with regard to the importance of their respective fields of research. The more radical representatives of both sides might actually think that the work of those on the other side was irrelevant. This disagreement was to some extent also due to the fact that the metropolitan historians usually originated in the nation of the colonial rulers while the others had been born as colonial 'subjects' and felt that they were continuing the freedom struggle by writing history. Moreover, some governments of newly independent nations commissioned the writing of national histories for political reasons. India is a particularly interesting case in point, as two rival 'master narratives' of the Indian freedom movement were produced in the 1960s. The influential education minister, Maulana **Abul Kalam Azad**, a famous Muslim scholar, initially commissioned Romesh Chandra Majumdar to write the 'official' history of this movement. Majumdar was a noted nationalist historian who had inspired many Indians with his work on the glories of ancient India. He took up his work with great enthusiasm. Being a Bengali Hindu he portrayed the freedom movement from a perspective which did not please the minister who had expected an emphasis on Hindu–Muslim cooperation in the freedom movement, as he himself had been a close associate of Mahatma Gandhi. The work was almost finished when the Government of India withdrew its patronage; Majumdar then published three massive volumes on his own for which he won acclaim from many nationalists.[9] In the meantime the minister had commissioned another official history, making sure that it would correspond to his point of view. The author of his choice was Tara Chand, an educationist from Allahabad, who already had a book on *The Influence of Islam on Indian Culture* to his credit which was first published in 1922. This showed him to be a Hindu scholar with a sympathetic interest in Indian Muslims. Assisted by a competent staff, Tara Chand produced four massive volumes on the freedom movement which were published by the Government of India.[10] Both Majumdar and Tara Chand took a long view and did not restrict their work to the twentieth century. Tara Chand constructed his narrative as a dialectical trilogy, beginning in the eighteenth century and showing how India had lost its freedom, then describing the colonial period and incipient nationalism and finally showing how India regained its freedom. He paid due attention to the nationalist Muslims whereas Majumdar had neglected them because he was attracted to Hindu communalism. The tensions between Hindus and Muslims which had led to the partition of India were thus reflected also in the field of historiography. The two comprehensive 'master narratives' literally exhausted the subject and discouraged younger scholars from contributing further studies to this field. Moreover, the younger generation of historians was inspired by Marxist ideas and nationalist historiography appeared old-fashioned to them. A new impetus to the study of the national movement was given only by the project *Towards Freedom* which was the Indian response to the great British publication of sources concerning *The Transfer of Power*. This will be described in the Guide to Sources and Secondary Reading.

Other African and Asian nations produced hardly any nationalist 'master narratives' of the Indian type. There are good reasons for this; India had experienced a long and intense freedom movement and it already had a tradition of Western-style historiography as several Indian universities had built up history departments and many Indian scholars had studied history in British universities before taking up teaching positions at home. There was thus a universe of modern historical discourse in India which was lacking elsewhere. In the absence of trained historians, poets and other intellectuals tried to project a vision of national history in those other countries.

Muhammad Yamin of Indonesia was a typical example of the 'myth-maker' who emerged as a national 'historian'. He was a noted poet who was close to **Sukarno**. In 1957 he dominated the first Indonesian national history conference where he was challenged by Soedjatmoko, a leading intellectual who defended rational rather than national historiography. Soedjatmoko had studied medicine and had then represented Indonesia in the United Nations. Yamin's views prevailed at that time, but among the participants there was a young historian, Sartono Kartodirdjo, who was dissatisfied with the proceedings and looked for new ways of writing history. In 1970 he chaired the second national history conference and launched a plan for a multi-volume national history to be written by a team of authors. Soedjatmoko put him in touch with the Ford Foundation and the team was able to work for some time at the University of California, Berkeley. Sartono was not satisfied with their product. He was also soon eclipsed by one of the members of his team, the military historian, Nugroho Susanto, who was close to President Suharto and glorified the role of the Indonesian army in his work. During Nugroho's hegemony, he more or less determined the writing of history. He was a military officer with suave manners who served as a minister and also held high university positions. New approaches to national history could only be articulated after Suharto's 'New Order' collapsed. Critical voices such as that of the younger historian, Bambang Purwanto, could now make themselves heard. It seems that Indonesian historiography will only now come into its own.

While Indonesian historians were busy with their self-centred historiography, some sympathetic 'ex-patriates' stepped in and produced their versions of Indonesia's national history. Among them were scholars who started their academic careers after decolonization and were dissatisfied with the metropolitan approach described above. A senior leader of this group of scholars was George McTurnan Kahin, born in 1918, who had completed his studies in the USA before the war and was almost dropped as a parachutist on to Java in 1945. This plan was cancelled, but he then did land in Indonesia as a Ph.D. student in 1948, collecting material for his book *Nationalism and Revolution in Indonesia* which has remained a classic ever since its publication.[11] He subsequently pioneered Indonesian studies at Cornell University and emerged as a strong critic of the Vietnam War. He was operating on the same wavelength as his Dutch colleague, W. F. Wertheim, and his Australian colleague, Herbert Feith, who both made major contributions to Indonesian studies. A younger German colleague, Bernhard Dahm, followed the same line of Indonesian studies, working first on a biography of **Sukarno** and then publishing a history of *Indonesia in the Twentieth Century*.[12]

The examples of India and Indonesia may suffice for an illustration of the historiography concerning the emancipation of Asian countries from colonial rule. A description of the historiography of other Asian countries in this field would more or less reflect the same pattern. A comparative study of national 'master narratives' would go far beyond the scope of the present chapter; it could be the subject of another book. The historiography of the emancipation of African nations is less extensive than that concerning Asia. Professional African historians were very rare at the time of decolonization. In the meantime their numbers have not grown greatly and some of the best of them are working abroad rather than in the countries of their origin. The institutional support for the study of history is insufficient in most African states. Of the few African historians of international stature working in their home countries one may mention Bethwell A. Ogot, University of Nairobi, a very productive scholar who published on numerous areas of African history. Among his books is one which is also dedicated to the subject under discussion here: *Decolonization and Independence in Kenya, 1940–1993*.[13] His Nigerian contemporary, J. F. Ade Ajayi, University of Ibadan, has also published widely. He stresses the continuity of African history and considers the brief period of colonial rule only as an episode. This is reflected in his essays on

Tradition and Change in Africa.[14] In francophone Africa, Joseph Ki-Zerbo of Burkina Faso followed a similar line in his *Histoire de l'Afrique Noire.*[15]

'Expatriates' have also chimed in and contributed to the history of decolonization in Africa. One of them is David Birmingham who has been a pioneer in studying decolonization from the perspective of local experience rather than from the metropolitan point of view. He has paid attention to social and economic history and has placed African movements into this larger context without adopting a deterministic approach. He has highlighted African 'agency' in all his books. The slim volume on *The Decolonization of Africa* provides a good insight into his method of historiography and is also a succinct survey of this subject.[16] The interested reader may then turn to his chapter on 'Images and Themes in the Nineties' which he contributed to a volume which he also co-edited with Phyllis M. Martin.[17] Since this volume is devoted to the history of Central Africa after 1960, Birmingham's chapter does not deal with the whole of Africa in a grand sweep, but shows at least for an important part of the continent what happened after decolonization.

Another historian of Africa, Frederick Cooper, has also taken the side of African 'agency'. His special subject is labour relations in British and French Africa from the 1930s to the 1960s. But he uses this topic as an entry into the wider sphere of social history as demonstrated in his book *Decolonization and African Society.*[18] His work is based on a great deal of archival research in France, Great Britain, Kenya and Senegal. The various strikes in Africa are analysed by him in detail; he also shows how militant labour was drawn into national movements and how trade unions were used as stepping stones to political power by ambitious leaders. Whereas labour in Africa was initially very often forced labour, organized labour progressed literally along the railway lines. Cooper also shows how labour was finally deceived by the logic of nationalism. Under colonial rule, labour had tried to appeal to the universal idea of equal pay for equal work, whereas after independence the workers and their unions had to subordinate their interests to the goal of national development as defined by their leaders. Cooper not only captures the assertiveness of African agency but also the constraints imposed on it by colonial as well as national rule.

A prominent 'expatriate' who took sides with the Africans in the field of historiography is Terence Ranger, who taught history in Zimbabwe and Tanzania before becoming Rhodes Professor of Race Relations at Oxford University. He had gone to Africa as a young lecturer, teaching European history, but was soon 'converted' to African history to which he made important contributions. An early work in this field was *The African Voice in Southern Rhodesia.*[19] He had not only sided with the Africans as a historian, but also as a citizen and was deported from Southern Rhodesia (Zimbabwe) in 1963, then finding a new academic home at the University of Dar-es-Salaam. In his later work he devoted attention to the 'invention of tradition' as he observed it in Africa.[20] This theme has since been widely discussed by scholars. It has also been subjected to criticism as it could be taken to mean that all traditions are invented, which is certainly not what Ranger had stated. In fact, he had made a contribution to the new field of 'discourse analysis', revealing the political motives behind certain types of 'traditionalism'. He had earlier devoted a regional study to this theme in his book *The Invention of Tribalism in Zimbabwe*.[21] Returning to Zimbabwe in recent years as a visiting professor, he was faced with the 'patriotic history' propagated by the government which fits into the pattern of 'invented tradition'.

INTERNATIONAL RELATIONS AND COLONIAL RETREAT

Decolonization was an integral part of world politics. The old discipline of diplomatic history was extended so as to encompass the interaction of various powers in this field. William Roger Louis, an American historian whose special field is British history, did pioneering work in this field. He bases his studies on very detailed archival research. In addition to the decisions of the main actors he pays close attention to the minutes and notes of bureaucrats and experts who have often strongly influenced those decisions. His first major book was *Imperialism at Bay*[22] whose tragic hero is President Roosevelt. Deeply convinced of the need to subject all colonies to international trusteeship so as to remove the causes of future wars, he was finally prevented from reaching this goal by the development of international relations at the end of the Second World War. This kind of trusteeship was not meant to perpetuate foreign rule but to prepare the way for independence. Louis traces the debates on this central theme and shows how and why Roosevelt's policy was bound to be stymied. Louis's second great book, *The British Empire in the Middle East*,[23] also has a tragic hero: Ernest Bevin, the British Foreign Secretary, who was a tough labour union leader and a great patriot. He wanted to uphold Great Britain's imperial position by converting the empire into a partnership with the people who had so far been treated as colonial subjects. An empire based on partnership was, however, a contradiction in terms and Bevin had to learn this the hard way: his policy was a failure. Again, Louis analysed this tragedy with great skill. Subsequently he continued this line of analysis of the process of decolonization in several major publications.

In recent years two younger historians have followed this path in different fields: Matthew Connelly and Piero Gleijeses. Connelly's book *A Diplomatic Revolution*[24] throws new light on Algeria's fight for independence. He explains how this fight was won in the field of diplomacy although it had practically been lost on the battlefield. The French military had crushed the Algerians but was not permitted to win the war because Algerian leaders mobilized international opinion in the **United Nations** and elsewhere very successfully. Like Louis's books this work is also based on very detailed archival research of French, British, American and many other archives. Gleijeses has matched this effort in a very different field in his *Conflicting Missions*.[25] He has reconstructed the Cuban campaigns in Africa, particularly in the Portuguese colonies, with great attention to detail. As he had access to Cuban archives, he can tell his readers the inside story. Earlier there had been a general impression that the Cubans acted as Soviet mercenaries in Africa, but Gleijeses can show that Castro and his followers were directing their own actions and initiated risky ventures while the Soviet Union watched and at the most lent its support when necessary. The Cubans have kept quiet about their achievements because they had promised their African friends that they would keep a low profile so as not to distract from the merits of African freedom fighters.

Similar work documenting this new approach to diplomatic history has been published in a volume on *International Diplomacy and Colonial Retreat* edited by Kent Fedorowich and Martin Thomas.[26] In his introductory contribution to this volume John Darwin mentions the impact of the Cold War on the process of decolonization but also stresses that now, after the end of the Cold War, the breakup of colonial rule once more emerges as the key event of the second half of the twentieth century. The other contributions to this volume highlight the impact of the Cold War as well as other factors which influenced the process of colonial retreat. The tangled skein of British–American cooperation and rivalry is portrayed in several contributions. These contributions are devoted to very specific themes such as the re-establishment of British rule in Hong Kong after the war, the Congo crisis, the Yemeni revolution, etc., but they all show that the process of decolonization must be analysed in the context of international relations. Thus they continue the work of Louis, Connelly and Gleijeses mentioned above. They are also based on very detailed archival research and thus demonstrate that the archives contain very valuable information which deserves to be explored.

A volume devoted to a specific region has been edited by Marc Frey, Ronald W. Pruessen and Tan Tai Yong: *The Tranformation of Southeast Asia. International Perspectives on Decolonization.*[27] It contains four chapters on different aspects of the role of the USA in Southeast Asia. Other chapters deal with the decolonization of Indo-China, Indonesia, Malaya, etc. The grand old master, Wang Gungwu, has contributed a perceptive afterword on the limits of decolonization. He feels that the meaning of the term 'decolonization' is sometimes expanded too much and that one must be careful not to overload it. He ends his afterword with a plea to 'distinguish between what decolonization did for transformation in Southeast Asia and what transformations actually occurred because a restructured international architecture had transcended the heritage of decolonization'.[28] This is a crucial point for the study of 'International Relations and Colonial Retreat'. Decolonization is in itself an aspect of international relations. To separate it analytically from other fields of international relations is a difficult task but it must be undertaken so as not to blur the meaning of decolonization. The work of the scholars mentioned here has contributed to an awareness of such analytical distinctions.

CHANGING THE FOCUS OF HISTORIOGRAPHY

The future historiography of decolonization may also wish to highlight other aspects than those mentioned here so far. In reviewing the historical debate on the end of the British empire, John Darwin has stressed the deficiencies of all standard approaches to this subject.[29] He has pointed out that those who trace the motives of decolonization to the domestic politics of the colonial powers as well as those who highlight the 'Onslaught of Nationalism' cannot provide adequate explanations of the process of decolonization. But he is also not satisfied with those who restrict their vision to economics or to international politics. He pleads for a mix of interpretations but does not provide a receipe for a proper mix. Perhaps the proper mix will have to be composed according to the particular constellation studied by the historian. Phyllis Martin in her article 'Beyond Independence' has mentioned another reason for changing the focus of historiography.[30] She feels that the life histories of those who experienced the attainment of independence rarely reflect the triumph portrayed in standard national historiography. She pleads for a 'decentring of decolonization' as reflected in such life histories. There is an element of postmodern resistance to structural explanations of history in her plea. However, the need for new narratives in the field of decolonization is very obvious. The rivalling master narratives of the smooth 'transfer of power' and of triumphant nationalism no longer find receptive audiences. A more comprehensive social and cultural history of decolonization is required. It will not produce a new master narrative but may contribute to a deeper understanding of the causes and consequences of decolonization. Mahmood Mamdani has opened up new lines of historical research in his book *Citizen and Subject* in which he discusses the legacy of late colonialism in Africa.[31] He tries to steer a middle course between structuralism and its postmodern critics. He states that whereas structuralism puts 'agency' into the straitjacket of the iron laws of history, its critics tend to diminish the significance of historical constraint in order to salvage agency. He wants to find out how the subject population was incorporated into the arena of colonial power. As he sees it, the colonial rulers operated a system of decentralized despotism by means of 'native authorities'. This system has been maintained by the post-independence state. But there are instances of peasant resistance movements. Such instances are of special interest to Mamdani and he has done field work in areas where such movements are in evidence. His approach may provide new insights into the process of crossing the threshold of decolonization.

In India Ranajit Guha and the historians who have produced a series of *Subaltern Studies* have explored the relation between colonial hegemony and 'subaltern autonomy'.[32] The categories of this line of historiography are derived from the work of Antonio Gramsci who has certainly much to offer to historians of decolonization. The Italy which Gramsci tried to analyse from a Marxist perspective had hardly reached an advanced stage of bourgeois capitalism when it was unified by the nationalist movement of the nineteenth century. This movement was supported by an educated service class whose hegemony the 'subaltern' class accepted. The situation of many colonies was very similar to that of nineteenth-century Italy. But although Guha adopts Gramsci's categories, he is sceptical about 'hegemony'. He doubts whether either the British colonial rulers or the national government of India have ever been able to establish a real hegemony in India.[33] On the other hand he has no doubt about the urge of the 'subalterns' to assert their autonomy and to make their voices heard. There are methodological problems in this type of research, but at least the quest for giving expression to the sufferings and the hopes of the 'subalterns' has been of great heuristic value. The authors of the *Subaltern Studies* have used police reports and court cases as source material for their reconstructions of the 'subaltern' voice. They have also used the modern method of discourse analysis to penetrate the surface of colonial texts. Historians of other ex-colonies could learn a great deal from these studies which help to 'decentre decolonization'.

Parallel to the work of *Subaltern Studies* there has been the new venture of 'post-colonial studies'. Whereas the scholars engaged in *Subaltern Studies* were interested in the muted voices of the lower classes, the 'post-colonialists' paid attention to the new African, Asian and Caribbean writers who expressed the quest for an identity which had been submerged by the colonial impact. The seminal work of Edward Said on *Orientalism* had stimulated 'post-colonial studies'.[34] Said had shown how the image of the 'other' projected by Western Orientalists had forced the 'Orientals' to think of themselves in terms constructed by scholars who served the colonial rulers. The anti-colonial freedom movements had fought for political self-determination, the 'post-colonialists' inspired by Said fought for the intellectual and spiritual self-determination of the people who had been subjected to colonial rule. Said was a professor of English literature and his methodology of discourse analysis naturally attracted the historians of literature who found a rich field indeed in the creative writings of authors such as Chinua Achebe, Vidiadhar Naipaul, Ken Saro-Wiwa, Salman Rushdie, to mention just a few. But the more ardent post-colonialists have not been satisfied with this kind of work; they have launched an attack on historiography as a Western construct. Dane Kennedy has provided an insightful survey of post-colonialism in his article 'Imperial History and Post-colonial Theory'.[35] He has criticized the excesses of the post-colonialists but also recommends some of their work as a corrective to conventional imperial history.

Cultural anthropologists have also made important contributions to post-colonial studies, sometimes without explicitly identifying themselves with post-colonialism. The work of Brackette F. Williams is a case in point; her study of the politics of cultural struggle in Guyana is a report on field work among poor people but also a treatise on hegemony and the quest for identity.[36] Her empirical work infuses her theoretical interpretations with a strong dose of realism which is often missing in the more rarefied contributions to post-colonial studies. In some respects, Williams's work is akin to that of Mamdani mentioned earlier.

The future study of decolonization will embrace these various currents of historiography and add new dimensions to it. The old limitations of political history stressing the institutional aspects of the devolution of power will be overcome and the 'cultural turn' of the social sciences is bound to affect the study of decolonization.

MAPS

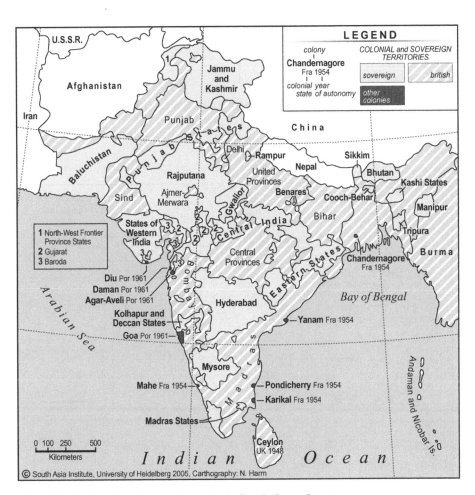

LEGEND

colony

Chandernagore
Fra 1954
colonial year
state of autonomy

COLONIAL and SOVEREIGN TERRITORIES

sovereign | british

other colonies

1 North-West Frontier Province States
2 Gujarat
3 Baroda

Map 1 **British India and princely states before independence**

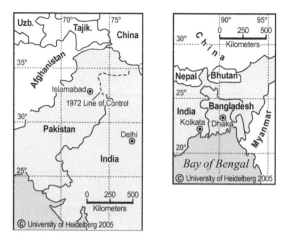

Map 2 **a) Partitioning the Punjab; b) partitioning Bengal (Radcliffe Award, 1947)**

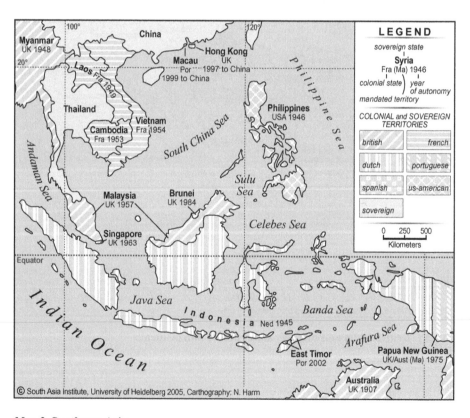

Map 3 **Southeast Asia**

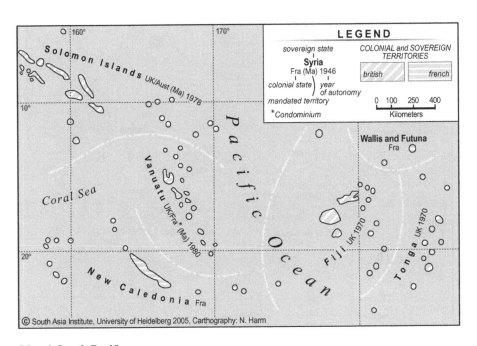

Map 4 **South Pacific**

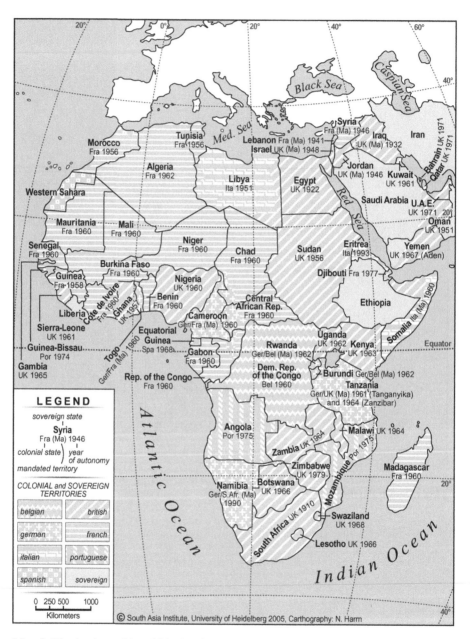

LEGEND

sovereign state
Syria
Fra (Ma) 1946
colonial state ⟩ year
of autonomy
mandated territory

COLONIAL and SOVEREIGN
TERRITORIES

belgian	british
german	french
italian	portuguese
spanish	sovereign

0 250 500   1000
Kilometers

© South Asia Institute, University of Heidelberg 2005, Cartography: N. Harm

Map 5 **The Arab world and black Africa**

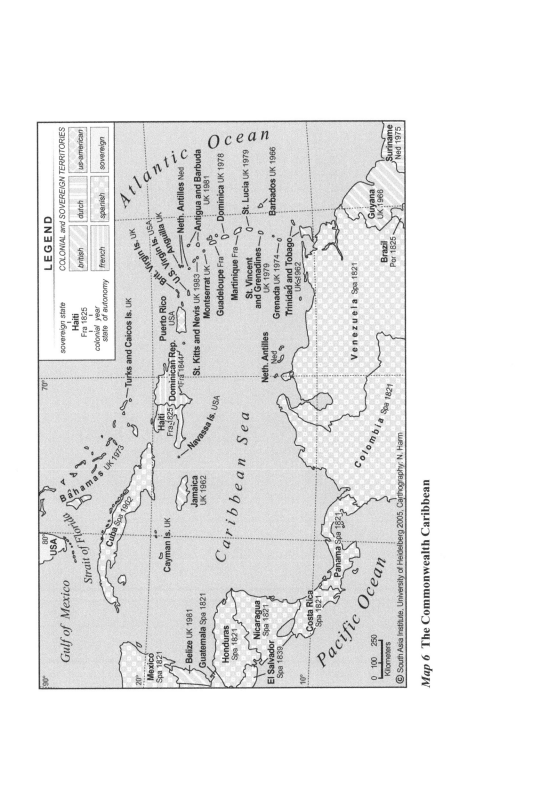

Map 6 **The Commonwealth Caribbean**

II
THEMES

THE CONTEXT OF DECOLONIZATION

THE DISINTEGRATION OF THE WORLD ECONOMY

Decolonization was precipitated by the disintegration of the world economy during the period from 1914 to 1945 which was marked by the sequence war–depression–war. Before 1914 the dominant countries were linked in a kind of economic world federation of the gold standard.[1] This federation had an unofficial capital, the City of London. According to economic doctrine, there was no monetary policy which supported the gold standard. The free flow of gold automatically adjusted international prices. Prices would rise in the country which attracted gold and decline in the country which had to export it. This would lead to a reversal of the flow in due course. The balance could be upset if a country which attracted gold decided to hoard it so as to maintain internal price stability. This is exactly what the USA did after the First World War. The war had put an end to the economic world federation of the gold standard, but then several countries adopted it again so as to restore the old stability. The USA, however, refused to follow the rules of the game and kept its gold locked up in Fort Knox. This was done for purely domestic reasons, but it deeply affected the world economy nevertheless.

In the 'golden age' before the First World War, the City of London could control the unofficial world federation because it was the clearing house for all major financial transactions and could maintain an uninterrupted flow of gold. This also helped to secure the British empire although the majority of British investment was made outside the empire than within its confines. Interest payments on these investments were so enormous that they provided the City of London with the critical mass required for keeping the 'world federation' going. This was drastically changed by the First World War from which Great Britain emerged indebted to the USA as well as to its own people as it had contracted a huge internal war debt. Moreover, the interest payments on investment abroad were reduced to less than one-third of their former dimensions. In spite of this Great Britain returned to the gold standard in 1925 at the pre-war parity to the US dollar which it maintained only with great difficulties until it was forced to abandon the standard under the impact of the Great Depression in 1931. The vain attempt at reviving the gold standard after the First World War proved to be a distaster.[2]

The 'Crumbling of Empire' was precipitated by the Great Depression, but at the same time the depression stiffened imperial resistance to decolonization. The depression years witnessed a contraction of international credit. Some countries defaulted on their debts, some devalued their currencies, others introduced strict exchange controls. The British economist Joan Robinson coined the term 'beggar thy neighbour' for the economic nationalism that prevailed in this period. Each sovereign state tried to improve its position at the cost of others. There was one exception: colonial governments could not default nor manipulate their currencies as they were controlled by their imperial rulers.[3] The fierce debates on the exchange rate of the Indian rupee and the action of the Secretary of State in dictating terms to the Government of India on behalf of the Bank of England in 1931 is a case in point.[4] The focus of colonial rule was narrowed to the interest of the creditor in controlling the debtor. The access to colonies as suppliers of raw materials was no longer of importance as the Great Depression had led to such a steep fall in the prices of raw materials that anybody could buy them cheaply in the world market. Trade in these commodities declined in terms of value but not of volume during the years of the Great Depression.

Since the control of trade in colonial commodities was no longer a lucrative affair, the metropolitan powers had to refine their methods of exacting a tribute from their colonies. As Moritz Bonn put it: 'currency control . . . may be a convenient cloak for downright coercive exactions'.[5] In adopting such methods, the colonial rulers provided grist to the mill of economic nationalists in their colonies. The quest for self-determination was enhanced by acute economic grievances which will be discussed in the chapter on colonialism and neocolonialism later on (p. 258). At this stage it may suffice to stress that the disintegration of the world economy accentuated the conflicts between the rulers and the ruled in the colonies.

The Second World War affected different levels of the colonial relationship. The most visible result was the participation of millions of colonial soldiers in the imperial war effort. Moritz Bonn had written in 1938: 'colonial levies are being employed in a European civil war'.[6] He could not yet know at that time what enormous dimensions these 'levies' would have. The British Indian army had about two million soldiers in the field at the end of the Second World War. Probably about half a million African soldiers were recruited by the British and the French in various colonies. Most of these soldiers had to be demobilized after the war. They had been trained in modern warfare and their loyalty could not be taken for granted. For many, their experiences during the war had been unpleasant and they told their countrymen about these when they returned home. Another result of the war was the change in credit relationships. India, which had earlier been kept on a tight leash by the British as it was a substantial debtor, emerged from the war as a creditor of Great Britain. This greatly facilitated the grant of independence to India which also had to shoulder the burden of taking care of the demobilized soldiers, a burden which the British were eager to relinquish. But even more important in the field of credit relationships was the abject dependence of the European powers on the USA which had funded most of the war expenditure and then also provided financial help for European post-war reconstruction. The cards were thus stacked against the European colonial rulers after the war.

THE CHANGING CONTOURS OF WORLD AFFAIRS
AFTER THE SECOND WORLD WAR

The period from 1945 to 1975 which encompassed the emancipation of the majority of former colonies was influenced by rapid changes in the global context of the respective policies. The years from 1945 to 1948, which witnessed the termination of Japanese rule in East Asia, the decolonization of South Asia by the British and of the Philippines by the Americans, saw at the same time the return of the Dutch and the French to their colonies in Southeast Asia and the rise of post-war imperialism in Africa. The Cold War also began at that time and changed American policies which had earlier encouraged decolonization but then became obsessed with checking the advance of Communism, which it now perceived in a global perspective. This American obsession was reflected in conflicting trends of American policy with regard to decolonization. On the one hand advances in decolonization were demanded so as to reduce the targets of Communist propaganda or intervention, while on the other hand there was an interest in maintaining military bases throughout the world. Strategic positions occupied by European colonial powers were valuable in this context. These powers were sometimes perplexed by the alternating currents of American policy. The Cold War turned briefly into a hot one in Korea. The Korean War then led to a sharp rise in commodity prices and this once more enhanced the value of colonies that produced raw materials. Colonial rulers made plans for stimulating production in their colonies in Africa. Post-war imperialism received a boost and further decolonization was postponed. But the commodity boom collapsed in the mid-1950s and dreams of increased colonial production also evaporated. At the same time the French experienced a terrible defeat in Vietnam and in the wake of this they also took initiatives to decolonize Tunisia and Morocco. However, they were then faced with the outbreak of a new war in Algeria.

In 1955 the **Bandung Conference** emitted a global signal of Afro-Asian solidarity and broadcast the demand for further decolonization. **Nasser** returned to Egypt from this conference greatly encouraged in his defiance of the British and the French who then wanted to teach him a lesson in 1956. The joint intervention of the British and the French at Suez in 1956 turned out to be the final act of imperial bravado. President Eisenhower's angry reaction to this conspiracy of the imperial powers changed British and French policies. So far they had profited from being NATO allies in an intensified Cold War. But now Eisenhower put them in their place and they were forced to reconsider their overseas expenditure on defence and colonial control. The wave of decolonization culminating in the early 1960s was due to this new constellation. It was an irony of fate that the USA got involved in the Vietnam War in the mid-1960s. This preoccupied the Americans to such an extent that they could not pay much attention to the unfinished business of decolonization. The Portuguese empire thus eluded international pressure for many years. Its sudden downfall was caused by internal developments rather than by global power relations. There was, of course, the attraction of joining the European Community which promised greater economic benefits to the Portuguese than clinging to the African colonies. Resistance to their rule in these colonies had caused enormous losses to the Portuguese. The revolution led by military officers in April 1974 was a reaction to these losses. The final phase of Portuguese decolonization in Angola in 1975 then led to a unique confrontation of Cuban troops and South African troops – a rather new dimension of international relations in the era of decolonization. The attraction of the European Community (EC) which had induced the changes in the orientation of Portugal had earlier influenced British and French decisions also. But whereas France belonged to the founder members of the EC, Great Britain had to wait because General de Gaulle successfully obstructed its entry to the club until it was finally permitted to join in 1971. Even before this date, however, British interest in the emergent EC had diminished the attachment to colonial rule. The European expansion which had fostered imperialism was not revived; economic growth within the EC was no longer based on colonial exploitation but on the profitable interaction of industrialized countries.

The 1970s marked the end of the period of decolonization in most parts of the world; there remained only some smaller colonies which were still held by the colonial rulers – some of them even to the present day. In some cases this was not due to the diehard perseverance of the colonial rulers but to the material interests of the colonized. Where they had free access to the metropolitan country and also derived other economic benefits from their continued status as a colony or 'overseas territory', they preferred this attachment to independence. The **United Nations** maintains a register of such territories and it received in 2002 an official request from the people of American Samoa who wished to be struck off that register because they had no intention of achieving independence. It should also be mentioned that some colonies have been so devastated by their colonial rulers by the testing of atom bombs, etc., that they are hardly in a position to survive on their own and continue to depend on their imperial masters.

NATIONALISM AND THE RESISTANCE TO COLONIAL RULE

Nationalism is a hybrid ideology which may show various characteristics from right-wing chauvinism to a radical quest for self-determination. Its origins have been traced by many scholars but their findings are rather disparate. In his pioneering study *Nationalism and Social Communication* Karl Deutsch has highlighted the importance of the print media in spreading the message of nationalism.[7] A more or less standardized national language and widespread literacy were preconditions for this kind of social communication. In dealing with African and Asian nationalism one is at a loss in this respect. If one adopts Deutsch's criteria, nationalism would not have had a chance in Africa and Asia. Benedict Anderson, an Indonesia expert, has tried to go beyond Deutsch in his book *Imagined Communities. Reflections on the Origin and Spread of*

Nationalism, but he also stressed print capitalism as an important factor in the spread of nationalism.[8] Strangely enough, his book contains no reference to Deutsch's work. Ernest Gellner in his *Encounters with Nationalism* has tried to trace the social foundations of this ideology, but like Deutsch he concentrates on Europe.[9] The social change caused by the bourgeois revolution and industrialization is seen by him as the major reason for the rise of nationalism. However, the most militant form of nationalism in Europe arose in a country which was rather backward and had hardly been touched by industrialization: Poland. This was highlighted by a contemporary British historian, Lord Acton, in his essay *Nationality*, published in 1862, one year before the Polish national revolt which was brutally suppressed by the powers which had partitioned Poland among themselves.[10] Marx and Engels had commented on the fate of Poland even earlier and had pointed out that the joint oppression of Poland was the common bond of Austria, Russia and Prussia.[11] It was the very denial of national existence which was the mainspring of Polish nationalism. In this way it had much in common with African and Asian nationalism.

This denial-driven nationalism was rather different from the established nationalisms of France and Great Britain which had experienced their national consolidation as a result of the emergence of royal power in earlier centuries. This self-assured nationalism was projected abroad; its most striking feature being a strong corporate solidarity. In fact, the maintenance of colonial rule was possible only because the members of the respective European nations subordinated their individual ambitions to the interests of their nations. This was clearly perceived by the subject people; they felt that the lack of such corporate solidarity among themselves had led to their subjugation. Therefore nationalists in countries under colonial rule turned to the cultural resources of their people in order to construct such a corporate solidarity. But indigenous traditions often included ideas and practices justifying vertical and horizontal segmentation rather than comprehensive solidarity. Therefore creative nationalists turned to a solidarity traditionalism, i.e. a selective interpretation of traditions which implied solidarity.[12] In India such attempts were based on Hindu monism which stresses the identity of the one and the many and thus cuts across social segmentation; in Africa concepts like *negritude* or *ujamaa* (community spirit) served the same purpose. Those who highlighted such concepts did not present them as modern reconstructions but as inherent qualities of the respective 'national character'. There was, of course, also the contrasting approach of liberal 'nation-builders' who realistically assessed the impediments to national solidarity and relied on political education and institution-building instead of conjuring up traditions. But both approaches could blend in the thoughts and actions of individual nationalists. Jawaharlal **Nehru** is a case in point. He was a rational nation-builder who knew about the importance of political institutions, but he was also influenced by the solidarity traditionalism derived from Hindu monism. Thus he used to speak of 'Indian socialism' as a cultural resource; this was similar to **Nyerere**'s reference to *ujamaa*.[13] The rhetoric of national agitation would often produce a syncretism of reconstructed traditions and rational nation-building. Whereas there were many debates on the nation as such, both Indian and African nationalists hardly discussed the national territory. The Indian nationalists looked upon it as a given fact and did not acknowledge that the actual boundaries of the India they lived in had been fixed by the British. Similarly African nationalists conceived of Africa as a given entity and initially thought of one united African nation. Pan-Africanism was their nationalist ideology.[14] This was an inspiring idea and helped them to forget about the dismal reality of artificial colonial boundaries. But as decolonization progressed, the African nationalists were caught in the net of these boundaries and had to accept them as defining the arena of their political life. While pursuing their quest for political power within such boundaries they still held on to such ideas as *negritude* or *ujamaa* (community spirit) which were related to Pan-Africanism. In this way African nationalism was unrelated to the deep attachment to the national territory which characterizes nationalism elsewhere. It retained the flavour of anti-colonial resistance and the general quest for self-determination. Unfortunately it was also used for endorsing the cohesion of dictatorial one-party states. As Mahmood Mamdani has pointed out, the colonial rulers had 'bifurcated' the state.[15] They controlled the upper level of centralized administration and had left the lower level to a 'decentralized despotism' of 'native authorities'. After independence, the African nationalists captured the upper level and for the most part retained the decentralized despotism at the lower level, justifying this practice by means of nationalist ideology. The denial-driven nationalism of earlier days was thus converted into an authoritarian doctrine in support of the powers that be. In many instances this was a rather rapid process; the same leader who had only recently been a freedom fighter turned into a dictator as soon as he came to power. This was also due to the fact that representative institutions had been introduced by the colonial powers in Africa only at a very late stage whereas they had been established in India several decades before independence.

AFRO-ASIAN SOLIDARITY AND NON-ALIGNMENT

The rise of Afro-Asian solidarity was a direct reflection of nationalism and the resistance to colonial rule. Nationalism did not only mean self-determination at home but the assertion of an independent role in world politics which had been denied to the people subjected to colonial rule. Jawaharlal **Nehru**, who had taken a keen interest in world affairs even at the time of the Indian freedom struggle, projected an active foreign policy when he was interim prime minister. He had sent his sister, Vijayalakshmi Pandit, who was a politican in her own right, as ambassador to Moscow in 1947.[16] At about the same time, in March 1947, he invited representatives of various Asian nations to an Asian Relations Conference in New Delhi.[17] **Nehru** thought at that time that Asia had always been a zone of peace and that the imperialists had projected their conflicts onto this area. Once they were gone, peace would again prevail. He had to learn some painful lessons in subsequent years, but in 1947 he was still an optimist in this respect. Future tensions already announced themselves when invitations were issued to the 28 nations represented at the conference. China initially objected to the invitation of delegates from Tibet; the Jews of Palestine participated in the conference and this was resented by the Arab nations. The Indonesians sent a big delegation, but as the conference was not supposed to pass resolutions, the Indonesian fight against the Dutch colonial rulers could not be explicitly endorsed. **Nehru** was interested in establishing a permanent secretariat of this conference, but the Chinese voted against it. They wanted to postpone the decision until the second conference to be held in China, hoping that they could then have the secretariat in their country. Finally **Nehru** did establish a secretariat in New Delhi, but it remained inoperative. The second conference was never held because by that time the Communists had captured China.

In January 1949 **Nehru** convened an altogether different conference in New Delhi which was exclusively devoted to the plight of Indonesia. Several Asian nations and Australia participated in this conference. This time resolutions were passed which asked the Dutch to release the Indonesian leaders and to grant independence to Indonesia by 1950. The **United Nations** Security Council passed similar resolutions following this conference whose participants had thus made a mark as an international pressure group. It is interesting to note that similar action was not taken with regard to the French in Indo-China. This was probably due to the fact that in Indo-China the Communists were the vanguard of the anti-colonial struggle. By this time the Soviet Union was supporting Communist movements in several countries and the Communists were perceived to be enemies of nationalists.

As both the USA and the Soviet Union were trying to recruit allies in the incipient Cold War, non-alignment became an attractive option for Asian and African nationalists. **Nehru** had already recommended non-alignment and in December 1952 a conference of 12 African and Asian states met in Cairo, invited by the leaders of the Egyptian revolution. Afro-Asian solidarity and non-alignment became practically synonymous at this conference. In subsequent years, however, the two terms emerged as labels for two different movements. The Indonesians took the initiative in convening the **Bandung Conference** devoted to Afro-Asian solidarity in 1955. **Nehru** had insisted that China should be invited to this conference, obviously with a view to taming the new Communist regime by making it adhere to the principles of peaceful co-existence. China was at that time still an ally of the Soviet Union and was, therefore, certainly not non-aligned; nor was Pakistan which had joined the US system of military pacts in 1954. The major achievement of those assembled at Bandung was that they demonstrated a common front against colonial rule and demanded rapid decolonization. Those who still lived under colonial rule got the message and felt inspired by it.[18]

The presence of aligned powers at Bandung meant that another forum had to be created for those who advocated non-alignment. In the summer of 1956 **Nasser**, **Nehru** and Tito met at Brioni, Yugoslavia, and decided to provide such a forum. It so happened that a few months later the Soviet reaction to the Hungarian revolt and the Suez crisis gave added importance to the rallying of the non-aligned. When the first conference of the non-aligned was convened in Belgrade in September 1961, the Cold War had entered a rather 'hot' phase as Khrushchev had ordered the building of the Berlin Wall and had resumed the testing of atom bombs. **Nkrumah** and **Sukarno** also used the **Belgrade Conference** for denouncing the colonial rulers and urging them to speed up decolonization. **Nehru** made a rather moderate speech, admonishing the non-aligned that they should remain non-aligned among themselves. The resolutions passed by the conference were not hugely important; the only dramatic gesture was that **Nehru** and **Nkrumah** were sent as emissaries to Moscow and **Sukarno** and **Keita** to Washington in order to plead with the superpowers to keep the peace.[19]

The border war between China and India in October 1962 practically ruined both the Afro-Asian solidarity and non-alignment movements. **Nehru** was forced to ask the USA and Great Britain for military aid against China, which provoked criticism from **Nkrumah**. India's claim that it was still non-aligned sounded somewhat hollow. In subsequent years frantic efforts were made to hold a second Bandung and a second Belgrade.[20] There was never to be a second Bandung, because India insisted that the Soviet Union should be invited in its capacity as an Asian power. This would keep out China which had in the mean time severed its ties with the Soviet Union. A conference in Algier, which was supposed to prepare the second Bandung, ended in frustration. There was, however, a second Belgrade convened by **Nasser** in Cairo in October 1964. **Nehru** was dead by that time and **Sukarno** dominated the show as the leader of the 'new emerging forces', mostly newly independent African nations enjoying **Sukarno**'s anti-imperialist tirades. The **Non-aligned Movement (NAM)** lingered on in subsequent years, but its original attraction was lost. As years went by, the memory of how Afro-Asian solidarity had been stymied faded into oblivion and the myth of the **Bandung Conference** was revived at its golden jubilee in 2005 which was celebrated at a convention of about 100 heads of governments in the Indonesian capital of Jakarta. They represented for the most part the 'decolonized world' and paid their respects to the message which had been propagated from Bandung fifty years previously.

MANDATE AND TRUSTEESHIP: FROM THE LEAGUE OF NATIONS TO THE UNITED NATIONS

The **League of Nations** owed its origin to the terrible experience of the First World War. Even when the war was still going on, French and British plans were circulated which proposed a **League of Nations** as an instrument for the prevention of future wars. These plans received strong support from the US president, Woodrow Wilson.[21] As the USA practically determined the outcome of the war and saved the British and the French, Wilson's ideas had to be respected. Unlike the European politicians who mainly thought in terms of mediation and arbitration and otherwise wanted to continue the old diplomacy of a 'concert of European powers', Wilson wanted to establish a new world order based on the principle of self-determination. The old diplomacy of secret deals should be replaced by a new style of open deliberations. The Covenant of the **League of Nations** adopted at the Versailles Peace Conference on April 28, 1920 was mainly based on Wilson's ideas. The **League of Nations** was also charged with the responsibility of administering the former German colonies as well as the provinces detached from the defunct Ottoman Empire. Wilson, while stressing their right to self-determination, admitted that these territories would need some interim administration and that the **League of Nations** by itself could not accomplish this task. It had to be entrusted to different European states which would administer these various territories under the supervision of the **League of Nations**. Wilson would have preferred that only small European nations, not tainted by imperialism, be entrusted with this task.

Unfortunately much of what was done with these territories after the war was predetermined by the old methods of European secret diplomacy during the course of the war. As early as 1914, when the war had just begun, the British and French had concluded secret treaties on how to divide the German colonies of Togo and Cameroon among themselves. In April 1915 British, French, Russian and Italian representatives had signed a treaty in London which practically settled the fate of all enemy colonies. In May 1916 the **Sykes-Picot Agreement** determined the division of the Arab provinces between the British and the French. It was, of course, a secret pact, but it was made public by the Soviets after the revolution of 1917 when they found a copy of it in the archives of the Tsar. This agreement contravened the assurances given by the British to the Arabs, although Mark Sykes, the British representative, perhaps did not see it that way: he did not have in mind a permanent annexation but instead a temporary British–French condominium. Sykes cherished the alliance of the two nations during the war and hoped to preserve it after the conflict had ended. The French welcomed his view, but they presumably did not share his idea of a temporary condominium. At any rate, the post-war years were characterized by rivalries between the French and the British rather than by harmonious cooperation. Another secret treaty concerned the German colonies in the Pacific which were supposed to be turned over to Japan.

If Wilson had not appeared on the scene, all these treaties could have been implemented immediately after the war. Now they had to be put into practice within the framework of the **League of Nations**. In anticipation of these developments General Smuts of South Africa had published an ingenious plan in December 1918: *The League of Nations: A Practical Suggestion*. Smuts was an influential member of the British war cabinet. But in suggesting the distribution of what were now termed the 'mandates' of the League, he also had South Africa's special interest in German Southwest Africa in mind. In fact, he was looking for an internationally acceptable formula which would permit South Africa to annex this territory. He therefore graded the mandates in three classes: A, B and C. Class A contained territories such as the Arab provinces of the former Ottoman Empire which would get the right of self-determination for the foreseeable future. Class B included almost all African colonies which would need considerable further development before they could stand on their own feet. Class C was reserved for colonies which were supposedly completely unable to govern themselves and should be annexed by a developed nation. This class was constructed for German Southwest Africa which was then, indeed, annexed by South Africa but not excluded from supervision by the **League of Nations**. In addition, Class C also included some German colonies in the Pacific.

Smuts's plan was enshrined as Article 22 in the Covenant of the **League of Nations**. Wilson did not like this as he could clearly see that the old colonial powers would use this arrangement as a cover for their imperial designs. But in order to get the **League of Nations** going at all, he was prepared to make this concession to the European powers. Unfortunately the strength of the **League of Nations** was soon sapped by the refusal of the USA to ratify the Covenant. At home, Wilson faced a Republican majority in the Senate as well as in the House of Representatives. The powerful Republican leader, Senator Henry Cabot Lodge, opposed the Covenant and wanted to get it amended. Wilson probably felt that these amendments would have reduced the effectiveness of the League to such an extent that it would be better to let the League go on without the USA instead of hobbling it from the very beginning. He therefore asked his Democrats to vote against the amended draft, thus excluding the USA from the League. This was the first blow suffered by the League, but worse blows were soon to come.

In 1926 Germany had been admitted to the League due to the skilful diplomacy of the German foreign minister, Gustav Stresemann. Unfortunately his achievement was not to last long; Hitler left the League in 1933. In the meantime the League had failed to restrain one of its members, Japan, from waging war against China, another member, in 1931. The most shameful failure of the League was its acquiescence in Mussolini's rape of Ethiopia in 1936. Old-style diplomacy had once more overtaken the ideas incorporated in the Covenant of the League. The British and the French abetted Mussolini's Ethiopian venture because they feared that not doing so would push Mussolini into the lap of Hitler. Mussolini enjoyed this support and when he had got what he wanted, he left the League in 1937 and allied himself with Hitler after all.

While the performance of the League in the field of power politics was dismal, its less noticeable activities were quite creditable. It sponsored the International Labour Organization and other special agencies which did very good work. It also regularly received reports on the administration of the **mandate territories**. The governments concerned had to observe certain standards under the constant supervision of the League. Actually its supervisory role was of a very peculiar kind as the League had not determined the territorial distribution of the mandates. The Treaty of Versailles did not mention the League and simply stated that the colonies of the defeated powers would be distributed among the victors. They could implement the secret treaties mentioned above; that they had agreed to report to the League was only due to the fact that they had ratified its Covenant. The League could do very little to take them to task except for exposing them to international criticism.

The heritage of the League was bequeathed to the **United Nations** which replaced it after the Second World War. In the course of that war President Roosevelt took up President Wilson's unfinished task. He wanted to put all colonies, not only those of the enemies, under a regime of international trusteeship to prepare them for independence. This would require a period of transition. Roosevelt was a gradualist and thought in terms of decades rather than of rapid decolonization.[22] Nevertheless, his ideas alarmed Churchill who was fighting the war not just to save Great Britain but also the British empire. When Roosevelt and Churchill signed the **Atlantic Charter** in 1941 they discussed the choice of words in detail. Roosevelt personally corrected the draft and entered the words: '. . . self-government may be restored to those from which it has been forcibly removed'. Churchill insisted on inserting 'sovereign rights' before self-government.[23] He must have thought that this term would definitely exclude colonies from the purview of the Charter as their sovereignty was vested in the respective metropolitan powers. When others interpreted the Charter in a different way, Churchill reacted very sharply and asserted that he had not become the King's First Minister in order to preside over the liquidation of the British empire.[24] Therefore he naturally resented Roosevelt's insistence on the submission of all colonies to a regime of international trusteeship. In fact, Churchill even hoped that the old mandate system would be abolished after the war so that the respective territories could be added to the colonies of the mandatory powers. The British were particularly annoyed by the right of inspection and visitation which the international trusteeship authority was supposed to have. This was more than the Permanent Mandates Commission of the **League of Nations** had ever had. It had merely received reports of the mandatory powers.

Some British officials involved in these debates tended to make fun of Roosevelt's ideas which seemed to be vague and unrealistic. However, as Justice Frankfurter asserted at one stage of the long debates on the term 'trusteeship', this term had a very definite meaning in Anglo-Saxon law and implied that the trustee did not judge his own acts.[25] Accordingly there had to be an authority to which the trustee was accountable. The principle of accountability was at the centre of Roosevelt's plan. The authority concerned would be the **United Nations** which Roosevelt had named and inaugurated in 1942. Of course, it did not yet have a Trusteeship Council at that time. This was established only after the San Francisco Conference of the **UN** in 1945. By that time Roosevelt had died and his original plan had been whittled down. It was now to apply to only three types of territories: 1) The earlier **League of Nations** mandates, 2) the former colonies of the Japanese and the Italians lost by them in the Second World War, 3) any territory which a colonial power wished to transfer voluntarily to the Trusteeship Council.

The whittling down of Roosevelt's original plan was not only due to persistent British opposition, but also caused by a peculiar problem faced by the USA at the end of the war. It had captured the Pacific islands held earlier by the Japanese, and in the process nearly 40,000 US soldiers had lost their lives. The US military insisted on the annexation of these islands.[26] The British supported this, the more so as it would convert the USA into an imperial power which could not put the British empire in the dock any longer. For this very reason Roosevelt insisted that the USA would occupy these islands only under a regime of trusteeship. He then acquiesced to the demand of the military to use the term 'strategic trust' which the USA would hold in the interests of world security. The British were willing to accept this scheme although they thought of it as a striking example of US hypocrisy. The **UN** Trust Territory of the Pacific Islands was created by the Security Council on April 2, 1947. It encompassed the Mariana, Caroline and Marshall Islands. Their decolonization in the 1980s will be described later on.

As part of the bargain the USA sidetracked Roosevelt's comprehensive plan. His death shortly before the San Francisco Conference made it easier for those who had to arrive at a compromise. Only the Australian Labour politican, Dr H. V. Evatt, upheld Roosevelt's idea in San Francisco. But this 'stormy petrel', as Roosevelt had once called him, fought for a lost cause. Many of the smaller nations sympathized with him whereas the US and British governments defended their compromise. The two strands of Roosevelt's plan were then embodied in separate chapters of the **UN** Charter. He had emphasized the eventual independence of dependent nations even shortly before his death.[27] This aim should have been mentioned in Chapter XI of the Charter, which dealt with non-self-governing territories, but in this general chapter the term 'self-government' was all that the colonial powers would accept. They acquiesced to the inclusion of the term 'independence' in the more specific Chapter XII dealing with the regime of trusteeship.[28] Since only a few territories were to be administered under this scheme, it was acceptable to state that these territories should eventually achieve independence. The old A, B, C classification was abolished and the Trusteeship Council was entitled to receive petitions from the people of the respective territories; it also had the right of visitation but only on invitation from the administration of the territory. These functions of the Trusteeship Council seemed to be rather limited, but unlike the Permanent Mandates Commission of the **League of Nations** which was manned by experts reading reports, the Trusteeship Council was a political body. There was another decisive difference: the USA was now in the 'driver's seat' and the **UN** General Assembly was joined by more and more members from Africa and Asia. These new members took an active interest in decolonization. For many leaders from trusteeship territories, their appearance before the Trusteeship Council in New York was a great chance to make a mark on the international scene. If they clashed with the colonial rulers at home or were even put into prison, this now attracted international attention. In some cases the **UN** even set time limits for decolonization and the respective 'trustees' had to abide by them.

THE END OF COLONIAL EMPIRES
IN ASIA

INDIA: SETTING THE PACE FOR DECOLONIZATION

The Conquest of India and the Origins of Indian Nationalism

India was by far the biggest and one of the oldest European colonies in Asia. It was called the brightest jewel in the British crown; and yet it was destined to set the pace for decolonization by attaining its independence on August 15, 1947. It seemed to be a foregone conclusion that once this had happened the emancipation of other colonies would only be a matter of time. By the mid-1960s decolonization was almost complete. The pace set by India's independence was a fast one. The story of this initial emancipation is therefore of special relevance.

India was conquered in the eighteenth century, at the expense of the Indian tax-payer, by the English East India Company founded in London in 1600. For a long time this company had remained restricted to maritime trade. It had established some bridgeheads in Asia, but it had not tried to make major territorial acquisitions. When the Mughal empire was still strong, all European powers looked small in comparison. In the eighteenth century India had a population of about 150 million people, whereas Great Britain had only about 5 million inhabitants at that time.

When the Mughal empire disintegrated, a commercialization of power spread in India. Troops who had earlier served the Mughals were available in a large military labour market. Any prince or usurper who could raise some money was able to hire troops and subdue his neighbours. The East India Company fitted very well into this new context. It had grown up in an atmosphere of the commercialization of power in England and could transfer its skills to India. Whereas Indian princes were soloists in the concert of power, the East India Company was a modern corporation with a corporate memory. It also knew how to finance military campaigns while Indian princes were often left by their troops when they had exhausted their funds. Moreover, Indian princes were used to cavalry warfare and despised the lowly foot soldiers, whereas first the French and then the British in India trained Indian infantry soldiers who were cheap and efficient when following the methods of European infantry warfare. It was not the technological superiority of weapons, which were anyhow freely available to all in the market, but financial organization and military drill which enabled the British to conquer India.[1] They started by capturing Bengal and its rich land revenue after 1757. By

1818 they had vanquished almost all Indian powers and controlled the major part of India's territory.

The British administered India with a very small group of expatriate civil servants. They urgently needed indigenous assistants and introduced at a very early stage colleges of the British type. They also educated large numbers of Indian lawyers, as they introduced courts all over the country. This was not an altruistic measure; the courts yielded additional revenue to the government due to high court fees. India was turned into a nation of litigants, while the Bar Associations of the lawyers also offered a forum for political debate. With this type of education, liberal ideas spread among the new Indian elite and nationalism emerged at a very early stage. In 1849 an Indian nationalist wrote in a Marathi newspaper that the British should listen to Indian opinions otherwise there would be a revolution in India and the British would lose it in the same way they had lost America.[2] In later years such a writer would have been tried for sedition, but in the first half of the nineteenth century the British were still so sure of themselves that they took such remarks very lightly. They felt that the Indians had to be grateful to them for introducing the benefits of civilization. Lord Macaulay, the Law Member of the Government of India, gave expression to these ideas in 1835 when he stated that the British should educate Indian gentleman who would be Indian only in blood but British in every other respect. This ideology of perfect assimilation was shattered by the Indian Mutiny of 1857.

For later Indian nationalists, the mutiny was 'The First Indian War of Independence', but it was neither such a war nor merely a mutiny of soldiers. The mutiny of British Indian troops gave rise to a rebellion of North Indian landlords and peasants who had been pressed by harsh land revenue settlements. They were forced to grow cash crops to pay the revenue. As a result the soil had been degraded and they found it difficult to raise sufficient funds. If they defaulted, their land was immediately seized and sold by the revenue collector. The soldiers had other worries: their British officers did not understand their religious and cultural habits and punished them severely if they did not obey orders. The British could have suppressed the peasants by a show of force, but they found it more difficult to deal with the soldiers whom they themselves had trained in modern warfare. When the British almost faced 'decolonization' at that time, they were saved by the Sikhs who had only recently been vanquished by the soldiers who spearheaded the mutiny. It was an opportunity for the Sikhs to take revenge, after which they remained the favourite 'martial race' for the British who recruited them for the army in great numbers after they had helped them to quell the mutiny.

The new Indian educated elite had not sympathized with the mutineers, who wished to restore the power of the Great Mughal who had lived in Delhi as a British pensioner before the mutineers had asked him to lead them. A restored *ancien régime* would have had no use for the new educated class. Incipient nationalism experienced a setback due to the mutiny. It was almost twenty years before nationalist trends made themselves felt once more. Queen Victoria, when taking over India on behalf of the Crown in 1858, had promised equal chances to all her subjects. In 1877 she became Empress of India; her advisers had suggested she adopt this title in order to replace the Great Mughal whose hollow sovereignty the East India Company had retained so as to acquire legitimacy for governing India on his behalf. India was thus not a Crown colony like Ceylon, but an empire – a colony in a class of its own. Educated Indians appealed to the Empress to keep her word concerning the equality of her subjects. One of the most senior Indian nationalists, Dadabhai Naoroji, who later also won a seat in Parliament in a British constituency on a Liberal Party ticket, emerged as a vocal critic of British rule. He published a book with the title *Un-British Rule in India*, contrasting the actual practice of the Government of India with British liberal thought. He also spoke of the 'drain of wealth' from India and provided facts and figures to prove it. The **Indian National Congress**, founded in 1885, served as a forum for nationalist protest. In its intial years it was dominated by moderate nationalists who still thought that the British connection was politically beneficial for India. They were soon challenged by radical nationalists who argued that India had been a nation long before British rule and would come into its own again if it threw off the imperial shackles. Terrorism spread among the young generation of nationalists, but the British held the monopoly of force and could easily crush terrorism, nor was the British system vitally affected by the occasional assassination of high officers.

Both 'moderates' and 'extremists' (as the radical nationalists were called) tried to explore religious and cultural elements of national solidarity. Neo-Hinduism provided a message of this kind, but it had the drawback of excluding Muslims who were a substantial part of the Indian nation. The Census of India which was conducted every ten years from 1881 showed for the first time the numerical strength of various religious communities. The Muslims, many of whom were still proud of the fact that they had once ruled India, had never given much thought to the significance of numbers. If India did finally progress towards parliamentary democracy, numbers would be all important and the Muslims became afraid of being at the mercy of a Hindu majority. The British made use of this fear and granted **separate electorates** to the Muslims in 1909. In doing so they did not realize that they had prepared the way for the partition of India. Actually, in the context of the constitutional reforms of 1909, separate electorates were quite harmless. The elected representatives could only voice their opinions in the Imperial Legislative Council, without being able to touch the irremoveable British executive. However, the next round of constitutional reforms introduced the principle of '**responsible government**', i.e. the appointment of Indian ministers responsible to their respective legislatures in which they would have to be supported by political parties. Separate electorates were incompatible with this system, as the British themselves admitted, but they also stated that by now the Muslims regarded those electorates as a political privilege which could not be taken away.[3] The **Muslim League**, led by M. A. **Jinnah**, was thus bound to try to capture all seats of those separate electorates, whereas the **Indian National Congress**, which did not wish to represent only Hindus but claimed to speak for all Indians, had to put up its own Muslim candidates competing with those of the **Muslim League**. This conflict of interests determined the further political development of India.

The Freedom Movement led by Mahatma Gandhi

After the First World War the **Indian National Congress** seemed to have found an altogether new way of constructing a national solidarity. Mahatma **Gandhi** was not interested in Neo-Hinduism or in the quest for a useful past; he worked in the present and looked to the future. His method of *satyagraha* (holding on to the truth), which he had evolved in South Africa, seemed to be applicable also to India.[4] *Satyagraha* always refers to conscious actions of individual human beings who bind themselves by vows not to resort to violence. Many such individuals can then constitute a mass movement, but this movement does not derive its strength from any kind of collectivism. It is based on the individual convictions of all participants. Such convictions would transcend the barriers of caste or creed. Hindus and Muslims could join in a common endeavour. Gandhi made a mistake, however, when he espoused the **Khilafat movement** of the Indian Muslims in order to foster national solidarity. The movement arose when the victorious British imposed harsh conditions on the Turkish Kalif whom the Indian Muslims revered as their spiritual head. Gandhi had no idea that he was supporting **Pan-Islamism** by joining this movement.[5] He was drawn to it because its Indian leaders such as Maulana **Abul Kalam Azad** advocated non-violent non-cooperation with the British just as he did. Finally the Turks themselves abolished the institution of the Khilafat and left the Indian Muslims high and dry. **Abul Kalam Azad** remained a loyal follower of **Gandhi** and an important member of the **Indian National Congress**, but other ardent Khilafatists became communalists and parted company with the Congress. **Jinnah**, who had warned **Gandhi** against getting involved with the Khilafatists, whose movement he considered to be reactionary, finally ended up as the leader of the Muslim communalists as no other constituency was available to him.

    Gandhi's non-cooperation movement of 1920–1922 was initially a great success, but it eventually lost its impetus, the more so as the British let it run its course and did not confront the movement. **Gandhi**'s main problem was that he could not find suitable unjust laws which he could transgress with his *satyagrahis* as he had done in South Africa. It was only during his second great campaign in 1930 that he identified a law which was both demonstrably unjust and could be easily transgressed in a spectacular way. This was the Salt Act which made the production and distribution of salt a government monopoly and thus provided the government with a handsome revenue. The consumption of salt is a physical necessity, particularly so in the hot Indian climate. Even the poorest had to buy it. In order to defend this monopoly, the authorities would even punish people who picked up salt on the beach, where it formed due to the evaporation of sea water. Gandhi staged a spectacular **Salt March** with a selected group of *satyagrahis*. The group took about two weeks to get from the interior of Gujarat to the beach at Dandi where **Gandhi** picked up a grain of salt, thus ceremoniously transgressing the Salt Law. The gesture was repeated all over the country and prisons could not hold the thousands who had to be arrested. It was a symbolic revolution of impressive dimensions.

When **Gandhi** had started this campaign, the impact of the Great Depression had not yet hit India, but it did so in July 1930 when the wheat price fell by about 50 per cent, followed by an even steeper fall in the price of rice in January 1931.[6] The peasants were mostly indebted and had to continue paying interest to the moneylenders as well as land revenue to the government. The **Indian National Congress**, which organized no-rent campaigns and also encouraged the peasants to withhold land revenue payments, emerged as a party of the peasants at that time. This broadened its social base and later on enabled it to achive success at the polls when more peasants were enfranchised. The British, who feared a peasant rebellion much more than the campaigns of urban nationalists, felt that their rule was seriously threatened. As a result, the Viceroy, Lord Irwin, concluded a pact with **Gandhi** in March 1931, spurred on also by the fact that in Burma Saya San's rebellion was in full swing at that time. Actually, Irwin gained much and **Gandhi** very little from this pact. Gandhi suspended his campaign and promised to attend the second Round Table Conference in London in September 1931, while Lord Irwin permitted the production of salt for individual home consumption. The Salt Act, however, was not abolished and the salt tax even increased in subsequent years. Land confiscated during the campaign from peasants who had refused to pay land revenue was not restored to them. The only benefit which Gandhi got from this pact was that the Viceroy negotiated with him on equal terms. Winston Churchill understood this very well and spoke of 'the half-naked faqir' who was permitted to talk to the representative of His Majesty, the King, as a partner to a pact.

Gandhi also cherished this pact for reasons which he could not state. He seemed to hope that when attending the Round Table Conference in London he could conclude a pact with the British prime minister, Ramsay MacDonald. It was known that MacDonald was a friend of India, but unfortunately, by the time **Gandhi** reached London, MacDonald's government had been toppled as it failed to cope with the impact of the Great Depression. Although MacDonald had remained prime minister, he now headed a 'national government' in which he was a hostage to the Conservatives who needed him to pacify the working class. When **Gandhi** finally got an interview with him, MacDonald appeared to him like a 'sphinx' as he could only give evasive answers.[7] Instead of being able to conclude a pact on a high level, **Gandhi** was forced to participate in the tedious debates of the Round Table Conference. **Gandhi** had never been interested in constitutional reform; rather he had wanted to build up the **Indian National Congress** as an alternative to the legislatures created by the British for the Indians. However, he was now forced to discuss the representation of minorities, the safeguards for British interests in India, etc.

On returning home, **Gandhi** expected to be received for an interview by the new Viceroy, Lord Willingdon, who had replaced Lord Irwin in 1931. Before **Gandhi**'s departure, Lord Willingdon had been on good terms with him as he did not want to be blamed for **Gandhi**'s cancellation of his participiation in the Round Table Conference. But actually Willingdon despised Gandhi and thought that his predecessor had made a pact with him unnecessarily and thus increased his political standing. Irwin had hoped that Willingdon would be an ideal successor to him as he had previously been Governor General of Canada and seemed to be the right person to inaugurate the next stage of India's constitutional reforms. Rather than relying on his Canadian experience, however, Willingdon harked back to his earlier impressions of India as Governor of Madras and Governor of Bombay at a time when **Gandhi** had not yet led the **Indian National Congress**. Instead of granting **Gandhi** an interview, he had him arrested and suppressed the **Indian National Congress** with a heavy hand.[8] He could have continued this policy of repression if there had not been elections for the Imperial Legislative Council in 1934. The **Indian National Congress** scored a great success in these elections which was repeated on a larger scale when in 1936 provincial elections were held under the **Government of India Act of 1935**. Jawaharlal **Nehru** conducted this election campaign in a dynamic manner although he himself was not running for office and was even altogether against accepting office. He saw in these elections a demonstration of popular support for the **Indian National Congress**, a continuation of the freedom struggle at the polls. In fact, his party won a majority in seven out of nine provinces. The remaining two – the Punjab and Bengal – had been won by local parties. **Jinnah**'s **Muslim League** had not been very successful at all. He had thought that he would win all the seats in the **separate electorates** for Muslims as he had practically the same programme as the Indian National Congress. Why should Muslims vote for a Congress candidate when they could cast their vote for a representative of the **Muslim League**? But there were Congress Muslims who captured many seats, and the local parties in the Punjab and Bengal also had their own Muslim clientele. **Jinnah** had hoped that the Congress would need the League as a coalition partner in at least some provinces.[9] It would have been an act of political wisdom to offer him the chance of entering coalitions in at least some provinces, even if his support was not essential. But **Jinnah**'s League seemed to be down and out, so why extend a helping hand to it? In subsequent years **Jinnah** would take revenge for having been slighted, but nobody could have foreseen this in 1937.

Against **Nehru**'s wishes, the **Indian National Congress** did accept office in the seven provinces where it had gained a majority of the votes. The British had enfranchised the upper strata of the peasantry at this election, hoping that they would vote for pro-British agrarian parties because they owed much to the tenancy acts that the British had introduced. This would broaden the social base of colonial rule. These acts put a limit on the enhancement of rents and protected the tenant against eviction as long as he paid the rent. If the Great Depression had not hit the peasants so hard, they would probably have done what the British wanted them to do, but now they had flocked to the Congress and expected further legislation in their favour. If the Congress had stuck to agitation and spurned the legislatures, the peasants would not have understood this.[10] The term of office of the provincial Congress ministries was cut short by the outbreak of the Second World War. The new Viceroy, Lord Linlithgow, signed the declaration of India's participation in the war without paying attention to India's leaders. With some diplomatic effort he could have convinced **Gandhi** and **Nehru** to side with the British. **Gandhi** never attacked his adversaries when they were under attack by others and **Nehru** was an ardent anti-fascist, but Linlithgow could not explain British war aims in a way which would have motivated Indian leaders. He was a staunch follower of Churchill, and Churchill was a diehard imperialist. Churchill fought the war to retain the empire, not to liquidate it.

The resignation of the Congress ministries meant that the Congress lost influence during the war, whereas **Jinnah**'s importance increased immensely. At the conference of the **Muslim League** in Lahore in 1940 he proclaimed his Two-Nations theory, according to which Hindus and Muslims were two nations 'by any definition of the term'. The Muslims were therefore entitled to have separate states of their own. The name 'Pakistan' was not mentioned by **Jinnah** at that time. It had been coined by Rahmat Ali in 1933 as an acronym formed by the first letters of Punjab, Afghan Province (Northwest Frontier Province), Kashmir and Sindh plus the last syllable of Baluchistan. Bengal was conspicuous by its absence in this scheme. When this was pointed out to Rahmat Ali, he coined the term 'Bangistan'. **Jinnah** had been against this scheme at first, because he was then still a representative of the Muslim minority provinces, the Muslim diaspora, which would be left isolated if the Muslim majority provinces seceded from India.[11] By 1940 the scheme had grown upon **Jinnah** and he supported it, but he still did not want to use the name 'Pakistan'. However, his followers did not hesitate to do so and the Lahore Resolution of 1940 was soon called the Pakistan Resolution.

During the war **Jinnah** was by no means an obedient collaborator. He trailed the Congress, but always remained prepared to talk to the British. He was a political friend of Churchill who had almost succeeded in sponsoring **Jinnah** as a Conservative candidate for a seat in Parliament. This did not work, but Churchill had remained **Jinnah**'s protector. When the Japanese pursued their triumphant military campaign and had almost reached the shores of India, Roosevelt urged Churchill to do something for India so as to enlist it in the war effort. At this stage Sir Stafford Cripps, a Labour politician who had just joined the war cabinet, offered to fly to India. Cripps was a friend of **Nehru** and hoped to win him over. For Churchill the 'Cripps Mission' was a good alibi. He saw to it that Cripps could make no attractive offer to the Indians and his faithful standardbearer, Lord Linlithgow, did nothing to help Cripps in his negotiations. The 'Cripps Offer' consisted of vague promises concerning independence after the war, provided the Congress joined a 'national government' immediately. The Viceroy would act like a constitutional monarch and not interfere with the work of this government.

If Linlithgow had endorsed this claim, Cripps might have succeeded in his negotiations. Instead, Linlithgow complained that Cripps wanted to deprive him of his constitutional rights. Cripps blamed the Congress for his failure, rather than Churchill and Linlithgow. He was peeved and never again looked at Indian affairs with the air of optimism with which he had arrived in India in the spring of 1942.[12]

Having rejected the Cripps Offer, the Congress leaders felt that they had to start an agitational campaign rather than lapse into sullen inaction. **Gandhi** was asked to design a campaign. The first thing he did was to coin the slogan 'Quit India' – addressed to the British. He argued that the Indians had nothing to fear from the Japanese and since the British were hardly in a position to defend India, they should rather leave it before it was too late. Before **Gandhi** could devise a programme for the campaign, he and all other Congress leaders were imprisoned. Linlithgow would have liked to deport them all to South Africa for the remainder of the war, but his governors dissuaded him from doing this, as it would have led to criticism abroad. With the Congress leader out of the way, the younger generation embarked on a violent revolution, storming police stations, removing railway tracks and cutting telegraph wires. Later referred to as the 'August Revolution', it lasted no longer than a month as the British knew how to deal with such rebellions. Like **Gandhi**'s earlier campaigns, this August Revolution also threw up a new group of leaders who became important in Indian politics after the war. In later years such leaders were called 'prison graduates' and India had an ample supply of them. They had proven that they were ready to risk their lives or at least their personal freedom in the service of the nation. Many other 'decolonized' nations lacked this type of manpower.

British Policy and the 'Transfer of Power'

The British have often tried to portray the granting of independence to India and Pakistan as an orderly transfer of power which they had planned well in advance. But this was not so; Churchill had never wanted to grant independence to India. If he had not lost the general election of July 1945, India would not have gained independence in 1947. Unfortunately the Labour Party which now formed the government failed to make a clear statement about its plans for the future of India. If it had set the pace immediately it could perhaps have prevented the partition of India. Prime Minister Clement Attlee was well informed about India because he had headed the India Committee of the war cabinet. He was a firm believer in self-determination, but for this very reason he did not want to transfer power in India to an elite oligarchy not legitimized by elections.[13] Cripps, who had also been a minister of the war cabinet and now belonged to the new Labour cabinet, was also well informed and highly influential. It must have been due to his prompting that the only clear statement the new government announced was that the 'Cripps Offer' was still open. This was an anachronistic statement and obviously showed that Cripps was still peeved at his failed mission of 1942. Ernest Bevin, the new foreign minister, who had drafted with Cripps in 1943 a plan for

India's future economic development, was also well informed about India. But he was by no means an ardent 'decolonizer' as was apparent from his actions in subsequent years. Lord Pethick-Lawrence, the Secretary of State for India, was a good-natured old gentleman with no previous experience of Indian affairs. He was a learned man and a social reformer who had worked for women's suffrage together with his wife. He had been a Member of Parliament for the Labour Party for many years. He was 74 years old in 1945 and had been made a Lord in that year. It seems the cabinet position given to him was a reward for past services. Entrusting him with Indian affairs indicated that this was not a high priority on the government's agenda. He proved to be helpless as was reflected in a response to the Viceroy, Lord Wavell, who suggested to him that in the absence of a declaration of the government's India policy he could at least employ the old parliamentary device of getting a question on a specific issue asked on the floor of the House to which he could then give an authoritative reply. The old man answered by writing to Wavell that he would rather not do that, because then other questions might be asked which he would not be able to answer.[14]

Lord Wavell had become Viceroy in 1943, having earlier held the post of Commander-in-Chief in India. He was thus fully acquainted with the country and was convinced of the need for decolonization. His role model was General Lord Allenby, under whom he had served and whose biography he had written. Allenby had been in charge of granting a circumscribed type of independence to Egypt in 1922. Wavell would have been glad to advance towards independence in India, but he was not supported by the British government in this and was increasingly frustrated. In May 1945 he went to London for talks with Churchill as he urgently needed an Indian national government to share the responsibility of demobilizing the huge Indian army. Churchill permitted him to call a conference at Simla in July 1945 in order to discuss the formation of such a government with all Indian leaders. Churchill later admitted that he had given this permission only because his advisers had assured him that the conference would fail anyhow. **Jinnah** torpedoed this conference by demanding that he should name all the Muslim ministers in the national government, a particular affront given that the Congress president whom he faced at the conference was Maulana **Abul Kalam Azad**. The Congress could not accept this demand and as Wavell was not permitted to ignore **Jinnah**'s veto, the matter ended there. Now Wavell drew up a cabinet list himself in which he included only one Muslim who did not belong to the **Muslim League**, a representative of the Unionist Party of the Punjab. Wavell was permitted to show this list only to **Jinnah**, who again vetoed it. Since Wavell's lips were sealed, **Jinnah**'s second veto raised his reputation even more than the first one. He had clearly demonstrated that nothing could be done in India of which he did not approve. The **Muslim League** then did very well at the polls at the beginning of 1946, capturing almost all the seats in the separate electorates – **Jinnah**'s unfulfilled dream of 1937. But now he was no longer interested in forming coalitions with the **Indian National Congress**. He wanted Pakistan, and he knew he could only get it from the British.

Wavell now felt that he had no other option but to draft a breakdown plan, which envisioned a phased withdrawal of British troops from India. He no longer believed in an orderly transfer of power. This plan alarmed the British cabinet so much that it decided to send three ministers to India. This 'Cabinet Mission' arrived in March 1946, consisting of Sir Stafford Cripps, Lord Pethick-Lawrence and Lord Alexander, the First Lord of the Admiralty. This should have been the right time to issue a declaration of the British government's intentions with regard to India. Instead there was only a secret Cabinet Directive defining the terms of reference of the Cabinet Mission. It stressed the need for India to take care of its own defence and internal security. British troops would not be available for these purposes to an independent India. The Directive also contained a clause forbidding the transfer of **paramountcy** over the Indian princes to an Indian government. There was no reference to the possibility of a failure of the Mission's endeavours.[15] Equipped with a secret Directive but no open declaration of the British government's intentions, the Cabinet Mission had no clear terms of reference and its constitutional recommendations remained mere suggestions. These recommendations were very complicated; they envisioned two groups of provinces and a limited central government with functions specifically entrusted to it by the provinces. The 'grouping' of provinces left options open to the provinces whereby they could opt in or out of their respective group. **Jinnah** accepted the scheme as he saw it as a step towards Pakistan, the Congress leaders initially agreed to work the scheme, but **Nehru** made a statement that once the constituent assembly was convened, it could arrive at its own decisions. **Jinnah** then withdrew his acceptance. In the meantime the Cabinet Mission had left India and Wavell was back to square one. He then cut the Gordian knot and appointed a national government with **Nehru** as interim prime minister. **Jinnah** was furious and announced a 'Day of Direct Action' for August 16, 1946. Since **Jinnah** had never organized any campaign of this sort, nothing happened on this day except in Calcutta which became the scene of the 'Great Calcutta Killing'. Shahid Suhrawardy, the Chief Minister of Bengal, had declared this day a public holiday and had invited criminal elements from outside. They killed large numbers of Hindus, while many of those who survived fled to Bihar from where they had come to work in the jute mills of Calcutta and other industrial enterprises. This is what Suhrawardy had intended to achieve by organizing the killing. He foresaw that Calcutta would only become a part of Pakistan if he could tilt the demographic balance in the city in favour of the Muslims. In spite of this, Calcutta remained in India. Wavell was once more thinking of a breakdown plan and sent a note on 'A Policy for India' to Pethick-Lawrence in September 1946. He warned that his administration was rapidly running down and even the army was deteriorating.[16]

While Suhrawardy had rightly guessed that Bengal and the Punjab would not be given to Pakistan undiminished, as Hindus were in a majority in West Bengal and in East Punjab, **Jinnah** still hoped that he would not have to be satisfied with a 'motheaten Pakistan', as he called it. But after all, his own Two-Nations theory required a partition along the lines of Hindu and Muslim majority districts.

Jinnah then approved of the appointment of Justice Cyril Radcliffe who would ascertain this line by looking at the Census data.[17] In the meantime Lord Mountbatten had replaced Lord Wavell as Viceroy in April 1947. Mountbatten had consulted Wavell often when he was in charge of the Allied forces in Southeast Asia. He thus knew what was at stake in India, but he was in line for being appointed First Lord of the Admiralty and feared that the viceroyalty would derail his navy career. Thus he could dictate his terms when Attlee urged him to go to India. The most important condition was that the government would finally issue the declaration concerning the independence of India which had been overdue.[18] A date was fixed for August 15, 1948, three years after Mountbatten had accepted the capitulation of Japan. Soon after he reached India, Mountbatten got this date moved to August 15, 1947. He was afraid that not much power would be left to transfer, if there was any further delay. Parliament passed the Independence of India Act as quickly as possible. It was essentially the Government of India Act of 1935 with some appropriate amendments. The same act was passed for Pakistan.

Before these acts were passed, Mountbatten had to settle the mode of partition. A scheme which was appropriately called 'Plan Balkan' was prepared by his advisers and then finalized in London. These final touches were crucial as the British government wanted to grant independence to the British Indian provinces. It was then left to them as to how they would form new states and there was no need for 'partition' as a British administrative act. The British also granted independence to the Indian princes. When Mountbatten showed this final draft to **Nehru**, he was surprised that **Nehru** rejected it furiously.[19] It could, indeed, have led to a Balkanization of India. It was much better that the British partition India by an administrative act. This is how Justice Radcliffe was asked to do his job, but there was one crucial omission in his terms of reference: he was to deal with the British Indian provinces only, not with the princely states. This proved to be a major handicap.

Lapse of Paramountcy: The Decolonization of the Princely States

When the British conquered India, they had entered into alliances with many princes who were then subjected to **indirect rule**. A British resident at their court would tell them what to do. Otherwise they enjoyed internal autonomy in their state. There were about 500 such princes, preserved like insects in amber, in the British-Indian empire. While only a few of them ruled large states such as Jammu and Kashmir, Hyderabad, Mysore, etc., there were many middling ones such as Alwar or Bhopal and so on. Applying the principle of 'divide and rule' to the princes, the British had finely graded them in ranks, expressed in terms of the number of shots fired as a salute when they attended an imperial meeting or visited the Viceroy. Some had high grades such as 19, 17, 15 shots, but there were many for whom not a shot was fired. They all owed allegiance to the Queen or King, called Empress or Emperor of India after 1877. This peculiar relationship was called **paramountcy**. Since the British did not have a written constitution they also wisely refrained from defining paramountcy in more concrete legal terms. The British exported this model of **indirect rule** to other colonies where they could find suitable sultans or emirs as in Malaya or northern Nigeria. In India the princely states covered about one-third of the territory, but they were conspicuous by their absence in the fertile plains. The British saw to it that most areas which yielded high revenue and cash crops were under their direct rule.

Under the Government of India Act of 1935 an attempt had been made to include the princely states in an Indian federation. There was even a specific federal section of the act, but it never became operative, because at least half of the princes would have had to join the federation to make it work. The Political Department of the Government of India, most of whose officers did not favour the federation, obviously told the princes that joining it would imply financial contributions. British policy makers had actually designed the federation so as to make the princes a conservative counterweight to the **Indian National Congress**. If the princes had joined the federation they could have got a much better deal than they actually did after India attained independence. They could not foresee, however, that this would happen so soon.

As mentioned earlier, a 'Plan Balkan' had been drawn up in London before the granting of independence. It implied that the provinces of India would achieve independence individually and could then decide how to unify under a central authority. This was avoided, however, by a transfer of power to central states at the price of partition, but it did not affect the princely states. When paramountcy lapsed on August 15, 1947, all of them achieved their individual independence. Lord Mountbatten urged them to sign instruments of accession to one or the other successor state of British India, but these were only recommendations. He could do no more than that, because the British government had shied away from taking a stand on this issue. Even the secret Cabinet Directive given to the Cabinet Mission had explicitly excluded the transfer of 'paramountcy' to an Indian government. Attlee was probably afraid of giving Churchill and his party a chance to start a campaign against Indian independence if the status of the princes was affected. Thus large states such as Jammu and Kashmir or Hyderabad, and coastal states such as Travancore could actually consider remaining independent. Some of the princes had started – even at the time of Mountbatten's arrival in India – to put in claims for separate dominion status for their states.[20] These claims, were, at least, firmly rejected by the British government. The other states, most of whom were small and landlocked, literally queued up at the office of the Indian Home Minister, Vallabhbhai Patel, to sign their instruments of accession, being promised a certain degree of autonomy and privy purses.

Two princes, however, did not sign up and created a great deal of trouble: the Maharaja of Jammu and Kashmir and the Nizam of Hyderabad. The Maharaja was a Hindu ruler of a state with a Muslim majority, while the Nizam was a Muslim who ruled Hindus. The location of the state of Jammu and Kashmir was such that the idea of an independent state, a kind of Switzerland in the Himalayas, was very appealing. It shared a long border with Pakistan, but since Gurdaspur district in the Punjab had been given to India at the time of partition, it also had a common border with India. The location of Hyderabad was less suitable, as it was land-locked in the middle of India. As a Muslim ruler, the Nizam could have thought of joining Pakistan, but he hated **Jinnah** and did not want to be subjected to him. Pakistan also did not covet Hyderabad, but it claimed Kashmir with its Muslim majority. The Maharaja delayed his decision and Pakistan sent terrorists across the border who nearly captured Srinagar, the Maharaja's capital. He asked India for help, but Mountbatten, who had remained in India as Governor General, insisted that he must accede to India first as the Indian army would otherwise have no legal standing in Kashmir. **Nehru** endorsed this, but also promised that a referendum could be held later on so that the people of Kashmir could exercise their right of self-determination. This was a rash promise that was never followed up. It would have been the first referendum in which Indian Muslims would be asked whether they prefer to live in India or Pakistan. In view of the fact that almost one-third of the Muslims of British India had remained in India after partition, it would have been an explosive issue. Moreover, with the exception of the Northwest Frontier Province, there had been no referendum of this kind when British India was divided.

The case of the Northwest Frontier Province was a very peculiar one. Its leaders had participated in **Gandhi**'s movement and the province had a Congress government at the time of partition. **Gandhi** advised the Congress leaders of the province to abstain from voting in a referendum. This was a painful decision for him, but he was aware of the problems which would arise if the province joined India. Pakistan would have been doomed from the very beginning. **Gandhi**'s position with regard to Kashmir was different. He even advised **Nehru** against taking the case to the **United Nations**. He had reluctantly agreed to the partition of India as a territorial sacrifice, but he could never accept **Jinnah**'s Two-Nations theory as he had worked for Hindu–Muslim unity throughout his life. Moreover, the logical conclusion of this theory would have been that India's large Muslim minority be expelled to Pakistan. **Jinnah** did not want this as it would have led to a collapse of Pakistan. Nevertheless, he pursued the annexation of Kashmir, sending regular troops after the terrorists who had not succeeded in captur-ing Srinagar. The Indian army defended Kashmir and finally a ceasefire line was agreed upon in 1949 which is still the de facto border between India and Pakistan.

The problem of Hyderabad was solved in 1948 by a 'police action' of the Indian army. Similarly, the more complicated case of Junagadh, a coastal state of Gujarat, was solved by sending Indian tanks into this small princely state. The Jam Saheb of Junagadh, a Muslim ruler, had actually opted for Pakistan and **Jinnah** had accepted his request.[21] Junagadh, however, is located at a considerable distance from Pakistan and has a Hindu majority. The Jam Saheb then fled to Pakistan and in this case a referendum was held after military action. Its result confirmed that the people wanted to join India.

Initially the princely states retained some autonomy and the rulers of larger states were appointed as governors under the Indian constitution. In due course, however, they were absorbed by the states of the Indian Union, e.g. Hyderabad became part of Andhra Pradesh, Mysore was absorbed by Karnataka, Travancore and Cochin plus the former British Indian district of Malabar formed the new state of Kerala in 1957. In 1969 prime minister Indira Gandhi abolished the privy purses of the princes. These were payments which they received from the government according to the agreements made when they signed the instruments of accession. Of course, the princes complained about this, but they retained their private wealth after all. Some of them also made a career in Indian politics, emerging as democratic leaders after having lost their feudal privileges.

From Creditor to Debtor: The Economic Implications of Indian Independence

India's attainment of independence so soon after the war was due to a war-time reversal of the position of creditor and debtor. Before the war there had been long debates about India's national debt which the nationalists wanted to reject, arguing that it had been imposed upon India by the colonial rulers. This nationalist recalcitrance made the British even more eager to maintain their rule, because they feared bankruptcy of Great Britain if India defaulted. All this had changed during the war when India's industrial production was geared to the British war effort. The British paid for this by printing Indian rupees and piling up the respective sterling reserves in the Bank of England. India was not permitted to draw upon these reserves during the war nor immediately thereafter. This amounted to a regime of forced saving. However, it resulted in India emerging from the war as a creditor rather than as a debtor of Great Britain.[22] Churchill would have liked to prevent this by presenting a bill for war expenditure to India. If India had been a dominion like Australia or Canada, it could have been asked for such contributions. But Churchill had denied this status to India and could not have it both ways. Moreover, President Roosevelt, who financed the British war effort, would have prevented Churchill from extorting money from India. Churchill often stymied Roosevelt's attempts to get political concessions for India during the war, but in financial affairs Roosevelt had the greater leverage and Churchill was aware of this.

Since it is much easier to grant independence to a creditor than to a debtor, India could derive political profit from its favourable financial position. But Great Britain was nearly bankrupt at the end of the war and it would have been unable to pay its debts to the newly independent creditor. Consequently, a last-minute moratorium was signed by the Indian interim government. British business interests would very much have liked to insert in the treaty some provisions which would have ensured a continuation of their earlier privileges in India. However, the British government told them that it was hard enough to get the Indians sign the moratorium and that it would be impossible to ask for more. The moratorium forced India to turn for credit to the World Bank and the International Monetary Fund, because India's sterling reserves could not be drawn upon. India also knew very well that it is unwise to drive a debtor to bankruptcy if one still hopes to get money from him.

India attained its independence at an auspicious time. A few years later the Korean War drove up the prices of raw materials and made colonial possessions attractive once more. In addition the Cold War increased the fear that the colonies would fall prey to the Soviet bloc. Many of the more tortuous processes of decolonization in the 1950s and 1960s were influenced by such apprehensions. Once India had set the pace, however, there would be occasional delays in the progress of decolonization but no return to old-style colonialism.

PAKISTAN AND SRI LANKA: FREEDOM WITHOUT STRUGGLE

The Construction of a New State: Pakistan

Pakistan is a unique case in the history of decolonization. It was not to be found on the map before it was created in 1947, whereas all other decolonized states corresponded in their territorial outlines to the areas delineated by the colonial rulers years, decades, even centuries earlier. The idea of separating Pakistan from India was thrust upon the British at the final stage of decolonization. Of course, the British had played the game of 'Divide and Rule' in India as far as Hindus and Muslims were concerned, but they had done this in order to maintain colonial rule, not because they intended to create Pakistan. In fact, they had always proudly stressed that India had been united only under their rule.

If the state was created against the wishes of the British, one would expect that they had to be forced to grant it after a long and fierce struggle. But this was not so. M. A. **Jinnah**, the founder of Pakistan, had never led a rebellion nor had he spent a single day in a British prison. As a brilliant lawyer, he had never transgressed the limits of legality and had derived his political leverage from the veto power which he had as a participant in the final negotiations preceding decolonization. It was a great paradox that **Jinnah** should become the founder of a Muslim state in northern India. He was not at all a pious Muslim, but a secularized and Anglicized member of the British Indian educated elite. By birth he was an Ismaili Khoja, a member of a Shia sect who were followers of the Aga Khan. He was a Gujarati like **Gandhi** and like him he had studied in London. He began his political career as leader of the Muslims of the diaspora, i.e. the Muslim minority provinces of British India. In those provinces the fear of the Hindu majority was naturally greater than in the Muslim majority provinces, Punjab and Bengal. As a diaspora leader, **Jinnah** was naturally averse to the Pakistan plan when it was first proposed by Rahmat Ali, a Punjabi, in 1933.[23] It was only during the Second World War, when the provinces that had been ruled by Congress ministries reverted to governor's rule and no longer offered any scope for political activities, that **Jinnah** shifted his attention to the Muslim majority provinces.[24] But they had their own political leaders who would only respect him as a leader at the 'national' level. Therefore, he had to define his nation and did it by means of his Two-Nations theory (see p. 59).

The social structures of the two Muslim majority provinces were very different; in fact, there could not have been a more striking contrast than between the Punjab and Bengal. In the Punjab the Muslim leaders were feudal lords who were often also heads of great clans. They controlled great landed estates and their descendants have continued to do so even up to the present day. Since landlords have common interests, the Punjab was for a long time dominated by a party of Muslim and Hindu landlords, appropriately named the 'Unionist Party'. In Bengal the Muslim politicians were leaders of tenants who cultivated the land of Hindu landlords. The dominant party there was the Peasants and Workers Party (*Krishak Proja Party*). There was, therefore, no place for the **Muslim League** in the provincial politics in the Punjab and Bengal. It made progress there only in the late 1940s due to the propaganda for Pakistan. Since this did not involve social issues, Punjabi landlords and Bengali tenants could rally behind the demand for Pakistan. Even in territorial terms **Jinnah** was careful to keep Pakistan as vague as possible, because once he put his cards (and maps) on the table, many people would recognize that Pakistan was not for them. As long as this vagueness persisted, many Muslims could believe that Pakistan would be wherever Muslims lived, a kind of territorial equivalent of the **separate electorates**. When **Jinnah** left Mumbai (Bombay) for Karachi to take up his new post of Governor General of Pakistan, he was asked by the local Muslims whom he left behind what they were supposed to do now. **Jinnah** admonished them to become good citizens of India but he did not tell them how this would be compatible with his Two-Nations theory.

Jinnah had insisted on becoming the Governor General of Pakistan, because he had to build up a new state from scratch – and he did not have much time left in which do it. He knew that he had cancer and that his days were numbered. He died in September 1948. Opting for the office of Governor General instead of becoming prime minister as **Nehru** did in India, **Jinnah** determined the future of his state. It would follow the viceregal tradition and would finally be based on an alliance of the bureaucracy with the army, but not on parliamentary democracy. The army was particularly strong in the Punjab, as the Punjabi Muslims were one of the 'martial races' which the British recruited for the British Indian army. Actually, the Pakistan army inherited the same British tradition of preserving political neutrality and taking orders from a civilian government, but whereas this worked in India, it was soon jettisoned in Pakistan.[25] The main reason for this was that the **Muslim League** was not at all a party like the **Indian National Congress**. The League had been used by **Jinnah** for promoting the demand for Pakistan; once Pakistan was created and **Jinnah** was dead, this party disintegrated.

Whereas the army was strong in Pakistan from the very beginning, the civil service was relatively weak. It was able to gain some recruits only because the educated Muslims from northern India who fled to Pakistan after partition joined its ranks. These refugees (*muhajeers*) initially played a dominant role in Pakistan but eventually, once 'locals' had grown up and began to compete with them, the *muhajeers* lost ground and even complained of discrimination. In East Pakistan (Bengal) the conditions were completely different. There were very few indigenous civil servants and even fewer military officers. The British had hardly recruited any Bengalis for the army. East Pakistan was soon governed like a colony of West Pakistan by Punjabi expatriates who were not liked by the Bengalis. In addition, the West Pakistanis told the Bengalis to abandon their own language and adopt Urdu, the language spoken by the Muslims of northern India, which had become the national language of Pakistan. A language movement consequently arose; students who participated in it were shot and then regarded as martyrs by the Bengalis. All such conflicts finally led to the secession of East Pakistan as Bangladesh in 1971. Pakistan, which had been a new state on the map in 1947, was also the only state to have experienced a secession after decolonization.

The war which led to the secession of Bangladesh was lost by the Pakistan army in a most spectacular way. The Indian army, which had contributed to the liberation of Bangladesh, held 90,000 Pakistani prisoners of war who were repatriated to West Pakistan after the meeting of the new Pakistani president, Zulfiqar Ali Bhutto, with the Indian prime minister, Indira Gandhi, at Simla in the summer of 1972. This was already the third war between India and Pakistan – all of them undeclared and all of them won by India. The first was the encounter in Kashmir in 1947–1948; the second, also concerning Kashmir, was started by Pakistan's President Ayub Khan in September 1965. **Nehru** had died in May 1964 and his successor, Lal Bahadur Shastri, seemed to be a weak and inexperienced man. Ayub Khan was proud of the Patton tanks which his American allies had supplied and thought that he could cut off the road from India to Kashmir with one swift attack in his 'Operation Grand Slam'. His plan failed, however, and Indian troops marched towards Lahore. After a ceasefire, Ayub Khan had to attend a conference at Tashkent in January 1966 and accept Soviet mediation. Shastri withdrew Indian troops only after Ayub Khan had signed a declaration in which he pledged that Pakistan would never again use force in order to settle disputes with India. As a military man, Ayub Khan was particularly affected by this defeat. Soon after he was faced with the Bangladeshi quest for constitutional autonomy. Pakistan's defeat in 1965 finally contributed to the secession of 1971.[26] Pakistan then wished to get even with India by becoming a nuclear power, as it could not hope to achieve parity in the field of conventional warfare. India then started its own nuclear programme and in 1998 both countries conducted large-scale nuclear tests.

When one considers the progression from **separate electorates** to partition and from there to the emergence of two rival nuclear powers, something had obviously gone wrong in the process of decolonization.

Sri Lanka: A Painless Emancipation?

Ceylon – as Sri Lanka was called at that time – achieved its independence as a dominion on February 4, 1948. There had been no freedom struggle in Ceylon and dominion status had been the declared aim of the national politicians. They had never asked for complete independence as had the Indians, who accepted dominion status only as a stage of transition in 1947. Ceylon remained a dominion for more than two decades. The painless transfer of power was due to the fact that national politics in Ceylon was in the hands of a small group of educated gentlemen who settled their problems in quiet negotiations rather than appealing to the masses.

Ceylon had already been blessed with the universal franchise in 1931, while Indian voters had to wait until 1952 for this. But the generous franchise was combined with a rather peculiar form of government. In order to circumvent the introduction of parliamentary democracy, the British had taken the London County Council as a model for the government of Ceylon. The Council consisted of the chairmen of seven committees which elected their chairmen themselves. The seven chairmen constituted a Board of Ministers. It is understandable that this structure facilitated the deliberations of cultured gentlemen. Even the Tamil minority could suitably represent its political interests within this framework. However, the problem of representing the Tamil minority was not solved by the new constitution. Before its introduction there had been **separate electorates** which had now been replaced by the universal franchise; this naturally favoured the majority. However, some of the seven committees elected Tamil chairmen which contributed to a political balance, although this was not mandatory. During the next period of office, beginning in 1936, all seven chairmen were Singhalese. The Tamils were furious about this. In the constitution which was framed immediately before the granting of dominion status, there was a closer approximation to the parliamentary model, with some modifications concerning the delineating of constituencies so as to accommodate the Tamils.

The man who led Ceylon during this period of transition was Don Stephen **Senanayake**. He had been a member of the council of seven ministers since its inception in 1931. He then became the head of the council in 1942 and the first prime minister of Ceylon in 1947. He negotiated the transfer of power and then remained prime minister until his death in 1952. His party was the **United National Party (UNP)**. Under his guidance, communal peace was maintained, but it broke down when election campaigns revealed the power of the Singhalese majority.

The gentlemen who had earlier dominated politics had all conversed in English, but after 1956 language conflicts surfaced. Solomon **Bandaranaike** and his **Sri Lanka Freedom Party (SLFP)** appealed to the '*swabhasha* educated', i.e. the people who had been to school in Buddhist monasteries and knew only Singhalese and no English, as this was not taught in those schools. They saw all the white-collar jobs going to the Tamils who had attended schools where they learned English well. When **Bandaranaike** made Singhalese the state language, he was sure to win over the '*swabhasha* educated', but in doing this he alienated the Tamils of whom very few had even an elementary knowledge of Singhalese. However, **Bandaranaike** did not go far enough for the more radical Singhalese and he was shot by a Buddhist monk in 1959. His widow, Sirimavo Bandaranaike, then became his successor following a tearful election campaign. In 1965 she lost to the **UNP**, but returned to power in 1970 when the **SLPF** championed the rejection of dominon status and the conversion of the country, which was now called Sri Lanka, into a Democratic Socialist People's Republic. The decolonization of the name of the country was long overdue. Sri Lanka was the original name of the country which had been mispronounced and misspelt by the colonial rulers (Cey = Sri, lon = Lanka). The qualifactions contained in the name of the republic corresponded to the political fashion of the time; it started to sound rather incongruous after the presidential regime introduced by Junius Jayewardene on behalf of the UNP in 1978 adopted a decidedly liberal course in its economic policy.

The Republic also got started on the wrong foot when the **SLFP** government introduced a quota system in higher education which benefited the Singhalese and discriminated against the Tamils. This discrimination spawned sectarian terrorism which has beset Sri Lanka ever since.[27] The Liberation Tigers of Tamil Eelam (LTTE) are among the world's most fierce terrorist movements. The emancipation of Sri Lanka, which seemed to be such a painless affair in 1948, turned into a very painful experience when the communal conflicts, earlier hidden under the placid facade of gentlemanly politics, surfaced.

THE DUTCH AND THE REPUBLIC OF INDONESIA

Dutch colonial rule in Indonesia was markedly different from British rule in India. The British had imposed their legal system on India at a very early stage. This had yielded handsome court fees which provided additional revenue to the colonial state, but also led to the rise of Indian lawyers whose Bar Associations provided a forum for political debate. Many of these lawyers had studied in England and returned as barristers. Prominent Indian leaders like **Gandhi**, **Jinnah** and **Nehru** were all barristers. Such lawyers were conspicuous by their absence in Indonesia under Dutch rule. The Dutch had carefully recorded Indonesian customary law and had published it (*Pandekten van het Adatrecht*). Jurisdiction under this customary law was left to native authorities. Accordingly there was only a very small Western-educated elite in Indonesia. Engineering or elementary medicine were the only subjects to be studied for a career in the colonial state. **Sukarno** was a civil engineer trained in Java but very few Indonesians obtained an academic degree in the Netherlands. Nevertheless, there had been some inspiring leaders; for instance, Raden Adjeng Kartini (1879–1904), a young lady belonging to the indigenous nobility; Tjipto Mangunkusumo (1886–1943), the founder of the movement *Budi Utomo* (Noble Endeavour) and Umar Said Tjokroaminoto (1882–1934) who established *Sarekat Islam* in 1912.[28]

The Dutch kept Indonesia under tight control, giving nationalism little chance to develop. However, they could not prevent the rise of youth organizations which debated national unity and initiated a quest for a national language. In 1928 a youth congress adopted a national pledge and advocated *Bahasa Indonesia* as national language. This was of great importance for the further development of Indonesian nationalism. Whereas other nations experienced intense language conflicts, there was no such conflict in Indonesia. *Bahasa Indonesia* in Latin script could be easily propagated and was generally appreciated. Although the name for this language had only been adopted in 1928 it was by no means a new or artificial language. It corresponded to coastal Malay which was widely used as a lingua franca. Even the Javanese, who had a venerable and highly complex language whose forms of address reflected the hierarchical order of their traditional society, were glad to adopt this lingua franca for everyday use. This greatly facilitated modern political discourse, the more so as *Bahasa Indonesia* easily absorbed foreign terms such as 'national' (nasional) or 'socialist' (socialis), etc.

While the Dutch did not interfere with the activities of the youth congress, they came down with a heavy hand on nationalist agitators like **Sukarno** who was arrested in 1929 at the age of 28 and spent more than a decade in jail in subsequent years until the Japanese freed him and used him to obtain popular support. The Japanese did not initially advocate Indonesian independence and perhaps even hoped to turn the country into a Japanese colony, provided they won the war. When the Japanese prime minister, Marshall Tojo, spoke of the independence of Myanmar (Burma) and of the Philippines during the war but did not mention Indonesia, this alarmed Indonesian nationalists.[29] It was only in September 1944, when Japan's defeat seemed to be a foregone conclusion, that the Japanese government also promised to grant independence to Indonesia. This at least saved the reputation of **Sukarno** and other 'collaborators' whose credentials were doubted by the revolutionary youth. But the young revolutionaries did not want to wait; they pressed **Sukarno** to proclaim independence before the Japanese would grant it. **Sukarno** knew that the massive presence of Japanese troops in Indonesia would make a revolution a suicidal adventure.

Finally, the Japanese appointed a Committee for the Investigation of Indonesian Independence which drafted a constitution. Subsequently a Committee for the Preparation of Indonesian Independence was formed whose chairman was **Sukarno**. In this capacity he flew to Dalat (Vietnam) to get the approval of Marshall Terauchi, the Japanese supreme commander in Southeast Asia.[30] **Sukarno** returned to Jakarta on August 14, 1945 to the news of the atom bombs dropped on Japan and the impending Japanese surrender. But still he hesitated in proclaiming Indonesian independence. He was then hijacked by some young revolutionaries who forced him to issue the proclamation. Even then he first secured Japanese approval, because he wanted to prevent the Japanese from slaughtering the young revolutionaries, which they were still in a position to do and were even obliged to defend the status quo under the terms of their capitulation. The Proclamation of the Independence of the Republic of Indonesia was then drafted, literally overnight, in the house of the Japanese Admiral Maeda. It was signed only by **Sukarno** and his close associate **Hatta** and read out by **Sukarno** on the steps of his own house on August 17, 1945, which was celebrated henceforth as 'Freedom Day' (*Hari Kemerdekaan*).[31]

While the Japanese had ruled Indonesia very harshly, they had made some contributions to Indonesian nationalism. They had prohibited the use of the language of the colonial rulers and had actively promoted *Bahasa Indonesia*. The Japanese not only supported secular nationalists, they also rallied the Muslim organizations and established a Muslim council (*Madjelis Sjuro Muslimin Indonesia = Masjumi*) which remained very important in subsequent times.[32] The Japanese had also raised a national army and had trained and commissioned 6,000 Indonesian officers, which was of enormous importance for Indonesia's subsequent political development. Although the Japanese were obliged under the terms of their capitulation to disband this army, **Sukarno** persuaded them merely to dissolve it into local commands responsible for preserving law and order. This decision turned out to be of crucial importance for the further political development of the Republic of Indonesia.

At the end of the war, Indonesia was in the British sphere of the Allied Command. This meant that the USA was not charged with taking over Indonesia from the Japanese. This process would probably have happened more quickly under US control, but it remains a matter of speculation what this would have meant for the decolonization of Indonesia. Since the British were responsible for occupying Indonesia, the supreme command over this operation was in the hands of Rear Admiral Louis Mountbatten. This young cousin of King George V had had a brilliant military career. He was only 39 years old when he accepted the Japanese capitulation in 1945, and he purposely fixed the date of India's independence on the same day two years later as the last Viceroy of British India. Mountbatten sympathized with Asian nationalists and was not at all interested in subjecting them once more to European colonial rule. But now he had to send British-Indian troops to Indonesia to replace the Japanese and he did not approve of **Sukarno**'s proclamation of independence.

When the British troops arrived in Indonesia, they did not have orders to occupy the whole country but only to secure the ports and some major cities and to protect the lives of Europeans who had been interned by the Japanese. They were shocked and surprised when they faced fierce Indonesian resistance in Surabaya, where their forces were almost defeated by revolutionary Indonesian troops under a charismatic leader, Sutomo, who was then only 25 years old. Sutomo was a bright and dedicated young man who had no official credentials. In fact, the leaders of the newly proclaimed Republic of Indonesia were taken aback by the 'Battle of Surabaya' which they nevertheless had to celebrate as a heroic deed in years to come. They had hoped to play off the British against the returning Dutch, but this game was spoiled by Sutomo.[33] The decentralized revolutionary troops did not have a unified command at that time nor were they at all under civilian control. The Republic of Indonesia was indeed a rather chaotic structure.

About six weeks after the proclamation of the Republic, the Dutch Governor General, Hubertus van Mook, arrived in Batavia/Jakarta. He was like a king without a realm as there were no Dutch troops to support him. He depended entirely on the British and could not be quite sure about their intentions. The British General Christison wanted to act as 'honest broker' and arranged a meeting between van Mook and **Sukarno** on October 23, 1945. The Government of the Netherlands did not approve of this meeting and ordered that it should be considered as not having taken place at all. Van Mook then moved the British military administration to tell the leaders of the Republic, in no uncertain terms, that the British were bound to respect Dutch sovereignty. This was the proverbial 'cold shower' that greatly dampened the enthusiasm of **Sukarno** and his colleagues.[34]

At this juncture the star of another Indonesian politician was rising: Sutan **Sjahrir**. He had been a critic of **Sukarno** as early as in 1931 when he had teamed up with **Hatta** and started working for a more substantial political education of the Indonesian people which differed from **Sukarno**'s agitational mode of operation. **Sjahrir** was a social democrat with a strong preference for parliamentary democracy. He had not collaborated with the Japanese and had remained 'underground' during the war. For this reason he was more acceptable to the Dutch than **Sukarno** and **Hatta** whom the Dutch despised as 'collaborators'. In November 1945 **Sjahrir** published his political manifesto 'Our Struggle' (*Perdjuangan Kita*) in which he made a plea for parliamentary democracy and attacked the presidential system introduced by **Sukarno** in his constitution of August 1945. In a kind of 'palace revolution' he forced **Sukarno** to appoint him prime minister in November 1945 and to change the constitution to a parliamentary one.[35] Almost parallel to this 'coup' conducted by **Sjahrir**, the revolutionary army also consolidated its position and elected General Sudirman, a former teacher, as their commander-in-chief. Since Sudirman was not appointed by the government but elected by the soldiers, he had his own source of legitimacy and would not take orders from civilians.[36] **Sjahrir** thus had to use all his diplomatic skills to wrest concessions from the Dutch on the one hand and to pacify the Indonesian soldiers on the other. He performed this risky balancing act for 18 months before he finally resigned.

Sjahrir started his negotiations with van Mook in November 1945. A British general presided at this meeting, clearly indicating the triangular constellation which **Sjahrir** wanted to use to his advantage. Van Mook had his own agenda. He had already drafted a plan for a federal Indonesia within a union under the Queen of the Netherlands. In this union the Republic of Indonesia would be only one state among other Indonesian states. This plan was kept a secret as the first step would have to be to 'tame' the Republic, for which **Sjahrir** seemed to be a useful partner. On the other hand van Mook also had to deal with his government at home, a coalition which encompassed right wingers totally opposed to decolonization. The troubles brewing in The Hague were increasing for van Mook. While he was sometimes on the verge of being dismissed, finally the Dutch government more or less abdicated its control over Indonesian affairs and entrusted it to van Mook.

In February 1946 the first Dutch troops landed in Indonesia and van Mook saw to it that they came to the outer islands first and not to Java. Their dispatch was urgent as the British had announced that they were going to withdraw their troops soon. Since these British soldiers were mostly Indians, and Indian nationalists had protested loudly against their deployment in Indonesia, Mountbatten had made an announcement in December 1945 about their withdrawal by March 1946.[37] But this had been postponed due to Dutch pleas. The Dutch cabinet then made a move prompted by van Mook and invited a delegation of the Republic of Indonesia to Hoge Veluwe in the Netherlands. The meeting ended without agreement but **Sjahrir** was so enthustiastic that he lost his caution and told one of his men that once they had their own state, they no longer needed **Sukarno**. With this remark he almost precipitated an Indonesian civil war.[38]

In June 1946 officers of the Indonesian army abducted **Sjahrir**. **Sukarno**, who must have heard about **Sjahrir**'s remark, declared an emergency which practically amounted to a dismissal of **Sjahrir**'s government. Thereupon troops loyal to **Sjahrir** marched to Yogjakarta, the capital of the Republic, and disarmed some of the troops there. Finally, **Sukarno** appointed **Sjahrir** as prime minister once more. He started his new term in October 1946. By now 91,000 Dutch troops were stationed in Indonesia and had captured the area from Batavia to Bandung. The British troops had now nearly disappeared but a powerful British representative had arrived in Indonesia who played an important role in subsequent negotiations: Lord Killearn (Miles Lampson). During the war he had been in Egypt and had become famous for his decision to force a prime minister amenable to British influence on King Faruq by surrounding the royal palace with tanks. This impressed Churchill so much that he would have liked to send him to India as Viceroy, but this did not happen. In Indonesia his activities were less flamboyant and more conciliatory. He presided over further negotiations between **Sjahrir** and the Dutch which finally led to the **Linggadjati Agreement** of November 1946,[39] in which the de facto sovereignty of the Republic was recognized and enshrined in a treaty. However, the document also included van Mook's federal plan which made the Republic part of a larger scheme.

Sjahrir immediately utilized this agreement in getting the Republic officially recognized by several foreign countries.[40] In April 1947 he attended **Nehru**'s Asian Relations Conference in New Delhi with a large Indonesian delegation. This was the climax of **Sjahrir**'s career which ended rather abruptly only three months later. The Dutch and the Indonesian armies were close to conflict and had actually fought each other for several months in many skirmishes. Ceasefires were negotiated from time to time when diplomatic endeavours progressed. Dutch hardliners felt that the enormously expensive deployment of Dutch troops should finally be made use of in a large-scale military action. Indonesian hardliners on the other hand felt that time was on their side as the Dutch government faced a severe financial crisis at that time. **Sukarno** calculated that the Dutch had to spend

3.5 million Dutch guilders per day to keep their troops in Indonesia and that they could not go on like this for much longer.[41] In the meantime **Sjahrir** talked to the British and US representatives in Jakarta and discovered that their governments would not support the Republic against the Dutch. The US could actually have used its superior financial power to bring about a settlement, but had no intention of doing so at this time. **Sjahrir** realized that further negotiations with the Dutch were necessary in order to avoid a war, but when he went to Yogjakarta to press this point, he found that he had lost the support of **Sukarno** and the Indonesian military. He was thus forced to resign. While the Indonesian military had always had a sneaking suspicion that the civilian government would use the Dutch to put them in their place, another important group distrusting **Sjahrir** were the Masjumi politicians who felt that his government was drifting towards the left.[42] As far as **Sukarno** was concerned he shared neither the suspicions of the military nor the prejudices of the Masjumi, but he had always regarded **Sjahrir** as a rival. **Sjahrir** spent the last years of his life in the 1960s under house arrest during the period of **Sukarno**'s dictatorial rule.

After **Sjahrir**'s diplomacy had failed, the Dutch launched their military action on July 26, 1946. The British Foreign Minister, Ernest Bevin, and the US Secretary of State, General Marshall, agreed not to intervene.[43] Strangely enough, one of the reasons for launching the military action was to demonstrate Dutch capability in using US grants for the improvement of the infrastructure in Indonesia. The disbursement of the grants had been delayed because the USA doubted that the respective projects could be carried out as the Dutch no longer controlled the country.[44] Militarily, the Dutch action was a full success. They captured a large part of Java. Van Mook and the Dutch military would have liked to go on and destroy the headquarters of the Republic in Yogjakarta, but by now the Dutch cabinet was on the verge of breaking up over this issue and thus the action was terminated on August 4, 1947.[45] Dutch politicians were afraid that the Security Council might vote for intervention by the **United Nations** as a resolution to this effect had been introduced by India and Australia. Moreover, the Dutch had good reasons to improve their image. The Marshall Plan had been announced on June 7, 1947, and the Netherlands could hope to improve its financial position with US help. So far, the USA had backed the Dutch who were their allies in Europe, but there were limits to their patience. In this context the Dutch also accepted the dispatch to Indonesia of a 'Commission of Good Offices' by the **United Nations**. It was headed by an American, Dr Frank Graham. The Commission arrived in Jakarta in October 1947 and aimed at a repeat performance of the **Linggadjati Agreement**. There was disagreement about the location of the meeting. The Dutch preferred Jakarta, while the government of the Republic wanted a venue outside the area controlled by the Dutch. Finally it was decided to meet on the US ship *Renville* near the Indonesian coast in January 1948.[46]

The **Renville Agreement** was much less favourable than the **Linggadjati Agreement** had been. The Republic had to agree to join the interim government of the Union long since advocated by van Mook. Moreover, the territory of the

Republic was now restricted to only about half of Java which had not been conquered by the Dutch. Prime Minister Sjarifuddin, who signed the agreement on behalf of the Republic, resigned immediately thereafter as he feared the stigma of having endorsed a capitulation. **Sukarno** then appointed a presidential cabinet under **Hatta** as prime minister. The new government faced a daunting task. The Republican army consisted of about 400,000 men. **Hatta** demobilized part of this army as it could no longer be supported from the slender resources left to the Republic. A large number of the demobilized soldiers joined a Communist-inspired uprising at Madiun in September 1948. Ex-Prime Minister Sjarifuddin, who had joined the opposition and wanted to dislodge **Hatta**, also joined the fray. Troops loyal to the government defeated the rebels and Sjarifuddin was executed.[47] This bloody affair turned out to be a blessing in disguise for the government. The USA, which was very apprehensive of the success of communism in Asia, took note of the fact that here was a goverment which did not hesitate to suppress the Communists.

In the meantime the Dutch government had gone ahead with its plans for the formation of the federal state. In this context the Governor General was replaced by a High Representative of the Crown. Van Mook left Indonesia after three turbulent years. The High Representative was the former Dutch prime minister, Louis Beel, a known hardliner who was bent on further military action.[48] He got his chance a few months after his arrival when constitutional negotiations broke down. The Dutch proposals for the integration of the Republic into the federal state amounted to an emasculation of the Republic to be followed by its liquidation. The Republic was to give up its army and its control over foreign policy and recognize the emergency powers of the High Representative. A final Dutch ultimatum on December 18, 1949, asked for an immediate reply which could not possibly be given at such short notice. One day later, Dutch paratroopers landed in Yogjakarta, seized **Sukarno**, **Hatta** and **Sjahrir** and whisked them away to a distant island. Dutch troops occupied strategic points of the Republic of Indonesia, which would have ceased to exist had international opinion not been so shocked by the Dutch action and the Security Council intervened. President Truman, who was just preparing the ground for establishing NATO, did not want to alienate the Dutch whom he needed for this new alliance. Senator Owen Brewster of the opposition, however, forced his hand, pointing out that the Dutch had actually used Marshall Plan aid for financing their military venture in Indonesia. Truman reluctantly suspended this aid. The Dutch were also hit by the reaction of their federal puppets who resigned because they did not want to be accused of taking an unpatriotic stand.[49]

Beel finally proposed a plan of his own: an early transfer of power to a United States of Indonesia in May 1949 to be preceded by a Round Table Conference in The Hague. The leaders of the Republic would be released but not permitted to return to Yogjakarta nor would the Republic be restored. The Security Council, however, insisted on the restoration of the Republic. When the Dutch were thus forced to restore the Republic, Beel resigned. He had hoped that by conceding a quick transfer of power he could still retain the fruits of military action, i.e. the liquidation of the Republic. In July 1949 the Republican leaders returned to Yogjakarta. They arrived at an agreement with the federalist leaders and then all parties attended a lengthy Round Table Conference at The Hague in August and September.[50] The agenda of this conference not only contained constitutional points but also tricky issues such as the settlement of the national debt of Indonesia. The Round Table Conference ended on November 2, 1949 and the formal transfer of power to the United States of Indonesia was effected on December 27, 1949. By decolonizing Indonesia the Dutch government saved a huge amount of money which could be invested in the economic development of the Netherlands. It has been estimated that US aid which the Dutch would have forfeited if they had continued to hold on to Indonesia amounted to more than 5 billion US dollars.[51]

Only a few months after taking charge of the United States of Indonesia, **Sukarno** dissolved it. Its parts were absorbed by the Republic of Indonesia. It seemed that a unitary national state had finally come into its own, but there were regional differences which surfaced in due course, following some early indications of such tensions. In August 1949, S. M. Kartosuwirjo had proclaimed a state called 'Dar-ul-Islam' in Western Java.[52] In the Southern Moluccas an independent republic was also proclaimed in April 1950. But these were minor irritations. More serious traces of regionalism emerged during the first democratic elections held throughout Indonesia in 1955. Democratic parties are supposed to work for aggregation of interests, but in Indonesia they failed in this and instead reflected regional strongholds. The Masjumi dominated Sumatra and Western Java, **Sukarno**'s **Partai Nasional Indonesia (PNI)** had its strongholds in Central Java. The Islamic party, Nahdat-al Ulema, had captured Eastern Java. It was difficult to form a national government on the basis of these results.[53] Trouble started brewing in West Sumatra where military officers and politicians formed the *Banteng* Council (Council of the Wild Buffalos) in November 1956 in opposition to the central government.[54] In March 1957, the military commander of Eastern Indonesia seized power in Makassar and proclaimed a 'United Struggle' (*Perjuangan Semesta = Permesta*) of all outlying provinces against the central government in Java. The *Banteng* in Sumatra then joined *Permesta*. Loyal troops under General Nasution defeated the rebels, but this also meant the end of parliamentary democracy in Indonesia. In July 1959 **Sukarno** proclaimed the restoration of his presidential constitution of 1945. In August 1960 he prohibited several political parties, among them the Masjumi and **Sjahrir**'s **Partai Socialis Indonesia (PSI)**. In 1962 an attempt was made to assassinate **Sukarno**, after which he ordered the arrest of prominent party leaders, among them his old rival **Sjahrir**. Indonesia now embarked on a long period of dictatorship.

If we compare Indonesia's fate with the political developments in India, where **Nehru** was able to lay a solid foundation for parliamentary democracy, we may ask whether **Sjahrir** could have become an Indonesian **Nehru** under more favourable circumstances. The cards were stacked against **Sjahrir** in many respects. He could not rely on a powerful party like the **Indian National Congress**, nor did he inherit a disciplined, unpolitical army subordinate to civilian control, but instead was faced with a highly politicized army which distrusted the politicians. He was faced with Dutch colonial rulers who were glad to use him while at the same time pursuing their own agenda.

While the Dutch finally had to accept the Republic of Indonesia as heir to their colonial empire, they left some unfinished business: West New Guinea, or Irian Jaya, as the Indonesians call it.[55] In the **Linggadjati** and **Renville** Agreements it seemed to be implied that sovereignty over this territory would not be contested. Of course, at that time the Dutch still believed in the incorporation of the whole of the Netherlands Indies in the federal Union which they had proposed. When the Round Table Conference was convened in the The Hague in 1949, the Dutch were no longer sure about the fate of the Union and insisted that at least New Guinea should remain under their sovereignty. The Indonesians on the other hand claimed that the transfer of power must also include New Guinea. The conference almost broke down on this issue. As both parties were interested in a successful conclusion to the conference, they agreed that the status quo should be maintained for the time being, and that further negotiations should be conducted one year after the transfer of power. The dispute then remained unresolved; the **United Nations** had to deal with the pleas from both parties for many years. Finally the Republic of Indonesia refused to continue their debt payments to the Netherlands, arguing that such payments could only be demanded from a successor state after the transfer of power, but since this transfer had been incomplete due to the Dutch insistence on holding on to Western New Guinea, Indonesia was not obliged to pay those debts.

The participants of the **Bandung Conference** of 1955 endorsed the Indonesian claim, but the Dutch could not be moved. In 1961 **Sukarno** was put to shame by the Indian action in Goa. When asked what he was going to do about the liberation of Western New Guinea, he gave the scurrilous answer that he had already appointed a governor of 'Irian Jaya' and this man had landed there, but his whereabouts had to be kept secret for security reasons. He then decided to follow the Indian example after all and ordered General Suharto to prepare for an invasion of New Guinea. Before any conflict could begin, the Dutch relented. In a face-saving move, they handed over the disputed territory to the **United Nations** which then transferred it to Indonesia.

INDONESIA AND THE INDEPENDENCE OF EAST TIMOR

Unlike Western New Guinea, Indonesia had never laid claim to the Portuguese colony of East Timor which remained an enclave of colonial rule in the Indonesian archipelago. The doctrine of the 'successor state' which Indonesia had stressed when dealing with the Dutch could not be applied to East Timor. West Timor had been part of the Netherlands Indies and was thus absorbed by the Republic of Indonesia, whereas East Timor had a chequered past. The Portuguese had captured it in search of slaves and sandalwood in the sixteenth century but had never ruled it very intensively. At one stage they had thought of selling it to the Germans, but nothing came of this. In 1930 East Timor was declared an overseas province of Portugal. The population of East Timor was different from that of West Timor. Malays had settled there before the Portuguese had arrived and in due course a mixed Portuguese-Malay group had emerged. Moreover, most of the East Timorese had become Catholic Christians. A nationalist uprising had been suppressed in 1959 and since then there had been no nationalist movement to speak of in this remote colony. The Portuguese revolution of 1974 then precipitated the independence of East Timor. Three different movements vied with each other for political control. Finally the **Frente Revolucionaria do Timor Leste Independente (FRETILIN)** subdued the others in a brief civil war. The Portuguese then abandoned the colony. It was only at this stage that Indonesia staked a claim to it. Stating that **FRETILIN** was a Communist organization which must be suppressed, the Indonesian army occupied East Timor and in July 1976 it was absorbed by Indonesia as its 27th province. The governments of the USA and Australia supported the Indonesian annexation of East Timor. **FRETILIN** took to the hills and waged a guerilla struggle against the Indonesians. A young poet, Xanana **Gusmao**, became its chief commander. He was captured in 1992 and imprisoned in Indonesia until 1999. In the meantime two other prominent leaders emerged on the international scene: Bishop Carlos Belo and José Ramos Horta. Bishop Belo returned to East Timor in 1981 after his ordination in Portugal. The Indonesian president, General Suharto, urged him to become the bishop of the Dili diocese, probably hoping that Belo would ensure the political stability of East Timor. However, after the 'Dili Massacre' of November 1991 where Indonesian troops had shot at people attending a funeral, Belo raised his voice against the Indonesian government. In 1996 he was awarded the Nobel Peace Prize jointly with Ramos Horta. Whereas Belo had lived in East Timor, Horta had fled in December 1975 a few days before the Indonesian army arrived. He remained abroad throughout and aroused world opinion against the Indonesian annexation of his country whose foreign minister he became onced it finally gained independence in 2002.

The final path to independence was a very tortuous one. With Suharto's resignation in 1998, it seemed to be a foregone conclusion that East Timor would soon be independent. But the Indonesian army sponsored Timorese militias opposed to independence. After a referendum was held under UN auspices, in which 98 per cent of the East Timorese opted for independence, these militias conducted a reign of terror, which was supported by the Indonesian military. Order was restored by an Australian peacekeeping force backed by the UN, which assumed control of East Timor in October 1999, setting up a UN Transitional Administration. On May 19, 2002 the UN finally handed over power to President **Gusmao**, who had won the preceding presidential elections, standing as an independent candidate. This was one of the last acts of decolonization.

THE FRENCH AND THE WAR IN INDO-CHINA

The French called their Asian colonial empire Indo-China, because it was a region which combined the cultural influences of both India and China. The establishment of French rule stopped a trend which had been dominant in this region since the fourteenth century. The Thai and the Vietnamese who had come from southern China had overwhelmed the Mon and Khmer who had earlier dominated this region. In fact, Thai and Vietnamese conquered the Southeast Asian mainland in a kind of pincer movement. The Thai progressed along the Menam river and the Vietnamese captured the coast of what the Chinese called 'Annam' (Peaceful South). Finally the Vietnamese occupied the fertile rice plains of the lower Mekong.[56] Without French intervention the Thai and the Vietnamese would in due course have absorbed the kingdoms of Laos and Cambodia. The French had first annexed Cochinchina in the plains of the lower Mekong. This was their only genuine colony; the other areas further north were only French protectorates. By 1900, however, the whole area was subjected to centralized French control, which made the distinction between colonies and protectorates almost irrelevant.

There were early traces of nationalism among the minority French-educated peoples of this region. One of these early nationalists was Phan Boi-Chau who visited the Chinese reformers Kang Yu-wei and Liang Qui-chao in Tokyo in 1904. They had fled to Japan after their political reform had failed in China. A year later Phan Boi-Chou founded the League for the Renewal of Vietnam (*Viet-Nam Duy-Tan Hoi*) in Japan. In 1907 the French established a university in Hanoi, but when they noticed that it had become a breeding ground of nationalism they quickly closed it down. It took another ten years before they opened it again, but the university never became an important centre of learning. Those interested in modern education went straight to Paris. Nguyen Ai Quoc, who later became known as **Ho Chi Minh**, had made the trip to Paris even before the First World War. He worked as a photographer in the French metropolis and became one of the founder-members of the French Communist Party in 1920. Later on he spent many years in exile in Russia and China. It was only at the very end of the period of colonial rule that he returned home and played a leading role in politics.

It may seem strange that a man who had lived abroad for such a long time had hardly any political rivals at home. This was because the French ruled Indo-China with a heavy hand and nipped all nationalist movements in the bud. A nationalist party founded in 1927, the *Vietnam Quoc Dan Dang*, which followed the example of the Chinese *Kuomintang*, was stamped out as it was accused of indulging in terrorist activities. The same happened to the Communists, who had taken care of a peasant rebellion in 1930 which had erupted without their help in a region in which the harvests had failed twice but where the tax collectors were still pressing the peasants to pay their poll tax. The Communists organized the peasants in Soviets, following the Russian example. But this only prompted the French colonial rulers to pounce on the peasants even more harshly than usual.[57]

In subsequent years Indo-China was affected by the steep fall in agrarian prices caused by the Great Depression. After returning to the gold standard in 1928, the French had tied the local piastre to the French franc. This link could only be maintained by deflationary measures which deepened the impact of the depression.[58] This should have caused further peasant unrest, but by now the peasants were so intimidated that they did not dare resist the colonial rulers. In Cochinchina, which was an area dominated by rich landlords, the depression further strengthened this class as small peasants sold their land to the landlords.

After Hitler had vanquished France, the French Vichy regime was forced to cooperate with the Japanese.[59] In September 1940 a treaty was concluded under which the Japanese were permitted to occupy North Vietnam. Thailand, which had a friendship treaty with the Japanese, was permitted to annex the two western provinces of Cambodia: Battambang and Siemreap. The German invasion of the Soviet Union forced the Japanese to halt their progress into Indo-China for a short time in June 1941, but when it seemed that Hitler would subdue Russia, the Japanese annexed the whole of Indo-China in July 1941. There ensued a strange condominium; the Vichy French administered Indo-China for the Japanese whose control was therefore much more ephemeral there than in Indonesia. The Japanese had no reason to patronize nationalists here or to raise an indigenous army. The French on the other hand, backed by the mighty Japanese, could continue to rule their colony as usual.

The collaboration between the Vichy French and the Japanese lasted until March 1945, when the Japanese terminated the alliance and ruled Indo-China directly. They became aware that many French in Indo-China were sympathizing with the Free French and, now that the Allies were liberating France, they could no longer be trusted. The Japanese sponsored nationalism towards the end of their rule over Indo-China.[60] **Bao Dai**, Emperor of Annam under French 'protection', now proclaimed the independence of his realm, and so did the kings of Laos and Cambodia. **Ho Chi Minh**, who had already started an armed struggle against the Japanese in north Vietnam with American support, refused to submit to **Bao Dai**'s rule. By the time the Japanese capitulated, **Ho Chi Minh** had captured Hanoi.

Ho Chi Minh had to wait for a long time for his great moment in history. He was 55 years old when he conquered Hanoi. In 1930 he had founded the Communist Party of Indo-China in Hong Kong. There had been three Communist parties in the three regions of Vietnam and it was **Ho Chi Minh**'s achievement to unite them in 1930. Initially the party was to be called the Communist Party of Vietnam, and it was only under the pressure of the Komintern that it was called the Communist Party of Indo-China. At the eighth plenary session of this party in 1941, **Ho Chi Minh** had inaugurated the Vietnamese Independence League (*Viet Nam Doc Lap Dong Minh Hoi* = **Vietminh**). This was a front organization aimed at providing a forum for all nationalists. **Vo Nguyen Giap** trained guerilla fighters for this organization who made a mark in taking action against the Japanese, helping **Ho Chi Minh** to capture Hanoi. After this successful 'August Revolution' of 1945, **Ho Chi Minh** proclaimed the independence of the Republic of Vietnam, only a fortnight after **Sukarno** had done so for the Republic of Indonesia. One may ask why **Ho Chi Minh** did not proclaim a Republic of Indo-China. After all, he was the leader of the Communist Party of Indo-China. He obviously realized that he could not claim the allegiance of the kings of Laos and Cambodia. Moreover, Vietnamese nationalists had long since stressed the name 'Viet'. Even the Vichy French had started to use this name rather than Annam. Their governor had made it a point to sponsor the separate cultural traditions of Vietnam, Laos and Cambodia.[61] Vietnamese nationalists who may have hoped to inherit the whole of Indo-China from the French were disappointed in this respect. **Ho Chi Minh**, however, was a realist – Laos and Cambodia were beyond his sphere of influence. He actually controlled only one-third of Vietnam at that time.

While **Ho Chi Minh** proclaimed the Republic of Vietnam in Hanoi, the Allied leaders assembled at the Potsdam Conference had very different plans for Indo-China. Chinese troops were asked to occupy Vietnam down to the 16th parallel and the British were put in charge of the rest of Indo-China.[62] They occupied Saigon in September 1945 and helped the returning French to gain control of their colony. In North Vietnam the Chinese let **Ho Chi Minh** rule his part of the country and did not admit the French. Only in February 1946 did the French and the Chinese arrive at an agreement which permitted French troops to enter North Vietnam. With the kings of Laos and Cambodia the French arrived at agreements which guaranteed internal autonomy to them to be exercised under the supervision of French governors. **Ho Chi Minh**'s republic was recognized as a free state within a federal union consisting of France and Indo-China. This was very similar to the **Linggadjati Agreement** between the Dutch and the Republic of Indonesia and it soon ran into the same kind of trouble. Moreover, there was a difference of opinion about the status of Cochinchina. Initially the Republic of Vietnam had been assured by the French that a referendum would be held there so as to decide about its merger with North Vietnam. This and other matters were discussed at a conference in Fontainebleau where the Vietnamese leaders met representatives of the French government in July 1946.

The conference at Fontainebleau was sabotaged by the French High Commissioner in Indo-China, Admiral Georges-Thierry D'Argenlieu, a former priest who was a hardliner of the type represented by Louis Beel among the Dutch. He had been sent to Indo-China in 1945, and was totally opposed to the recognition of the Republic of Vietnam and now wanted to create a Republic of Cochinchina run by collaborators. The French government was obviously unable to discipline him. The Vietnamese leaders left Fontainebleau and on returning home, they resumed an armed struggle against the French.[63]

In March 1947 **Ho Chi Minh** declared that he would be willing to cooperate with the French if they acted like the USA in the Philippines or the British in India. The French replied by insisting on their sovereignty and now supported **Bao Dai** who was supposed to form a government for the whole of Vietnam. In this way the French wanted to undercut **Ho Chi Minh**. Of course, they did not grant sovereignty to **Bao Dai**. It was very obvious that he was to be a mere instrument in the hands of the French and, therefore, he hesitated in accepting their offer. He finally agreed in March 1949 and took up his new post at the end of that year. In February 1950 his government was recognized by the British and the USA, but even before they did this, the Soviet Union, China and several East European states had recognized the Republic of Vietnam. Vietnam thus became deeply involved in the Cold War.

Bao Dai proved not to be the obedient puppet which the French had wanted him to be. He soon demanded full sovereignty as vigorously as **Ho Chi Minh**. The kings of Laos and Cambodia chimed in, but the French turned a deaf ear to all these pleas. The USA was in two minds about the course of developments in Indo-China. This was reflected in contradictory statements made by Secretary of State Dean Acheson in 1949. In September he told his French counterpart, Robert Schumann, that the French presence in Indo-China was the only guarantee against chaos. Only four weeks later, at a hearing of the American Senate, Acheson said that the USA would get nowhere by supporting the French as a colonial power in Indo-China. Perhaps the proclamation of the People's Republic of China on October 1, 1949 – midway between these two statements – had made him change his mind. However, the Korean War then forced the USA to support the French in Indo-China once more. This was clearly shown by their increasing share of French military expenditure in Indo-China. From 1946 to 1949 this expenditure had increased from 100 to about 170 billion francs, which came completely from the French budget. In 1950 this military budget had been augmented to 285 billion francs, of which the USA shared 15 per cent. In terms of US dollars, this Indo-China war cost the French 10 million, twice the amount they had received as American aid under the Marshall Plan. In spite of this massive investment the French were routed by **Vo Nguyen Giap** at Dien Bien Phu on May 7, 1954. The French had chosen this place near the border of Laos because they thought they could easily defend it. They had not expected **Vo Nguyen Giap** to be able to move heavy artillery through the jungle and thus make their position untenable. Dien Bien Phu fell one day before the **Geneva Conference** started its proceedings. It had been convened in order to discuss Indo-China. The French had hoped to score some points there, but after the resounding defeat at Dien Bien Phu they could only capitulate and the conference had to record this fact. It then tried to find ways and means for the further peaceful development of Indo-China. The conference was attended by the French and all the states of Indo-China, plus representatives of the USA and China. The USA were actually opposed to the transactions at this conference,[64] after which President Eisenhower stated that the USA did not consider itself to be bound by the decisions taken in Geneva. This announcement was advance notice of US interest in building up South Vietnam as a client state and making its own arrangements for the defence of the region. This policy was diametrically opposed to **Nehru**'s vision of a neutralized region which could be kept out of superpower rivalry. India had not been invited to the **Geneva Conference**, but Krishna Menon, **Nehru**'s emissary, had played a decisive role behind the scenes. He had urged the members of the conference to appoint an international control commission made up of delegates from Canada, India and Poland which would tour the region regularly and see to it that peace was maintained. A commission was appointed, but soon thereafter the USA sponsored the Southeast Asia Treaty Organization (SEATO) as a part of their global system of military pacts to which India was opposed.[65] The commission worked nevertheless for many years, but it could not prevent the escalation of military conflicts in this region.

Bao Dai, who had finally reached the goal of full sovereignty in 1954, appointed a prime minister, Ngo Dinh Diem, who deposed the unfortunate **Bao Dai** in April 1955 and then proclaimed the Republic of South Vietnam. Ngo Dinh Diem was a devout Catholic who had earlier served as a civil servant under the French and had then collaborated with the Japanese. In the early 1950s he had spent some time in the USA and in Europe, only returning to Vietnam in 1954. He helped to instigate the exodus of Vietnamese Catholics from North Vietnam to the South; nearly one million people from North Vietnam fled, most of whom were Catholics.[66] Initially the Vietnamese bishops had supported **Ho Chi Minh's** government after the proclamation of the Republic in 1945, but subsequently they had been forced to pursue an anti-communist line. At the **Geneva Conference** it was agreed that the Catholics would be able to practise their religion in North Vietnam. However, many priests and the CIA spread rumours that this agreement was not to be trusted and that the USA would soon bomb North Vietnam. For Ngo Dinh Diem the refugees were a useful clientele in South Vietnam. Many South Vietnamese regarded them as a fifth column of his regime which became more and more dictatorial. Massive US military aid was poured into South Vietnam for the fight against North Vietnam. By 1958 the expenditure amounted to 687 billion francs, of which about 80 per cent was contributed by the USA. Ngo Dinh Diem was opposed by the Buddhists who protested against his rule; Buddhist monks immolated themselves in May 1963. Finally a military coup put an end to Ngo Dinh Diem's regime. The USA had orchestrated this as he had become an embarrassment to them. He was murdered in November 1963. From now on one military ruler after another tried to control the country which became more and more involved in the Vietnam War. The war started when the North Vietnamese allegedly attacked ships of the US Navy in the Gulf of Tonkin in August 1964. North Vietnam pleaded several times in vain for a reconvening of the **Geneva Conference**, but events had progressed too far and the Vietnam War had to run its fateful course.

CAMBODIA AND LAOS

The two small kingdoms of Cambodia and Laos were the remnants of ancient empires which had almost been reduced to insignificance by the Thais and the Vietnamese.[67] Their kings became clients of their mighty neighbours who frequently interfered with their affairs. While the Lao are related to the Thais, the Khmer of Cambodia are a people with a distinctive language of their own and a great cultural tradition which is still reflected in the mighty ruins of Angkor. The modern educated elite in both the countries was very small under French rule. National movements arose only at a late stage and were then supported by the Western powers in order to fight against the Japanese. In Cambodia the **Khmer Issarak** and in Laos the **Lao Issara** made a mark in this way. When the Japanese broke with the Vichy French in March 1945, the young King **Sihanouk** of Cambodia proclaimed the independence of his realm, as did King Sisavang Vong of Laos one month later. The returning French did not want to recognize these proclamations, but they had to contend with nationalist forces which had gained ground in the meantime.

The course of events was different in the two countries. The quick-witted Norodom **Sihanouk**, who liked to call himself 'Little Prince', alluding to Saint-Exupery's famous book, finally abdicated and made his father ascend the throne while he became a 'bourgeois' prime minister in 1955. As head of a party called *Sangkum Reastr Nium* (Socialist People's Community), he won 80 per cent of the vote in 1955 which enabled him to rule his country for the next 15 years. When his father died in 1960, **Sihanouk** also assumed the position of head of state but did not again ascend the throne. The political development of Laos was less smooth. There were three royal half-brothers, **Phetsarat**, **Souvanna Phuma** and **Souphanouvong** who determined the fate of their nation in different ways. **Phetsarat**, the 'Iron Prince', had not only risen to the position of the highest civil servant under French rule, but was also Viceroy and practically ruled Laos. He was an ardent nationalist who headed the **Lao Issara** and had worked hard to unite the various principalities of Laos. He was also extremely popular among his countrymen. His hour of greatness came on October 12, 1945 when the returning French who wished to subdue Laos once more forced the weak King Sisavang Vong to abdicate. **Phetsarat** once more supported the independence of Laos, defying the French, who forced him to flee to Thailand. From there he organized the armed resistance against them, appointing **Souphanouvong** as the commander of the troops of his movement.[68] **Phetsarat** remained in exile in Thailand and did not return to Laos until 1956, about two years before his death. His last service to his country was that he persuaded his half-brothers to form a coalition government, claiming no position for himself. Unfortunately, this coalition did not last.

Souvanna Phuma had worked as an architect and civil engineer in Vientiane after returning from his studies in France; **Souphanouvong**, who believed that Laos had no future, joined the French colonial service as a civil engineer in Vietnam. In September 1945, shortly before **Phetsarat** reconfirmed the independence of Laos, **Souphanouvong** was taken by US agents to Hanoi where he was warmly welcomed by **Ho Chi Minh** who supplied him with arms for the struggle against the French in Laos. He then joined **Phetsarat**'s **Lao Issara**. However, a split soon emerged in the ranks of the **Lao Issara** when **Souvanna Phuma**, who was originally with **Phetsarat**, decided to work with the French rather than join the armed struggle. This split was of crucial significance to the further political development of Laos. **Souvanna Phuma** became prime minister of Laos in 1951 with French support. **Souphanouvong** formed a government in exile in Vietnam, now calling his movement **Pathet Lao** (the Land of the Lao). In 1953 he was able to conquer two provinces in northern Laos with Vietnamese help. The **Geneva Conference** of 1954 tried to mediate between to two brothers. They agreed to a ceasefire and, as mentioned earlier, they formed a coalition government in 1956 as **Phetsarat** had prompted them to do. **Souphanouvong** converted his militant **Pathet Lao** into a democratic party called *Neo Lao Haksat* and became an active minister in his brother's cabinet. The USA, however, did not like this coalition, as they still regarded **Souphanouvong** as a communist who could not be trusted. Therefore they saw to it that the coalition government was toppled in 1958 and replaced with a government more amenable to US influence.

In subsequent years Laos's politics became more and more chaotic. Captain Kong Le captured Vientiane with his troops in 1960 and tried to reinstate the coalition government. He did not succeed at that time, but finally the USA agreed to the resurrection of the coalition government, obviously after making sure that **Souvanna Phuma** would now toe their line. Although **Souvanna Phuma** had earlier sympathized with the **Non-aligned Movement**, he now became a follower of US policies as he realized that nothing could be done in Laos without US support. **Souphanouvong** finally left the coalition government in 1963 and the civil war resumed. The small country was soon dragged into the Vietnam War, as was Cambodia. When the USA started bombing villages in northern Cambodia in 1965, **Sihanouk** broke off diplomatic relations with the USA, who in turn then supported the military coup of General Lon Nol who became their puppet in Cambodia throughout the Vietnam War.

THE LIBERATION OF BURMA (MYANMAR)

The British had conquered Burma in three wars, the first of which, in 1823–27, was the longest and bloodiest. The British claimed that it was a defensive war as the Burmese army, under its young and aggressive general, Mahabandula, trespassed on territory only recently colonized by the East India Company.[69] The British used steampowered gunboats for the first time in this war and managed to defeat the Burmese who had to yield the coastal provinces of Arakan and Tenasserim to the East India Company. The second war of 1851 was due to the warmongering private British traders in Lower Burma who found in the British naval officer, George Lambert, an eager advocate of military intervention. Again the Burmese were defeated and had to yield the province of Pegu in 1852. This province encompassed the fertile plains of the lower Irrawaddy which became a fabulous rice-producing area under British rule.[70] In earlier times its potential had not been used to a great extent as the centre of Burmese power had always been the upper Irrawaddy valley which still remained under Burmese control and proved to be a viable state under the resourceful King Mindon and his successors.[71] The third and final war of 1885 lasted only two weeks and ended in the total annexation of Burma by the British. The main reason for waging the war was the increase of French activities in Southeast Asia. This was the period of the **Scramble for Africa**. The British and the French were about to divide the world between them and Burma became a victim of this rivalry. Neighbouring Thailand only escaped the same fate because its diplomatic kings managed to secure their realm as a buffer state between the British and the French.

The **Indian National Congress** condemned the British annexation of Upper Burma at its first session in 1885. It stated that India wanted to live in peace with its neighbours,[72] but the resolution was also passed for another reason: the Indian nationalists knew that once again a British imperialist adventure was to be financed by the Indian taxpayer. The war was short, but the pacification of Burma proved to be a lengthy and costly affair. In subsequent decades the **Indian National Congress** took no notice of Burma. The Indians were not liked in Burma. The most conspicuous Indians there were the Tamil Chettiars who operated as graintraders and moneylenders in the fertile rice areas and exploited the Burmese peasants.

British-Indian constitutional reforms also applied to Burma. In 1919, however, the British did not want to extend the reforms of that year to Burma but faced such a storm of protest that they finally introduced more generous reforms in Burma than they had done in India. An expanded legislature was established in 1923 and the franchise was granted to all heads of households, male or female, above the age of 18. It is likely that the British were so generous in Burma because the authorities there would have found it difficult to adapt the complicated Indian property qualifications for the franchise to Burmese conditions. When the Burmese were told that the next constitutional reforms enshrined in the Government of India Act of 1935 would not apply to Burma as it would be separated from India in 1936, they did not like this at all. They saw in this separation not an achievement but a means to deprive them of constitutional advancement. Burmese nationalists only acquiesced when they were assured by the British that they would enjoy the same constitutional rights as the Indians.

Before separation Burma had experienced a massive peasant rebellion lead by the charismatic **Saya San**, a former Buddhist monk who finally recommended himself as a righteous Buddhist king. The outbreak of the rebellion in 1930 was triggered by a fatal conjunction of the decisions of the British administration and of the Chettiar moneylenders. The fertile rice area of Lower Burma yielded a triple revenue income to the British administration. The peasant had to pay land revenue as well as a poll tax, in addition to which a rice export duty was collected in the port. The poll tax was due before the harvest and thus acted as an incentive to produce as much rice as possible for the market. The Chettiars would gladly give the peasants credit for paying the poll tax as they could recover it with interest after the harvest. But they stopped doing so in November 1930 as they already knew that the rice price would fall dramatically when the winter harvest came to the market in January 1931.[73] The British tax collectors nevertheless demanded the poll tax from the peasants without showing any mercy. **Saya San**, who had earlier studied agrarian conditions in the rice region, submitted petitions to the government on behalf of the peasants. When this had no effect, he led the peasants in a bloody rebellion which British troops needed almost a year to suppress. **Saya San** was captured in August 1931. The lawyer who defended him, Dr **Ba Maw**, gained great popularity as a result of his trial, and later became president of Burma. His client **Saya San**, however, was executed in 1937. He remained a national hero and **Aung San** subsequently referred to his ideas, particularly to the vision of a righteous Buddhist king who would solve the problems of the people.

The political development of Burma reached a new stage in 1937 when provincial autonomy was introduced and Dr **Ba Maw** became prime minister. While **Ba Maw** was a moderate politician, there was also a rising group of young radical nationlists who had organized a student group at the University of Rangoon in the 1930s. Among them were **Aung San**, **U Nu** and **Ne Win** who rose to prominence later on. Thirty of these young radicals, among them **Aung San** and **Ne Win**, went to Japan in 1940 in order to receive military training. They returned to Burma in 1942 as members of the Burmese Independence Army sponsored by the Japanese. In 1943 the Japanese even conceded the establishment of a Burma National Army to **Aung San** and declared that Burma was now independent.[74] This declaration was identical with that issued for the Philippines at the same time.

The changed attitude of the Japanese was a response to the advance of the British-Indian army in northern Burma. It was a tragedy that Indians now had to fight Indians on Burmese soil as **Subhas Chandra Bose**'s **Indian National Army** was fighting on the Japanese side, hoping to free India from British rule in this way.[75] The Burmese followed up the declaration of independence by forming a national government with Dr **Ba Maw** as president and **Aung San** as minister of defence. **Aung San** soon recognized that siding with the Japanese would not augur well for Burma's future and from the end of 1943 he played a double game. On the one hand he supported **Ba Maw** in his collaboration with the Japanese, while on the other hand he contacted British agents without informing **Ba Maw**. Lord Mountbatten, as commander of the Allied forces in Southeast Asia, was obviously eager to support **Aung San** at an early stage. Finally **Aung San** officially changed sides in March 1945. His party was now the **Anti-Fascist People's Freedom League (AFPFL)** which had been secretly established in August 1944. After the Japanese capitulation, **Aung San**'s Burma National Army was permitted by the British to participate in the celebrations in Rangoon, flying their own flag. At the same time **Ba Maw** had to flee the country with the departing Japanese. From then on, **Aung San** was the undisputed leader of the Burmese, but since the returning British rulers were not as farsighted as Lord Mountbatten, the **AFPFL** was not yet permitted to form a government.

In August 1946, General Rance, who had worked with Lord Mountbatten during the war, was appointed Governor of Burma. He made **Aung San** his interim prime minister in October 1946. In January 1947 **Aung San** and members of his government negotiated with Prime Minister Attlee in London. U Saw, who had been prime minister of Burma under British rule, was a member of the delegation. **Aung San**, who was convinced of Attlee's good intentions, signed an agreement which did not yet contain a declaration of independence but represented a great step forward. U Saw, his rival, who obviously wanted to appear to be the more radical nationalist, refused to sign. Other Burmese politicians also criticized the agreement, but **Aung San** was greatly strengthened by the **AFPFL**'s success at the polls in April 1947. He had established good relations with the ethnic minorities of Burma, even offering them the option of drafting the constitutional provisions referring to them.[76] But he did not live to pursue this path. On July 19, 1947, he was assassinated together with six other members of his cabinet. It is assumed that the murderers were paid by the ambitious U Saw.

General Rance immediately appointed **U Nu**, the vice president of the **AFPFL**, as **Aung San**'s successor as prime minister.[77] **U Nu** was a pious Buddhist who was not interested in power. Now political responsibility was suddenly thrust upon him. Under his government, Burma achieved independence on October 17, 1947. In January 1948 Burma inaugurated its new constitution. This was followed by rebellions of the ethnic minorities which only **Aung San** could have tamed. The jurisdiction of the government was now restricted to the immediate environment of Rangoon. **U Nu**'s modesty and sincerity helped to mollify the minorities. The new republic would hardly have survived without him. But the government could not hope for any revenue income and had to rely on the rice export tax which was collected in the port of Rangoon. Since Burma was the greatest exporter of rice in the world and prices increased due to the Korean war, **U Nu**'s government survived for some time. However, when the rice price fell very rapidly in the years 1954 to 1956, **U Nu**'s government was in serious financial trouble. He was forced to hand over power to General **Ne Win** who considered himself to be the true political heir of **Aung San**. The **AFPFL** then split into a 'clean' faction and a 'stable' faction. **U Nu** led the 'clean' faction in the election campaign of 1960. He appealed to the respect for Buddhism which he wanted to make the 'state religion'. He won the election, but aroused the opposition of the ethnic minorities who did not agree with his religious policy. Once more the survival of the republic was at stake. General **Ne Win** then staged a military coup on March 2, 1962, which put an end to Burmese parliamentary democracy. From then on the army played a decisive role in Burma. Like the Indonesian army, it was politicized and deeply influenced by the impact of the Japanese.

THE DELAYED DECOLONIZATION OF MALAYA AND SINGAPORE

Malaya, the western part of the present state of Malaysia, was an early target of colonial conquest, because its main port, Malacca, controlled the straits that were the main maritime trade route to East Asia. As early as 1515, the Portuguese traveller Tomé Pires had written in his *Suma Oriental*: 'He who holds Malacca has his hands at the throat of Venice'.[78] The Portuguese captured Malacca in the sixteenth century and it fell to the Dutch in the seventeenth century. The British had occasionally had contact with the area, establishing an outpost on the island of Penang in 1786. But it was only when they took over Indonesia from the Dutch at the time of the Napoleonic Wars, that they showed a deeper interest in Malaya. Stamford Raffles, who ruled Indonesia until it was returned to the Dutch, had discovered the strategic location of Singapore at that time. He concluded a treaty with the local ruler, the Sultan of Johore, and established a trading station in 1819 which became the bridgehead of British rule over Malaya.[79]

Malaya, however, was not very well suited to centralized control. Its interior regions were covered by huge forests, while the small coastal towns were rather distant from each other and served as the headquarters of small principalities which were subdued by the British. The petty sultans retained autonomy but had to accommodate British residents whose advice they had to follow. In 1896 the four sultans of Perak, Selangor, Negri Sembilan and Pahang joined in a federation whose Resident General was Frank Swettenham, who had done much for the construction of this particular type of British colonial rule.[80] His headquarters were at Kuala Lumpur. The Sultan of Johore did not join the federation nor did the sultans of Kedah, Perlis, Kelantan and Trengganu. These latter four states had earlier belonged to Thailand and had only been subjected to British rule in 1909. Thus Malaya was a curious patchwork which could hardly give rise to a common spirit of nationalism. Malayan nationalists rather looked across the straits to Sumatra and were receptive to political currents from there, the more so as they spoke the same language.

Another peculiar feature of 'British Malaya' was the rapid expansion of Chinese economic activities which had started with the exploration of tin mines on the Malayan east coast. Both entrepreneurs and workers were Chinese; they were joined by Indians who mostly worked in the rubber plantations. The Malays were not interested in this type of work. Their number was small and they could easily make a living from agriculture. As a result they almost became a minority in their own country,[81] which later became of great political importance as the Malays insisted on their right as 'sons of the soil' (*bumiputra*).

In 1942 the Japanese invading forces struck Malaya like a whirlwind and persecuted the Chinese there who fled into the forests and formed the **Malayan People's Anti-Japanese Army (MPAJA)**. They were at first supported by the British who regarded the ca. 7,000 guerrilla fighters of the MPAJA as useful allies in fighting the war against the Japanese. But once the war was over, most guerrilla fighters did not hand over their arms and continued to remain in the forests. The Chinese trade unionists affiliated to the Communist Party then made common cause with the MPAJA.[82] This created a major problem for the British who proclaimed a state of emergency in 1948 which was to last until 1960. An elaborate counter-insurgency campaign was waged against the guerrillas who hid in the forests and drew sustenance from scattered rural settlements of Chinese people. Most of these rural Chinese did not sympathize with the guerrillas but could not refuse to help them. The British forcibly resettled them in about 500 'new villages'; more than one million people were resettled in this way. But it was only when General Gerald Templer conducted the campaign from 1952 to 1954 that the guerrillas faced defeat. He combined tough military forays with 'Operation Service' in which the military and the police instilled confidence in the rural people.[83] The same strategy was then used for suppressing the Mau Mau rebellion in Kenya.

In addition to this 'emergency' the British were also beset with the problems of the Malayan Union which they had wished to impose upon an unwilling population. Under this Union the citizenship rights of the Chinese and Indians were to be recognized and the privileges of the sultans curtailed. Moreover, Singapore was to be separated from Malaya.[84] The protest against the Malayan Union led to the rise of the **United Malays National Organization (UMNO)** which has remained a decisive force in politics until the present day. Faced with this protest, the British shelved their plan and instead created in 1948 a Federation of Malaya in which the rights of the sultans and of the Malays were respected. The goverment was headed in the interim by a British High Commissioner and the parliament initally had only nominated members; from 1955 half of them were elected. The autonomy of the sultans for which the Malays campaigned has led to a peculiar construction: the sultans provide the head of state by rotation. The incumbent now bears the title King of Malaysia.

The separate development of Singapore permitted a more rapid progress of decolonization in that city-state. By 1955 the first indigenous Chief Minister, David **Marshall**, took office. An Iraqi Jew born in Singapore, who was a patriotic citizen of this great emporium, he had made a mark in the city as its most brilliant criminal lawyer. During the period of transition he served as an impressive Chief Minister. He resigned in 1956 because the British refused to transfer power. The Chinese majority of the citizens soon rallied behind **Lee Kuan Yew** and his **People's Action Party (PAP)**.[85] **Lee Kuan Yew** became the first prime minister of independent Singapore in 1959.

Malaya's multi-ethnic composition delayed its decolonization. The founder of **UMNO**, Dato Onn bin Ja'afar, had intended to broaden the social base of his party by admitting non-Malays, but this was resisted by the Malays. Onn had to resign as president of **UMNO** in 1951. He then founded the multi-ethnic Independence of Malaya Party which soon disappeared. Tunku **Abdul Rahman**, who had become president of **UMNO** in 1951, then succeeded where Onn had failed. As son of the Sultan of Kedah, the Tunku had a prominent position in Malay society. He preserved **UMNO** as a purely Malayan party but formed an alliance with ethnic organizations such as the Malayan Chinese Association (MCA), founded in 1949, and the Malayan Indian Congress (MIC), founded in 1946. This policy was highly successful. Heading this alliance, the Tunku became the first prime minister of independent Malaya in 1957 and continued to hold this office until 1970.

Having succeeded in ethnic alliance-building, the Tunku launched an initiative to unite Malaya, Singapore and Sarawak with Sabah on Borneo in a Federation of

Malaysia, a plan that had been discussed by the British for quite some time. Known as the 'Grand Design',[86] it had been mooted earlier in the 1950s, but the British did not pursue it as the Malays were reluctant to adopt it. The Singapore leaders were keen on a merger, because they could see that their city-state would not be viable in isolation. But the Tunku feared the addition of a large Chinese population which would upset the ethnic balance of Malaya. Only when he began to fear that Singapore could become a 'Cuba' on his doorstep and only when he was sure that the British would add Sabah and Sarawak to Malaysia, which would somehow help to restore the ethnic balance, did he finally opt for the 'Grand Design' in a speech on May 27, 1961. The British were glad to broker this deal and saw to it that the Tunku would be credited with the initiative.

Lee Kuan Yew knew that he needed British support for maintaining the economy of Singapore and he had stated this openly. This had alienated the radicals in the **PAP** who left the party and formed a socialist front (*Barisan Sosialis*). After a by-election in July 1961, this new party had only one seat fewer that the **PAP** in the legislative assembly. **Lee Kuan Yew** therefore looked upon the Tunku as a convenient ally. In 1962 a referendum was held in which Singapore endorsed the merger. Now the central government of Malaysia could deal with the *Barisan Socialis*.[87] However, the merger proved to be a short marriage of convenience which broke up in 1965 because Singapore's Chinese majority had disturbed the delicate ethnic balance of that state. But by now **Lee Kuan Yew** had consolidated his power. The *Barisan Socialis* had dwindled to insignificance and the **PAP** has remained dominant ever since. **Lee Kuan Yew** could proceed to modernize his city-state by authoritarian methods, but even David **Marshall** had to admit that his old rival had eradicated corruption and was running a clean and efficient administration.

The Federation of Malaysia had from its very beginning a deadly enemy: **Sukarno**. He saw in this new state a device of British neocolonialism on his doorstep. He was not too far wrong in this assessment as the British had sponsored Malaysia in order to protect their interests in Southeast Asia. **Sukarno** adopted a policy of **Konfrontasi**, harassing Malaysia by sending his soldiers disguised as 'rebels' across the border of Indonesian Kalimantan. This involved the British and their clients in costly guerrilla warfare. They finally managed to defeat **Sukarno**, but this war of attrition contributed to the British government's decision to cut its losses and withdraw from 'East of Suez'.[88]

In Malaysia the Malays turned against the other ethnic groups and the end of Tunku **Abdul Rahman**'s period of office was overshadowed by race riots in 1969. The Malays simply could not understand that in spite of having political power and special privileges for the 'sons of the soil' (*bumiputra*), they nevertheless could not share the riches that the Chinese amassed before their very eyes. Multiethnic harmony, which had enabled the Tunku to lead the country to independence so very smoothly in 1957, had finally broken down. In subsequent years policies which gave the Malays a better chance to share the fruits of economic progress helped to restore ethnic harmony to some extent.

BRUNEI: A SPECIAL CASE OF LATE DECOLONIZATION

The present Sultan of Brunei, Hassanal Bolkiah, is the 29th ruler of a dynasty which began in the 1360s with Awang Alak Betatar, who embraced Islam and was then known as Muhammad Shah. At the zenith of their power the sultans of Brunei controlled large parts of Borneo and the Philippines. When British influence spread in western Borneo, Brunei's territory dwindled. In 1888 the sultan agreed to the establishment of a British protectorate and in 1906 a British resident arrived who controlled the sultan's government in keeping with the well-known practice of **indirect rule**. After the Japanese interregnum, the British returned in 1945 and the sultan resumed his reign in 1946. In 1950 a reformist sultan, Muda Omar Ali Saiffuddin III, ascended the throne and during his reign made good use of the oil wealth which accrued to Brunei. The British granted internal autonomy to Brunei in 1959. The British resident was now called High Commissioner and the sultan promulgated a constitution.

The British were eager to incorporate Brunei in their 'Grand Design' – Malaysia – but the sultan hesitated. Moreover, Brunei was faced with a rebellion in December 1962. A. M. Azahari, leader of the People's Party of Brunei, had scored an electoral success, but as he could not exercise any political power, he became a rebel and formed the North Kalimantan National Army (NKNA). He also opposed Brunei's merger with Malaysia and could rely on Indonesian support. The sultan appealed for help to the British whose troops soon defeated the rebels, but then '**Konfrontasi**' tied these troops down for several years. This considerably delayed decolonization as the sultan depended on British support. In 1967 Sultan Saiffuddin III resigned in favour of his son, Hassanal Bolkiah, who continued the policies of his father. It was only in 1984 that Brunei attained independence and joined the Association of Southeast Asian Nations (ASEAN). The idea of a merger with Malaysia was no longer considered. The viability of tiny Brunei as an independent state was by now well established, owing to its enormous wealth.

THE USA AND THE PHILIPPINES

The Philippines were acquired by the USA following their victory in the Spanish-American War of 1898. There were nationalists in the Philippines at that time who at first welcomed this liberation from Spanish colonial rule, but who became deeply disappointed when they realized that the new rulers were not at all willing to grant independence to their country. These nationalists had been inspired by the liberal revolution in Spain which had forced Queen Isabella II to abdicate in 1868. The most prominent nationalist leader in the Philippines was José Rizal (1861–1896), a physician who had studied in Spain and Germany and had also become famous as a writer.[89] His novel *Noli me tangere* became a manifesto of Philippine nationalism. He also translated Schiller's play *Wilhelm Tell*, which celebrated the Swiss freedom fighter, into Tagalog, the most important language of the Philippines. Rizal had returned home in 1892 and started a national movement, the *Liga Filipina*, but he did not advocate open rebellion against Spanish rule at that time. When a rebellion nevertheless broke out in 1896, Rizal was arrested and executed. The leader of the rebellion, Andreas Bonifacio (1863–1897), was the founder of the secret society *Katipunan*.[90] Because he was the son of poor parents, Bonifacio has been described as a proletarian revolutionary by some historians, whereas Rizal was seen as the representative of the educated elite. Bonifacio had led the rebels in the province of Cavite and while he eluded capture by the Spanish, he fell victim to his own comrades. Emilio Aguinaldo (1869–1964), who had joined Bonifacio, accused him of treason and had him executed by his henchmen. Aguinaldo was a competent military leader, but even he could not vanquish the Spanish. Finally he arrived at an agreement with them which enabled him to leave the Philippines for Hong Kong with some of his followers in 1897. From there he returned home on a US ship, as the USA regarded him as an ally in fighting the Spanish. In 1898, Aguinaldo proclaimed the independence of the Philippines.[91] When the USA did not respect this, he waged a war against the USA which ended with his capture in 1901. He subsequently swore allegiance to the USA and spent the rest of his long life in retirement.

After the militant fighters had been eliminated, the civilian politicians forged ahead. They tried to negotiate with the USA so as to reach their goal. The most prominent among them was Manuel Luis **Quezon** who became president of the government formed under US auspices in 1935.[92] The USA had granted independence to the Philippines in 1934, stipulating that there should be a ten-year period of transition. **Quezon** was re-elected in 1941, fled to the USA when the Japanese occupied the Philippines and formed a government in exile in Washington, where he died in 1944 before he could see his country once more. His effort to gain independence for his country by means of peaceful negotiations was supported by many Americans who opposed colonial rule. They did this not for altruistic reasons, but because products of the Philippines such as sugar competed with US products. This problem was highlighted during the Great Depression when US sugar producers would have liked to be rid of the Philippines. President Roosevelt could count on the support of these people when he signed the act of independence in 1934. During the period of transition, the Philippines still had free access to the US market which greatly helped to see them through the years of the depression.[93]

Japanese occupation hit the Philippines hard. US and indigenous troops had put up stiff resistance to the Japanese onslaught and had to give up their last position near Manila on May 9, 1942. This was a relatively late victory for the Japanese if one considers that they had overrun Singapore in February and Indonesia in March 1942. The Japanese installed José Laurel (1881–1959) as president of the Philippines and they made him declare war on the Allies. Laurel was a legal luminary who had always been in the shadow of **Quezon**, serving as his vice president. This may explain why he succumbed to the temptation of being installed by the Japanese. After the war he was accused of being a collaborator but an amnesty saved him. In the last year of the war, the Philippines were the scene of a massive US invasion. US troops landed at Leyte in the eastern part of the Philippines on October 17, 1944. On July 4, 1946, President Truman granted independence to the Philippines, referring to the earlier act of 1934. The first president of the independent republic was Manuel **Roxas** whose term of office was cut short by his untimely death.[94]

While other new states in Southeast Asia were plagued by ethnic tensions, the Philippines suffered instead from a kind of class struggle between landlords and peasants. The cause of the peasants was championed by the *Huks*.[95] These were the armed guerillas of the 'army'(= *hukbo*) which had liberated whole regions of the interior of the country from Japanese occupation during the war. In those regions the *Huks* had introduced radical agrarian reform which was then abolished after 1945. The *Huks* continued their struggle from 1946 to 1954 and threatened the government which supported the landlords. The government argued that the *Huks* were communists who must be crushed although their links with the Communist Party were very tenuous. Louis Taruk, the leader of the *Huks* and the son of poor sharecroppers, had already led peasant movements in the 1930s. In the first elections after the war, in 1946, he won a seat in the Philippine legislature, but the established parties (Liberals and Nationalists) saw to it that he was deprived of his mandate. This contributed to the *Huk* rebellion. Taruk was arrested in 1954 and kept in prison until 1968.

After the *Huks* were suppressed, unrest began in another region. The Muslim minority of the southern provinces of Mindanao and Sulu had become more and more discontented due to its treatment by the central government. The Spanish had hardly touched these provinces, but under US rule the migration of people from the northern islands was actively encouraged. President **Quezon** also favoured it. After independence roads were built and the land was surveyed in order to attract more settlers. Those *Huks* who surrendered were given free land by the government in Mindanao. The Muslims of that province had no idea of land titles and individual ownership. They regarded the land as communal property to be distributed by the clan heads (*datus*) to the cultivators according to their needs. Most Muslims were analphabets and resented 'Christian' education. The *datus* retained their traditional power and some of them collaborated with the government and enriched themselves. When land encroachment increased and party politics entered the countryside, tensions finally led to the emergence of a Mindanao Independence Movement. Weapons were freely available in the countryside ever since guerrillas fought the Japanese during the war. In keeping with US ideas, nobody had dared to disarm the people after the war. Unrest could therefore easily turn into armed rebellion.

The USA had retained many privileges after granting independence to the Philippines. They made the new government sign a commercial treaty which accommodated their interests. They also insisted on an amendment of the constitution which granted the same rights to US citizens as to Philippines citizens. Later on the USA also established military bases in the Philippines. They had handled the decolonization of the Philippines much more adroitly than other departing colonial rulers in their respective colonies. The transfer of power was smooth and US privileges were taken care of. It was a tragedy that after such a skilful performance, the USA then got themselves involved in the bloody Vietnam War in which they lost not only men and money but also their prestige.

THE TERMINATION OF JAPANESE RULE IN TAIWAN AND KOREA

The surrender of the Japanese on August 15, 1945, also put an abrupt end to their colonial rule in Taiwan and Korea. Whereas elsewhere 'decolonization' was often a tortuous process extending over many years, the end of Japanese rule was very sudden. Its aftermath, however, was problematic, as new masters appeared on the scene.

Taiwan had been annexed by the Japanese in 1895 after winning a war against China.[96] But even before the Japanese troops could reach Taiwan, an independent republic was proclaimed by the Taiwanese, the first of its kind in Asia. This was crushed by the Japanese who ruled their new colony with a heavy hand. Initially they were mostly interested in Taiwan's agricultural production which served as a useful supplement to Japanese production at home. The Great Depression, with its dramatic decline in agrarian prices, also affected Taiwan, but with the Japanese industrial drive towards re-armament in the 1930s, Taiwan was also industrialized in a decentralized fashion which served it well subsequently. The Japanese also equipped Taiwan with an advanced banking system and economic efficiency was maintained by a tough police state.[97] In 1945 Taiwan was returned to China but there was not much difference between Japanese and Chinese rule. In fact, the Chinese nationalist government took over the Japanese police state in Taiwan and used it for its own purposes. In 1947 the Taiwanese rebelled once more and proclaimed an independent republic which was as shortlived as the first one. The repression of the rebellion was brutal and thousands of Taiwanese died. When the *Kuomintang* government lost its base on the mainland in 1949, it shifted to Taiwan where nine million Taiwanese were now faced with two million 'mainlanders'. The total detachment of the 'imported' government from the local population enabled it to introduce rigorous agrarian reform and to advance industrialization by authoritarian means. Economic development was encouraged in this way, but the freedom for which the Taiwanese had hoped when they were liberated from Japanese rule remained out of sight.

The fate of the Koreans was not much better. The Japanese cabinet had stated as early as 1904 that Korea was predestined to supply produce and raw materials to Japan. Since it was sparsely populated, it would also be an ideal immigration colony for the Japanese. After winning the war against Russia in 1905, the Japanese first made Korea a protectorate and finally annexed it in 1910.[98] The plans made by the cabinet in 1904 could now be implemented, but there was not as much Japanese migration to Korea as the cabinet had hoped for. By the end of the colonial period there were about 700,000 Japanese in Korea and as many Koreans in Japan. Whereas the Koreans in Japan were mostly labourers, the Japanese in Korea were administrators, businessmen and landlords, but hardly any cultivators. The Japanese landlords in Korea amassed a great deal of land which was cultivated for them by poor Korean tenants.

The Japanese acquisition of Korean land was greatly facilitated by the cadastral survey which the colonial authorities conducted between 1910 and 1918. It turned land titles into marketable commodities and also enabled the authorities to collect the land revenue efficiently. If Korea had been an independent country, this survey would have been of great benefit to it, but under colonial rule it only helped the immigrant Japanese landlords who by then controlled a large part of the arable land and enhanced rice production which led to an increase of rice exports.

After the First World War, Korean nationalists were inspired by Woodrow Wilson's message of self-determination. A rebellion against the Japanese, which became known as the March First Independence Movement, broke out in 1919, shortly after the death of Korea's last emperor Kojong who had reigned from 1864 to 1907. There were rumours that he had been poisoned by the Japanese. His public funeral triggered the rebellion which had broad popular support. A Korean delegation presented a declaration of independence to the Japanese Governor General. The Japanese were taken unawares by this rebellion and then suppressed it brutally. International opinion turned against the Japanese and they tried to make their rule look more liberal and enlightened in subsequent years. However,this merely hid the iron fist by putting on a velvet glove.

In their drive towards re-armament and industrialization the Japanese did a great deal for the development of infrastructure and industrial production in Korea. This heritage undoubtedly contributed to the Korean economic miracle in later years, as did the methods of authoritarian economic policy which the Japanese had introduced and which were later followed by Korean governments.[99] The Japanese were past masters in the field of 'colonial development' but, of course, this was not a result of altruism. The colonial economies were carefully geared to providing essential inputs for the Japanese economy. Social welfare in the colonies did not keep pace with the increase in production. Korean rice output increased from 2 million tonnes in 1910 to 4 million tonnes in 1940. About half of the production of 1940 was exported. In the meantime the Korean population had also increased substantially and the availability of rice per capita had declined. Poor Koreans, therefore, had to subsist on coarse grains while their rice fed the Japanese.

The fate of Korea after the termination of Japanese rule was decided by the Allies whom the Soviet Union had joined at the last moment. President Roosevelt had made plans for imposing a regime of international trusteeship on Korea after the war. At the Yalta Conference he discussed this idea with Stalin who agreed with him. They envisaged a period of trusteeship administration of about 20–30 years which was to be a joint project of the USA, the Soviet Union and China. Stalin felt that the British should also be invited to participate.[100] No further arrangements were made during the war. The Soviet Union then occupied North Korea and the USA South Korea. The idea of international trusteeship was then discussed again but the South Korean leaders rejected it. They felt that trusteeship was applicable to a backward people, not to the Korean nation. Thus the plan was dropped.[101] The fate of Korea was, therefore, left in the hands of the two powers which had occupied it and which then guided it according to their respective visions of the future.

North Korea had been the more highly industrialized part of the country under Japanese rule. It also held most of the mineral wealth. As a client state of the Soviet Union it suffered from the introduction of a socialist economy. South Korea profited from US aid which was stepped up after the Korean War when South Korea emerged as a bastion of the West in the Cold War. Unlike other ex-colonies which could stress Afro-Asian solidarity and later on joined the **Non-aligned Movement**, the Japanese ex-colonies had no such options. They were immediately caught in the vice of the superpowers which determined their fate.

IMPERIAL SUNSET: HONG KONG, 1997

The booming tea trade of the eighteenth century brought many British sailors and merchants to China. The British demand for tea increased dramatically and yet the price of tea fell because the Chinese supply of it grew even faster. In some provinces of China every suitable piece of land was converted into a tea garden. Due to the regulation of foreign trade, the British were restricted to Canton as the only port where they could do business. They wanted access to ports closer to the tea producing areas. In 1793 Lord Macarteney was sent as a special ambassador to China to plead with the Chinese emperor for freer access to Chinese ports. His mission was unsuccessful. The emperor wrote a letter to the British king, telling him that China did not need the goods of foreigners; he also warned him that Chinese territories were accurately delimited and if the British tried to tresspass these limits they would be driven away by force. The emperor surely knew about the British conquest of India and wanted to prevent the British from penetrating China. Thus they had to stick to their trading station in Canton, but since they always got sufficient tea at low prices they could tolerate these restrictions. The only problem was the increasing amount of silver required for the purchase of tea, the solution to which was found in selling Indian opium to the Chinese in ever increasing quantities. This trade was illegal and while the production was a monopoly of the East India Company, the shipping to China was in the hands of British private traders. The emperor repeatedly condemned this trade. Finally a Chinese official seized a large quantity of opium and had it burned. The British government, always eager to defend the property of its citizens, then waged the Opium War against China in 1839. The British made use of their latest technological achievements; gunboats driven by steam engines went up the rivers and bombarded Chinese cities. The emperor capitulated and permitted the continuation of the opium trade. Emboldened by this success, the British went one step further. In 1841 a detachment of British soldiers occupied the small island of Hong Kong which was at that time inhabited only by fishermen and pirates. Located near the mouth of the Pearl river, it soon proved to be of strategic importance.

By means of an 'unequal treaty' the Chinese were compelled to yield Hong Kong to the British in perpetuity.[102] Soon the British were not satisfied with the small island and claimed adjacent Kowloon on the mainland. This was ceded to them by the Convention of Peking, signed in 1859 following a joint invasion of China by British and French forces. After a few decades the 'New Territories' beyond Kowloon were attached to Hong Kong. This time the treaty signed in 1898 did not provide for a grant in perpetuity but only for a 99-year lease. The signatories probably did not foresee that the date set in this way would actually mark the British imperial sunset in Asia.

The revolutionary governments of China after 1911 were neither willing nor able to drive the British away. On the contrary, British influence in China grew during the 1920s and 1930s. During the Second World War the Japanese occupied Hong Kong. The British were not sure whether they would ever be able to recover it. Chiang Kai-shek insisted on it being returned to China after the war and Roosevelt encouraged him in this. When Chiang's credentials as a military leader faded at the end of the war and Roosevelt died, the British hoped to get Hong Kong back. Attlee, who was otherwise sceptical about the value of the empire, was adamant about restoring British rule in Hong Kong. The British then managed to capture Hong Kong in a daring act soon after the Japanese capitulation, outsmarting Chiang who had insisted on taking over the city from the Japanese.[103] Subsequently the communist seizure of power in China in 1949 could have meant the end of British rule, but it soon turned out that Mao found Hong Kong as a British port very useful. Whenever an embargo was imposed on China, the clever traders of Hong Kong would find ways and means to circumvent it. When China opened up in the late 1970s, Hong Kong performed another useful function for China, acting as its commercial hub and linking it to an expanding world market.

As the expiry of the lease of the 'New Territories' drew nearer, the British had to make up their mind whether they wished to hold on to a much reduced Hong Kong 'in perpetuity' or hand it over gracefully to the Chinese, along with the New Territories, in 1997. The political environment had changed in the meantime. Hong Kong was no longer needed for the circumvention of an embargo and in its new role as commercial hub it would also prosper after 1997. The transfer was sweetened by the Chinese as they suggested the formula 'one country, two systems' and assured Hong Kong of the continuation of its laws and its free economy for another 50 years. These were the main points of a treaty signed with the British in 1984, but there remained one contentious issue. The British always prepared the 'transfer of power' to their colonies by establishing a democratic framework such as an elected legislative council and a 'leader of government business' who could then become prime minister. In Hong Kong, however, power was to be transferred to the Chinese government and not to the people of Hong Kong. Since this government was not a democratic one, it wished to prevent any advance towards democracy in Hong Kong. The Chinese emphasis was more on 'one country' than on 'two systems'.

The British governors of Hong Kong had traditionally been senior civil servants or diplomats who did what they were told to do. But it so happened that Chris Patten, the last governor who took up his post in 1992, was a practising democrat and not a civil servant. He had been a Member of Parliament, a minister in the British government and finally the chairman of the British Conservative Party. He wished to introduce at least the rudiments of parliamentary democracy in Hong Kong before handing it over to the Chinese government. Naturally this government did not support Patten's activities at all, nor did the rich Chinese businessmen of Hong Kong sympathize with him. They felt that he might upset the status quo and spoil their business prospects. Patten, however, was liked by those citizens of Hong Kong who believed in democracy and wanted to see to it that the formula of 'one country, two systems' would not remain a mere platitude. In institutional terms, Patten did not achieve much and the man to whom he had to transfer power in 1997 was a Chinese businessman handpicked by the Chinese government. Despite this Patten had strengthened Hong Kong's civil society which then successfully protested against any abridgment of its civil liberties attempted by the Chinese government. In doing so the citizens of Hong Kong set an example for Chinese citizens elswhere. Appointing a practising democrat as governor of Hong Kong at the time of the imperial sunset was a good idea after all.

THE ARAB WORLD: FROM THE
FERTILE CRESCENT TO THE SAHARA

THE BRITISH, THE FRENCH AND THE DECLINE OF
THE OTTOMAN EMPIRE

When the Ottoman Turks besieged Vienna in 1529 and again in 1683 they terrified Europe. By the nineteenth century, however, the sultan in Istanbul was a sorry figure who was pitied rather than feared. European powers vied with each other in detaching limbs from his far-flung empire. In the sixteenth century this empire had expanded at a rapid rate and became one of the so-called 'gunpowder empires'. 'Field artillery states' would be a more accurate term, as the success of these empires was based on their mobile artillery which could be deployed on the battlefield. The Safavids of Persia and the Great Mughals of India also belonged to this category. The descendants of the Islamic warriors on horseback, who had conquered the area from the fertile crescent to Morocco, were subdued by the artillerists. Those who were used to cavalry warfare felt that artillery was a lowly weapon unfit for true warriors. But Selim I, who was rightly called 'The Cruel', made very efficient use of his artillery and subdued all those who detested it. His son, Suleyman II, who was called 'Qanuni' (the lawgiver), consolidated the empire during his long reign (1520–1566). It was he who besieged Vienna. He also conquered Basra and thus attached Iraq to his realm. In addition he subjected the states of the Mediterranean coast. Only the Sultan of Morocco resisted the Ottomans for any length of time, but even he had to recognize Ottoman suzerainty by signing a treaty in 1582.

Istanbul was at a great distance from these far-flung provinces of the empire. Some provinces even seceded from it at times; for example, Iraq from 1623 to 1639. But by and large the empire proved to be cohesive and imposed its institutions on all Arab provinces. This was also true of the administrative reforms (*tanzimat*) which were introduced in 1839. These reforms were aimed at opening up the empire to Western influences so as to catch up with Europe. Modern education was introduced with the help of Europeans, but the British and the French were not satisfied with such cultural influence. They wanted to advance their economic interests. The opening of the Suez Canal in 1869 was an important event in this context. It literally cut across the Ottoman Empire and facilitated the spread of European colonialism. Initially the building of the Suez Canal was a matter which concerned only the Khedive of Egypt who was a kind of viceroy of the Ottoman sultan. However, he did not inform the sultan about the details of his plans. It soon appeared that the Khedive had run into debt by participating in this venture. The British bought some of his shares in the Suez Canal Company and saw to it that Egypt was put under the financial tutelage of its foreign debtors. The sultan then deposed the Khedive who was succeeded by his son, Taufiq. The new Khedive was soon threatened by a military revolt led by Colonel Ahmad Urabi who was celebrated as a hero by the people. He was called a protector of Islam and a Bismarck of Egypt. In order to get rid of him, Taufiq conspired with the British whose fleet appeared at Alexandria. Instead of frightening the Egyptians, this infuriated them even more. Finally the British occupied Egypt in 1882, under the guise of helping the Khedive. Urabi was defeated by the British; Taufiq wanted him executed but instead the British deported him to Ceylon. The sultan in Istanbul had supported Urabi against Taufiq and was now a loser in the game which Taufiq and the British had won.

The French had also scored points in this kind of game even before the British arrived on the scene. They had conquered Algeria after 1830 and established a French protectorate in Tunisia in 1881. In 1912 they also attacked Morocco. When the Ottomans joined the side of the Germans in the First World War and were defeated, their empire was completely dismantled, the British and the French distributing the remnants among themselves by way of mandates of the League of Nations. During the war they had encouraged Arab nationalism as an ally against the Ottomans, but after the war they disappointed the high hopes of those nationalists. The British nevertheless made good use of the Hashimites who became their clients and ruled Iraq and Transjordania for them.

IRAQ AND TRANSJORDAN: THE BRITISH AND THEIR HASHIMITE CLIENTS

The Hashimites became British clients after the British had disappointed Hussein of Arabia who had joined them in their fight against the Ottoman Empire in the First World War. Hussein had expected to unify the Arab world under his command; he not only failed to achieve this aim, but was also deprived of his home territory in Arabia by Ibn Saud. Hussein was thus a tragic figure who could only bequeath his lofty ambitions to his sons Faisal and Abdullah who then played important roles in the British game of controlling the Arab world. The Hashimites claimed to be descendants of the Prophet, which provided them with legitimacy but not necessarily with political power.

Faisal had tried to claim the throne of Syria in 1918, but he was soon chased away by the French who had no use for a monarch in their mandate territory, as will be discussed below. The British found a new job for the unemployed king; they installed him in Iraq which had been entrusted to them as a mandate. This was a fatal decision as the Hashimites never gained the allegiance of the Iraqi people. It was obvious that they ruled only on behalf of the British. The credit for keeping this fragile political structure in good repair goes to **Nuri al-Said** who had served as an Iraqi officer in the Ottoman army and proved himself to be a consummate politician – and a friend of the British.

Iraq was a Class A mandate, i.e. destined for early independence. The British accordingly granted formal independence to Iraq in 1930, tying it down with a treaty which preserved British rights such as access to the oil fields, maintenance of military bases, etc. The continued rule of King Faisal I seemed to guarantee the stability of this arrangement. It was unfortunate for the British that Faisal died in 1933 and that his successor, Ghazi, met with a fatal car accident in 1939. Faisal II ascended the throne as a child which meant that the government had to be led by a regent, his uncle Prince Abdul Ilah. This prince, a nephew of Abdullah of Transjordan, was a weak and timid man. However, there was **Nuri**, the prime minister, who could be trusted to maintain the status quo.

The Second World War contributed to a reassertion of British power in Iraq but also put it to a severe test. In 1941 a group of Iraqi officers led by Rashid al-Ghilani staged a coup and tried to get Hitler's support.[1] They were not Nazis themselves but rather Arab nationalists who wanted to get rid of the British and their Hashimite clients. They had a great deal of popular sympathy which lingered on after they had been crushed by the British. **Nuri**, who had also secretly tried to establish contact with Hitler, then opted for the British who knew nothing of his devious tactics. He emerged as the strong man of Iraq on whom the British relied.[2]

After the war Bevin tried to make Iraq a showcase of his new policy of partnership with the Arab world. **Nuri** had gone into semi-retirement as president of the senate and his protégé, Saleh Jabr, had become the first Shia prime minister of Iraq in March 1947. The British were hopeful that this young politician could lead his country into a brave new era in which the British would remain respected partners. To this effect a new treaty was drafted which was designed to replace that of 1930 which Arab nationalists regarded as a British imposition. The new approach was mainly one of a change of terminology. There was to be a Joint Defence Board which masked the continuation of undiluted British military presence. The British military bases were also to be retained. Saleh Jabr welcomed the British gesture and went to Portsmouth to sign the new treaty on January 15, 1948.[3] He stayed on in Great Britain for some time. In the meantime serious unrest broke out at home. There had been a bad harvest, making bread scarce and expensive. The people were restive and on top of this there was nationalist criticism of the 'sell-out' represented by the new treaty. The regent, Prince Abdul Ilah, was so scared that he announced that he would not ratify the treaty. On returning home, Saleh Jabr had to resign. Bevin's policy of partnership had failed dismally. He did not make any attempt at revising the treaty but simply announced that the old treaty of 1930 would remain valid.[4] This did not augur well for British–Iraqi relations. To Arab nationalists, 'independent' Iraq remained a British colony in disguise.

When **Nasser**'s influence made itself felt throughout the Arab world, **Nuri** tried to counteract it by designing the Bagdad Pact which linked Iraq with Turkey, Pakistan and the British in 1955. No Arab nation joined this pact. For **Nuri** this was a Pyrrhic victory. The pact did not add anything to the security of Iraq as it was protected by the British anyhow. On the other hand, the pact confirmed the views of Arab nationalists, that **Nuri** was a puppet of the West. He had practically invited the retribution which subsequently put an end to his life as well as to the lives of the young king and his family in July 1958.[5]

For a long time Transjordan remained the last bastion of British power in the Arab world. **Abdullah**, who was born in 1871, reached a ripe old age before he was assassinated in 1951. His realm had been created for him by the British who detached the southern part of their mandate territory, Palestine, in the 1920s. Churchill, who was then the colonial minister, assured **Abdullah** that it would remain an Arab territory to which no Jewish settlers would be admitted.[6] Formal independence was granted to Transjordan in 1946, prior to which the British had promoted **Abdullah** from 'Amir' to 'King'. The British referred to him as 'Mr Bevin's Little King'. Transjordan had the same treaty relations with the British as Iraq had. After the experiment with a revised treaty had ended in disaster in Iraq in 1947, **Abdullah** pleased Bevin by signing a new treaty in 1948. As a special feature, this treaty included the British guarantee of a continued subsidy for the legendary **Arab Legion**. **Abdullah** was, of course, keen to preserve this special relationship. The **Arab Legion** was not only crucial for the defence of Transjordan, it also protected **Abdullah** against any coup, as the Legion was in the hands of the trusted British general, John Glubb, and would certainly not try to overthrow the king. Glubb had taken up the command of the **Arab Legion** in 1938 and had made it the finest fighting force in the whole region. In the beginning it had consisted of only 1,200 soldiers, but by the end of the Second World War, there were 8,000 troops and by 1956 it had grown to 25,000.[7] It was, however, disbanded in 1956 under pressure from **Nasser**, and Glubb had to return home after 18 years of service. Prime Minister Eden's decision to attack **Nasser** in 1956 was influenced by the departure of Glubb's **Arab Legion** from this region, in which it had represented the last remnant of British imperial glory. It must be mentioned, however, that Glubb had also managed to 'Arabize' the officer corps and to transform what was once a colonial 'special force' into a national army.

Transjordan, an artificial creation of the British, nevertheless survived as a national state. It also survived as the realm of the last Hashimite monarchy. **Abdullah**'s vision of a 'Greater Syria', however, remained a pipe-dream. He had devoted much energy to the propagation of this idea. In 1947 he even published a White Paper on the issue in which he described Syria and Transjordan as parts of one country.[8] Syrians tended to hold this view, too, but to them Transjordan was a Syrian province which would one day return to Syria. They were completely opposed to a 'reunification' under a Hashimite king, whereas **Abdullah** was convinced that his throne should stand in Damascus. The British were embarrassed by the ambitions of their protégé. In general they did not object to plans of Arab unity as long as they were made by Arabs and not attributed to some sinister British motive. They also had misgivings about the stability of Syria as they had been deeply involved in its fate during the war and in the immediate postwar period. However, they certainly did not believe that **Abdullah**'s plans had any chance of success.

SYRIA AND LEBANON: REPUBLICS OF FRENCH DESIGN

Both Syria and Lebanon owed their republican constitutions to the French who had obtained the mandate to administer these territories. They had seen off King Faisal and enlarged the province of Lebanon which they then separated from Syria. Both republics were characterized by ethnic plurality and the French had great difficulties in controlling the many rebellious ethnic communities. The Druzes, a heretic Islamic group which had originated in the eleventh century AD, had been persecuted by many Islamic rulers before managing to find refuge in the mountains of Lebanon as well as in adjacent parts of Syria. In 1925–1926 the French suppressed a rebellion of the Druzes and then established a democratic republic in Syria with a multiparty system which actually attained some political importance.

One of the Syrian parties was the **Baath Party**, founded in 1940 by Michel **Aflaq**, a Syrian Christian and a staunch Arab nationalist. 'Baath', meaning 'rebirth', referred to a secular Arab nationalism with a socialist tendency.[9] The party gained many adherents among young intellectuals and also among young army officers. It especially appealed to the Alawites, a Shia community, which had earlier belonged to the lower classes and had risen by entering modern professions and also as officers in the army.

The French had ambivalent feelings about the republics which they had fostered. After all, they also provided a fertile breeding ground for Arab nationalism. They added fuel to this fire when, in 1941, an emissary of the **Free French** promised independence to Syria and Lebanon. The British who occupied the area during the war also promised independence in 1943 and the USA followed suit in 1944.[10] In 1943 elections had been held and Shukri Al-Quwatli became Syria's first president. He feared that the British and the French had concluded another secret agreement like that of Sykes and Picot during the First World War, but Churchill assured him that no such agreement existed. The French seemed to respect the independence of the republic and even saw to it that Syria and Lebanon were invited to become founder-members of the UN in 1945. However, in May 1945, French troops suddenly landed in Syria. The British were perplexed but could not prevent it. They knew that this move was aimed at restoring French influence and to prevent the British from including Syria in their sphere of influence. The French were deeply suspicious of British motives and were also aware of the actual position of power which the British had in this region. The new French government was obsessed with its duty to reassert French imperial might. In view of the fact that the French had sponsored Syrian independence, their brutal methods of asserting their military presence came as a surprise. They even bombed Damascus at the end of May 1945. The British felt compelled to intervene and imposed a ceasefire. General de Gaulle was outraged and told the British ambassador to France: 'We are not in a position to open hostilities against you at the present time. But you have insulted France and betrayed the West. This cannot be forgotten'.[11] It seemd that de Gaulle wanted to punish the British at some time in the future if he had an opportunity to do so. Relations between the French and the British remained tense until they finally agreed to withdraw their troops simultaneously in 1946. It was only then that Syria and Lebanon became truly independent.

Lebanon followed in the footsteps of Syria towards decolonization. It achieved its formal independence on January 1, 1944, and its actual independence in 1946 when the French and the British withdrew their troops. The French were particularly attached to the Lebanon and posed as the protectors of its Maronite Christian minority. The small Lebanese nation which consisted of communities which were always in conflict with each other could hardly ever live in peace. The Maronite Christians, the Druzes and the orthodox Sunni Muslims could not easily achieve a political balance.[12] There was a constitutional provision that there should always be a Christian president and a Muslim prime minister. This seemed to work when Camille Chamoun was president, but in 1958 a civil war erupted because the Muslims feared that Chamoun intended to change the constitution to perpetuate his rule. Under the Eisenhower Doctrine, the USA had intervened in the Lebanon in 1958 which Chamoun had welcomed. After the USA withdrew, conflicts persisted and finally the Chief of Staff of the Lebanese army, General Fuad Shihab, was elected president. The old rule of having a Christian president was thus abandoned. Further trouble was brewing and the Lebanon became a scene of recurrent civil war.

PALESTINE AND ISRAEL: THE SQUARING OF THE CIRCLE

During the First World War Palestine had been occupied by British troops under General Allenby and Arab troops under the Hashimite Prince Faisal. After the war, the British and the French had delimited their respective mandate territories according to their convenience. The district of Mossul which had belonged to Syria was transferred to the British mandate territory of Iraq. Palestine was also taken away from Syria in 1920 and became another British mandate territory. In Palestine the Zionist Jews intended to establish a state of their own. Initially they just raised a claim for areas to be settled in agreement with the Arabs of Palestine, the justification for which was the Balfour declaration of November 1917. Arthur James Balfour, the British foreign minister, had stated in a letter to the Zionist leader, Lord Rothschild, that the British government would grant a home to the Jews in Palestine. As there was no legal definition of 'home', it was open to various interpretations. The deliberate vagueness of Balfour's declaration was in keeping with its immediate purpose. It was aimed at securing the good will of the Jews in support of the British war effort. Balfour had drafted it in order to pre-empt a similar declaration from the German side. After the war there was no pressing need to be more precise about the Balfour Declaration. It remained a vague assurance at the time when the British were given the mandate of the

League of Nations to administer Palestine. The immigration of Jews was permitted at the same time as the rights of the Arabs were to be respected. This proved to be an attempt at squaring the circle.

In the early years Jewish immigration had been rather limited. As a result of Hitler's persecution of the Jews, immigration increased in the 1930s, leading to violent reactions from the Arabs of Palestine. The British felt obliged to curtail immigration and to announce that the original promise of providing a home to Jewish settlers had been kept, but that further immigration had to be phased out. In a British government document published in 1939 it was stated that immigration would be permitted until 1944. After this the Arab veto would be taken into consideration. The Arabs acquiesced in this decision. During the war, Palestine was under British military control. After the war immigration started again and the British administration in Palestine faced great pressure to accommodate more Jewish refugees. The British public had been shocked by the terrible evidence of Nazi atrocities discovered by British troops when they freed the inmates of the German concentration camp Bergen-Belsen. Added to this was the pressing problem of Jewish refugees crowding camps of displaced persons in Europe. President Truman, who respected the interests of his American Jewish voters, was made aware of this problem but hesitated to relax US immigration laws in order to admit thousands of Jewish refugees to the USA. Instead he put pressure on the British to settle 100,000 Jewish refugees in Palestine. This became a highly contentious issue between the British and US governments. Great Britain was financially dependent on the USA after the war, but the British government did not want to take orders from Truman when major British interests were involved.

Ernest Bevin, the British foreign minister, was deeply concerned with Arab sympathies for a continued British role in the Middle East. He wanted to change the British role from that of a colonial ruler to that of a partner of Arab nations. In this context he was very apprehensive at alarming the Arabs by sending large numbers of Jews to Palestine. He also knew that the British had to terminate their mandate in due course; for a peaceful transfer of power he envisaged a binational state in Palestine in which Jews and Arabs would live together. Admitting large numbers of Jews at this stage would certainly spoil this plan. However, it soon became apparent that Bevin was fighting an uphill battle against Truman in which he was bound to be defeated.

The alternative to Bevin's plan for a binational state was the partition of Palestine, which had been suggested by a British committee as far back as 1937. But the creation of a Jewish state was anathema to Bevin, even worse than admitting thousands of refugees. The Arabs would be up in arms, which is what Bevin wanted to prevent at any cost. In order to get some breathing space he agreed to a joint British–American committee which proceeded to examine a large number of witnesses and also toured Palestine.[13] Somewhat rashly, Bevin told the committee that he would accept its verdict provided it was unanimous, probably assuming that unanimity could never be reached in view of the contentious issues involved. But to everybody's surprise, the committee did arrive at unanimous recommendations. They contained an endorsement of Truman's demand for the admission of 100,000 Jews to Palestine but also of Bevin's proposal for a binational state. Truman gladly accepted the approval of his demand but kept quiet as far as the other recommendations of the committee were concerned. Bevin was stuck with the verdict. He had suffered his first defeat – but more was to come.

On July 22, 1946 Jewish terrorists of the **Irgun Zvai Leumi** blew up the British headquarters in Palestine, the King David Hotel in Jerusalem. Many people died and British public opinion was incensed. The Jewish terrorists had succeeded in enhancing British frustrations. There were about 100,000 British troops in Palestine. The cost of maintaining this force strained the British budget and in spite of this massive military presence, the disaster at the King David Hotel could not be prevented. There was a growing feeling that the British should leave, which is just what the Jewish terrorists wanted to achieve.

In order to regain the initiative, Bevin took the case to the **United Nations**. He hoped he could avoid US pressure in this way and get support from the Arab states and other Third World nations. He presumed that they would support his plan of a binational state. He also relied on US–Soviet rivalry which would produce the usual deadlock. Later on he was greatly surprised when the Soviet Union endorsed the same resolution as the USA. The UN had appointed a special committee in May 1947.[14] To Bevin's discomfiture, the committee came up with a partition plan of its own and did not endorse the idea of a binational state. Looking at the map produced by the committee, observers spoke of 'fighting serpents' as Jewish and Arab territories were intertwined in a very complex pattern. The subsequent resolution debated in the UN General Assembly, which also contained the partition plan, was passed in November 1947, with 33 nations voting for the plan, 13 against it and 10 abstaining.[15] Following this second defeat, Bevin now recommended that the British terminate their mandate on May 15, 1948. He had the full support of Prime Minister Attlee in this decision. Attlee had indicated as early as September 1947 that a firm date for a British withdrawal should be fixed and he had cited the Indian precedent where the British had also announced a date for the granting of independence in advance and had stuck to it.[16] There was a flaw in this analogy, however; in India and Pakistan there were governments ready for a transfer of power, whereas in Palestine no such orderly transfer could be hoped for. There was the rudimentary Zionist state of Israel, of course, but the British were not yet reconciled to handing over power to Israel, the more so as there was no equivalent Arab state in sight. In fact, the Arabs were so shocked by the British decision that they pleaded with them to retain their mandate.[17]

The British decision also put the US government on the spot. General Marshall, the Secretary of State, clearly saw that the British wanted to manoeuvre the US into a position which they no longer wanted to hold.[18] The somewhat simple-minded President Truman was out of his depth in dealing with this problem, but he was sure that he did not want to send US troops to Palestine to impose the partition plan which he otherwise endorsed. When the State Department suggested that the UN should temporarily set up a trusteeship administration to give Jews and Arabs a chance to reach an agreement among themselves, Truman agreed to this. However, when the US representative at the UN made a speech only a few days later in which he made this proposal, Truman complained that 'the State Department had pulled the rug from under him'.[19] His furious reaction was due to the fact that one day before that speech, Truman had had one of his meetings with Chaim Weizmann whom he respected very much. He had assured Weizmann of his support for the partition plan. After the speech he felt that Weizmann would now think of him as dishonest. To compensate for this, Truman wrote a secret letter to Weizmann on April 23, 1947, informing him that he would recognize Israel immediately after the termination of the British mandate. Truman did not even tell Marshall about this secret promise.[20]

In the meantime the British had also made arrangements for their impending departure from Palestine. They trusted their faithful ally, King **Abdullah** of Transjordan, whose **Arab Legion** under the command of the British general, John Glubb, was the only well-trained military force in the Arab world. **Abdullah** would quickly capture the Arab parts of Palestine as soon as the mandate expired. In February 1948 Glubb and **Abdullah**'s premier Taufiq, had a private meeting with Bevin in London. It was agreed that the **Arab Legion** would occupy the part of Palestine allotted to the Arabs by the UN immediately after the termination of the mandate. Bevin endorsed this but urged that they should not invade the areas allotted to the Jews.[21] The British colonial minister, Arthur Creech-Jones, met Moshe Shertok, who would soon become Israel's first foreign minister, in New York shortly before the mandate expired. He told him that the **Arab Legion** would advance but avoid clashes with the Jewish troops 'without appearing to betray the Arab cause'.[22] This was good news for the Jews in Palestine as they did not have to heed the USA's appeal for a truce with the Arabs before the expiry of the mandate and they could rely on **Abdullah** to mop up the Palestinian Arabs and keep them under control. On May 4, 1948, a memorandum of the State Department predicted that **Abdullah** would cut across to the sea at Jaffa, give some territory in the north to Syria and leave only the coastal strip from Tel Aviv to Haifa to Israel.[23] In May 1948, however, **Abdullah** was not feeling very comfortable at all. He met Golda Meir, who was at that time a member of **Ben-Gurion**'s provisional Israeli government. She had to disguise herself as an Arab on this secret mission. Her task was to persuade **Abdullah** not to attack the Jews. At an earlier meeting in November 1947 he had assured her that he would not do this, but now she found him exhausted and disconcerted. He told her that he must attack because he was no longer alone and his Arab allies would expect him to act. **Abdullah**'s position had become more difficult after the Jews had forcibly occupied several areas allotted to the Arabs in April, even before the mandate expired. Thus **Abdullah** was forced to wage a war which he had wanted to avoid.

Truman ensured that he kept his promise to Weizmann and recognized the new state of Israel almost simultaneously with **Ben-Gurion**'s proclamation on May

15, 1948. The Soviet Union soon followed suit. It was a rare case of joint action in the Cold War. Before the proclamation of the state of Israel, there had been debates about how the partition should be enforced and who should do it. However, it now became a do-it-yourself project for the Israelis. The war of partition started immediately. The Arabs had sworn that they would push the Jews into the sea, but it soon appeared that the real problem was how to stop the Israelis from seizing the whole of Palestine or even going beyond that. In the first round of the war 19,000 Israeli troops faced 23,000 Arab troops. **Abdullah** tried his best to do what the British and the USA had expected from him at this stage, but instead he was stymied by rapid Israeli advances. General Glubb admitted that a military stalemate had been reached and a truce was arrived at on June 11, 1948. The UN appointed a mediator, the Swedish Count Folke Bernadotte. There were high hopes that he would prove to be the Mountbatten of Palestine but, before he could do anything about it, the 'Nine Days War' of July 9–18, 1948 intervened. It soon became obvious that the Israelis had made good use of the breathing space obtained by this first truce. They had prepared their new offensive very well and made more territorial gains in this brief war. In the midst of the war, Bevin informed **Abdullah** that he would do anything for him except supply ammunition.[24] The British and the USA had agreed on an arms embargo. If Britain had supplied arms and ammunition to the Arabs, the USA would have done the same for the Israelis. There was thus a danger of an Anglo–US proxy war developing, which Bevin wanted to avoid. The Israelis, who had received Czech armaments in large quantities before May 15, 1948, benefited from the Anglo–US stalemate at this point.

Abdullah had seen to it that the other Arab powers had made him the commander-in-chief of the Arab forces. Actually, he would have been satisfied with the position achieved at the time of the first truce and would have liked to sign a separate peace treaty with Israel. This incensed the Arabs as well as the British, because **Abdullah** would have blatantly betrayed the Arab cause. When he was forced to fight again on July 9, 1948, he did so in spite of himself, the more so as the British could give him only 'moral' support but no military aid. He therefore tried to make use of Bernadotte and dictated a plan to him which was then incorporated in a UN resolution of July 15, 1948. According to this plan the Israelis would retain Galilee but leave the Negev to the Arabs. Jerusalem would become an international city.[25] The plan, which became known as the 'Bernadotte Plan', already looked anachronistic by the time of the second truce. The Israelis had made further territorial gains which they had no intention of giving up. Nevertheless, Bernadotte pursued his plan until he was assassinated by Israeli terrorists on September 18, 1948.

In October 1948 the war took on a much larger dimension. The Israelis had so far won the war of partition and the Arabs were fighting with their backs to the wall. By now Israel had 100,000 troops in the field and launched an attack on Egypt. This ended in a complete collapse of the Egyptian army which was defeated in the battles of December 1948 to January 1949. Bevin wanted to intervene in order to rescue the **Arab Legion** and informed Truman accordingly who then warned his Israeli clients. This had the desired effect. The war of partition ended with the resounding victory of the Israelis and a political defeat of the British.[26]

The fate of Palestine was grim: it was practically erased from the political map and its leadership had been dismal. There was a brief attempt at forming a Palestinian government with the Mufti of Jerusalem as its president, but he was obviously the wrong choice. The Mufti had openly sided with Hitler during the Second World War and was hated by the British and their Hashimite clients. When the Israelis started their war of partition, about 700,000 Palestinians had to flee. Their places were taken by Israeli settlers. From 1870 to 1947 only 216 Jewish settlements had been established in Palestine. In the short period from 1948 to 1950 246 settlements were added to this number.[27] While Israel consolidated its hold on the area it had occupied, **Abdullah** did the same on his side. He ordered elections to be held in his own state of Transjordan and in the region to the west of the Jordan occupied by him. The joint parliament then ratified the annexation of West Jordan, which is what **Abdullah** had wanted to achieve by means of a separate peace treaty with Israel but which he was unable to conclude. **Abdullah** could not offer a home to the large number of Palestinian refugees who then spread throughout the Arab world. When Israel became a member of the **United Nations** in November 1949, it endorsed a UN resolution which asked for the return of the refugees to their homes. But this resolution – a faint echo of the failed plan for a binational state – was never implemented. Israel became a powerful national state, but the problem of the displaced Palestinians was to haunt it for a long time to come.

EGYPT: FROM LIBERALISM TO MILITARY DICTATORSHIP

Egypt was similarly rudely awakened from the Arab dream of national unity sponsored by the British during the First World War. At the same time Woodrow Wilson's message of self-determination reached Egypt after the war and fired the imagination of liberal nationalists. Saad **Zaghlul**, a prominent politician who had been a minister before the war, proclaimed Egypt's independence in November 1918. The British were not amused; he was arrested and deported. They also tried to prevent him from attending the Versailles Conference in 1919, but he finally managed to get there with an Egyptian delegation (= *wafd*). The members of this delegation formed the nucleus of the **Wafd Party** founded by **Zaghlul** in the same year. In 1921 he was again arrested and deported, and once more in 1923. But due to popular pressure, the British released him and his party won the elections of January 1924.

In the meantime the British High Commissioner, General Lord Allenby, had been permitted to grant formal independence to Egypt in 1922. Allenby had been eager to do this, but unfortunately he himself demonstrated only two years later that this independence was a sham. The British commander had been murdered and Allenby adopted draconian measures to restore 'law and order'. Moreover, he blamed **Zaghlul** for the assassination who then resigned in November 1924 having been prime minister for less than a year.[28] **Zaghlul** remained president of his party until his death in 1927 when Mustafa al-**Nahhas** succeeded him.

While the **Wafd Party** remained the most important party, King Fuad did not support it and even though it had won another election in 1925, it was not permitted to form a government. **Nahhas** got a brief chance at leadership in 1930 but also had to resign after a short time. It was only in 1936–1937 that he was able to remain prime minister for long enough to negotiate a new treaty with the British. After the Italian invasion of Ethiopia, the British were eager to get the Egyptians on their side. King Faruq, who ascended the throne in 1936, clashed with **Nahhas** who finally had to resign. It was only during the **Second World War** that Nahhas got another chance. General Rommel's troops were coming close to Cairo and Faruq was ambivalent about remaining loyal to the British. He appointed a prime minister who was suspect to the British. At this point the British ambassador, Miles Lampson, had Faruq's palace surrounded by tanks and forced him to appoint **Nahhas**. After the British had defeated Rommel in 1944, Faruq was permitted to get rid of **Nahhas** whose popularity had suffered due to his being imposed on the king by the British. In order to gain legitimacy, **Nahhas** had espoused the cause of Arab unity at that time and had taken steps to establish the **Arab League**.

After the war, the British retained their military control of the Suez Canal zone which caused great resentment in Egypt. With the benefit of hindsight one could say that the British should have withdrawn from Egypt by 1946 and thus saved themselves a great deal of trouble.[29] There were riots which the Egyptian government had to suppress, making it very unpopular. Nevertheless, Prime Minister Siddiqui, who headed the government at that time, achieved some success when he signed a new treaty with the British under which they were obliged to remove their troops within three years. Now Egyptian politics seemed to return to the old liberal mould. **Nahhas** became prime minister once more in 1950, but this was his final period of office. The British failed to honour the terms of the treaty and greatly embarrassed **Nahhas** who felt compelled to revoke it in 1951. In doing so, however, he opened the floodgates of radical action. An armed rebellion against the British was crushed; many people were killed and this only caused more disturbances. Faruq then dismissed **Nahhas** in 1952. Four helpless prime ministers followed in quick succession until a military coup in July 1952 put an end to Egyptian democracy.

The British had spoiled their relations with Egypt in many ways. In the early days of his period in office, Bevin had even offered to evacuate the military base at Suez but he soon retracted as the huge base with its ten airfields became an important asset in the Cold War. Another point of disagreement was the future of the Sudan, which the Egyptians claimed and to which the British obviously intended to grant independence as a separate state.[30] These issues were still not settled when the military coup changed the politics of Egypt fundamentally. Bevin was dead by now; a new Conservative government was in power and Anthony Eden was the new foreign secretary who had to tackle the Egpytian problem.

The leaders of the coup called themselves 'Free Officers'. The most resourceful among them was Colonel Gamal Abdel **Nasser**. However, he did not seize power immediately. During a transitional period the popular general Muhammed Naguib became the head of state. King Faruq had to abdicate; he then left the country. Naguib wanted to reintroduce parliamentary democracy, but **Nasser** disagreed and overthrew Naguib in 1954. **Nasser** had his first great international debut at the **Bandung Conference** of 1955. Subsequently the triumvirate of **Nehru–Nasser–Tito** emerged and sponsored the new **Non-aligned Movement**. But this did not prevent **Nasser** from cultivating good relations with the Soviet Union, just as **Nehru** did at that time. The Western powers consequently cancelled their financial support for **Nasser**'s pet project, the huge Assuan Dam on the Nile. In 1956 **Nasser** took revenge by nationalizing the Suez Canal Company in which British and French private capital had been invested. Sir Anthony Eden had just become British prime minister at that time. He had been foreign secretary when Prime Minister Neville Chamberlain had 'appeased' Hitler in Munich in 1938 and had resigned for this reason. Eden now saw in **Nasser** another Hitler who should not be appeased. He obviously forgot that the British had contributed to **Nasser**'s rise by their prevarication which had undermined Egypt's democratic government. In fact, Eden himself had negotiated a new treaty with Egypt in 1954 which also proved to be of little use.[31] In taking action against **Nasser**, Eden was supported by the French who hated **Nasser** for aiding the rebels fighting against them in Algeria. Israel was also keen to teach **Nasser** a lesson, as he was the first leader who seemed to be strong enough to rally the Arabs against Israel. The British and the French played a perfidious game by encouraging Israel to attack Egypt so that they could intervene on the pretext that they wanted to restore peace.[32] The USA were not taken into confidence at all as they were after all the protectors of Israel. President Eisenhower was furious and expressed his displeasure in no uncertain terms. Eden had to resign under US pressure and was quickly replaced by Harold Macmillan. This was the beginning of what may be called the 'Suez syndrome' in British foreign policy: never again would the British dare to act against the USA; henceforth they would bend over backwards to cultivate the 'special relationship'.

For **Nasser** the Suez War ended in military defeat but a resounding diplomatic victory. The nationalization of the Suez Canal Company was not cancelled; its owners received compensation. The canal was repaired with the help of the **United Nations**, but it remained closed to Israeli ships. Moreover, **Nasser** now emerged as the undisputed leader of the Arab world. In 1958 Egypt and Syria announced their merger as the United Arab Republic (UAR). The state did not last long; the UAR was dissolved in 1961. But **Nasser** was surely at the zenith of his power during those years. His decline began in 1967 when he lost the war against Israel. He survived this defeat for only a few years and died in 1970.

THE FRAGMENTED SUDAN

The Sudan is the largest country in Africa; its size surpasses even that of the Congo. Culturally it is a bridge between the Arab world and black Africa, but its political history has militated against this bridging of a cultural divide. The Sudan's ethnic fragmentation has given rise to persistent tensions. British colonial rule and the process of decolonization have enhanced these tensions.

In ancient times the Sudan was intimately related to the Egyptian civilization. When Egypt became a stronghold of Islam, it served as the base from which this religion could penetrate northern Sudan but it did not reach southern Sudan. In the nineteenth century, Ottoman Egypt conquered most of the Sudan. After the British entrenched themselves in Egypt, they also inherited its tenuous control over the Sudan. At about the same time as the British intervened in Egypt, the Mahdi, a Muslim visionary, inspired his countrymen in the Sudan to an extra-ordinary military endeavour. In a short time his forces controlled northern Sudan and defied the British. General Charles Gordon, who was ordered to subdue them, was defeated in 1885, and then murdered in his house. The British public was horrified and saw in Gordon a Christian martyr whose death should be avenged. This took some time, as the state built up by the Mahdi proved to be very resilient although the Mahdi himself had died soon after Gordon's death. In 1898 a British-Egyptian army under the command of General Kitchener conquered the Sudan and put an end to the Mahdi's state. The Sudan was then ruled as a British-Egyptian condominium, a smoke-screen behind which the British built up their colonial rule. When Egypt was granted limited independence in 1922, this smoke-screen vanished and the British then practically ruled the Sudan as they did their other colonies.

A nucleus of future Sudanese nationalism was created by the British when they established Gordon Memorial College in Khartoum. Inaugurated by Kitchener in 1902,[33] this 'Eton of the East' produced an educated Sudanese elite. Its 'old boys' had an *esprit de corps*. The Old Boys' Association was the forerunner of the Graduates' General Congress founded in 1940 whose Secretary General, Ismail **Al-Azhari**, was destined to lead the Sudan to independence. The Gordon Memorial College, whose languages of instruction were English and Arabic, was guided by its British mentors so as to produce modern Arabs who would keep in touch with their tradition. The southern Sudan, however, was not influenced by British educational policy. In fact, the British started a 'Southern Policy' in 1930 which deliberately divided the south from the north. At that time, the British policy makers were convinced that the southern Sudan would fit in better with the adjacent East African colonies than with the Arabic northern Sudan. This policy was reversed in 1946, when the British asserted that both parts of the Sudan belonged together and should have a common legislature. This legislative assembly was convened in 1948; 76 seats were given to the North and only 13 to the South, while 6 were reserved for British officials.

Even before this legislative assembly was inaugurated, political parties had been formed in northern Sudan. The two main parties were the Ashigga Party and the Umma Party. The first favoured a union with Egypt, the second stood for complete independence. The descendants of the Mahdi were still very active in politics and they controlled the Umma Party, while the Ashigga Party was supported by those who feared a resurrection of the Mahdi state.[34] The political development of Egypt was soon to have a decisive impact on Sudanese politics. In 1953 the British and the Egyptians arrived at an agreement which ended the facade of the British–Egyptian condominium and paved the way for the independence of the Sudan. Parliamentary elections were held in the Sudan in that year and the contours of the political landscape emerged very clearly. The most important party was the National Unionist Party (NUP) led by Ismail **Al-Azhari**. The NUP was the successor to the Ashigga Party and retained the aim of a union with Egypt. The Umma Party (UP) had not done well at the polls, winning only 23 of a total of 142 seats, whereas the NUP had captured 97. A newly formed Southern Party had won 16 out of the 22 seats reserved for the South. Based on these election results, the NUP were able to form a government and **Al-Azhari** became prime minister in January 1954. The people of the South felt neglected under the new dispensation. They made up about one-third of the Sudanese population but neither the seats reserved for them in the legislature nor their share in the civil service reflected their numbers. When the British had vacated all civil service positions in 1953, Sudanization was carried out in such a way that of a total of 800 posts the southerners got only 4. The plea of the Southern Party to establish a federal state with some degree of autonomy for the South had also been rejected by the northern politicians. In 1955 the government of **Al-Azhari** was faced with a mutiny of southern army officers which marked the beginning of a civil war which was to continue for decades.

On January 1, 1956, Sudan achieved independence and **Al-Azhari** continued as prime minister. His earlier plans of a union with Egypt had been shelved. He now headed a coalition of the NUP and the UP, but soon thereafter he lost his post because he advocated secular policies which were opposed by the conservative wing of the NUP. The party split and the conservatives formed the People's Democratic Party (PDP); together with the UP they brought down **Al-Azhari**'s government. In the election of 1958 **Al-Azhari**'s party won only a quarter of the seats and remained in opposition. But the PDP and the UP could not enjoy their victory for long. There was a military coup and the dictator, General Ibrahim Abboud, dissolved all political parties. One coup then followed another. From 1965 to 1969 there was an interlude of civilian rule, with **Al-Azhari** holding the largely ceremonial post of president. When another military dictator took over in 1969, however, **Al-Azhari** was thrown into prison where he died within a short time. It seemed that democracy in the Sudan had finally died with him.

A COLLAPSED STATE: ADEN AND YEMEN

The fortified port of Aden, held by the British since 1839, was of great strategic importance to them. In order to control its hinterland, they had established a protectorate there, which was secured by treaties with several small Arab rulers. The adjacent North Yemen had become independent in 1918, having been under Ottoman rule for a long time. It was ruled by the Zaidi Imams. In 1948 Imam Yahya had been assassinated by rebels who wanted to put an end to feudal rule. His son Ahmad defeated the rebels and continued ruling the country. From 1958 to 1961, North Yemen was part of the United Arab Republic consisting of Egypt, Syria and Yemen. Soon after the breakup of this precarious state, Ahmad died. His son, who succeeded him, was immediately overthrown in a military coup whose leader, Colonel Abdullah as-Sallah, proclaimed the Yemen Arab Republic. There followed a civil war in which the new republic was supported by Egypt and the royalists by Saudi Arabia. The republicans won this war and Egyptian troops withdrew in 1967. Soon after President Sallah was deposed by a Republican Council.

In the meantime, Aden and South Yemen had been decolonized in a rather chaotic fashion.[35] For a long time the British had clung to Aden because of its strategic position. In order to secure Aden, the British had created a federation of the Arab rulers of the hinterland in 1959, which was renamed the Federation of South Arabia in 1961. The Arab rulers then urged the British to include Aden in this new state. The British initially resisted the merger but then found it convenient for the control of the people of Aden who asked for more political rights. Finally, the decision about the merger almost coincided with the revolution in North Yemen in 1962. The British, of course, detested the new revolutionary regime supported by **Nasser** and refused to recognize it. President Kennedy urged Prime Minister Macmillan to recognize the new regime so as not to stir up trouble in the area which might attract Soviet intervention. The USA did recognize the new regime in 1962, but Great Britain still refused to do so. In this respect it was at one with Saudi Arabia which renewed its diplomatic ties with Great Britain at that time. These ties had been severed due to the Suez affair of 1956. Macmillan provided substantial financial aid to the royalists in the Yemenite civil war. The USA was obviously not pleased about this, but it was even more perturbed when the new British prime minister Harold Wilson decided in 1964 that the British should withdraw from South Arabia altogether. Macmillan's government had already decided to grant independence to South Arabia by 1968, but Wilson now announced that the British would not contribute to the defence of South Arabia after independence. The USA was not at all happy with the British withdrawal from the region 'east of Suez'.[36] Eventually the Federation of South Arabia collapsed in 1967 and the British pulled out in a hurry. It was perhaps the most ignominious act of decolonization.

The rebels who had driven away the British established the People's Republic of Southern Yemen in November 1967. A few years later, in 1972, an open war began between the two states of Yemen. This time the North was backed by Saudi Arabia and the South was supplied with arms by the Soviet Union. The conflict was occasionally interrupted by negotiations concerning a merger of the two states which was finally achieved in 1990.

BRITISH PROTECTORATES IN THE PERSIAN GULF: KUWAIT, OMAN, THE UNITED ARAB EMIRATES, BAHRAIN AND QATAR

In the nineteenth century, when the British established protectorates encompassing about a dozen small Arab states in this area, these states were poor and, at the most, of some strategic interest as they were close to the maritime connections which linked Great Britain with India. Kuwait was in a special category as it had a tenuous relationship with the Ottoman Empire, and while stressing its independence, occasionally collaborated with the imperial authorities. 'Kuwait' means a fortress near the water and this was about all that this small principality amounted to in its early days. It emerged as a thriving port during the nineteenth century. In 1899 Sheikh Mubarak al Sabah al Sabah signed a treaty with the British and henceforth enjoyed the protection of the Royal Navy. After the First World War, when the Ottoman Empire was dismantled, Ibn Saud, the founder of Saudi Arabia, posed a threat to Kuwait, but British protection helped to ward him off. When oil was discovered in the 1930s, British commercial interests were added to the strategic ones. However, once India had been decolonized and commercial interests in Kuwait could be protected in more indirect ways, full sovereignty was restored to Kuwait in 1961.

Oman, at the other end of the chain of British protectorates, attained its sovereignty even earlier, in 1951. The rulers of Oman had established a far-flung maritime empire in the eighteenth century, controlling much of the East African coast including Zanzibar. The British concluded a treaty with Oman as early as 1798 and have been on good terms with this state ever since. In contrast, British relations with Oman's neighbours were more problematic. The British called the coast to the north of Oman the 'Pirate Coast' because the petty rulers of this area harboured ships which interfered with their ships bound for India. Finally, the British converted this troublesome area into 'Trucial Oman' by arriving at a truce with one ruler after another in around 1820. In 1853 these trucial relationships were embodied in a Treaty of Peace in Perpetuity which meant that the British henceforth controlled the quarelling local rulers. Ibn Saud would have liked to incorporate these petty states into his realm, but the British presence discouraged him. The petty sheiks survived in their traditional states which did not have clearcut territorial boundaries until the British delineated them, particularly when oil was found in the area and claims had to be defined. Earlier the British had not paid much attention to the internal political affairs of these petty states, but in 1951 a Trucial States Council was set up under the chairmanship of the British Political Agent at Dubai. This was the first step towards the establishment of the United Arab Emirates. It was an irony of fate that the poorerst of these states, Abu Dhabi, soon became the richest due to its new oil wealth which transformed it within a few years.

After the British had beaten a hasty retreat from Aden and Yemen in 1967, they announced in 1968 that they would withdraw from the Gulf states by 1971. This shocked the rulers who had become accustomed to British protection and at first did not know how to manage without it. As independence drew near they agreed to form a federation, the United Arab Emirates (UAR), to be led by Sheikh Zayed of Abu Dhabi. They readily opted for his leadership as, with the exception of Abu Dhabi and Dubai, none of the other small principalities were blessed with oil wealth. Bahrain and Qatar, however, which were originally part of the federal scheme, decided to attain independence separately as they could afford to go it alone. Observers doubted whether the rather fragile construction of the UAR could survive for any length of time, but due to clever diplomacy the UAR got along quite well and proved to be one of the more successful British-sponsored constructions of the age of decolonization.

THE MALDIVES: A SULTANATE IN THE ARABIAN SEA

The Republic of the Maldives is now a member of the South Asian Association of Regional Cooperation (SAARC), but its decolonization was achieved in the context of the British withdrawal from military bases 'east of Suez'. It was originally a sultanate of a similar type to the Arab emirates of the Persian Gulf. The sultanate had been established in around 1150 AD. The Portuguese and the Dutch had occupied the Maldives for some time until the British captured Ceylon in 1796 and then added the Maldives to their possessions. Since the Maldives were administered from Ceylon, they had to be separated from it when Ceylon became independent in 1948. The British wanted to hold on to the Maldives because of the strategic position of these islands in the middle of the Arabian Sea. They had used Gan Island as an air base during the Second World War but in the immediate post-war era, the base had not been used. In 1952 internal autonomy was granted to the Maldives which in 1953 opted for a republic led by Amin Didi, who was celebrated as the 'father of Maldive nationalism'. He was overthrown and killed in 1954 and the sultan was reinstated. By now the Cold War had affected British strategic thinking. Gan Island once more became an important base for which a 100-year lease was granted by the sultan in 1956. The Royal Air Force built a runway of 2.6 km on this island which is itself only 3 km long. The first airforce plane landed in 1962 on the new airfield. The sultan's prime minister, Ibrahim Nasir, had wished to curtail the lease and to enhance the amount to be paid as rent by the British. In 1960 the lease was shortened to 30 years and the British agreed to contribute £750,000 to the economic development of the Maldives for the period from 1960 to 1965. In the meantime some politicians in and around Gan Island, where the people profited economically from the British base, had started a secessionist movement and proclaimed the United Suvadivan Republic which existed from 1959 to 1962 when Nasir put an end to it. The British granted formal independence to the Maldives in 1965. In 1968 the sultan was overthrown by Nasir who once more established a republican government and ruled the islands with an iron fist. While he was in office, British troops left the Maldives in 1975 and the Royal Air Force gave up Gan Island in 1976. This led to a steep decline of the Maldives economy which affected Nasir's popularity. He stepped down in 1978 and fled to Singapore. His successor, Moumoon Abdul Gayoom was re-elected several times. He survived a coup in 1988 when the Indian army and navy rescued him.

LIBYA: THE REALM OF THE PIOUS KING IDRIS

Libya was an Italian colony occupied during the Second World War by the Allies. Though the Italians had changed sides during the war and were with the Allies at its end, they were not allowed to recover their colony. The British then played a decisive role in Libya as they wished to build it up as an alternative to Egypt which seemed to be escaping from their control. The British government was still convinced after the war that it had an important role to play in the Arab world. In Libya the USA also maintained a huge military air base at Wheelus Field. In general they advocated decolonization, but their security interests sometimes militated against their convictions.

Libya's progress towards independence was conditioned by its complex past. It had been a province of the Ottoman Empire which the Italians had seized in 1911. The Italian influence was restricted to Tripolitania, the most attractive part of Libya and home to two-thirds of its population. After the First World War, nationalists had proclaimed a short-lived republic there. This reflected the aspirations of the urban educated classes of this part of the country. The Cyrenaica to the east of Tripolitania had a completely different social and political profile. In the nineteenth century an Islamic leader from Algeria, al Zanussi, had settled there. His disciples were all referred to as Zanussi. They were not a tribe, but rather a congregation of different tribes united by their loyalty to their religious leader. While the Zanussi resisted Italian rule, they befriended the British who had driven away the Italians. Their head, **Idris** al-Zanussi, who had lived in exile in Egypt since 1922, returned to Libya in 1947. The British wanted to establish a Cyrenaica state under him, in which they could establish their military bases. However, the fate of Libya had to be determined by the **United Nations** and therefore the British could not pursue their plans without its support. Deliberations over the fate of the ex-Italian colonies was rather tortuous, involving all kinds of bargains, one of them also affecting Somalia where the British wanted to create a Greater Somalia. They finally had to agree to Italian trusteeship of a part of Somalia so as to get what they wanted in Libya.[37] Ernest Bevin, the British foreign minister, took a personal interest in the Libyan question which he considered to be vital for the strategic position of Great Britain. He thus spent a great deal of time and effort on the issue.

Bevin was an old trade union leader with little formal education but a powerful personality. Prime Minister Attlee, an educated man, who was for the working class but not of it, trusted and respected Bevin, the authentic labour leader. Appointing him foreign minister, however, was perhaps not the best idea, as Bevin knew little of the world abroad and depended on the advice of his staff at the Foreign Office.[38] Most of these men were still imperialists who thought like Churchill and looked for ways and means to defend Great Britain's position as a great power. Libya fitted into their schemes, but they wanted to divide the country, leaving precocious Tripolitania to the Italians, while depending on a reliable Cyrenaica. However, there were riotous demonstrations in Tripolitania when the people there heard about a possible return of the Italians. Even the USA had backed the British, who had submitted a draft resolution concerning the division of Lybia to the General Assembly of the United Nations. **Idris** had supported the British plan by proclaiming that he was the Emir of the Cyrenaica.[39] But the resolution was rejected by a narrow margin by the General Assembly in May 1949. Bevin's plan had failed to impress the General Assembly which finally decided in November 1949 that an undivided Libya should be granted independence by 1953.

Bevin quickly adjusted his position and now worked for a federal Libya under King **Idris**. The leader of the Tripolitanian nationalists, Beshir Saadwi, also changed his mind in July 1950 and suddenly backed Bevin's plan, although he had earlier advocated a unitary republic. By the end of the year, however, Beshir had reversed his position once again and organized demonstrations against the British and the US in Tripoli. It was said that Beshir was supported by Egypt in this action, and the British would liked to have got rid of him, but they did not wish to take any political risks and waited until **Idris** had him deported in 1952. **Idris** had been permitted to proclaim the independence of Libya at the end of 1951, but, of course, there was more form than substance to this independence. The new state was completely dependent on the subsidies paid by the British and the USA who were permitted to retain their military bases in Libya. Nobody had any idea at that time that Libya would soon be an oil-rich state.

In their secret files, the British often referred to **Idris** as a weak ruler; they would have liked to deal with a moderate and cooperative nationalist rather than with the head of a religious brotherhood. However, they could actually be quite satisfied with his performance. He kept the country quiet and permitted the British to maintain their military presence, just as Bevin had hoped he would do. **Idris** was very well aware of his risky position and when King **Abdullah** of Jordania was assassinated in July 1951, **Idris** feared that he would be the next victim. However, he survived the coup of 1969 by which Libyan revolutionaries deprived him of his throne.

TUNISIA: THE REPUBLIC OF HABIB BOURGUIBA

Libya's early independence fired the imagination of its neighbour, Tunisia, but this country had to wait for quite some time before the French set it free. Tunisia was ruled by the Bey of Tunis whose forefathers had been governors imposed on the country by the Ottoman Empire. In 1883 Tunisia had become a French protectorate. The French obviously wanted to protect their investments which had flowed into the country since 1881, the British having given their approval to the French for this. French and Italian settlers had also flocked into the country. The Bey had established a legislature with limited functions in the late nineteenth century and the citizens had acquired some national consciousness. These political currents were represented by the Destour Party which split in 1934, its more radical wing being led by Habib **Bourguiba**. His Neo-Destour Party soon became the dominant political force in Tunisia.

Bourguiba determined the political fate of his country for a very long time. He was basically a moderate politician who corresponded to the French ideal of an 'assimilated' colonial citizen. He seemed to be a good partner with whom to negotiate – at least this is what the French foreign minister, Robert Schumann, must have thought when **Bourguiba** visited Paris in 1950 and submitted his rather 'reasonable' demands. Schumann then dispatched a liberal French resident to Tunis, but he was only able to implement very limited reforms. The French elections of June 1951 had led to a swing to the right and further reforms were put on hold. Schumann remained foreign minister, but while the right-wing politicians let him have a free hand concerning his policy for European unity, they did not permit him any progress towards decolonization. The French settlers in Tunisia also objected to reforms which they regarded as treason. A new political climate ensued in 1954 when French confidence was shattered by the defeat in Vietnam. Prime Minister Pierre Mendès-France made use of this crisis and took some decisive steps towards decolonization. He belonged to the Radical Socialist Party which was far less radical than its name would suggest, but Mendès-France was an exceptional politician. He achieved a great deal during the short period in which he was permitted to serve as prime minister. He accepted the recommendations of the **Geneva Conference** on Indo-China and also secured the transfer of the French colonies in India to the Indian government, thus avoiding the fate of the Portuguese who were forcibly thrown out of Goa in 1961. Finally, he paved the way for Tunisian independence with a dramatic gesture. He flew to Tunisia without any prior announcement and proclaimed that the country would have full internal autonomy. His cabinet had passed the respective resolution only a few hours before he took the plane. He also managed to take the conservative governor of Morocco, Marshal Juin, along on this flight so that it did not appear to be a partisan move.

With this lightning action, Mendès-France prevented a disaster in Tunisia. A strong guerrilla movement was about to attack the government; **Bourguiba** had been imprisoned and no other politician was prepared to head the government at that time. After Mendès-France made his announcement, the guerrillas handed over their arms and **Bourguiba** was once more ready for negotiations. France showed no gratitude for the courageous initiative of Mendès-France, and he was toppled in February 1955. **Bourguiba**, however, was satisfied with the granting of internal autonomy as a first step towards independence which was eventually achieved in March 1956. **Bourguiba** had had great difficulty in controlling the more radical members of his party who had clamoured for immediate independence, but the course of events had proved him right. Independence came earlier than expected and in April 1956 **Bourguiba** was elected prime minister. In 1957 he forced the Bey to abdicate and converted Tunisia into a republic which became a one-party state. **Bourguiba** became president and remained in power until 1987.

The peaceful transfer of power was, unfortunately, followed by a violent episode, as France wished to punish Tunisia for supporting the Algerian rebels. France had retained a military base at Bizerta in Tunisia and had rejected Tunisian demands for the withdrawal of these troops. There were clashes and in February 1958 French bombers attacked Tunisian army camps. **Bourguiba** once more had to face the challenge of controlling his more radical comrades. He prosecuted some of them while at the same time making more determined demands for the withdrawal of French troops. Bizerta was finally given up only in 1963, after which **Bourguiba** had a free hand in expropriating foreign landlords in Tunisia. He adopted a radical profile in 1964 and renamed his party the Socialist Neo-Destour Party. The conflict with France over Algeria may have contributed to **Bourguiba's** radicalization, but his new stance also reflected the attitudes of his followers. After 1959 he increasingly operated like a dictator, but he also knew how to adjust to the political currents of his time.

MOROCCO: THE SULTAN AS NATIONAL HERO

While Morocco had become a French protectorate before the First World War and thus had the same status as Tunisia, the Sultan of Morocco held a much stronger position than the Bey of Tunis. Sultan **Mohammed V** got along very well with the nationalist movements in his realm. Both he and the **Istiqlal Party** founded in 1943 hoped for the attainment of independence after the Second World War. The sultan had supported the '**Free French**' under General De Gaulle and expected to be shown some gratitude for this, but he was to be disappointed. The French prevaricated and then even tolerated a coup staged in 1953 by French settlers and the Pascha of Marrakesh. The sultan fled to Madagascar where he lived in exile for some time. However, this coup started a chain of events which eventually led to the reinstatement of the sultan and the attainment of independence.

The French cabinet of Prime Minister Laniel had neither publicly supported nor condemned the coup. François Mitterand, who was a minister at that time, resigned in protest against the attitude of the government. His cabinet colleague Edgar Faure did not resign but at least registered his protest. The French government did nothing to get the sultan back to Morocco but instead saw to it that he was replaced by his uncle, Mohammed Ben Arafa. This led to a national rebellion which was even joined by the Berber tribes which the French had tried to get on their side. The French soon realized that they could only pacify the country by arranging for the return of the sultan. However, this required them to get rid of Ben Arafa in a diplomatic manner.

Mendès-France could not solve this problem in the eight months in which he was permitted to serve as prime minister; it was left to his successor, Edgar

Faure, to tackle. Faure had at least protested against his government's inaction. He now visited Morocco personally and talked to the nationalists. He was deeply impressed by them and stated that they represented French civilization much better than the reactionary leaders who had masterminded the coup.[40] Faure persuaded Ben Arafa to resign voluntarily. The sultan then returned in November 1955 and in March 1956 the French gave up their protectorate and granted independence to Morocco. Having become a national hero, **Mohammed V** was able to increase his power as the head of state and adopted the title 'King of Morocco'.

CONFLICTS IN THE WESTERN SAHARA: MAURITANIA AND THE POLISARIO

Morocco's southern neighbours had an uneasy relationship with the sultan's realm. Morocco claimed that much of the terrority beyond its southern border had once been part of Morocco. Actually, Mauritania could have made a counter-claim as in medieval times the Almoravids of Mauritania had conquered Morocco and southern Spain. Mauritania is a bridge between the Arab world and black Africa. Even now this is reflected in the composition of its population of which about 60 per cent are Arabs while the rest consists of various African tribes such as the Wolof and the Soninke. The Arabs of Mauritania have ethnic ties with their neighbours in western Sahara and the African tribes with the people of Senegal. Mauritania used to control the trade routes from the African kingdoms to the Mediterranean, which is why the Almoravids were able to rise to prominence from their strongholds in Mauritania.

The Almoravids were neither a dynasty nor a single tribe but a fundamentalist Islamic movement guided by a charismatic leader who not only 'rectified' their conduct but also instilled in them a zest for power and expansion. The old glory has long since disappeared, but the social structure of Mauritania still reflects its medieval origins. The upper strata of its society consist of the old warrior nobility and of the families of religious leaders. The man who led the country in the period of decolonization, Moktar Ould **Daddah**, was born into one of these aristocratic families. He became the first Mauritanian lawyer educated in Paris and returned from there with a French wife, the daughter of General de Gaulle.

The French had conquered Mauritania early in the nineteenth century, but they had not penetrated the interior of the country. The Mauritanians retained their medieval lifestyle and even practised slavery, which was abolished only in 1981. In a highly hierarchical society it was not easy to introduce democracy, but in 1956, due to the **Loi cadre**, Mauritania was blessed with universal suffrage and in 1958 dutifully assented to remain within the **French Union. Daddah** was one of the most prominent pro-French leaders in Africa and enjoyed the support of his father-in-law. He was also very diplomatic and established good relations with the various ethnic groups of Mauritania. In 1958 he was elected president of the Executive Council and then became prime minister in 1959. After Mauritania attained independence in 1960, **Daddah** became its president in 1961. By the end of that year he had managed to unite the four major parties of the country. His new party was called the Mauritanian People's Party. It served as a platform for converting Mauritania into an authoritarian one-party state in 1964.

Daddah reached the zenith of his political career in the early 1970s. He was elected president of the **Organization of African Unity (OAU)** in 1971 and then re-elected for a second term. In 1976 he won the presidential elections in his country once more, but by that time his downfall was imminent. His nemesis were the armed brigades of the **POLISARIO** which attacked his capital, Nouakchott, in July 1977. He then had to rely on his small army which overthrew him in a coup in July 1978. He was imprisoned but later released in 1979 due to French pressure. He then moved to France where he lived in exile and founded a new party, Alliance pour une Mauritanie Democratique, a name which sounded incongruous as his one-party state had certainly not been a model democracy.

The **POLISARIO (Frente Popular para la Liberación de Saguia el Hamra y Rio de Oro)** was founded in 1973 to take up an armed stuggle against Spanish colonial rule. Spain had annexed the barren territory on the African coast opposite the Canary Islands in 1884, mainly because the **Scramble for Africa** was on and the Spanish did not want to permit any other European country to occupy this territory. The inhabitants were mostly nomads and the colonial capital, Al-Ayun, was no more than a large village. In 1969, however, very rich phosphate deposits were discovered at Bu Craa, about 100 km from the coast. International corporations moved in and invested a great deal of capital. A conveyor belt was built which connected the mines with the coast. All this changed the social conditions of the country and also gave rise to militant nationalism. The Spanish brutally suppressed this militancy but the Portuguese revolution of 1974, which raised the aspirations of all those who were still under colonial rule, caused the Spanish government to think about decolonization. In 1975 the International Court of Justice ruled in favour of the self-determination of the people of this Spanish colony, but the Spanish preferred to make a deal with Morocco and Mauritania. The Madrid Agreement of 1976 stipulated that Morocco would get two-thirds and Mauritania one-third of the Spanish colony.[41] Bu Craa was situated in the Moroccan share of the country and the agreement contained a clause guaranteeing one-third of the profits from the phosphate mines to Spain. The two beneficiaries of the agreement sent their troops into the area while **POLISARIO** proclaimed an independent Democratic Arab Saharawi Republic with a government-in-exile based in Algeria. In spite of Moroccan and Mauritanian occupation, **POLISARIO** managed to liberate many parts of the country and even attacked the Mauritanian capital.

Mauritania finally sued for peace in 1979 and gave up its claim to the territory allocated to it by the Madrid Agreement. However, the King of Morocco, who had already dispatched many Moroccan settlers into the area claimed by his country, now sent his troops into the Mauritanian part and claimed that too.

Many African countries recognized the Saharawian Republic which became a member of the **OAU** in 1984. In 1989 Morocco and the **POLISARIO** agreed on a ceasefire and in 1991 the UN Security Council appointed a mission for the organization of a referendum in the territory. Morocco insisted that the settlers who had been sent into the territory should also be permitted to vote in this referendum, an issue which has practically stymied all further progress in this matter. Even the former US Secretary of State, James Baker, as envoy of the Secretary General of the **United Nations**, could not make any headway with a plan to secure autonomy for the territory and for a referendum to be held thereafter. Morocco is not willing to give up what it calls its 'Southern Provinces' and the Saharawian Republic has still to wait for its independence; meanwhile about 160,000 Saharawian refugees live in camps near Tindouf in western Algeria where they have been now for almost three decades. The sad story of this erstwhile Spanish colony reminds one of the sufferings of East Timor, but whereas East Timor attracted a great deal of international attention, hardly anyone takes note of the Saharawis.

THE 'WIND OF CHANGE' IN BLACK AFRICA

DE GAULLE AND MACMILLAN IN AFRICA

The British and the French had divided most of Africa between them during the nineteenth century, while other European nations had obtained only bits and pieces in the famous **Scramble for Africa**. German colonial rule remained a mere episode which was quickly terminated at the end of the First World War. The Belgians left Africa hastily in 1960, whereas the Portuguese stayed on until 1974. Their diehard empire will be discussed in a separate chapter. Almost all the territorial borders of the colonies had been demarcated arbitrarily. They hardly reflected African conditions but rather the political contingencies of annexation. The control of coastal areas had preceded the penetration of the interior parts of Africa by some decades. This had a great impact on the social structure of the respective colonies. Along the coasts arose an indigenous 'anglophone' or 'francophone' elite of traders and middlemen, whereas the interior was dominated by chiefs and local rulers supported by the colonialists who often preferred **indirect rule** to the more costly and demanding procedures of direct rule. The chiefs were often appointed by the colonial powers and no longer enjoyed the legitimacy of earlier local rulers.

Christian missions played an important role in the colonization of Africa, where the number of converts was much larger than in Asia. The innumerable African religions succumbed more easily to the missionary impact than the religions of Asia. The Africans often had a rather flexible approach to Christianity. Moreover, adopting the religion of the white man became an instrument of social advancement for many Africans. The most important activity of the missions was the running of mission schools which attracted young people. The medium of instruction was often the mother tongue of the missionaries but African languages were also used. The German missionaries, for instance, used Swahili in their schools in East Africa. The colonial governments took hardly any interest in the primary education of their subjects. This task was left almost entirely to the missionaries. There were only a few colleges sponsored by colonial governments which produced a small African francophone and anglophone elite. African Christians started their own movements and churches which combined African myths with Christian ideas of salvation. These African Christian movements often prepared the ground for incipient nationalism. Later on they sometimes spearheaded resistance to African governments, too.

The administrative structures of the various colonies differed with regard to their systems of taxation. Some colonies had a poll tax or hut tax which required an organization for the collection of such taxes in the interior of the country. However, tax collection was usually entrusted to the native authorities and not to colonial government servants.[1] Land revenue, such as that collected from Asian peasants by the colonial rulers, was practically unknown in Africa.[2] The most important revenue income for the colonial rulers was derived from customs duties which were collected at the port of entry. Sometimes export duties were also levied so as to tax the flow of African commodities which entered the world market.[3] If the ports remained the only places of revenue collection, there was no need to train and educate a large staff of African officials. There was also no need to train African lawyers. Thus there would be hardly any social groups which could support the rise of modern nationalism. There was only sporadic unrest caused by events such as the fall in prices of export products. This type of unrest could be suppressed using the small contingents of African troops recruited by the colonial rulers.

The only field of modern organization open to the Africans was the trade union movement of railway workers. Railways had played an important role in the **Scramble for Africa**. The **Berlin Conference** of 1884–1885 had made effective occupation the chief criterion of the recognition of territorial claims of European powers. This called for a strategic expansion of railways even before they were needed for the shipment of increasing amounts of agricultural produce. The main period of railway construction was from 1895 to 1914. The typical pattern was the extension of a line from the coast as far as possible into the hinterland. There were hardly any cross-connections and thus no real network. Actually this should have meant a decentralized administration and a fragmented structure of unions. However, in French West Africa, in particular, the railway administration was highly centralized and there were common standards for the workers. Moreover, after the Second World War, French governments proclaimed the equality of workers without giving the same pay to white and black workers. This merely invited strikes for higher wages throughout the system. In October 1947 such a strike was organized for the entire French West African railways by a brilliant union leader, Ibrahim Sarr, who managed to maintain the solidarity of the workers for a long period.[4] The strike lasted nearly half a year and ended with concessions by the French administration. African politicians then tried to take over the trade union movement, but for the unionists this presented a dilemma. The benefits that they had gained for the workers depended on the administration which had granted them. Decolonization would undermine that administration. Nevertheless, the social dynamics evident in such strikes were important for the further political development of the colonies.

Railway workers were not the only ones who could strike; dock workers and workers in the mines owned by European companies could also combine and make use of their strategic position. During the Second World War and in its immediate aftermath prices rose and real wages declined, which led to strikes in many African colonies. Moreover, concessions made by colonial governments to the workers were often disregarded by the employers. The French *Code du Travail* of 1953,[5] which granted essential benefits to African workers, was often transgressed by employers. Thus workers had added reasons to strike.

Representative institutions were still in their infancy in Africa when the European powers felt compelled by changes in world affairs to accelerate the decolonization of their empires. The French and the British were starting from altogether different premises in this respect. The French had adopted the attitude that their colonies were integral parts of their state, although they imposed regulations which restricted the rights of Africans who would otherwise have constituted the majority of the citizens of the **French Union**. Thus only a small number of African representatives were elected and took their seats in the French national parliament. Some of them even became cabinet ministers in French governments. Whereas this highly visible African participation in French politics was quite impressive, democratic representation in the colonies was rather limited. This was changed only by the **Loi cadre** (Framework Law) of 1956.[6] This was an enabling act and as such a clever device to get around a constitutional impasse. The momentous changes made at that time would have required a constitutional amendment which was impossible due to the political weakness of the Fourth Republic. The **Loi cadre**, however, empowered the French president to issue decrees addressed to the individual African colonies. The decrees equipped them with territorial assemblies based on adult suffarge and executive councils (conseil du gouvernement) composed of members of those assemblies. The arena of representation was shifted from the French parliament to those assemblies which would also control their own budgets and thus be responsible for paying their African civil servants. This could have been a potentially explosive issue, because many members of those assemblies were also civil servants. They could hardly be expected to vote for a reduction of their own payscales. However, since the payscales of those employed at that time were protected, the transition was smooth.[7] The old federations of French West Africa and French Equatorial Africa were bypassed in this way and strong links were forged between Paris and the respective territorial governments.

The British never had to face such problems. They had only an unwritten constitution which they did not need to amend. The constitutions of their colonies were constructed and revised individually. A uniform labour code did not exist, neither did the British provide for representation of the colonies in their parliament. There were a few Members of Parliament born in the colonies, but they had won their seats by direct elections in constituencies in the United Kingdom. They could win these seats only if a British party fielded them as its candidate in those constituencies. For the British the decolonization of African colonies was a process of a transfer of power into suitable African hands. The Indian example has shown that this would be the result of a long process. In Africa such processes had hardly begun when decolonization had to be precipitated, largely due to external pressures. The French and the British then entered into a kind of competition as to who would accomplish this task first. In 1956 they had jointly participated in the Suez venture which had shown them that the assertion of imperial rule was no a viable option for them.

The British prime minister, Harold Macmillan, owed his post directly to the Suez disaster, as his predecessor, Anthony Eden, had been forced to resign owing to US pressure. Charles de Gaulle became president of France only two years later as a result of the Algerian problem which he solved with consumate skill. Both de Gaulle and Macmillan took the initiative in Africa in order to be able to set the agenda of decolonization before it was too late. They both made spectacular journeys to Africa in order to project their views on the spot. In this respect de Gaulle was ahead of Macmillan. He wanted to submit the new project of the **French Community**, which replaced the **French Union**, to a referendum in Africa.[8] Starting his African journey in August 1958, de Gaulle offered the Africans a simple choice. If the majority of the voters in their respective colony assented to the new constitution, they would remain part of the **French Community**; if they rejected it, they would immediately attain independence, but all connections with France, including economic aid, would be cut. De Gaulle landed first in the capital of Chad, Fort Lamy (N'Djamena). During the war, the governor of this colony had been the first one to opt for the **Free French**. From there de Gaulle proceeded to Madagascar and then reached Brazzaville, the capital of French Congo, on August 23, 1958. This city had been, on occasion, his headquarters during the war when he led the Free French. In Brazzaville de Gaulle proclaimed his intention to grant independence to all French colonies which voted 'no' in the referendum, but he made it very clear that he did not expect such negative votes. When he landed at Abidjan, the capital of the Ivory Coast, on the next day he met with no opposition. In nearby Guinea, however, he had to listen to Sekou **Touré** who indicated that this colony would vote 'no'. Proceeding from there to Senegal, he hoped to hear of 'yes' votes from Léopold Sedar **Senghor**, who was known to be pro-French. However, this shrewd politican was visiting France at that time, probably because he wanted to avoid meeting de Gaulle. A positive statement from this famous man would have meant much to de Gaulle. Since other politicians of this area were inclined to vote 'no', Senghor was keen to avoid a commitment.

Once Guinea had voted 'no' in September 1958, De Gaulle treated it with cold contempt. He firmly believed that the newly independent state would soon collapse and thus prove to everybody concerned that it was fatal to leave the **French Community**.[9] When this did not happen, however, de Gaulle felt compelled to adopt a more lenient attitude to the other colonies that had voted 'yes'. In December 1959 he once again visited Senegal and made the surprising announcement that he was now prepared to retain in the **French Community** even those colonies who opted for independence. The transfer of power was to be accompanied by a cooperation agreement, which defined the relation of the African state to the Community.[10] De Gaulle assured those states of further French economic aid which he had earlier denied to Guinea. This change was obviously related to the shift in his Algerian policy as he had offered self-determination to

Algeria in September 1959. De Gaulle's statement of December 1959 amounted to an invitation to all French colonies in Africa to opt for independence; and most of them actually took up this invitation in 1960 which thus became the year of the 'wind of change'. The newly independent states concluded treaties with France which contained clauses that enabled France to retain its influence on matters of defence, economic development and educational policy in its former colonies. Critics called this 'neocolonialism' and there was some truth in that. The leaders of the new states agreed to the treaties because the French connection stabilized their rather precarious political position.

After de Gaulle had set the pace, Macmillan appeared in Africa in January 1960. Initially the British were a step ahead of the French in black Africa by granting independence to Ghana (Gold Coast) in 1957. After this no other British colony had attained independence. Macmillan could clearly see the effect that de Gaulle's announcement would have and now saw the need to precipitate decolonization. He had been an imperialist in earlier years but had changed his mind after the Suez crisis. Great Britain was facing bankruptcy once more and was bereft of US support. Therefore, determined to cut British losses, Macmillan had put his staff to work on an agonizing reappraisal of British commitments to overseas defence and colonial rule. On his whirlwind tour of Africa, he first visited Accra, the capital of Ghana, on January 10, 1960, where he delivered his famous 'wind of change' speech.[11] He stressed that the peoples of Africa were now becoming nations and that it was important to go along with this development. He repeated his speech in Lagos, Nigeria, and then in the Federation of Rhodesia and Nyasaland. The white politicians there did not receive his speech well; to them the 'wind of change' appeared rather to be a hurricane which would blow them off their feet. A few days later he gave his speech in South Africa where, of course, it was not appreciated at all.

Only two British colonies, Somaliland and Nigeria, attained independence in 1960, whereas nine French colonies in black Africa plus two French mandate territories could celebrate this year as their date of birth as a free nation. The other British colonies, some of whom had white settlers, posed problems for Macmillan whose term of office ended in 1963 before he could set them free. Only Sierra Leone and the British mandate territory of Tanganyika attained independence in 1961 when Macmillan was still prime minister. De Gaulle had remained ahead of him in the march towards decolonization. Macmillan's speech was more of an incantation than the anouncement of a policy to be implemented immediately.

In tracing the decolonization of black Africa in detail we shall first turn to the vanguard – Ghana, Sierra Leone and Guinea – and then study the many others which attained their independence in due course.

THE VANGUARD: GHANA, SIERRA LEONE AND GUINEA

The Gold Coast, as Ghana was called as a colony, had attracted European attention at an early stage. Even today the fortresses which the Portuguese, the Dutch, the Danes and finally the British had constructed on this coast are testimonies of times gone by. Fort Elmina, the oldest fortress, was built by the Portuguese and then taken over by the Dutch. Fort Christiansborg is a reminder of Danish rule, later serving as the residence of British governors and finally as the home of Kwame **Nkrumah** who then had to bear the 'curse of Christiansborg' as Dickson Mungazi called it.[12] This so-called 'curse' converted **Nkrumah** into an autocrat who lost touch with the people.

In Ghana the people of the coast always had a rather tense relationship with the mighty Ashanti who ruled the hinterland. In Kumasi, about 200 km to the north of the coast, resided their great chief, the Asantehene. In the early nineteenth century his armies had several times tried to conquer the coastal areas. The Ashanti country became a British protectorate as late as 1896. While the prosperity of the Ashanti had formerly been derived from the trade in slaves and gold, they had turned to growing cocoa in the twentieth century. However, this meant that they were dependent on the fluctuation of prices in the world market and the services of middlemen living on the coast. Further into the interior of the country were the Northern Territories with Tamale as the provincial capital. This was a poor area mostly inhabited by Muslims who served the colonial rulers as policemen and soldiers.

Political opinion was mainly influenced by the coastal elite. One of the earliest and most influential institutions of Western education in Africa was the Prince of Wales College at Achimota, founded in 1925.[13] The educated elite of the coast established the United Gold Coast Convention as a political party in 1947. The founder of this organization was Joseph **Danquah**, a leading lawyer deeply interested in the history of his country. It was he who suggested the name Ghana for the Gold Coast, thus reviving the memory of an old African kingdom which was located in the north, beyond the borders of present-day Ghana. **Danquah** had founded the Gold Coast Youth Conference in 1930 and had henceforth been active in politics. He was a spokesman of the bourgeois elite which had experienced a setback in the elections to the Legislative Council of 1946, in which the chiefs, meanwhile, had done well. The elite thus realized that a modern political organization was required. The foundation of the United Gold Coast Convention was a first step in this direction. In need of a competent secretary general to built up the party, **Danquah** hit upon Kwame **Nkrumah** who had spent twelve years in the USA and Great Britain. He was an admirer of George **Padmore**, a black intellectual from Jamaica whose **Pan-Africanism** influenced many African politicians. At first **Nkrumah**, who was a radical votary of **Pan-Africanism**, had hesitated to serve a party founded by conservative senior citizens. But in December 1947 he accepted their invitation, as he saw in this a convenient entry into the political life of his country. He was so successful in making this entry that after only two years he broke with his old employers and founded his own party, the **Convention People's Party (CPP)**. This party projected a radical profile. It stood against chiefs and the conservative elite and attracted frustrated young people who felt that they had no future in the narrowly circumscribed society of this British colony.

Nkrumah had founded his party at the right moment. In 1950 constitutional reform was introduced which provided for a legislature with 75 seats, of which 37 were reserved for the people of the coast and 19 each for the Ashanti and the people of the Northern Territories. Before the elections, to be held in 1951, **Nkrumah** had urged his followers to take 'positive action'. He particularly appealed to the trade unions. There were riots and **Nkrumah** was put into prison, but at the elections his **CPP** scored an overwhelming success. He was released and made 'leader of government business', i.e. he was de facto prime minister, a title which was then bestowed upon him in 1952. It was a bonus for **Nkrumah** that the British governor, Charles Arden-Clark, supported him fully. In keeping with the British idea of the transfer of power, Arden-Clark believed that he had found the right man in **Nkrumah** in whose hands Ghana would be safe. He was keen to complete this transfer of power during his period of office and did not support any opposition to **Nkrumah**.[14]

At first it had seemed that **Nkrumah** was universally appreciated by the people of Ghana, but soon there was a conflict with the Ashanti. As **Nkrumah** was a man from the coast and had no connections with them, the Ashanti felt that they were not sufficiently represented in Ghana politics and also had economic reasons for being dissatisfied with **Nkrumah**'s policies.[15] The main issue was the price of cocoa which was fixed by the government at a level far below its price on the world market. During the war, the British had organized Marketing Boards in many colonies so as to control produce and raw materials for the war effort. These continued to operate after the war. In Ghana the Marketing Board was of particular importance because it dealt with the buying and selling of cocoa. Rather than abolishing this colonial institution **Nkrumah** had gone one step further by establishing a Cocoa Purchasing Company which was controlled by the **CPP**. In this way **Nkrumah**'s party prospered at the expense of the Ashanti. This measure did not just affect a small group of big landowners, but all of the Ashanti, many of whom were sharecroppers whose livelihoods depended on the price of cocoa. When the government fixed the price of cocoa at a very low level in August 1954, the Ashanti rebelled. Many of them left the **CPP** and became members of the National Liberation Movement (NLM), founded in September 1954, which soon became a powerful opposition party. The NLM was initially supported by the same kind of people who had earlier contributed to the rise of the **CPP**. Many of them had learned the art of political organization in the **CPP**. While the Ashanti youths participated in militant actions against the government, at the same time the NLM organizers managed to get the support of the Asantehene by appealing to Ashanti solidarity. However, this conservative, pro-British chief disapproved of militancy and tried to take the movement along a constitutional path. He found a good opportunity to do so when three prominent **CPP** members of the legislature left this party and joined the NLM. The Asantehene saw to it that one of them was made secretary general of the NLM. In this way it was possible to restrain militancy and proceed along the parliamentary path. As the Ashanti region did not offer a sufficient base for obtaining a majority in the legislature, however, attempts had to be made to gain support among the conservative citizens of the coast, who had been sidelined by **Nkrumah**, and to find partners in the Northern Territories. It seemed that the new party could seriously challenge the CPP. Moreover, the claim of the NLM that it would dissolve the centralized **CPP** state and establish a federation composed of three autonomous regions (the coast, the Ashanti and the Northern region) sounded reasonable and was even appreciated by some politicians in London. The NLM even threatened that there would be another Pakistan if the British rejected the federation, which is why new elections were held in 1956, before Ghana could become independent.

Nkrumah then launched a counter-attack. In 1955 he introduced an act which enabled chiefs who had been deposed by the Asantehene to appeal to the government and get themselves reinstated.[16] At first this appeared to be an unnecessary provocation of the Asantehene, but **Nkrumah** had obviously correctly perceived the tensions within Ashanti society, as this act damaged Ashanti solidarity. When elections in all 104 seats were held, the **CPP** won 71 and the NLM only 33. The NLM had been unable to win any seats on the coast and it captured only 13 of the Ashanti seats, whereas the **CPP** managed to win 8 Ashanti seats. For **Nkrumah** the decision of the NLM to adopt the parliamentary path and reject militancy was of great advantage. Now the NLM had to accept the election results and could not revert to militancy. No further obstacles held up Ghana's progress to independence, which was achieved in March 1957. Supported by his victory in the elections, **Nkrumah** could forget about federalism and rely on the centralized state which he had established. He was, however, not too sure whether he could continue to rule this state undisturbed by the opposition. Therefore he undermined this opposition in various ways which led him finally to the establishment of a one-party state. He assumed dictatorial powers and did not hesitate to imprison his old mentor, Joseph **Danquah**, when he opposed him.

At his official residence, Christiansborg, **Nkrumah** received nationalist politicians from all over Africa and supported them with good advice or even financial contributions. He hosted the **All-African People's Conference** in Accra in December 1958, which was presided over by the young labour union leader Tom **Mboya** of Kenya. He compared this conference to the **Berlin Conference** of 1884, which had marked the high tide of the **Scramble for Africa**, whereas the conference in Accra marked the end of the era of colonial rule. Not all African politicians flocked around **Nkrumah**, however, and his plan to establish a United States of Africa remained a dream. African leaders could only agree on the establishment of the **Organization of African Unity (OAU)**. This was not what **Nkrumah** had in mind and it was actually established against his wishes. The more he was frustrated and disappointed, the more he became a megalomaniac who lost touch with the reality around him. Only the union of Ghana and Guinea remained as a poor remnant of what **Nkrumah** had in mind for Africa. In 1966, when **Nkrumah** was on a visit to North Vietnam, the military at home seized power and he could not return to his country. Sekou **Touré** offered him asylum in Guinea and the symbolic post of vice-president. **Nkrumah** thus spent the last six years of his life in Guinea, but his active political life had been terminated by the coup of 1966.

The other former British colony which can claim to be in the vanguard of decolonization is Sierra Leone. It was a rather unique colony, established as a settlement of freed slaves. The name of Sierra Leone's capital, Freetown, refers to this origin. The land around Freetown was bought by English philanthropists from local chiefs in 1787 in order to settle the freed slaves there. In 1808 Sierra Leone became a British colony and in 1827 Fourah Bay College was established as the first institution of Western higher education in Africa.[17] The ancestors of the freed slaves had come from Nigeria and other places, thus the new settlers in Sierra Leone had no connections with the people of this area. They prospered as traders and produced an educated elite that looked down upon the people of the hinterland. In 1896 the hinterland became a British protectorate whose integration with the coastal colony remained a problem. Actually, Sierra Leone should have been way ahead of Ghana in its political development, but political progress was made only by the coastal 'Creoles' who jealously guarded their privileges.[18] The National Council of British West Africa, led by Dr Herbert Bankole-Bright, was renamed the National Council for the Colony of Sierra Leone (NCCSL). When a new constitution was introduced in 1946, which granted a majority of seats to the people of the protectorate, the NCCSL protested against it and thus alienated a large part of the electorate.

This provided an opportunity to a new party, the Sierra Leone People's Party (SLPP), founded in 1951 by Dr Milton **Margai**. He belonged to the Mende people and was not a Creole. As a senior medical officer he had served in many districts of the hinterland and knew the people well. In founding the new party he was joined by his half-brother Albert, a lawyer, and Siaka Stevens, a prominent trade unionist. They won the elections in 1951 and played an important role in the executive council composed of six members, who were referred to as 'ministers' in 1953. In 1954 Milton **Margai** became chief minister.[19] Thus a kind of cabinet system was gradually introduced. The tensions between colony and protectorate still prevailed and a new constitution had to be imposed by the British in 1956, which also provided for a widening of the franchise for the elections which were then held in 1957. A large number of the Creoles of the colony abstained from voting and the people from the protectorate who resided in Freetown supported the SLPP enthusiastically. Milton **Margai** became prime minister. It seemed that independence would soon be achieved, but at this stage the victorious SLPP was torn apart by internal dissensions. Finally, Albert Margai and Siaka Stevens formed the People's National Party (PNP) in 1959.[20] This was a dramatic setback for Milton **Margai**, but a United Front Coalition was then formed under his leadership. However, in 1960 Stevens left this coalition and established the All Peoples Congress (APC), a radical party; he stymied progress towards independence by demanding new elections. Milton **Margai** had Stevens arrested and independence was granted in April 1960. Milton **Margai** died in office in 1964. He was succeeded by Albert Margai who was then defeated in the elections of 1967 by Stevens. Before Stevens could form a government, however, there was a military coup led by Brigadier Lansana, a follower of Albert Margai. Immediately after this coup there was another coup of junior officers which succeeded in removing the Governor General and suspended the constitution. Within a year, there was yet another coup, this time led by warrant officers who helped Stevens to return to power. He introduced a republican constitution in 1971 and became Sierra Leone's first president.

In Guinea, Sekou **Touré** had risen to prominence at about the same time as **Nkrumah** had done so in Ghana. Samory Touré, allegedly Sekou **Touré**'s grandfather, had established a large empire in the late nineteenth century which reached far beyond the borders of Guinea. This illustrious ancestry is probably a myth, but Sekou **Touré** made good use of it. His real strength was not based on myth but on the position he held as a trade union leader of dock workers and government employees.[21] One of his initial successes was a large strike in 1953, which lasted for two months and ended with the official concession of limiting working hours to 40 per week. The unions led by **Touré** were affiliated to the French Communist union CGT, which also supported the political Parti Démocratique de Guinée (PDG) whose secretary general **Touré** had been since 1952. In Africa the PDG was affiliated to the **Rassemblement Démocratique Africain (RDA)** which Félix **Houphouet-Boigny** had founded in 1946.

The French colonial government did everything to prevent **Touré**'s rise, but inadvertently contributed to his popularity in this way. Guinea was shaken by serious unrest from July 1954 to February 1955 and then again in the autumn of 1956 and the spring of 1957. This unrest was provoked by the African chiefs appointed by the French government, who often abused their power by shamelessly exploiting their subjects. If a chief wanted to buy an expensive car or needed money for a pilgrimage to Mecca, he made his subjects pay for this. The chiefs could rely on the support of the colonial rulers who, in turn, depended on their support. When elections were held under the **Loi cadre** in March 1957, the PDG had a resounding success and **Touré** became head of government. **Touré** abolished the institution of government-appointed chiefs with the concurrence of the colonial rulers who then depended completely on him. He had thus turned the tables on them and this was manifested in the referendum of September 1958 when over a million voters voted 'no' to de Gaulle's new constitution and only about 50,000 voted 'yes'.

Sekou **Touré** must have thought that de Gaulle's announcement of the withdrawal of all support from Guinea if it voted negatively in the referendum was only a bluff. He had hoped to negotiate with the French from a position of strength.

If he had obtained any concessions in this way they would also have benefited the other French colonies. De Gaulle knew this and reacted with the utmost severity. All French citizens left Guinea immediately. Even the uniforms of soldiers and medical stores were removed. As far as diplomatic affairs were concerned, de Gaulle also proved to be very vindictive. He could not prevent other nations recognizing Guinea, but he tried his best to delay its admission to the **United Nations**. As a result of his machinations, however, Guinea was admitted to the **UN** much faster than any other newly independent nation.[22] The lesson which de Gaulle wanted to teach Guinea rather became a lesson which he had to learn. Only a few months later he behaved very differently in the case of Senegal's independence and actually started to woo African nationalists.

Having won Guinea's independence by democratic means, **Touré** subsequently abolished democracy, established a one-party state and survived as president and dictator until his death in 1984. Although Guinea had not collapsed in 1958, its economic position was poor in subsequent years. It had to rely on Soviet aid, and **Touré** saw to it that there was no unrest.

FRANCOPHILE TRENDSETTERS: SENEGAL, MALI AND THE IVORY COAST

Senegal and the Ivory Coast offered a programme in contrast to Guinea's abrupt departure from the **French Community**. This was mainly due to the two eminent political leaders of these two colonies: Leopold Sédar **Senghor** and Félix **Houphouet-Boigny**. Their backgrounds were rather different, but they had both been ministers in the French government as elected African representatives of their respective countries. **Senghor** was a famous poet whose French poems had won universal acclaim. In his old age he even became a member of the Académie Française in 1984. He was thus one of the forty 'immortals' who represented the greatness of the French nation. He had by no means flattered the French; rather, he had challenged the 'civilization française' by stressing 'negritude' as a cultural and spiritual value. While very eloquent, he could also keep quiet and let his political rivals get entrapped in their own intrigues. When once asked about not having commented on an important issue, he replied: 'A hunter does not cough when he is stalking his prey'.[23]

Senegal was one of the oldest French colonies and had a very peculiar constitutional position. The inhabitants of four cities were rated as 'citoyens' and could send representatives to the French parliament. 'Citoyens' with a right to vote numbered only a few thousand, while the majority of the Senegalese in the countryside were 'sujets' and therefore did not have the right to vote. **Senghor** came from the countryside and was thus a 'sujet', which happened to be an advantage when he began his political career. He had never thought of such a career; his greatest aim in life was to become a professor in France. He managed to get a scholarship from the colonial government and studied linguistics in Paris in the 1920s. He was the first black African to pass the highest academic exam, the 'aggrégation'. Thus he corresponded to the French ideal of an 'assimilated' subject who had absorbed the blessings of French civilization and had turned from a 'barbarian' into an educated gentleman. **Senghor**, however, became a critic of 'assimilation' as his experiences in Paris had shown him that he was and would always remain a black man. Rather than accepting this as a stigma, he turned it into a virtue and propagated the blessings of 'negritude'. The word had been coined by his black Caribbean friend, Aimé Césaire, in discussions with **Senghor**, who then became the prophet of 'negritude'. **Senghor** was influenced by the ideas of the German anthropologist, Leo Frobenius, who had praised the great value of African culture. **Senghor** also adopted the German distinction between 'culture' and 'civilization'. He protested against the emphasis on French civilization whose spread appeared to him to be very one-way. The idea of 'negritude' also had its problematic aspects. Critics accused **Senghor** of racism. Moreover, if 'negritude' was an attribute of all black people it would not fit in with cultural pluralism as advocated by Frobenius. As a participant in the Second World War, **Senghor** ended up in a German prison camp where he spent his time reading the works of Goethe. This turned his attention to a humanist universalism. When he subsequently edited a political magazine, he did not call it *Negritude* but *La Condition Humaine*.[24]

Senghor was converted from a scholar into a politician rather suddenly and unexpectedly. Lamine **Guèye**, who represented the 'citoyens' in the French parliament and was a close family friend of the Senghors, was looking for a political partner among the 'sujets'. A franchise reform had just given the right to vote to the 'sujets'. Only one seat had to be filled and **Senghor**, a 'sujet', was the most suitable candidate. He left his academic career with great misgivings and consented to stand as a candidate for the French Socialist Party in 1945. At first he remained in the shadow of his great mentor, Lamine **Guèye**, and just like him he refused to attend the inaugural session of the **Rassemblement Démocratique Africain (RDA)** at Bamako in the autumn of 1946. Félix **Houphouet-Boigny**, the founder of this movement, had opted for an affiliation with the French Communist Party, not because he was a communist, but because other French parties already had their African clients. Lamine **Guèye** had opted much earlier for the French Socialist Party and so did **Senghor**, which is why they did not turn up at Bamako. **Houphouet-Boigny** thus became **Senghor's** most important African rival.

As a political novice, **Senghor** was initially a loyal follower of his mentor, Lamine **Guèye**, but in October 1948 they parted company. **Guèye** still followed the old pattern of patron–client relations which tied him to his 'citoyen' electorate. **Senghor**, however, who represented the 'sujets', had to tour the countryside and identified with the rural people. He had been born in a village and remembered his childhood, all of which was of great political benefit to him when the colonial government widened the rural franchise, having exclusively favoured the cities until then. **Senghor's** political weight increased greatly as a result. In 1952 he was able not only to win the elections himself but also to help a hitherto unknown canditate to dislodge **Guèye** who again wished to represent the 'citoyens'.

Paradoxically enough, **Senghor** could also rely on the support of the powerful Muslim brotherhoods of Senegal. Belonging to the Catholic minority, **Senghor** could not rival the Muslim leaders who helped him, because they knew that he depended on them and could not challenge them.

When the **Loi cadre** introduced universal suffrage, **Senghor**'s influence increased even more. He founded a new party, the Bloc Populaire Sénégalais (BPS), in which he managed to include even Lamine **Guèye** whose position he had earlier undermined. The elections for the territorial assembly of March 1957 resulted in a huge success for the BPS, which captured 78 per cent of the seats.[25] **Senghor** was a master of compromise, which is how he avoided a confrontation with de Gaulle. However, after Senegal had voted 'yes' in the referendum of 1958, **Senghor** surprised de Gaulle with a request which then contributed to de Gaulle's remarkable shift in strategy. The logic of the **Loi cadre** had led to closer con-nections between France and its individual colonies and to the dissolution of older structures such as the French West African Federation which had its capital in Dakar. **Senghor** shared **Nkrumah**'s fear that the process of decolonization would lead to a Balkanization of Africa. It so happened that Modibo **Keita**, prime minister of the French Sudan, was prepared to join Senegal in a federal state called Mali, named after an old kingdom which had once been ruled by **Keita**'s ances-tors. Other neighbours, such as the Ivory Coast led by **Houphouet-Boigny**, were not willing to join this federation; **Houphouet-Boigny** feared that his rich state would only have to make financial contributions to such a federation without deriving any benefit from it. He not only boycotted the federation but also saw to it that Dahomey and Upper Volta, which had shown an interest in joining the federation, did not pursue this option. However, the two willing partners, **Senghor** and **Keita**, applied to de Gaulle in September 1959 to permit the establishment of an independent federal state called Mali. This did not fit in with de Gaulle's policy of creating small African states which would continue to depend on France. Moreover, the request that Mali be granted independence immediately would make de Gaulle's recent punishment of Guinea look rather ridiculous. De Gaulle then revised his policy in a striking manner. In December 1959 he visited Dakar and gave a friendly speech in which he made the famous announcement that independent states could also remain members of the **French Community**. This was a victory for **Senghor** who led his country to independence in 1960, while remaining on good terms with de Gaulle.

The Mali Federation, however, did not last long. **Keita**, who headed its gov-ernment, resided in Dakar and threatened to become more powerful than **Senghor**.[26] Elections for the president of the federation were pending and **Senghor** also aspired to this office. There were rumours that **Keita** planned to overthrow **Senghor**. It was not just a matter of personal rivalry but of essential differences of political opinion. **Keita** was much more radical than **Senghor** and de Gaulle did not want to see **Keita** assuming more power. **Senghor**, the old 'hunter', was on his guard and did 'not cough' when he had **Keita** and his followers arrested and then shipped in a sealed train to Bamako from where they had come. Senegal remained Senegal, but Mali retained the name which **Senghor** had given to the new state when he was still in alliance with **Keita**.

At a later stage, Senegal became part of another federation: Senegambia. Senegal includes the small enclave of The Gambia. It was a British colony which attained independence in 1965 and at that time added the article 'The' to its name. It was an old colony occupied by the British in 1820 and initially governed jointly with Sierra Leone. It is comprised merely of narrow strips of territory on both banks of the Gambia river. It produces mainly groundnuts and thus competes with Senegal in this respect. Nevertheless, the idea of Senegambia was supported by both partners, but their partnership was shortlived, lasting only from 1982 to 1989.

In Senegal, **Senghor** had established a one-party state of the type now found in many parts of Africa. He also became a dictator, but his style was less brutal than many of the other African leaders. After becoming president he left the daily work to his loyal prime minister, Mamadou **Dia**, but after some time, **Senghor** started having doubts about **Dia**'s loyalty. **Dia** was a Muslim who, merely because of his faith, emerged as a threat to the conservative heads of the Muslim brotherhoods. He wanted to establish rural cooperatives which would have broken the quasi-feudal control of the land by these brotherhoods. **Senghor** had paid lipservice to the idea of African socialism which he propagated without being too serious about it. **Dia** wanted to take socialism seriously and thus also aroused the fears of French capitalists who continued to play an important role in independent Senegal. The young people of Senegal soon regarded **Senghor** as an old man who constantly repeated his slogans but actually preserved the status quo. They turned to **Dia**, but once again **Senghor** proved the qualities of the old 'hunter'. **Dia** was accused of planning to subvert the state and was sentenced to a long term in prison.[27] Ibrahim Sarr, who had once organized the famous railway strike, shared **Dia**'s fate. **Senghor** could have saved **Dia**, but he obviously saw in him a rival and was glad that he was behind bars. He continued to rule Senegal until 1980 when he resigned voluntarily. By that time the younger and more radical citizens of his country saw him as a collaborator with the French neocolonialists. He embodied the past and not the future of Africa.

Félix **Houphouet-Boigny**, **Senghor**'s political rival, led the Ivory Coast to independence in almost the same way as **Senghor** led Senegal. He was a physician but not a scholar like **Senghor**. However, just like **Senghor**, he represented the countryside. He was a chief of the Baoulé who were like the Ashanti of Ghana in the business of producing cocoa for export. They also grew coffee. **Houphouet-Boigny**, himself a substantial rural capitalist, had founded the Syndicat Africain Agricole in 1944, a modern organization which represented the interests of African farmers. As a medical doctor he was a member of the French-educated elite. He held a seat in the French parliament for many years and was also minister in several French cabinets. But he was by no means a tame collaborator; for some time he was even at loggerheads with the French governor. At the beginning of his political career, however, he had the good fortune that the first post-war French governor, André Latrille, was close to the French communists and supported **Houphouet-Boigny** in establishing the **Rassemblement Démocratique Africain (RDA)** in 1946. Although **Houphouet-Boigny** had no contacts with trade unions, his leadership of the **RDA** made him look like a champion of the working class. Actually he later proved to be a votary of economic liberalism. However, Latrille's conservative successor regarded **Houphouet-Boigny** as a communist and obstructed his political activities. In doing so he actually did him a favour, enabling him to emerge as a leader of the opposition. At the end of 1950 he parted company with the communists, but he was still head of the **RDA** with its disciplined and loyal cadres who held the fort for him even while he pursued his political career in distant Paris. In his days as a French minister he also had a hand in formulating the **Loi cadre** which corresponded to his approach to decolonization. His ideal was the incorporation of individual autonomous African states in a **French Union**. He once stated that the French would not follow the misguided British precedent of creating independent African states. He was thus caught on the wrong foot when de Gaulle reversed his policy in December 1959, but subsequently he led his country to independence in 1960 as all the others did. He quickly introduced a presidential constitution and a one-party state which cemented his political position for a long time to come.[28]

As **Houphouet-Boigny** had always relied on farmers rather than workers, no strong trade union could emerge under his rule. He led the Ivory Coast to economic prosperity which also benefited the French. In fact, even after independence he was surrounded by French advisers, some of whom were ministers in his cabinet. More white expatriates resided in the Ivory Coast after independence than before it. Under **Houphouet-Boigny**'s protection they enjoyed life in a neocolonial paradise. In 1963 he survived a military coup and quickly restored his hold on the levers of power. In 1971 he even established cordial political relations with his old rival **Senghor**. Unlike **Senghor**, however, he did not consider resigning and remained in office until his death in 1993.

DIVIDED TOGO

The great explorer of Africa, Gustav Nachtigal, had annexed Togo in 1884 on behalf of Germany. After the First World War it was divided into two mandate territories, one under British and the other under French administration. The British part was governed as a part of Ghana and thus took part in its political development, which had a direct impact on the French part where the possibilities of political participation were at first very restricted. The Ewe, an African people living in both parts of Togo and beyond, played a leading role in Togo's political life. They were very mobile and active. Around 1600 they had left their original habitat around Notsie in order to escape from the tyranny of King Agokoli. They had migrated to the west and had participated in the slave trade. But they were also good farmers and skilled artisans. In the years after the First World War they prospered by supplying food to their neighbours who specialized in cash crop production. At the same time they profited from smuggling cash crops to the Togo port of Lomé in which they were not subjected to the usual export taxes.

After the Second World War when Togo had become a trusteeship territory under the auspices of the **UN**, the Ewe campaigned for the reunification and decolonization of their country. They found some sympathizers in the **UN**, but the British were adamant about not against making any concessions to the Ewe. They argued that they never encouraged ethnic territorial claims and pointed out that the Ewe were minorities in both parts of Togo, amounting to only one-fifth of the population. When, in 1956, a referendum was held in the British part, the majority there voted for amalgamation with Ghana. The Ewe voted against it, of course, but once the issue was settled they gave up their interest in reunification and concentrated on the independence of the French part. The French then tried to placate the Ewe by accelerating Togo's political development.[29] There were two prominent leaders in Togo, Nicolas **Grunitzky** and Sylvanus **Olympio**, who were rivals as well as brothers-in-law and were destined to take turns in governing their small nation. **Olympio**'s grandfather had been born in Brazil as the son of a Portuguese father and an Afro-Amerindian mother. He had come to Togo as a slave trader. He and his sons had then prospered in all kinds of business, and thus belonged to the rich elite of Togo. **Grunitzky** had inherited his name from his Polish grandfather. He had lost the election to the French parliament in 1946 but had remained in favour with the French who suspected **Olympio** of being a British agent, because he represented the United Africa Company in Lomé until 1952. The French had a hand in his losing that job. **Olympio** had won his fame when he represented the Ewe at the **UN**, a move that was also frowned upon by the French. When the chances of a reunification of the Ewe appeared to be slight, **Olympio** changed his course and asked in 1951 for the independence of Togo within five years. The French then tried to undermine **Olympio**'s strategy by extending the franchise, thus hoping to get ahead of **Olympio**'s nationalists. This led to the strange situation whereby the nationalists protested against the widening of the franchise. They were, however, quite right in their apprehensions, because the enlarged electorate supported **Grunitzky** who now rose very rapidly as a political leader. He represented those parts of Togo which resented the hegemony of the coastal Ewe. He won the 1951 and the 1956 elections for the French parliament. In September 1956 he became prime minister of an 'autonomous' Togo which remained part of the **French Union**. The French had not as yet asked the **UN** for a termination of their trusteeship. Some critics in the **UN** protested against the French move which seemed to indicate that Togo was to be tied to France while the granting of independence was delayed. The French subsequently declared that they would hold new elections and terminate the mandate in 1958. These elections were the first under universal suffrage and a team of **UN** observers certified that they were free and fair. **Grunitzky** was expected to win this election, but to everybody's surprise **Olympio** gained a majority and became prime minister. Formal independence was then granted in April 1960.

Olympio's victory seemed to be so conclusive that **Grunitzky** left Togo and lived in exile for some time. Togo became a one-party state under **Olympio**'s rule, but soon he was faced with financial difficulties. One of them was the claim of former colonial soldiers to continued employment in the small Togo army. **Olympio** denied this claim and thus made a fatal mistake. A small group of soldiers from northern Togo murdered him in January 1963. Not wanting to seize power themselves, they invited **Grunitzky** to return to Togo. He then governed the country until 1967 when he was also overthrown by a military coup led by Colonel Eyadéma. Togo had been a model country as far as the French transfer of power was concerned, but soon it was no longer such a model. It succumbed to military rule just one year after neighbouring Ghana.

MALE RIVALRY IN THE LAND OF THE BLACK AMAZONS: DAHOMEY/BENIN

Dahomey was famous for its female army units known to the world as the Black Amazons. King Agaja of Dahomey, who ruled from 1708 to 1732, had introduced the practice of recruiting female soldiers who proved to be much fiercer than their male colleagues. The French, who had to fight against them, attested to that. Being engaged in constant warfare, the kings of Dahomey always had a great supply of prisoners of war whom they could sell as slaves; for this reason this part of the coast became known as the Slave Coast. This attracted the Europeans: the British built a fort at Ouidah in 1650, the French also established a foothold there and the Portuguese founded Porto Novo, renaming an old royal town. During the period of the **Scramble for Africa** the French were eager to get ahead of the British and the Germans. They defeated King Behanzin in 1893 and dispatched him to the distant island of Martinique. Subsequently they extended their territorial rule further to the north and in 1904 Dahomey became part of French West Africa.

After the Second World War local leaders were able to enter politics and there emerged a dramatic rivalry between three men who vied with each other for the control of Dahomey: Sourou **Apithy**, Hubert **Maga** and Justin **Ahomadegbe**. Each had their strongholds in different parts of the country. **Apithy** was at home in Porto Novo, **Maga** was a northerner from Parakou and **Ahomadegbe** was a labour leader in the port of Cotonou and had strong ethnic ties with the people around the old royal capital of Abomey. All three had their own parties which reflected their regional leadership. Initially **Apithy** held the advantage.[30] He had studied in France, was a member of the French Constituent Assembly in 1946 and had participated in launching the **Rassemblement Démocratique Africain** at Bamako in 1946. He was, so to speak, of the class of **Houphouet-Boigny** and **Senghor** and was a close associate first of one and then of the other. He seemed to be destined to lead his country to independence as both **Houphouet-Boigny** and **Senghor** did. But whereas these leaders had no serious rivals in their respective countries, little Dahomey produced more ambitious men. It had been a centre of French colonial education and the educated people of Dahomey had filled many administrative positions in other French colonies. In the quest for supreme leadership, **Apithy** was soon joined by **Maga** who captured the second seat in the French parliament in 1951. In the elections under the **Loi cadre** in 1957, **Apithy**'s party won the majority of seats, while **Maga**'s and **Ahomadegbe**'s parties trailed behind. **Apithy** formed a government as the first premier of Dahomey. He had not supported the federalist plans of **Senghor** and others.[31]

In January 1958 Dahomey was affected by an ugly strike. The leading trade union opposed the government even though one of its members was a minister in that government.[32] Such problems existed elsewhere but they loomed large in the tense political atmosphere of Dahomey. In the next elections of 1959, **Apithy** was defeated by a coalition led by **Maga** and **Ahomadegbe**; **Maga** became premier. When independence was granted new elections were held in 1960. This time **Maga** and **Apithy** formed a coalition and became president and vice-president respectively. **Ahomadegbe**'s party had won no seats at all and Dahomey became a one-party state ruled by the coalition named Parti Dahoméen de l'Unité (PDU).

In 1963 a coup toppled **Maga**'s government, but when the dust had settled **Apithy** emerged as president with **Ahomadegbe** as vice-president, the latter becoming president for two years (1964–1965). After a chaotic period during which there were several coups, the three old rivals were given a chance to form a triumvirate, taking turns at serving as president. This experiment started in 1970 and ended in 1972. The military, led by Mathieu Kérékou, then took over and the three rivals were imprisoned. The military dictator adopted a left-wing profile in keeping with the spirit of the times. He also renamed Dahomey in 1975, calling it Benin after an old northern kingdom of this area. He thus followed the example of Ghana and Mali in harking back to pre-colonial traditions. After their active political careers of earlier years, the three old rivals played no further role in the politics of their country.

THE DESERT STATES: BURKINA FASO, NIGER, CHAD

During the late nineteenth century the French penetrated the hinterland of their coastal colonies. This part of Africa did not offer many economic attractions. The discovery of uranium in Niger was a rather late event and the respective mines were opened up only in the 1970s. In colonial times this hinterland provided a labour force for the plantations in the coastal colonies. The Mossi of Upper Volta (Burkina Faso) were recruited for work in the Ivory Coast. In earlier centuries these desert states had been the scene of mighty empires such as those of Songhai in the west and Bornu in the east. Later on the Mossi had carved out a kingdom of their own, ruled by the Mogho Naaba, whose descendant is still recognized as a kind of divine king in present-day Burkina Faso.

Maurice **Yaméogo**, who belonged to the Mossi people, led Burkina Faso to independence in 1960. He had attended a Catholic seminary but was not ordained as a priest. After becoming president in 1960 he held on to office until 1966 when he was overthrown by a military coup. This coup was followed by several others in due course. In 1983 Thomas Sankara staged another coup and tried to give his country a new direction. It was he who changed the name of the country from Haute Volta (Upper Volta) to Burkina Faso (Land of the Honest), in keeping with his political intentions. He was assassinated in 1987.

The neighbouring state of Niger was led for a long time by Hamani **Diori**, a staunch ally of the French. He belonged to the group of African leaders who had become members of the French parliament in 1946. His leadership in Niger was challenged by a radical trade union leader, Djibo Bakari, who aspired to become Niger's Sekou **Touré**. At the time of the elections to the French parliament in 1956, **Diori** narrowly defeated Bakari. However, Bakari had his revenge when the elections to the territorial assembly were held under the **Loi cadre** in 1957. His Mouvement Socialist Africain won 41 out of 60 seats. With such a strong position, Bakari thought that he could easily make Niger vote 'no' in the 1958 referendum. He hoped to attach Niger to Nigeria if he opted out of the **French Community**. The French worked hard, however, to frustrate Bakari's campaign, giving full support to **Diori**, who forged an alliance with the conservative chiefs. In the end only 22 per cent voted 'no' in Niger.[33] Bakari had to resign and the territorial assembly was dissolved. From then on **Diori** led Niger. Even Bakari's trade union was banned. In 1960, when Niger achieved independence, **Diori** became president and held on to office until 1974 when he was overthrown by the military. There had been an earlier attempt at a coup, but at that time **Diori** was saved by French troops stationed in Niger. He had concluded a defence treaty with the French which permitted them to retain a garrison in Niamey, the capital of Niger. **Diori** was surrounded by French advisers; critics could point to him as a henchman of French neocolonialism. The French, of course, loved him and celebrated him as one of the great supporters of Francophonie. In 1970 **Diori**, **Senghor** and **Bourguiba** had founded the Agence de Coopération Culturelle et Technique in Niamey, which subsequently became the Agence Intergouvernementale de la Francophonie, with branches in many countries. Under normal circumstances the French would have surely saved **Diori** again in 1974, but at that time President George Pompidou had just died and there was an interregnum in France. Moreover, **Diori** had been too sure of himself and had phased out the French garrison in Niamey, thus leaving nobody to help him when he needed it most.

In neighbouring Chad, President Ngarta **Tombalbaye** also enjoyed a long period of office. He even surpassed that of **Diori** by one year. He belonged to the Sara, an ethnic group predominant in southern Chad. Since 22 per cent of the population of the state are Sara and the rest is composed of numerous small groups, his political power increased with universal suffrage. **Tombalbaye** had remained for a long time in the shadow of Gabriel **Lisette**, the co-founder of the Chad Progressive Party. **Lisette** had been posted in Chad in 1946 as a French civil servant; he was a black West Indian and adapted very well to Chad politics. It was only when he climbed to the very top that his foreign origin was held against him. Under the **Loi cadre** he had led his party to a great success in the elections to the territorial assembly, winning 47 of 65 seats. He encouraged his party to vote 'yes' in the referendum of 1958 and continued as prime minister until 1959. At this stage his rival **Tombalbaye** ousted him and led Chad to independence in 1960. **Lisette** spent the rest of his life in exile.

Like **Diori** in Niger, **Tombalbaye** relied for a long time on French support. Some parts of Chad were administered by French civil servants until 1965; French troops helped to suppress rebellions against **Tombalbaye**'s dictatorial rule. His downfall began with his campaign for African cultural 'authenticity'. In this context he changed his first name from Francois to Ngarta in 1973. He also forced civil servants to undergo initiation rites which were not even common among all Sara but were typical for his own local ethnic group. This caused a great deal of resentment. He also persistenly neglected the north which soon fell prey to various warlords.[34] Several French military interventions did not make much difference to the sad fate of Chad. The coup in which **Tombalbaye** was overthrown in 1975 also cost him his life.

All three desert states had rather fragile political structures. Whereas other African states had produced dictators only some time after gaining independence, these three states became dictatorial regimes almost immediately in 1960. The French did not seem to mind as these dictators depended on them for their survival. The critics of neocolonialism could strengthen their arguments by using the history of these states as striking examples.

NIGERIA: FROM NATIVE AUTHORITIES TO FEDERALISM

Nigeria is inhabited by about one-quarter of the total population of Africa. Its several territories were ruled by the British in different ways. Only the area around Lagos was a British colony; the other parts of the country were British protectorates. In the northern territories the British practised a system of **indirect rule** which Governor Lord Lugard had introduced in the early twentieth century. He believed so firmly in the virtues of indirect rule that he turned this system into an ideology which he preached with great fervour. It was once said that if all the Nigerians left the country the British administrators in the north and the south would still continue their debates about the best system of colonial government. Lugard had found in the northern territories a very suitable foundation for the system of **indirect rule**. This region was the home of the Fulbe and Haussa who had established a series of Muslim emirates which assured political stability. The Fulbe were mobile herdsmen who lorded it over other people. They had conquered many Haussa states during the course of the nineteenth century. For state formation in this region, ethnic ties were less important than the common experience of participating in an Islamic *jihad*. Once such states had been formed they also provided a platform for political negotiations with the colonial rulers, both in terms of collaboration and resistance. In northern Nigeria the British simply spread another layer of political control over the layer established by the

Muslim emirs. This was efficient and also saved expenditure. Under the system of **indirect rule** the emirs lost some of their sovereignty but were recognized as **'native authorities'** with a large degree of autonomy. In order to control their budget, native treasuries were established which received the taxes collected from the people. The model proved to be successful and the British wished to extend it to southern Nigeria. But this was difficult due to the totally different social structure of the peoples of the South.

The two dominant peoples of the South, the Yoruba in the west and the Ibo in the east had never been subjected to Muslim rule. Their political traditions were of a different nature. The Yoruba had formed many small kingdoms with a high level of urban culture. All these kingdoms traced their origin to the kingdom of Ife whose ruler was universally respected among them. However, he was more of a spiritual head than a temporal ruler. If it was almost impossible to introduce the Northern system of native authorities among the Yoruba, it proved to be totally absurd among the Ibo. Like the Kikuyu of Kenya, the Ibo had no chiefs but an elaborate structure of age grades and elders. This was a highly decentralized system of governance, but it suited local conditions. The British could establish native authorities only by nominating chiefs, but this was the very opposite to building on indigenous traditions as advocated by Lord Lugard. The system was criticized by the educated elite who had mostly been trained in mission schools and had been converted to the Christian faith.

In spite of the absurdities inherent in this system, the British tried their best to make it work. This system was not at all suited to a smooth transfer of power, but when it was introduced such a transfer was not a consideration. In 1946 a constitutional reform was introduced in Nigeria which provided for a majority of African representatives in the legislature, but they were elected indirectly. The **native authorities** elected representatives to be sent to the three regional councils (north, west and south). These councils would then elect representatives to be sent to the Nigerian legislature. The executive was retained in British hands. The autocratic north had never had any kind of democratic representation. Seen from the British point of view this reform seemed to be a bold experiment, but the African educated elite was, of course, dissatisfied with the system. It campaigned for further reform which was then started in 1948 and implemented in 1951. While the nationalists aimed at genuine parliamentarianism, the British wanted to democratize the **native authorities** and thus directed the political activities of the nationalists into local and regional arenas. This meant that political parties working under such conditions would have a local and regional bias and this would not contribute to interest aggregation at the national level. The **National Council of Nigeria and the Cameroons (NCNC)**, led by Nnamdi **Azikiwe**, was bound to become an Ibo party in this way; the **Action Group (AG)**, led by Yoruba chief Obafemi **Awolowo**, concentrated its attention on the western region; and Abubakar Tafewa **Balewa**'s Northern People's Congress indicated its regional identity by its name. These three prominent nationalists did not belong to the traditional elites but owed their careers to Western education. **Azikiwe** had studied and taught political science in the USA; **Awolowo** had studied law in London and had been appointed by the British as Yoruba chief; **Balewa** was a teacher and had also studied in London. Their political careers would have been different under a parliamentary system, but the system which the British had imposed on Nigeria forced them to look for political support exclusively in their regions of origin. Via their ethnic identification they also managed to bridge the gap between urban and rural areas. The peasants often distrusted urban intellectuals; their confidence had to be won and nurtured. Ethnic solidarity was a means to that end. The constitutional form and opportunities for political mobilization thus converged at the regional and not at the national level.[35]

The constitution of 1951 clearly showed the profile of a federal state with three autonomous regions and a marked preponderance of the north. The British were keen to back the conservative north, but the north also saw to it that it would get the lion's share by threatening to secede from Nigeria. The new constitution not only reformed the legislative but also the executive branch of government. It provided for Nigerian ministers who were at first treated as unwelcome guests by the British civil servants. By 1954 a further reform had taken another step in the direction indicated by the previous one. The autonomy of the three regions was strengthened; they only delegated specific functions to a federal centre. Democratization was enhanced by the introduction of universal suffrage. In the north this was restricted to men only. The next step could have been the dissolution of the federation and the granting of independence to the three regions. With the benefit of hindsight, this may have been better, as the defence of the federal state caused much bloodshed and enormous conflict which might otherwise have been avoided. The British and the Nigerian nationalists, however, steadfastly pursued the aim of maintaining a federal state, whereby every step in this direction was accompanied by greater concessions to the north.

The consolidation of regional political power was further enhanced by the elections held in May 1956 in the Western Region, in November 1956 in the Northern Region and in March 1957 in the Eastern Region. In the Northern Region the election results confirmed the predominance of the Northern People's Congress. In the Western Region, **Awolowo** had conducted a spirited election campaign and had secured the support of his ethnic group, the Yoruba, for his **Action Group**, which won 48 of 90 seats, whereas the **NCNC** which had earlier been stronger in this region had to be satisfied with the remaining 32 seats.[36] It was typical of the trend of ethnic accentuation of the vote that the **NCNC** won its seats only in the non-Yoruba constituencies. The election results in the Eastern Region were a mirror image of those of the Western Region. The **NCNC** won 65 of 84 seats, reflecting the strength of the Ibo vote. The **Action Group**, which had not put up candidates in the Eastern Region in earlier elections, captured 15 seats in non-Ibo constituencies.[37]

The constitution of 1959, which preceded the granting of independence, provided that the north would get 174 of a total of 312 seats in the Nigerian federal parliament. This meant that **Balewa** would automatically become prime minister of independent Nigeria in October 1960. **Azikiwe** had entered into a coalition with **Balewa**, although **Balewa** would have been able to go it alone. As a reward, **Azikiwe** got the ceremonial post of Governor General.

Awolowo and his **AG** were left in opposition. **Balewa** was not satisfied with his overwhelming power and tried to undermine **Awolowo**'s position by cultivating a dissident member of his party, Samuel Akintola, who had joined the **AG** after returning from London in 1950. Akintola split the **AG** in 1962 and became prime minister of the Western Region. **Awolowo** was accused of treason and thrown into prison.

These moves reflected **Balewa**'s general political course. He had tried to remain in favour with the British after independence and thus reward the British for having built him up all along. However, it was not easy for **Balewa** to steer this course, as the British had imposed a defence treaty on Nigeria which was highly unpopular. **Awolowo** as leader of the opposition had attacked the pact and **Balewa**'s pro-British attitude. He had also demanded that Nigeria should sever the connection with the British Crown and become a republic. India had done this in 1950 while still remaining a member of the British Commonwealth. Nigeria actually did the same in 1963. **Azikiwe** became president of Nigeria and **Balewa** remained its prime minister.

The Ibo distrusted the new alliance between **Balewa** and Akintola, a Yoruba, which excluded them. This led to the first military coup of many which shaped Nigeria's further political development. **Balewa** and Akintola were murdered in 1967 and General Ironsi, an Ibo officer, seized power. He abolished the federal state in favour of a unitary one. This incensed the officers of other ethnic groups. General Ironsi was murdered by them and the pattern of military coups continued. Since the Ibo now feared that they would be marginalized, and since the oil was gushing from their soil, they supported a secessionist coup in favour of a new state: Biafra. The secession was suppressed. Nigeria's federal character was preserved at the cost of many lives. It changed this character several times in subsequent years, but one essential feature remained: the control of a strong central government over the region rich in oil which the Ibo had wished to capture.

CAMEROON: RADICAL NATIONALISM AND CONSERVATIVE REACTION

Cameroon had been a German colony which came under British and French mandate administration after the First World War. The smaller part was attached to Nigeria, while the bigger one was left to the French who introduced a highly centralized administration. The differences in social structure were as important here as they were in Nigeria. The north was dominated by Muslims, Fulbe and Haussa, while the southern coastal region was inhabited by the Duala, who had for a long time been in contact with Europeans and had profited from trade with them. The western part of the country was settled by the Bamileke who were more numerous than the Duala. Since the Duala were politically more advanced, however, the colonial rulers regarded them as more troublesome. The Duala had sent petitions to the League of Nations in the 1920s. In 1945 they had produced a manifesto asking the French for political reforms. Their paramount chief, Alexandre Manga Bell, had been given a seat in the French parliament, but his collaboration with the French had made him unpopular among his own people.

The leader of the radical nationalists of Cameroon was Um Nyobé who belonged to the Bassa people. He was one of the four vice-presidents of the **Rassemblement Démocratique Africain (RDA)** and in 1948 he had founded a party called Union des Populations de Cameroun (UPC), affiliated to the **RDA**. The Duala played no role in this new party; in fact, during its first phase when the party tried to get official recognition from the French, the participation of the Duala would have been a handicap. The party was finally registered but could not enjoy its recognition for very long. The French distrusted it, although Nyobé had left the leadership of the party to innocuous moderates to be on the safe side. In 1950 when **Houphouet-Boigny** parted company with the French communists, Nyobé had retained the communist connection. But it was less this formal connection than his radicalism which angered the French. Nyobé had openly advocated the independence of Algeria and Vietnam. The French then manipulated the elections in such a way that the UPC did not get any seats in the Cameroon legislature. However, they could not prevent Nyobé from petitioning the **UN**, which was responsible for terminating the mandate and setting Cameroon free. In 1952 Nyobé was invited to address the **UN** in New York. The French had seen to it that Alexandre Manga Bell was also heard by the UN at that time, but Nyobé's arguments were much more effective. The attention he received in New York was of no avail, as the French did not budge an inch in Cameroon.[38] They adopted a very oppressive policy, provoking riots in 1955 which they repressed with violent measures. The UPC was prohibited and Nyobé and his followers had to go underground. Nevertheless, Nyobé tried again and again to participate in the political life of the country and requested an amnesty when he wanted to contest the elections of 1956. The French tried to keep up democratic appearances and wanted to establish a 'state under mandate administration' in Cameroon. This was absurd and Nyobé said so. His party remained prohibited and his followers then attacked the polling booths. They had to resort to guerrilla warfare.

The elections resulted in a solid conservative majority. Ahmadou **Ahidjo**'s Union Camerounaise (UC) and André-Marie Mbida's Democrates Camerounais (DC) formed a coalition government. **Ahidjo**, a Fulbe from northern Cameroon, represented the biggest party but had to be satisfied with the post of home minister, whereas Mbida, whose stronghold was the Catholic coastal region around Yaounde, became prime minister. Mbida was reactionary and pro-French to such an extent that even the French could not tolerate him. They forced him to resign in February 1958 and replaced him with **Ahidjo**. By now the French had realized that it was time to terminate the mandate and set Cameroon free. They accepted a resolution of the Cameroon legislature to that effect. Nyobé tried once more to get recognition for his party, but without success. He remained underground, but in September 1958 he was betrayed and the police arrested him. He was not tried but murdered. His followers continued their guerrilla activities.

Only a few months after Nyobé's death, the **UN** declared that Cameroon could attain independence without further elections. This enabled the French to transfer power to **Ahidjo** immediately. After independence on January 1, 1960, **Ahidjo** invited French troops to help fight the rebels. The first elections in independent Cameroon gave **Ahidjo** a solid majority (59 of 100 seats). The UPC meanwhile had split, one wing of it becoming the official opposition with only 13 seats. **Ahidjo** became president and his former finance minister, Charles Assalé, who was much senior to him, became prime minister. Assalé had been a member of the UPC in earlier years, but had left it in order to join with the winning party.

In 1961 **Ahidjo** achieved another aim for which **Nyobé** had campaigned – the reunification of Cameroon. The people of the southern part of the British mandate territory voted to join Cameroon, while the northern part remained with Nigeria. **Ahidjo**, who had become president when he was only 36 years old, retained this office until 1982. The methods he used for remaining in power were similar to those of most other African presidents; he was not a military dictator but under his rule Cameroon became a police state. Ahidjo was also an expert in the politics of patronage. The French backed him throughout his political career and he was widely regarded as a French puppet.[39]

'LATIN AFRICA': THE CENTRAL AFRICAN REPUBLIC, CONGO-BRAZZAVILLE, GABON

Barthélemy **Boganda**, whose untimely death in a plane crash in 1959 prevented him from leading his country, the Central African Republic, to independence had a vision of a 'Latin Africa' which ideally would have included all of French Equatorial Africa, the Congo and even Angola.[40] As a Catholic priest he was imbued with Latin culture and wished to see it preserved in Africa. He had been a member of the French parliament since 1946. At home he founded the **Mouvement d'Évolution Sociale de L'Afrique Noire (MESAN)** which won 97 per cent of the vote in the elections under the **Loi cadre** in 1957. **Boganda** became prime minister and under his leadership the Central African Republic voted 'yes' in the referendum of 1958. His followers attributed his death in a plane crash in March 1959 to the machinations of the French settlers who rejoiced after he had crashed. They feared that he was opposed to their economic interests.

David **Dacko**, who was a relative of **Boganda** and used to emphasize this, was quick to grasp the mantle of leadership and negotiated a pragmatic settlement with the French.[41] He was not a charismatic idealist like **Boganda**, but a clever politician. After he became president in 1960 he used **MESAN** as his political base and established a one-party regime in 1962. In 1966 his government was overthrown by the army chief, Jean-Bedel Bokassa, who also claimed to be related to **Boganda**. **Dacko** himself had promoted his 'cousin' whom he had underrated and did not fear. Bokassa first made himself lifetime president and then appointed **Dacko** as his personal adviser in 1976. In a strange perversion of **Boganda**'s earlier dream of a Latin Africa, Bokassa founded a Central African Empire in 1977 and had himself crowned as emperor in a very expensive ceremony. The French contributed lavishly to this megalomaniac venture. President Giscard d'Estaing befriended Bokassa who obviously thought of himself as an African Napoleon. The diamond wealth of his state helped him to corrupt people who could be useful to him. Only when he descended to the depths of bloody cruelty, were the French convinced that they should get rid of him, helping **Dacko** to topple him in 1979. **Dacko**, who knew the art of political survival, became president once more until he was overthrown by the military in 1981. Bokassa, who had fled the country, dared to return later on. He was tried and sentenced to death, but his sentence was commuted to a term in prison, after which he died as a free man and was honoured by a state funeral. It was a terrible irony of fate that the country of **Boganda** became one of the most corrupt in Africa, suffering under a fantastically cruel dictatorship. Its diamond wealth was not a boon but a curse. Since diamond mining was a decentralized affair, it lent itself literally to 'widespread' corruption.

The national leader of Congo-Brazzaville, Fulbert **Youlou**, was also a Catholic priest like **Boganda**, but he had no idealist dreams and was more interested in political power. He gave up the priesthood but still preferred to be addressed as 'Abbé'. Initially a parish priest in Brazzaville, he emerged as a local politician in 1955. His party, the Union Démocratique pour la Defense des Intérêst Africaines (UDDIA) was rivalled by the Mouvement Socialiste Africain (MSA). In 1956 he had agreed to form a coalition with his rivals, but he broke this agreement and then persecuted the MSA politicians. Since Brazzaville lies across the Congo from Kinshasa, the proximity of the two capitals led to the rise of one of Africa's most important urban centres, the more so as the population of Congo-Brazzaville became one of the most urbanized in Africa.

Unfortunately, one of the first significant events in the life of the new capital of Brazzaville were bloody riots in February 1959. About 100 people were killed and the memory of this massacre hung like a dark cloud over the nation as it progressed towards independence, the more so as **Youlou** and the French colonial authorities had obviously provoked these disturbances. Even before independence, **Youlou**, who prided himself on being Africa's staunchest opponent of communism, had practically assumed dictatorial powers. After independence was achieved in 1960, **Youlou** was elected president in 1961 with a high margin of votes, having co-opted the leader of the opposition who then joined his government. Nevertheless, **Youlou**'s position was precarious and he had to resign in August 1963 following a revolt which was later remembered as 'The Three Glorious Days'.[42] Trade unionists whom **Youlou** had persecuted as 'communists' were in the vanguard of this revolt. The French did not intervene; they accepted Alphonse Massamba-Debat who replaced **Youlou**. The new president adopted a leftist course, but social unrest continued until the army seized power in 1968.

Congo-Brazzaville was blessed with oil wealth just like its neighbour Gabon. But whereas this wealth had not contributed to political stability in Congo-Brazzaville, the leaders of Gabon obviously managed to make better use of it and kept their state under control for a long time.

Gabon prided itself on being the oldest French colony in this region and did not show much interest in gaining independence. In fact, in 1960 the French almost had to impose independence on a reluctant Gabon. Just as de Gaulle had deeply resented a 'no' to his referendum in 1958, he now did not tolerate exceptions to the granting of independence in 1960. The leader of Gabon at that time was Léon **M'Ba**, a staunch friend of France. He had become Gabon's first prime minister in 1959 and in 1961 he was elected Gabon's first president. He seemed to have his country firmly under control, but in 1964 a group of young military officers staged a coup and installed another civilian politician who seemed to be acceptable to the French. However, **M'Ba**'s French connections were stronger and French troops appeared on the scene and reinstalled him. Gabon not only has oil but also uranium and the French were interested in keeping it under their control. They were also not sure that **M'Ba**'s successor would be as amenable to their influence as the deposed president. After being reinstated **M'Ba** served only four more years in office; he died in 1967. He had taken care to build up a successor, Albert-Bernard Bongo, who had been director of the president's personal office since 1962 and was vice-president when **M'Ba** died. Bongo was a consummate tactician who obviously made good use of his state's oil wealth. Oil – unlike diamonds – lends itself much better to the support of central power and patronage. Gabon emerged as an African Kuwait with Bongo as its sheikh. Actually, he did embrace Islam, made the pilgrimage to Mecca and now called himself El-Hadj Omar Bongo.[43] Under his leadership, Gabon joined the Organization of Petroleum Exporting Countries (OPEC) and enjoyed windfall profits from rising oil prices. Bongo saw to it that his civil servants earned good salaries. Migrants from neighbouring countries were easily integrated. Intellectuals were kept happy by generous expenditure on university education and research institutes. It was only when oil prices fell that Bongo had to use all his skills as a political tactician in order to stay in power. He managed to do so for a very long time.

Gabon's tiny neighbour, Equatorial Guinea, a Spanish colony, attained its independence in 1968 and joined the same French-African currency system as its neigbours.

THE CHAOTIC DEPARTURE OF THE BELGIANS FROM THE CONGO

The Belgian Congo was initially the private property of King Leopold II of Belgium. It was called a 'Free State', i.e. free of any control of the Belgian government. Around 1900 international opinion, mainly informed by black American missionaries, was concerned with the cruel practice of forced labour in this colony. King Leopold II lost his reputation and turned over his colony to the

Belgian government in 1908. In fact, he was obliged to do so as the Belgian parliament had granted a credit to him. The decline in the price of rubber had reduced the profitability of the colony but the discovery of rich ore deposits in the Katanga province made the colony more attractive in later years. These deposits were then exploited by the Union-Minière de Haut-Katanga. During the First World War the Belgians annexed the German colonies of Rwanda and Burundi which they were permitted to govern as mandate territories.

Belgian rule in the Congo was much more intensive than European rule elsewhere in Africa. On the eve of independence there were about 10,000 Belgian civil servants, 1,000 military officers, 6,000 missionaries and several thousand European managers of various companies stationed in the Congo. Africans had been almost totally excluded from all important positions.[44] Forced labour, which had been criticized earlier, was abolished by the Belgian government, but it had been replaced by taxes which the poor peasants could not pay. In this way forced labour continued in a different guise. After the First World War a popular religious movement arose in the Congo which referred to the Bible when protesting against the cruel colonial rulers. The movement was led by Simon Kimbangu, a Protestant religious teacher who claimed to have experienced an awakening in 1921 and was venerated as a Messiah by the people. The colonial rulers persecuted him and sentenced him to death. The king converted this sentence into life imprisonment. Kimbangu died in prison in 1951. Since his followers still remained active, the Belgians brutally suppressed all such religious movements.

During the years of the Great Depression in the 1930s, the Belgian colonial authorities resorted to the forced cultivation of cash crops. The whole colony was run like one big plantation in which the colonial rulers determined what the peasants grew.[45] The Belgian civil servants argued that they had to educate the Africans as far as proper agriculture was concerned so as to legitimize their brutal regime. The Belgian administration survived the years of the depression in this way much better than other colonial administrations which also put a heavy burden on the peasants in those years. Other colonial powers even admired the Belgians for this achievement. They did not know that the Belgian methods led to a large-scale migration of frustrated people from the countryside to the urban areas. The towns of the Congo thus became powder kegs.

The Belgians continued to congratulate themselves on their efficient colonial management. They did not introduce even the rudiments of representative government. There were no elections and the few Africans holding political positions were nominated by the government. The first local elections were finally held in 1957. In the meantime, other African colonies had made some progress and the Congolese politicians took note of that. The most important political leader of the older generation was Joseph **Kasavubu** who had founded the Association des Bakongo (ABAKO) in 1950. His leftist rival was the young Patrice **Lumumba** who established the Mouvement National Congolais (MNC) and looked to Kwame **Nkrumah** as his friend, philosopher and guide. **Lumumba** published his manifesto 'Le Congo, terre d'avenir, est-il menacé?' (Is the Congo, the land of the future, in danger?) in 1957. He pleaded for cooperation with the Belgians in the interest of the future development of the Congo. In a letter to a Belgian author, he stated at that time that the Congo was not yet ready for independence as it had no trained manpower. He wanted to found a nation in the Congo in which there was no discrimination in terms of race and religion.[46] He was soon disappointed by the subsequent course of events. In December 1958 he attended the **All-African People's Conference** in Accra. His increasingly radical views were confirmed at this conference. In 1959 unrest broke out in the Congo. The Belgians decided to go ahead with decolonization, but at the same time they suppressed the political movements in the Congo. **Kasavubu, Lumumba** and several other politicians were imprisoned.

In planning for rapid decolonization, the Belgians were influenced by a realistic appreciation of their limited military capability. Belgian soldiers could not be sent to the Congo unless they volunteered to go there. The African colonial military, the Force Publique, had mutinied during the Second World War and could not be relied upon. The impending achievement of independence accentuated ethnic tensions instead of fostering national unity. This greatly perturbed **Lumumba** who wanted to preserve national unity. His MNC was represented in all parts of the Congo, whereas **Kasavubu**'s ABAKO was based on an ethnic stronghold in the lower Congo valley. But even **Lumumba** had followers who cultivated their own ethnic preferences. Albert Kalonji, who led the MNC in the Kasai province, sided with **Kasavubu** in advocating a federal state while **Lumumba** remained a centralist.[47] In January 1960 the Belgian government convened a conference in Brussels to which the various political parties of the Congo were invited. Here **Lumumba** was able to carry the day against the federalists. By now the Belgian government had also opted for a centralist position whereas it had earlier sided with the federalists. In May 1960 the new constitution of the Congo was inaugurated. It provided for a central state headed by a president and a prime minister. The central legislature would have two chambers and there were six provincial legislatures. Elections were held soon after the constitution was proclaimed. They showed a fragmentation of the political landscape. **Lumumba**'s MNC obtained only 26 seats in the central legislature, but it was nevertheless the biggest party. In Katanga Moishe **Tshombe** announced his plan to secede from the Congo even before the central legislature could be convened. **Kasavubu** formed a central government in June 1960 from which he excluded **Lumumba**'s MNC. **Lumumba** then threatened to form a rival government. Finally a compromise was arrived at: **Kasavubu** became president and **Lumumba** prime minister. Formal independence was granted to the Congo on 30 June 1960. Even before that date, **Tshombe** had proclaimed the secession of Katanga.

At this crucial juncture there was a mutiny in the Force Publique which wanted to oust its Belgian officers. General Janssens, the Belgian commander of this force, had demonstrated his views to his soldiers by writing an equation on a blackboard: 'After independence = before independence'.[48] This cynical provocation contributed to the outbreak of the mutiny. The new government dismissed the Belgian officers but then faced the problem of replacing them with African ones. A young African colonel, Joseph Mobutu, was made the chief of staff and thus attained a key position in the future political development of the Congo. The Belgians who still lived in the Congo were alarmed by the mutiny; thousands of them fled across the borders. At the time of independence about 10,000 Belgians were serving as officers, judges and administrators in the Congo. They had been promised equivalent positions at home if the situation in the Congo deteriorated. Now they all left at once and the Congo was bereft of all administrative personnel. While Belgium had hesitated to send troops to the Congo before independence, it sent them now in order to protect Belgian citizens. Thereupon the Congo government declared war on Belgium and appealed to the **UN** Security Council. This was the beginning of the most infamous chapter in the history of the **UN** which, for the first time, sent troops to a country which were bound to interfere with its internal affairs. The **UN** avoided sending troops of Western powers and initially asked troops from Ghana and Tunisia to do the job. Later on Indian troops were also asked to participate and India became the leading actor in this unfortunate game.

While the **UN** was careful as far as the composition of the troops were concerned, it could not prevent the USA from taking the lead in managing this conflict. These events took place at the height of the Cold War and thus the Americans saw the Congo imbroglio purely in this context. Among the many natural resources in the Congo, there was also uranium, which provided a strong motive for the CIA to get involved in Congo's affairs. **Lumumba**, who was anyhow suspect to the USA, confirmed their prejudices when he appealed to the Soviet Union for aid. Moreover, the Western powers were not interested in **Lumumba**'s central government; rather they wanted to deal with the provincial governments which were more amenable to their influence.

In September 1960 the political conflict in the Congo reached its zenith. **Lumumba** and **Kasavubu** deposed each other. Mobutu, who had worked very closely with the USA, staged a coup and saw to it that **Kasavubu** remained in office while he had **Lumumba** arrested. **Lumumba** fled, was caught and taken to Katanga where he was murdered, allegedly with the help of the CIA. **Lumumba**'s followers remained active, but the real power was now in the hands of Mobutu and the military. The **UN** saw to it that a new central goverment was formed in August 1961. **Kasavubu** remained president; the new prime minister was Cyrille Adoula who was considered to be a frontman for the USA. The **UN** then tried their best to revise the secession of Katanga and subject it once more to the Congo govern-ment. **Tshombe** had ensconced himself in this rich province which housed the mines operated by the Union Minière Congolais. With the help of his own ethnic group and aided by European mercenaries, **Tshombe** could defend his position very well. Moreover, Roy Welensky, the prime minister of the Federation of Rhodesia and Nysaland sympathized with and supported him.

The **UN** military intervention in Katanga ended in the defeat of the **UN** forces by **Tshombe**'s mercenaries. Dag Hammerskjöld, the **UN** Secretary General, wanted to meet **Tshombe** personally on the Ndola airfield in northern Rhodesia. But Hammerskjöld never arrived in Ndola, his plane crashing nearby. There were rumours that the plane had been hit by bullets, but according to Welensky's report it was nothing but an accident. The plane had flown in a large circle around Katanga, gained radio contact with the Ndola airfield and its lights had even been seen there, but then it vanished in the dark. The **UN** lost not only its Secretary General but also its reputation in this venture.

It took two years of fighting before the UN troops and those of the Congo government were able to occupy Katanga. **Tshombe** went abroad to live in exile, but after his departure and that of the UN troops, the civil war in the Congo continued. The central government controlled only about one-third of the country; the rest was in the hands of **Lumumba**'s followers or other provincial warlords. In July 1964 **Kasavubu** invited **Tshombe** to return and become his prime minister. The USA was allegedly behind this surprising deal. They knew that **Tshombe**'s troops, the Katanga Gendarmes, who had taken refuge in neighbouring Angola could help to win the civil war. In the spring of 1965 there were elections which **Tshombe** won. However, now that the rebels had been defeated, **Kasavubu** thought that he could do without **Tshombe** whom the nationalists regarded as a tool of the Western powers. **Kasavubu** deposed **Tshombe** and nominated another prime minister who was not accepted by the legislature. At this point Mobutu intervened, seizing power in a bloodless coup, and became president in 1966. He held this office for several decades.[49] It seemed as though the Congo had come full circle, as Mobutu, just like Leopold II, treated the country which was now called Zaire as his private property.

THE EVOLUTION OF TANZANIA

When German East Africa became a British mandate territory after the First World War, it needed a new name. A British officer suggested 'Tanganyika'. It is not a name hallowed by old traditions like Ghana, Mali or Benin, but a rather prosaic term. The Swahili word nyika means 'savannah'. Tanganyika is a dry land with low rainfall. Vast areas of the interior are plagued by the tsetse fly and the sleeping sickness which it spreads. The land is very sparsely populated and there are hardly any dominant ethnic groups. Most of these groups are very poor with the exception of the Chagga who live on the slopes of Mount Kilimanjaro and are prosperous coffee farmers.

The German colonial rulers had not acquired a prosperous part of Africa here, which is why they tried even harder to spread the cultivation of suitable cash crops such as cotton and sisal. They provoked the resistance of the population and were finally faced with a bloody rebellion which came to be known as the Maji-Maji rebellion of 1905. 'Maji-Maji' means 'water-water' and refers to the magic water which medicine men spread throughout the countryside, claiming that it would make those who sprinkled it on themselves invulnerable to the bullets of the colonial troops. They were mowed down by the machine guns of those troops.

More than 100,000 rebels are supposed to have died. Hunger and diseases ravaged those who had survived the shower of bullets. The memory of this heroic uprising remained alive in Tanganyika and inspired those who campaigned for the independence of their country.[50]

The British administration was more cautious and avoided such provocations. Governor Donald Cameron's period of office (1925–1931) was of special importance in this respect. He warded off attempts to include Tanganyika in an East African Federation which was at that time propagated by white settlers who saw in it an instrument of the consolidation of their power. Cameron was able to point out that this was incompatible with the mandate status. Having earlier served in Nigeria, Cameron had learned from Lord Lugard about the system of **native authorities**. He introduced it also in Tanganyika, but here it was even more difficult than in Nigeria to find suitable chiefs. They had to be appointed by the British, whereas the Germans had run the country with the help of *akidas*. These were people from the coast who remained strangers in the interior of the country. However, they did contribute to the spread of Swahili as the language of administration which subsequently became the lingua franca throughout Tanganyika. Swahili is a Bantu language in its grammar and basic vocabulary, but it includes many Arabic loanwords and has proved to be a very flexible means of communication.

The years of the Great Depression also brought poverty and misery to Tanganyika as the prices of export crops dropped. The British tried to make up for this by introducing new cash crops and enhancing taxation. This produced resistance which at first could not be articulated because the country lacked an educated leadership. Julius **Nyerere** was the first man from Tanganyika to return to his country with a foreign degree. It would be wrong to suggest that because of this he was predestined to become Tanzania's first president; there were more qualities needed for that than just a foreign degree. However, the scarcity of higher education in Tanganyika demonstrates that the mandate administration had shown little interest in promoting it. The missionaries did more for education than the government. **Nyerere** had attended a Catholic mission school in Tanganyika before attending Edinburgh University. He always remembered gratefully what the missionaries had done for him.

The political atmosphere in Tanganyika after the Second World War was influenced by Governor Lord Twining who served there from 1949 to 1958. Although he was appointed by a Labour government, he was an old-style colonial ruler who regarded nationalists as a nuisance. **Nyerere** said later on that he had to be grateful to Twining, because he had roused the resistance which then bred a national movement. Having returned in 1952, **Nyerere** served as a teacher and contacted his old friends. He managed to revive the Tanganyika African Union, which had been led by some moderate older men, and transformed it in 1954 into the **Tanganyika African National Union (TANU)**. At first **TANU** was small and poor, but it nevertheless raised enough money to send **Nyerere** to New York in 1955 where he addressed the **UN** Trusteeship Council. Unlike other African leaders who bombarded the UN with sonorous rhetoric, **Nyerere**'s speech was precise and to the point and left a deep impression on his listeners. At home he was received triumphantly and **TANU** spread all over the country. In organizing the party, **Nyerere** was supported by the Secretary General, Oscar Kambona. He was more radical than **Nyerere** who had won many friends among Europeans and Asians by refraining from racist propaganda.

The decisive year for **Nyerere**'s political career was 1958. Fortunately the new governor, Richard Turnbull, who arrived in that year, was quite different from his predecessor. Like his colleague Arden-Clark in Ghana, who had backed **Nkrumah**, Turnbull did the same for **Nyerere**. Elections were to be held in Tanganyika, but because the franchise was very restrictive, **TANU** intended to boycott them.[51] Instead the party wanted to launch a non-cooperation movement. **Nyerere** would have been in a good position in this respect. He had been sentenced to a term in prison or ordered to pay a fine for a political article he had written. Since it was almost a badge of honour for African politicians to serve a term in prison, this sentence was a boon to **Nyerere**. But Turnbull persuaded him to pay the fine and participate in the elections and **Nyerere** managed to convince **TANU** to do this. The elections led to a victory for **TANU** and paved the way for a further stage of constitutional reform. **Nyerere** became prime minister of a **TANU** government in 1960. Then he persuaded the British that the conference which preceded independence and was to be held in London should instead be held in Dar-es-Salaam. The constitution was suitably and speedily revised and Tanganyika attained independence in December 1961.[52] The rapid progress of events was due to the good relations between Turnbull and **Nyerere**, but Macmillan had also contributed with his 'wind of change' speech.

Shortly after the attainment of independence, **Nyerere** resigned as prime minister and left this office to his loyal follower, Rashidi Kawawa. **Nyerere** knew that the joy of independence would soon turn to disappointment as there would be no sudden change for the better. Moreover, **TANU** had provided a platform for winning an election, but it was not a party with dedicated cadres who would help him to govern the country. He spent a whole year working at the grassroots of the party. After this he produced a presidential constitution and then got himself elected as president. Tanganyika was not yet a one-party state at this stage, but the opposition won only a very small number of votes at the presidential election. **Nyerere** subsequently transformed Tanganyika into a one-party state. He stressed his ideology of African socialism for which he coined the term *ujamaa* (community spirit). He felt that Tanganyika could not afford the competition of many parties, but promised to introduce democracy within the party. In addition to internal affairs, he was also concerned about Tanganyika's relations with its neighbours.

Nyerere supported the idea of a federation of three independent East African states: Kenya, Tanganyika and Uganda. There was already a common market in existence, as well as the East African Common Services Organization. But he was convinced that this federation should be established quickly before the three states took their seats in the **UN** and would then perhaps be relunctant to give up some of their national sovereignty. **Kenyatta** agreed with him. **Nyerere** even tried to move the British to speed up the granting of independence to Kenya so that a federation could be formed. In the end, however, it was Uganda that proved to be the stumbling block, as its independence was delayed due to internal problems.[53] Looking back in 1965, **Nyerere** regretted that this chance had been missed and stressed that the cooperation of the three East African states had been more intensive in 1963 than it was two years later. He also still shared **Nkrumah**'s hope for a United States of Africa, but stated that there were serious obstacles to unification, among them the relations of different states with rivalling foreign powers and the competition for development aid.

Nyerere did, however, manage to establish a federation with Tanganyika's small neighbour, Zanzibar, which with only 300,000 inhabitants, had as yet hardly been affected by external events. The Sultan of Zanzibar, whose dynasty had its origins in Oman, had recognized German suzerainty, but then the Germans had traded Zanzibar in 1890 for Heligoland, an island in the North Sea. Since that time Zanzibar was a British protectorate. The Arabs, who made up only about 10 per cent of the population, dominated the other people of Zanzibar. Another influential group consisted of Indian Muslim traders; and there was also an old group of immigrants from Persia, the Shirazi, who had intermarried with black Africans and could hardly be distinguished from them. An Afro-Shirazi Party (ASP) had been formed under the old mariner, Abeid Karume, who had made a career in local politics. The Arab minority was split, a radical wing having deserted the Zanzibar National Party which represented the Arabs. The leader of this radical wing was Abdul Rahman Mohammed, called Babu, a Marxist who tried to unite all ethnic groups under his banner.

When Zanzibar attained independence at the end of 1963, tensions increased, but at first the continued rule of the Sultan of Zanzibar seemed to promise stability and nobody took much interest in the innocuous new state. In January 1964, however, Zanzibar came to international attention due to a sudden revolution. An obscure ex-policeman, John Okello, who soon called himself Marshall, staged a coup. The Sultan fled and a revolutionary council formed the new government. Okello had come from Uganda and had served as a policeman in Zanzibar. He had then joined the ASP but subsequently he sympathized with Babu's movement. Okello made use of the fact that some policemen who had come from the mainland like him had lost their jobs after independence. He organized them in a disciplined gang under his command. They seized the armories of the police as well as the radio station. Okello did not wish to head the revolutionary government himself, but he drafted in Babu and Karume for this purpose.[54]

Soon after this successful coup, the black soldiers of Kenya, Tanganyika and Uganda also mutinied for the same reasons as the soldiers of the Force Publique had done in the Congo. They wanted better pay and the dismissal of their white officers. In Tanganyika the mutiny started on January 20, 1964. The soldiers locked up their British officers and then went to see **Nyerere**, but no doubt with thoughts of Sylvanus **Olympio**, who had been murdered by his soldiers only a few months ago, **Nyerere** refused to see the soldiers and left the negotiations to his defence minister, Oscar Kambona. **Nyerere** and Kambona held different views about Africanization. A few days before the mutiny, **Nyerere** had given a speech in which he stated that now that all those who wished to stay in the country had acquired Tanganyikan citizenship, there was no reason why special preferences should be given to black Africans because of their race. This must have disappointed the soldiers. Kambona, however, had made some hasty attempts at Africanization which must have raised their hopes.[55] Now they were not sure whether they would be able to get rid of the British officers and thus wanted to do something about it. Kambona managed to pacify them. He quickly arranged for an airlift to get the British officers out of the country, but he also asked for British troops in order to disarm the mutineers. **Nyerere** was at first not willing to make this request, but eventually he agreed. The British troops put down the mutiny very quickly.

Nyerere was mortified at having to call in colonial forces so soon after having got rid of them. He arranged a special meeting of the **OAU** in Dar-es-Salaam where he apologised to the other African heads of government for taking this action.[56] He asked them to send him African troops from their countries to replace the British soldiers as soon as possible. Soon thereafter Nigerian troops were airlifted to Tanganyika, using British planes as Nigeria had no planes. **Nyerere** not only imported soldiers, but also judges and civil servants from Nigeria and Ghana because he was now forced to proceed with rapid Africanization but lacked sufficient trained personnel in Tanganyika.

Zanzibar remained a challenge to law and order even after the mutiny had been overcome. **Nyerere** solved this problem by creating the state of Tanzania (Tanganyika + Zanzibar) with the help of Karume who became first vice-president of Tanzania while Kawawa, who had been vice-president, became second vice-president. Karume stayed on in Zanzibar while Babu joined **Nyerere**'s cabinet as minister of planning. This was a great diplomatic victory for **Nyerere**, as Zanzibar under a revolutionary government could well have become a Soviet bridgehead. Some Soviet allies, among them the German Democratic Republic, had already initiated activities in Zanzibar. **Nyerere** had obviated this danger and in this way he also prevented Zanzibar from being used as a base for subversive forces. He was once more fully in control of his state and could forget about the humiliation he had experienced in January 1964.

UGANDA: THE DECLINE OF THE KINGDOM OF THE KABAKA

The tensions between Uganda and the kingdom of Buganda, which was included within it, had a strong impact on the history of Uganda from the nineteenth century until 1966 when prime minister Milton **Obote** ordered his troops to storm the palace of the Kabaka of Buganda. The kingdom of Buganda was the largest of a series of kingdoms in Uganda, whose rulers were probably descended from northern herdsmen who had conquered the land of the local tribes. The Baganda had a long tradition of kingship with dynasties with pedigrees of more than thirty generations.

Buganda had never been conquered by the British. The British had arrived in this area when the Kabaka was subjecting several of his neighbours. He gladly accepted British aid in this enterprise and absorbed about a quarter of Uganda with their help. He thought of himself as an ally and not as a subject of the British. The Uganda Agreement of 1900, which will be explained in detail below, was a unique treaty concluded between the Kabaka and the British Foreign Office. It did not just define the terms of the alliance but also the internal order of the kingdom of Buganda with regard to property rights and taxation. This treaty between equal partners was the pride of the Baganda, but it very much complicated the process of decolonization later on. In contrast to other colonies, problems with white and Asian settlers did not arise in Uganda.

Captain Lugard had come to Uganda in 1890 at a very opportune moment. There had been a struggle for power among Christian and Muslim groups, which had been decided in favour of the Christians who heartily welcomed Lugard. It was he who helped the Kabaka to extend his kingdom. Lugard had come to Buganda as an agent of the British East Africa Company which went bankrupt a few years after he had left the country. The British government inherited what was left of the company's acquisitions and was eager to collect taxes in Africa to recoup its liabilities. It also wanted to forestall further German advances in East Africa.

Henry Johnson, an emissary of the Foreign Office who arrived in Uganda in 1900, had already served in other parts of Africa and was credited with having invented the hut tax, which he now also introduced in the kingdom of Buganda. Each owner of a hut had to pay 3 rupees annually and if he owned a gun he had to pay twice that amount. The chiefs who collected the tax received a percentage of it and so did the Kabaka, but the British got the lion's share. Furthermore Johnson divided the land of the kingdom so that almost half of it was reserved for the British Crown, 40 per cent was distributed among 4,000 chiefs, the Kabaka got a small share of about 3 per cent and the Church also got a small allocation. This arrangement was stipulated in the Uganda Agreement which became a kind of basic law in Buganda.[57] The economic consequences of this regulation were enormous. The land allocated to the chiefs, called Mailo-land, was private and hereditary property, which could also be alienated by the chiefs. The old clan heads (*bataka*) had not been taken into consideration in the agreement, only the administrative chiefs (*bakungu*) appointed by the Kabaka. These chiefs became a kind of landed nobility. With the increase in the cultivation of cash crops (cotton, bananas, etc.), the chiefs and their tenants prospered and were interested in maintaining the status quo. They therefore supported the Kabaka loyally.

The kingdom of Buganda had its own parliament, the *lukiko*, and a prime minister, the *kattikiro*, as well as an administrative bureaucracy. It was to some extent a modern state. The Kabaka, Edward Frederick Mutesa II, born in 1924, had ascended the throne at the age of 14 and had then studied at Cambridge. He was known to the British public as 'King Freddie' and enjoyed great popularity. He was a member of the Anglican Church which played an important role in Buganda. Despite being the 33rd monarch of his dynasty, he was not an old-style king but a modern, Western-educated young man. It was an irony of fate that the liberal governor, Andrew Cohen, finally deported him as a result of a clash with him over issues which could be traced to the Uganda Agreement.

Andrew Cohen was a bright star of the British imperial system during the period of decolonization. In 1943, when he was just 34 years old, he had become head of the Africa division of the British colonial office. After 1945, when the Labour Party had formed a government, he had practically formulated its Africa policy. He was convinced that decolonization had to proceed rapidly and he relied for the tranfer of power on the British-educated class of Africans. He was opposed to the old policy of **indirect rule** and had no respect for chiefs, emirs and kings. He was also averse to ethnic nationalism and wanted to encourage African leaders to convert the heterogenous peoples in their respective territories into modern nations. When the Conservatives won the British elections, Cohen had to vacate his key position in the colonial office and was sent as governor to Uganda in 1952.[58] This place was certainly not congenial for a man of his views. It bristled with ethnic tensions and he was faced with a traditional ruler of a dominant ethnic group, who was an educated young man who had studied in Cambridge some years after Cohen had graduated from there.

Initially the relations between the Kabaka and the governor seemed to be harmonious. Cohen asked for a democratization of the *lukiko*. The Kabaka was not an autocrat and readily agreed to raising the number of representatives of the people. However, there was bound to be conflict when Cohen also wanted to broaden the base of the legislature of Uganda. This could only mean a dilution of the number of the representatives of Buganda in that legislature. Baganda resistance to the extension of the jurisdiction of the Uganda legislature had a long history which Cohen ignored. Moreover, distrust of British constitutional plans had increased in 1953 due to the establishment of the Federation of Rhodesia and Nyasaland. Cohen was not interested in federal plans for Uganda which he wanted to see become a unitary state at the time of independence. But this would also lead to a conflict with the Kabaka. A clash was inevitable and finally Cohen saw to it that the Kabaka was deported to London in November 1953.[59] This led to unrest in Buganda. Cohen had underestimated the solidarity of the citizens of that kingdom. In 1955 he had to ask for the return of the Kabaka, whose popularity was thus greatly enhanced, just like that of the Sultan of Morocco who had also been chased out of his country in 1953 and then returned as a national hero in 1955. The Kabaka agreed to restrict his role to that of a constitutional monarch. The powers of the *lukiko* were enhanced, but this revived the conflict with the Uganda legislature. The *lukiko* resolved that Buganda should boycott the elections to that legislature. This boycott was rather successful and resulted in the new

Democratic Party of Uganda, led by Benedicto Kiwanuka, winning the elections and forming a government. Kiwanuka was from Buganda, but he was regarded as a traitor by his people. He was a Catholic whereas the Kabaka and his people were Protestants; denominational differences enhanced political ones. A new party was established in Buganda with the programmatic name *Kabaka Yekke* (Only the Kabaka). Cohen had unwittingly contributed to this development, but did not stay on to see what he had done as his period of office came to an end in 1957. He had stimulated exactly the kind of ethnic nationalism which he detested and which he had tried to discourage throughout his career. When elections were held for the *lukiko* in 1962, the new party *Kabaka Yekke* swept the polls. It thus became an attractive partner for the opposition party in the Uganda legislature.

The leader of the opposition was Milton **Obote**. He had founded the Uganda People's Congress in 1960 which was supported by the Protestants who were opposed to Kiwanuka. **Obote** was from the north of Uganda. He had no sympathies for the secessionist tendencies of Buganda, but he was a shrewd man who knew how to cultivate people as long as he needed them. He encouraged the Kabaka who decided to support him, as *Kabaka Yekke* dominated the *lukiko* of Buganda but not the legislature of Uganda where it would need a partner to form a coalition government. Thus **Obote** became prime minister of Uganda in March 1962. He pretended to be a federalist now and when Uganda became an independent republic in October 1962, he remained prime minister while the Kabaka became the president of Uganda. As president the Kabaka had no powers under the constitution which was a parliamentary one in which the prime minister was in charge of the executive. Once the Kabaka had helped **Obote** to this position, he no longer needed the Kabaka and did not even consult him on important matters. When **Obote** had to deal with the mutiny of the troops in Uganda in January 1964, he called in the British troops without even informing the Kabaka.

With all this high-handedness, **Obote** was not sure of his position and only trusted some loyal followers from the north, among them Colonel Idi Amin. In May 1966 **Obote** ordered Amin to storm the palace of the Kabaka who then fled to London. **Obote** usurped the office of the president and jettisoned the property rights established by the Uganda Agreement. He confiscated the land of the Baganda chiefs and divided Buganda into several administrative districts. He also had the sacred drums of the Kabaka burned so as to destroy any vestige of his rule. During his exile in London, the Kabaka wrote a book, *The Desecration of my Kingdom.*[60] He died in exile in 1969. **Obote** did not enjoy his victory for long, as Idi Amin overthrew him in 1971 and subjected Uganda to a regime of terror.

RWANDA AND BURUNDI: BREEDING GROUNDS OF GENOCIDE

The kingdoms of Rwanda and Burundi were proud of their old traditions which were similar to those of Buganda. Their dynasties could be traced back for many centuries. They also possessed sacred drums which embodied the magic legitimacy of the kings. The kings belonged to the Tutsi, an ethnic group of cattle herders who lorded it over the Hutu, a peasant people. Nowadays social scientists tend to doubt this 'mythology' of ethnic cleavage, but in popular perception the Tutsi/Hutu divide has remained important. In both kingdoms the Tutsi constituted only about 15 per cent of the population. In a democratic age they would become a minority under Hutu majority rule, but as long as feudal tradition prevailed, the Tutsi nobility remained in control. When German colonial rule was extended to this area from German East Africa, the German administration was rather ephemeral. Unlike the British, inspired by Lugard, the Germans had no ideology of **indirect rule**, but in Rwanda and Burundi they used the indigenous monarchy to keep the area under control just as the British did elsewhere. When the Belgians accepted the mandate of administering Rwanda and Burundi in the 1920s, they followed the same practice. They also continued to use the Tutsi as the Germans had done.

More important than the influence of colonial rulers in this area was that of the Catholic Church represented by the order of the White Fathers. This church had established its dominant position in 1900 and from then on had enhanced it. Unlike the colonial rulers who relied on the Tutsi, the missionaries also worked among the Hutu and tended to sympathize with what they considered to be the downtrodden majority. This was particularly so in Rwanda where the Church started publishing, in 1933, the journal *Kinyamateka* in the local language, Kinyarwanda. In the 1950s a young Hutu catechist, Grégoire **Kayibanda**, used this journal as its chief editor to highlight the social problems faced by the Hutu.[61] He was the main author of the 'Hutu Manifesto' of 1957 in which demands for equal rights were highlighted. The Tutsi ruling elite reacted sharply to this appeal and stated unequivocally that the Tutsi held their position by right of conquest and though they were Christians themselves, they would not accept claims of equality based on Christian doctrine. This finally provoked the Catholic bishop, André Perraudin, to publish his 'open letter' of February 11, 1959, in which he stated that special privileges for some social groups are not compatible with Christian morality. He was born in Switzerland and when he had arrived in Rwanda he was appalled to see the ingrained practices which regulated even the recruitment for the clergy. The Tutsi had monopolized the Catholic priesthood in this way and the bishop felt that this would damage the Church which also had to take care of the Hutu. His letter was an expression of genuine concern and not an attempt at political interference. However, it exploded like a bomb and rocked the politics of Rwanda.[62] The year of 1959 thus became one which deeply influenced the fate of the country. The bishop's letter was not the only factor in this development, but it was certainly the most conspicuous evidence of ethnic and political conflicts.

Two political parties were established in 1959: Union National Rwandaise (UNAR) and Parti du Mouvement de l'Emancipation Hutu (PARMEHUTU). The UNAR campaigned for immediate independence under the Rwandan monarchy, while the PARMEHUTU, led by **Kayibanda**, advocated independence at a later date, and obviously not under the monarchy. King Rudahigwa died suddenly in 1959 under mysterious circumstances. Many in Rwanda believed that the Belgians had a hand in it. Moreover, the Belgian Colonel Logiest appeared on the scene at that time as a Special Resident and inspired some Hutu to attack the Tutsi. The seeds of genocide were thus sown. The Belgians then suddenly organized elections in 1960, which PARMEHUTU won; they then installed a provisional government with **Kayibanda** as prime minister in 1960. In 1961 the Belgian administration organized a referendum held under **UN** auspices concerning the abolition of the monarchy. This cleared the way for **Kayibanda** to become president and lead the country to independence in 1962. These events were accompanied by continuous massacres of Tutsi, many of whom fled to neighbouring countries, particulary to Burundi.

In Burundi, which also had a traditional Tutsi monarchy, political development had initially seemed to be more harmonious. The king, Mwami Mwambutsa IV, who had ascended the throne as a child in 1915 and reigned until 1966, provided political continuity. But in the years prior to independence, the Crown Prince, Louis **Rwagasore**, was far more active in politics than the king. **Rwagasore** was a radical nationalist and a close friend of Patrice **Lumumba**. He founded his own party, Unité et Progrés National (UPRONA), in 1959 which was officially registered in 1960. It included both Tutsi and Hutu and if **Rwagasore** had lived he would probably have been able to overcome the ethnic cleavage. The Hutu social revolution of 1960 in Rwanda and the exodus of many Tutsi to Burundi forced the Belgian administration to speed up the political process in Burundi. Elections were held in Burundi in 1961. UPRONA won 58 out of 64 seats in the National Assembly, half of these 58 won by Hutu representatives.

Rwagasore was elected prime minister, but before he could lead the country to independence in 1962 he was murdered on October 13, 1961. The culprits were found and tried, but it has remained a mystery as to who had instigated the assassination. Followers of **Lumumba** tend to believe that the same forces that were behind **Lumumba**'s murder also killed his friend **Rwagasore**.

After **Rwagasore**'s death, G. A. Muhirwa, a Hutu, became prime minister, but under his weak leadership the Tutsi and the Hutu in UPRONA drifted apart. The hope that this party could bridge the ethnic gap soon disappeared. In the meantime the **UN** General Assembly voted in June 1962 to cancel the Belgian mandate and to grant independence to the two countries, Rwanda under the Hutu government of **Kayibanda** and Burundi under the constitutional monarchy of Mwami Mwambutsa IV. The subsequent history of the two decolonized countries was flawed by increasing ethnic tensions which led to mutual genocide among the Tutsi and the Hutu.

In Rwanda, **Kayibanda** remained president until 1973, running the state under a one-party system. Periodic massacres of Tutsi and Tutsi attempts at attacking Rwanda from outside continued throughout this period. In 1973 **Kayibanda** was overthrown by his defence minister, Major-General Juvenal Habyarimana, who established a military dictatorship. Massacres continued, though to a lesser extent.

They flared up again in 1994 when Habyarimana died in a plane crash. Meanwhile Burundi had also experienced political upheavals. Mwanbutsa IV was deposed in 1966 by General Micombero who then installed the king's only surviving son, Ntare V, as head of state. But soon after this Micombero deposed him, too, and he went into exile. When Ntare V returned to his country in 1972, he was killed. This triggered a civil war in which first Tutsi were killed by Hutu and then even more Hutu were killed by Tutsi army leaders. Coups and massacres punctuated the further history of Burundi. Both Rwanda and Burundi were haunted by repeated genocide. Ever since the 'Hutu social revolution' of 1959, the Tutsi as a threatened minority seemed to have been at the receiving end of persecution and genocide. However, they struck back and by the late 1990s they were in power in both Rwanda and Burundi by controlling the military governments of those countries. Exile in Uganda, where the Tutsi finally made up a large part of the army under their kinsman, President Yoweri Museveni, had provided the Tutsi with a base from which they could capture power at home. Paul Kagame, who supposedly belonged to a Rwanda royal family, had been Museveni's chief of military intelligence before he became president of Rwanda. Unfortunately all this amounted to a see-saw power struggle and there was no attempt to establish the kind of political cooperation between Hutu and Tutsi which **Rwagasore** had in mind when he founded UPRONA.

SOMALIA, DJIBOUTI, ERITREA: OVERLAPPING PATTERNS OF COLONIALISM

This region was characterized by a very complicated pattern of colonial rule in which the Italians, the British and the French played their respective roles at various times. Moreover, Ethiopia, an independent kingdom which is not a subject of this book, laid claims to the entire area as it had supposedly belonged to the Ethiopian empire in earlier times. Ethiopia itself had been conquered by the Italians in 1936, but after the Italians had been driven out by the Allies, the Ethiopian emperor Haile Selassi II had again raised the old claims in which he firmly believed, although they were largely fictitious. These claims were rejected by Somali and Eritrean nationalists. The four-cornered contest between three European colonial powers and the Ethiopian emperor had a decisive impact on the political development of the region.

The French had been the first colonial power to stake its claims in the region. In 1862 they arrived at Obok, near the future colonial town of Djibouti, in order to establish a stronghold opposite British Aden. Initially this seemed to be quite a useless colony whose only purpose was to enhance French prestige. But after the opening of the Suez Canal, Djibouti was built up as a port serving Ethiopia. The ambitious plan of a railway from Djibouti to Adis Ababa fascinated the French. It required a track of 781 km in length which was completed in 1917. Stressing the Djibouti–Ethiopia link, the French relied on the Afar, an ethnic group which had strong ties with Ethiopia and a tradition of ruling the hinterland of Djibouti. The ethnic group which controlled the immediate environs of Djibouti, however, were the Issa who were proud of their Somali heritage. They resented French rule, the more so as it relied on the Afar who profited from the French connection.

The Italians, who also wanted to participate in the **Scramble for Africa**, had entrenched themselves at opposite ends of this region. In the north they had established a stronghold at Massawa on the coast of Eritrea in 1885. Their further expansion into Ethiopia was stopped by Ethiopian troops at the battle of Adowa in 1896. After this humiliating defeat the Italians had been satisfied with holding on to the Eritrean coast. In the south they had annexed Somalia in 1887, after arriving at an agreement with the Sultan of Zanzibar who claimed to be in charge of the entire East African coast. Meanwhile the British had established a protectorate over the area between Djibouti and the border of Italian Somalia, which became known as British Somaliland. This more or less stabilized colonial rule in the region until Mussolini revived old Italian dreams of the time before the battle of Adowa in 1896. He conquered Ethiopia in 1936 and for the first time united most Somali areas under one political rule. The huge Italian colony which emerged was shortlived. In the Second World War the Allies vanquished the Italians and Ethiopia was restored. Italian Somalia was put under British military administration in 1941. The British would have liked to receive it as a trusteeship territory under the mandate of the **UN**. In the British Foreign Office plans were made for a 'Greater Somalia' in December 1942.[63] However, the other Allies distrusted British intentions. In 1945 there were acrimonious debates in the British cabinet as Bevin was eager to acquire Somalia while Attlee considered it to be a 'dead loss'.[64] Moreover, the British wanted to get US, French and Italian support for their strategic plans in the Cyrenaica (Libya) which is why they had to accommodate the Italians in Somalia. Finally the **UN** General Assembly, in a resolution of November 1949, entrusted Somalia to Italy with the proviso that the country should become independent by 1960.

The eight years of British rule from 1941 to 1949 had been of some consequence for the political development of Somalia. There were still many Italians who were interested in the restoration of Italian rule and as an antidote the British encouraged Somali nationalism. The first modern political party of Somalia, the Somali Youth Club (SYC), was established with British support at Mogadishu in 1943. In contrast with their usual practice of prohibiting civil servants from joining political parties, the British encouraged Somali civil servants and policemen to join the SYC which expanded its membership very rapidly. It was renamed the **Somali Youth League (SYL)** in 1947 and campaigned for a reunification of all Somalis. Its leadership was keen to appeal to all Somalis regardless of their affiliation to various clans. The **SYL** was vehemently opposed to the return of the Italian colonial rulers but then had to tolerate them during the period of trusteeship from 1949 to 1960. The Italians first tried to fire civil servants belonging to the **SYL**, but under UN supervision they had to work with the **SYL** and also had to establish democratic institutions in which the **SYL** would soon have a majority. The first elections of 1956 ended in a victory for the **SYL** whose leader, Abdillahi

Ise, became prime minister. The new government used the time until 1960 very productively. The civil service was indigenized, the franchise was extended to women and a draft constitution was prepared in view of the impending merger with British Somaliland. The **SYL** advocated a unitary constitution and rejected federal plans. There were differences of opinion about a clause in the constitution which referred to the plans for a Greater Somalia which would include some parts of Ethiopia and Kenya. The radical wing of the **SYL** wanted to stress this very explicitly, but the moderate majority saw to it that the wording would not upset their neighbours. It was stated that there should be 'a reunification of the dismembered nation by peaceful means'.

Political progress in Somalia forced the pace of constitutional reform in British Somaliland. Initially the British were not at all convinced that they should grant independence to their colony so that it would coincide with the independence of Somalia which had been scheduled for 1960 by the **UN**. It was only after considerable pressure from Somali nationalists that a legislative council was established in Somaliland in 1957. It was a decidedly old-fashioned institution consisting of only six clan heads nominated as members of the council by the British governor. The first truly representative elections were held only in 1960. They were won by parties allied to the SYL. Obviously the 'wind of change' had reached this British colony only at the last minute, but once Macmillan had made his point, Somaliland could not stay behind when Somalia became independent. The merger of the two states proceeded very swiftly. A national assembly of 123 members was elected which was dominated by the **SYL** and its supporters from Somaliland. The new Somali Republic was inaugurated on July 1, 1960, with Aden Abdullah Osman **Daar** as president and Abdirashid Ali Shermarke as prime minister. **Daar** had earlier been the leader of the **SYL** in the Somali legislature and Shermarke had distinguished himself as a modernist in that party.

The smooth merger was deceptive. North–South conflicts surfaced subsequently. There was even a mutiny of young northern military officers who did not like serving under southern officers. There were also changes in the party alignments. A new party, the Somali Democratic Union (SDU), emerged in 1962. It contained disgruntled people from the north and a faction of the **SYL** which disagreed with its leadership. This actually helped to create a party system which bridged the North–South divide, but the clan structure of Somali politics resurfaced in subsequent years and led to many conflicts.

The French had managed to hold on to French Somaliland (Djibouti) for a long time, by backing the leader of the Afar, Ali Aref, and resisting the efforts of the Issa who sympathized with Somali nationalism. By forcing some of the Issa to flee, the French got a positive result in a referendum which confirmed the continuation of French rule in 1967. As a concession to the two ethnic groups, the French changed the name of the colony to the 'French Territory of the Afar and Issa'. But the Issa continued their nationalist quest under the leadership of Hassan Gouled **Aptidon** and his party, Rassemblement Populaire pour le Progrés (RPP), which was then renamed Ligue Populaire Africaine pour L'Independence (LPAI).

It was supported by the **OAU** which was very much concerned with one of the last remnants of colonialism in Africa. After Portugal had given up its colonial empire in the mid-1970s, French colonial rule in Djibouti appeared ever more anachronistic. Finally, in 1977, Hassan Gouled **Aptidon** was permitted to lead Djibouti to independence as its first president. He managed to hold on to this post for a long time, but since his regime privileged the Issa, he had to face several Afar rebellions. A civil war rocked the country in the 1990s, but **Aptidon** continued to rule his country until 1999 when the octogenarian retired voluntarily. He was succeed by his nephew.

The most difficult case of decolonization in this region was that of Eritrea, the former Italian colony which had come under British military administration in 1941. The four Allies (USA, Soviet Union, Great Britain and France) could not agree about what to do with Eritrea. A **UN** commission was sent there in 1950 and worked out a plan according to which the British administration would cease in 1952 and Eritrea would then become an autonomous state within a loose federation with Ethiopia. An election was held by the British prior to their departure in 1952. A representative assembly of 68 members, equally divided between Christians and Muslims, accepted the **UN**-sponsored constitution in July 1952 and it was ratified by Emperor Haile Selassi II in September. As his subsequent actions showed, he would have preferred an outright return of this territory to Ethiopia as he regarded it as a part of his empire which had been illegally occupied by the Europeans. Faced with international constraints, however, he played the constitutional game to which he had been invited. He relied on US support as his realm had become of strategic interest to the USA. The UN General Assembly gave its blessings to the federation, but the federal government headed by Haile Selassi soon transgressed its rather limited functions and started to undermine the autonomy of Eritrea. Political parties were proscribed and the principle of parity between Christian and Muslim officers was abandoned. Amharic was imposed as the official language. The Eritrean Assembly approved by a unanimous vote in November 1962 that Eritrea would become an Ethiopian province. There were rumours that the representatives had been bribed, all of which contributed to the rise of the Eritrean Liberation Front which had been established in 1960. This organization then spawned several militant groups which vied with each other for popular support. The guerrilla activities of these organizations spread to such an extent that, by 1977, nearly the whole of Eritrea was controlled by them rather than by the Ethiopians. Meanwhile there had also been several revolutionary changes in Ethiopia and with cleavages among the Eritrean nationalists and political instability in Ethiopia, there was virtually no chance of arriving at an early solution of the Eritrean problem. Eritrea had to wait for its independence until 1993.

MADAGASCAR: FROM VIOLENT REBELLION TO PEACEFUL INDEPENDENCE

Most processes of decolonization in Africa had been relatively peaceful affairs as the colonial rulers were eager to quit and found suitable leaders to whom power could be transferred. The exceptions were countries with white settlers who resisted decolonization, which will be discussed in a later chapter. Madagascar also had a community of about 35,000 white settlers. Their presence did create problems, but the cause of the violent rebellion which rocked Madagascar in 1947 was the intense conflict between the French colonial rulers and the Merina, the dominant ethnic group. The Merina were descendants of Malay seafarers who had arrived in fairly large numbers in Madagascar about 1,000 years ago. In due course they established their control over the island and lorded it over the people who came from the African mainland as settlers or as slaves. They lived in the lowlands along the coast, whereas the Merina occupied the highlands in the centre of the island. The Merina had produced a rather well organized kingship and had maintained the independence of the island for a long time. They established diplomatic relations with the British and adopted Protestantism in its various forms. In fact, the Merina monarchy tried to emulate the relationship between Church and State that prevailed in England in order to legitimize its position. It also welcomed Western missionaries, particularly those who could transfer technical skills.[65] The British did not establish colonial rule and left that to the French who finally subjugated the island with military force. The Merina queen, Ranavalona III, did not recognize the French protectorate established in 1894 and was deported by the French in 1895, first to Réunion and then to Algeria.

From the very beginning the French considered the Merina to be their enemies and the people of the lowlands their natural allies, because these people had been oppressed by the Merina and 'saved' by the French.[66] Colonial policy in Madagascar was much more than the usual 'divide and rule'; it was marked by a hostile and vindictive attitude towards the Merina. Occasional revolts confirmed the French in this attitude. In the meantime a small French educated elite had grown up in Madagascar. One of its leading figures was Jacques **Rabemananjara**, a noted poet and friend of **Senghor** with whom he edited the review *Présence Africaine* in Paris. He was not a Merina but a man from the coast, and he was destined to work closely with the two Merina leaders **Raseta** and **Ravoahangy** whom he first met in Paris in 1946, where they jointly founded the **Mouvement Démocratique de la Rénovation Malgache (MDRM)**.[67] The three men were deeply committed to the idea of a free and independent Madagascar. These were exciting times and the immediate post-war period raised hopes for the liberation of Africa. The second **Brazzaville Conference** in 1944 had propagated the idea of a **French Union**. But the actual practice of post-war French colonial administration disappointed African nationalists.

Madagascar had been occupied by the British in 1942 in order to ward off a potential Japanese invasion. In 1943 the British had returned Madagascar to the **Free French** whose administration was geared to squeezing the country in the interests of the war effort. The rationing of rice proved to be a major problem. Many people went hungry and resented the conduct of the French administration. At the end of the war, about 80,000 Malgache soldiers who had served in the French army returned home and reported their negative experiences. Moreover, the French administration, even if it considered itself to be liberal, showed the old anti-Merina bias. All this provided grist to the mill of the newly founded **MDRM**, whose nationalist message spread like wildfire. The founders of this movement did not encourage a violent uprising, but the rank and file grew impatient and on March 29, 1947, a rebellion broke out which soon engulfed large parts of the island. The French sent 30,000 troops to Madagascar and attacked the rebels with great brutality. They even resorted to the cruel method of hurling live prisoners out of planes so that they crashed to death in the middle of villages. This was supposed to serve as a warning but probably stoked the flames of violent revenge. About 80,000 rebels are supposed to have died in 1947. Not all of them were the victims of direct attacks; many fled into the forest and died there.

In the summer of 1947 the French parliament debated the events in Madagascar as well as the plea of the French government for the cancellation of the parliamentary immunity of **Rabemananjara**, **Raseta** and **Ravoahangy**. Almost all African representatives spoke and voted against this measure, but the French conservative members in particular showed their hatred for the accused whose guilt could not be established. They were nevertheless condemned and, while according to the verdict, they should have spent the rest of their lives in prison, they were finally released in 1956. During his years in prison, **Rabemananjara** wrote some of his finest poetry.

The terrible massacres in Madagascar and the prosecution of the three leading politicians restored law and order with a vengeance in the tormented country. The **MDRM** which had been banned in 1947 could not be revived and the field was now open for new political forces, the more so as the widening of the franchise favoured the people of the coast. Their leader was Philibert **Tsiranana** who had founded the Parti des Deshérités de Madagascar in 1946.[68] The name of the party was directed against Merina hegemony and it was quietly encouraged by the French colonial rulers. In 1956 **Tsiranana** changed the name of his party to Parti Social-Démocrate. He could appeal to a wider public in this way and was enormously successful at the polls. He, of course, supported de Gaulle's referendum in 1958 and was rewarded by being permitted to become president of Madagascar in May 1959. The transition to independence was thus very peaceful in Madagascar. A cynic might say that the massacre of 1947 served the French colonial rulers well. The rebels had raised their heads and they were cut off. Further political development could then follow the French plans. Unfortunately democratic government survived only a little longer in Madagascar than it did in other African countries. **Tsiranana** was overthrown in 1972 when a military dictator seized power.

TROUBLED PERFUME ISLANDS: THE COMORES

At one time, the Comores were an important trading station in the Indian Ocean. They attracted Arab and Shirazi merchants, Malay seafarers, Bantu people from the African mainland and many others. When the opening of the Suez Canal turned the southern Indian Ocean into a backwater, the Comores were almost forgotten. The French then subjected the islands to their colonial rule and established their headquarters on Mayotte (Maore), the island closest to Madagascar, in 1841. They subsequently made the other major islands, Grand Comoro (Ngazidji), Anjouan (Nzwami) and Mohéli (Mwali) French protectorates in 1886. The earlier cultivation of sugar was given up and vanilla and plants yielding scents for perfumes were grown to an increasing extent. Thus the Comores became known as the Perfume Islands. In contrast to the sweet smell of such scents, the politics of the islands left a bitter taste. Initially an independence movement was launched by Cormorans living in Tanganyika, but it was of no consequence. Only after most other African countries had become independent was there a belated attempt at claiming independence for the Comores. The French made arrangements for a referendum in 1974 which gave a surprising result. While three islands registered a vote of 95 per cent for independence, Mayotte opted to remain under French rule. It was the richest island with the longest tradition of French colonial rule and its citizens did not want to share the poverty of the other islands. They already resented the shift of the colonial capital from Mayotte to Moroni, the main town of Grand Comore, in 1962. The French were puzzled and postponed the granting of independence, but on July 6, 1975, 'President' Ahmad Abdallah issued a unilateral declaration of independence for the three islands which had voted for it. At the same time he claimed Mayotte on behalf of his government and the UN endorsed this claim while admitting the Comores as a member. Subsequently the politics of the Comores became a game of subterfuge. Ahmad Abdallah was overthrown in a coup only three weeks after his declaration of independence. It is said that mercenaries supported by French commercial interests were responsible for this coup. Abdallah fled to his home base, Anjouan, and plotted against Ali Soilih who had become president in January 1976. Soilih pursued a radical reformist policy and alienated both French commercial interests and the traditional Islamic elite. Abdallah had learned what could be done with mercenaries and hired a French adventurer, Bob Denard, who led a force of 50 mercenaries who ousted Soilih. Abdallah became president once more. He improved his relations with France and in 1978 introduced a new constitution of the Federal Islamic Republic of the Comores, granting both more autonomy to the three islands and more powers to the president. Denard remained a power behind the leader, building up a presidential guard and serving as a link between South Africa and **RENAMO** in neighbouring Mozambique. When Abdallah thought that he had consolidated power, he wanted to dismiss Denard in 1989. The conflict which ensued ended with Abdallah being shot and killed and Denard practically ruling the country. He finally surrendered after being granted safe passage to South Africa.

The subsequent history of the Comores continued to be rather tortuous. Anjouan and Mohéli declared their separation from the Islamic Republic of the Comores in 1997, wishing to revert to the status of French colonies. They thus greatly embarrassed the **OAU** which is pledged to uphold the sovereignty of the existing African states. After long negotiations a new constitution of the Union of the Comores was adopted in 2002. Each of the three islands got its own president, while Mayotte remained a French 'Collectivité Départmentale de la République Française'.

SOUTHERN AFRICAN STATES: BOTSWANA, LESOTHO AND SWAZILAND

These three states had a common fate; their peoples had to resist the advance of the Boers and their rulers asked for British protection. The British proclaimed the respective protectorates for Botswana (Bechuanaland) in 1885, for Lesotho in 1884 and for Swaziland in 1903 . At this time, the three territories were economically not very attractive. Botswana consisted mostly of deserts and was of importance to the British only because it controlled the transit routes from South Africa to what was to be Rhodesia. Lesotho was a small kingdom surrounded by mountains inside the future Union of South Africa. Swaziland was a marginal enclave bordering on Mozambique. The 'wind of change' reached these protectorates fairly late. In Lesotho (Basutoland) and Swaziland the British relied on the paramount chiefs. The huge protectorate of Bechuanaland had no paramount chief but a group of chiefs among whom the Ngwato chief, Khama III, was the most assertive. When the British government wanted to turn over Bechuanaland to the British South Africa Company, Khama III took the initiative and visited London, together with two other chiefs, in 1895. They made a deal with the British and gave them the land for a railroad on the condition that the rest of the protectorate would remain under the jurisdiction of the chiefs. The British accepted this arrangement but actually intended to attach this territory to Rhodesia. But this did not happen; instead, Bechuanaland remained a kind of frontyard to the Union of South Africa.

These events subsequently dictated the fate of the young Ngwato chief, Seretse **Khama**, who had studied in London and married Ruth Williams, a British woman, in 1948. In the Union of South Africa such a mixed marriage was a crime and the white South Africans were not prepared to tolerate this on their doorstep. The British government caved in; instead of 'protecting' Seretse **Khama**, they saw to it that he abdicated and was exiled to Great Britain were he lived from 1951 to 1956. After returning to his home country he worked as a farmer for some time before turning to politics. He founded the Botswana Democratic Party (BDP) in

1962. The British initially did not wish to grant independence to Botswana, arguing that it was much too poor and could not afford to maintain an independent state. They were also worried about the relations of an independent Botswana with the Union of South Africa. Finally the British relented in 1964 and built up a new capital, Gaborone, as until then the protecorate had been administered from Mafeking, a town located in the Union of South Africa. In 1965 Seretse **Khama** became prime minister of independent Botswana; in 1966 a republican constitution was adopted and he became president. Botswana's transition to democracy owed much to **Khama**'s leadership, but it was also based on the indigneous tradition of free speech addressed to the chief in the communal assembly.[69]

Khama turned out to be an honest and efficient ruler, making good use of the diamond wealth discovered in 1967 for the rapid economic development of Botswana. Annual growth rates ranged above 10 per cent. Under such favourable conditions **Khama** was re-elected several times in fair and free elections. He died in office in 1980 and was succeeded by Vice-President Quett Masire. In contrast with most other parts of Africa, Botswana under **Khama** provided a striking example of good governance and democratic freedom.

Lesotho, earlier Basutoland, is a mountain refuge of the Sotho people who were hard pressed by Zulu and Boer expansion in the nineteenth century but then valiantly defended themselves under their king, Moshoeshoe I. He finally asked for British protection and his land was initially attached to the British Cape Province, but it escaped incorporation in the Union of South Africa by having attained the status of a separate British protectorate in 1884.

Self-government developed slowly in the 1950s. Elections were held for a Legislative Council in 1960 and in 1966 Basutoland attained independence and changed its name to the Kingdom of Lesotho. It was now a constitutional monarchy under King Moshoeshoe II. The first prime minister, Leabua Jonathan, lost the elections of 1970, but instead of accepting the verdict of the electorate, he suspended the constitution, expelled the king, banned the opposition and ruled Lesotho as a one-party state. In 1983 he made the mistake of criticizing *apartheid*, thus incurring the wrath of the Union of South Africa which retaliated by economically strangulating the landlocked country. There were also disputes about the access to the water resources of Lesotho which were needed by the Union of South Africa. In 1986 Jonathan was overthrown by the military. South Africa denied having a hand in this coup, but the new military ruler no longer offended his mighty neighbours.

The Swazi people were, like the Sotho, victims of Zulu and Boer expansion. They defended their Swaziland as best as they could and finally also opted for British protection. A Swaziland Convention of 1881 was supposed to assure them of their territory, but contests between the British and the Boers continued until the British won the Boer War and established an uncontested protectorate over Swaziland in 1903. Swaziland remained an absolute monarchy and independence was granted to the king in 1966 under a British-made constitution. In 1973 King Sobuzha II abrogated this constitution because he held that it was not compatible with Swazi culture. In 1977 he promulgated a new constitution which vested absolute power in the king. He was succeeded in 1986 by King Mswati who continued the tradition of absolute monarchy. Such a traditional monarchy was a rare phenomenon in a 'decolonized' world which was otherwise ruled by democratic governments or military dictators.

WHITE SETTLERS IN AFRICA: RESISTANCE TO DECOLONIZATION

EUROPEAN TITLES TO AFRICAN LAND

Most parts of Africa were subjected to European colonial rule by expatriates who would return home after retirement. White settlers like those who had gone to America were rare in Africa, because there were very few places suitable for such settlement. South Africa was the great exception, but it is not within the scope of this book because it attained its independence before the period of post-war decolonization. The few places which attracted white settlers elsewhere in Africa were Algeria, the 'white highlands' of Kenya and some parts of Rhodesia and Namibia (formerly German Southwest Africa). These settlers were mostly farmers who required landownership of the European type. Africans did not own land as a marketable commodity. Their land laws regulated the access to land for the purpose of cultivation. Colonial authorities respected African 'customary law' and actually used to keep Africans literally in their place.[1] 'Custom' also sanctioned coercion which the colonial rulers applied when recruiting forced labour or compelling African peasants to cultivate cash crops for export. Whereas this was very convenient for the colonial rulers, they had to forget about customary law if they wanted to accommodate European settlers who were used to 'land titles' which could be bought and sold. The colonial authorities established such titles by imposing their own laws and delineating areas in which Europeans could acquire land. In many cases this was done by declaring lands that the indigenous people considered to be communal property as 'vacant'. Since their property rights depended on the continuation of colonial rule, the white settlers were bound to be completely opposed to decolonization. At the time when such land titles had been created, nobody had thought of decolonization. When it became imminent, however, the recalcitrant settlers proved to be a major problem, the more so as they often had sympathizers in the metropolis.

The phenomenon of European occupation of African land was by no means uniform; it varied according to ecological and political circumstances. The Algerian coast, for instance, was ecologically very similar to the European Mediterranean and politically Algeria was considered to be a part of France, administered by the French Home Ministry since 1881. Between 1871 and 1919 the French authorities transferred 215 million acres to European settlers, of whom about a million had flocked to Algeria.[2] There were only a few large landholders among them, whereas most were small farmers and urban artisans. The native Algerians were not citizens but subjects whose lives were governed by a 'code' (*indigénat*) which severely restricted their rights. They could not dare to compete with the settlers. The ecological setting of 'white' agriculture in Kenya was very different. It was in the heart of Africa, but its highlands offered an ecological niche whose climate was similar to that of temperate Europe. The comparatively few settlers who managed a very productive agriculture in this area were landlords rather than farmers and cultivated their estates with African labour. The conditions in Rhodesia were similar to this, but in northern Rhodesia there was also a substantial European minority connected with work in the mines. In what was to become Namibia, the land titles of German settlers had survived the demise of German rule, because it was practically annexed by South Africa under the special conditions of a C mandate of the **League of Nations** as explained earlier. The Union of South Africa did not think of itself as a colonial power and was therefore immune to the wave of decolonization.

In most cases the white settlers left the colonies at the time of independence or at least they lost their political influence. There were only very few exceptions: for example, the first minister of agriculture in independent Tanzania was a white settler who addressed the legislature in fluent Swahili. Unfortunately, this was a rare case and Tanzania had very few white settlers. Wherever these settlers had attained a critical mass, they had lorded it over the black majority in such a way that they were hardly welcome in independent African states.

ALGERIA: THE VIOLENT SEPARATION FROM FRANCE

The French had captured Algeria in 1830. At that time, it had a population of about 3 million, which for a long time did not grow much. The French had actually exterminated about one-third of the population in their fights against Algerian resistance.[3] These conflicts brutalized the French. Even their great intellectual luminary, Alexis de Toqueville, drafted plans of how to starve the Algerian rebels to death.[4] Some of his contemporaries were even more rabid in their desire to exterminate the Algerians. Echos of these brutal sentiments could be heard again during the Algerian war of the 1950s. After Algeria had been 'pacified' at the end of the nineteenth century, its population increased between 1891 and 1921 from 3.5 to 5 million. In 1947 the population consisted of about 1 million Europeans and 7.8 million Algerians.[5] Since the Muslim population continued to grow at a fast rate, the French raised the spectre of overpopulation. The white settlers feared that they would be swept away by a flood of Muslims. More than half of the Europeans lived in towns. Settler agriculture had expanded while ownership was consolidated and the pattern of cultivation had shifted. Food crops declined and wine was produced by the settlers in increasing quantities. Algerian peasants were pushed into the dry highlands. There was also considerable emigration of Algerians to France.

During the First World War, many Algerians had served in the French army. One of them was Messali **Hadj**, who became one of the first radical Algerian nationalists. He spent several years in Paris and in 1926 created the organization **Étoile Nord-Africaine** with others who strove for the independence of Algeria, Morocco and Tunesia.[6] **Hadj** was inspired by Rousseau and the ideals of the French Revolution. He attended the Congress of Oppressed Nations in Brusseles in 1927 where he met **Nehru** and **Ho Chi Minh**. In the meantime, **Ferhat Abbas**, who was a reformist rather than a radical at that time, felt inspired by the ideas of Kemal Atatürk and the 'Young Turks' and published *Le Jeune Algerien* in 1931. Both **Hadj** and **Abbas** were thrilled when the Front Populaire under Léon Blum formed the government in France in 1936. But they were soon disappointed by the plan of that government to grant full rights of citizenship to only 21,000 Algerians. Even this meagre concession met with a loud protest from the settlers. The **Étoile Nord-Africaine** rejected this offer and demanded full independence. Thereupon the organization was dissolved on the orders of the French government in 1937. Messali **Hadj** then founded the Parti du Peuple Algérien. This party also attracted younger people who longed for more radical action. One of them was Ahmed **Ben Bella** who later rose to fame.

When the Second World War began, both **Ben Bella** and **Abbas** joined the French army, **Ben Bella** as a young recruit and **Abbas**, twenty years senior to **Ben Bella**, as a volunteer as he was convinced of the need to fight the fascists. After Hitler had defeated France, **Abbas** returned to Algeria. Shortly before General de Gaulle arrived in Algeria on behalf of the **Free French** in 1943, **Abbas** drafted the 'Algerian Manifesto' asking for independence after the end of the war.[7] He was supported by Messali **Hajd** whom the French had imprisoned. In April 1945 **Abbas** and his followers held the first congress of the Friends of the Manifesto and of Freedom (Amis du Manifeste et du Liberté). Soon thereafter their high hopes were disappointed by a wave of French repression followed by violent clashes between Europeans and Algerians on May 8, 1945, the day when the war in Europe ended. More than 100 Europeans and several thousands of Algerians were killed in this orgy of violence. This terrible event did not augur well for Algeria's post-war political development.[8] **Abbas** nevertheless organized the Union Démocratique du Manifeste Algérien (UDMA) in April 1946 and a few months later **Hadj** launched his Mouvement pur le Triomphe des Libertés Démocratiques (MTLD). The MTLD subsequently proved successful in elections but also established a secret organization (Organisation Spéciale (OS)) for armed struggle. **Ben Bella**, who could make use of his military experience, soon became a leader of the OS.

In 1947 the French government introduced an Algerian Statute according to which all Algerians would have full French citizenship. They would be represented in a legislature in which the Algerians and the European settlers would have a parity of sixty seats each. This parity of majority and minority was, of course, resented by the Algerian nationalists. The French authorities, however, did not give this very restrictive democratic exercise a chance. After the nationalists had done well in municipal elections, the authorities first delayed and then manipulated the elections to the legislature so as to thwart the advance of the nationalists. The democrats among them now had to yield control to the radical young activists who advocated armed struggle. They founded the Comité Revolutionnaire pour l'Unité et l'Action (CRUA) in April 1954, which then transformed itself into the **Front de Libération Nationale (FLN)** on November 1, 1954, a day which was marked by a wave of terrorist attacks in several towns in Algeria.[9]

After suffering defeat at the hands of the Vietminh at Dien Bien Phu in May 1954 and accepting the verdict of the **Geneva Conference** in June 1954, the French now had to face another terrible colonial war on their doorstep. Pierre Mendès-France, who had boldly faced the consequences of the defeat in Vietnam and then granted independence to Tunisia, reacted very sharply to the events in Algeria and asserted that he would defend the French position in Algeria with firm determination.[10] François Mitterand, who had resigned from the previous government in protest against French connivance in the coup in Morocco, was now home minister and responsible for Algeria. He immediately dispatched troops to Algeria. The MTDL was dissolved on the order of the government and many of its members were arrested. Messali **Hadj** founded a new organization, Mouvement National Algérien, and criticized the **FLN** as he disagreed with its terrorist activities. **Abbas**, however, who would have preferred to remain a reformist democrat, joined the **FLN** in 1956 after the French assembly had passed the 'Special Powers Act', which marked the point of no return.[11]

Severe repression kept the **FLN** at bay. It held its first and only congress during the war in Soumman Valley in August 1956. The delegates present there stressed the importance of political initiatives as against the sole reliance on armed struggle.[12] **Ben Bella**, who had not attended this congress, protested against its resolutions, but he nevertheless participated in secret negotiations with the French on behalf of the **FLN**. A meeting was arranged in Tunis in October 1956 where **Bourguiba** was to act as a mediator. However, the Moroccan plane which was to take **Ben Bella** and several of his colleagues from Rabat to Tunis was intercepted and forced to land in Algiers. Robert Lacoste, the governor of Algeria, proudly displayed his prominent prisoners and his action was acclaimed by the European settlers.[13] A last chance at a potential compromise was therefore lost. **Ben Bella** and his colleagues remained French prisoners until the end of the war.

In Algeria a new wave of repression was launched by Generals Salan and Massu. The French prime minister Guy Mollet, who had indulged in the disastrous Suez adventure, did not want to accept defeat in Algeria. The generals there had 350,000 French troops at their disposal. The combat troops of the **FLN**, under the command of Houari **Boumedienne**, could not operate in Algeria. They were stationed across the border in Tunisia and the French had constructed a veritable 'iron curtain' along that border. The guerrilla forces of the **FLN** inside Algeria had nevertheless increased in spite of – or because of – severe repression. The number of guerrillas increased from about 5,000 in mid-1955 to 20,000 by the end of 1956; it remained at that level until November 1959 and then declined very rapidly.[14] In the meantime the French had 'resettled' about two million Algerian peasants, some in supervised 'model villages' but most of them in camps surrounded by barbed wire. Rural guerrilla warfare was made impossible for the **FLN** which had to concentrate on urban terrorism, particularly in Algiers. This led to the 'Battle of Algiers', waged by the French generals Salan and Massu in January 1957.[15]

Although the generals won the battle of Algiers, they lost the war. Massu had conducted his operations in Algiers with extreme cruelty. He had resorted to torture to such an extent that the police chief of Algiers, Paul Teitgen, resigned in protest. Teitgen had been tortured by the Nazis and did not want to condone the same methods under his jurisdiction.[16] The very cruelty of the war spoiled race relations beyond repair and drove more and more Algerians into the arms of the **FLN**.

It is a striking paradox of this war that it was accompanied by a rising tide of Algerian migration to France. In a way this migration helped to fill the gap caused by the drain of French manpower during the war years. As many as 500,000 young French soldiers were stationed in Algeria during the most crucial years of the war. The Algerian migrants not only replaced French manpower, however, they also made substantial contributions to the **FLN**.[17] Some of this money may have been extorted by agents of the **FLN**, but much of it was donated voluntarily. Algerian nationalists hoped that most migrants would return to an independent Algeria in due course. But this did not happen; on the contrary, more migrants left Algeria even after the war was over.[18]

In 1958 the French Fourth Republic was on the brink of collapse and the French generals temporarily seized power in Algeria. They appealed to General de Gaulle who then declared on May 15 that he was ready to govern the republic. The generals and the European settlers hoped that they would find an ally in de Gaulle. At first it seemed that their hopes would be fulfilled. In a famous speech in Algiers on June 4, he said, 'I have understood you'. The settlers thought that he was taking their side. Another speech given a few days later in which de Gaulle even used the famous slogan *'L'Algérie Francaise'*, seemed to confirm this impression.[19] There have been many debates about de Gaulle's intentions at this stage. His own comments in later years tend to disguise rather than reveal what he thought in 1958. After he was forced to give Algeria to the Algerians he tried to give the impression that he had wanted to do this all along. However, it seems that in 1958 he still felt that he could win the war. He stated that, first of all, the French must make themselves 'masters of the battlefield'.[20] In this he was successful. The number of **FLN** guerrillas fighting in Algeria dropped very fast. The French army had once more established its control over Algeria, but this also enabled it to challenge de Gaulle when he tried to recover his freedom of manoeuvre in the political field. In this arena he had to face the challenge of the Algerian nationalists who ironically grew in international stature at the very time when they had lost out on the battlefield.[21] They had formed a Provisional Government of the Algerian Republic (GPRA), headed by Ferhat **Abbas**, on September 19, 1958. De Gaulle appealed to the nationalists and offered 'a peace of the brave', but the GPRA rejected this offer as it did not contain the promise of independence for Algeria.

After de Gaulle had been elected president of France in December 1958, a large number of Algerian political prisoners, among them Messali **Hadj**, were set free in January 1959, but **Ben Bella** and his colleagues remained imprisoned. In September 1959 de Gaulle shocked his supporters in Algeria by announcing a referendum on the self-determination of Algeria.[22] In that month **Senghor**, the leading francophile politician of Africa, had addressed a request to de Gaulle which made it clear to him that he had to accept the independence of the colonies if he wanted to preserve their ties with France. A few months later de Gaulle announced his new policy during a visit to Senegal. His statement on Algerian self-determination had heralded this new approach. For the European settlers in Algeria this meant that they would be abandoned by France. No negotiations with the Algerian nationalists would rescue them once it was certain that France was no longer going to stand by them. The GPRA on the other hand was also not satisfied with de Gaulle's announcement as it did not contain a timetable for the achievement of independence. Moreover, the war in Algeria had been intensified under de Gaulle, who obviously wanted to humble 'the brave' before making peace with them. By now half a million French troops were deployed in Algeria while **Boumedienne** and his troops were still stuck in Tunisia. **Abbas**, who was still president of the GPRA, was in difficulties. While he could not accept de Gaulle's offer as yet, he had to live with the fact that the **FLN** now nominated **Ben Bella** as its chief negotiator. The contours of the coming power struggle in independent Algeria thus began to emerge.

General Massu, who had once appealed to de Gaulle in the hope that he would salvage Algeria for France, now turned against him. In a newspaper interview of January 1960 he confessed that he no longer understood de Gaulle's policy and boasted that the army had the forces to defend its position.[23] De Gaulle immediately relieved Massu of his post, but he could not replace all the generals at once. They and the settlers all agreed with Massu and radical elements among the settlers rebelled against the French government. De Gaulle now had two adversaries to deal with: the **FLN** and the European rebels who could count on sympathizers in the army. In January 1961 he held a referendum in Algeria which led to an overwhelming vote for self-determination. Soon thereafter French army officers founded the Organisation Armée Secrète (OAS) which adopted terrorist methods against all those who supported Algerian independence and negotiations with the Algerian nationalists.

Soon after French negotiations with the GPRA were announced, the generals in Algeria seized power. De Gaulle suppressed the coup and commenced negotiations with representatives of the GPRA at Evian. Throughout the year 1961 the OAS intensified its activities and in September de Gaulle narrowly escaped an assassination attempt. In the meantime, the GPRA had changed tactics and replaced **Abbas** with Ben Khedda as its president. A pharmacist like **Abbas**, Ben Youssef Ben Khedda was 21 years junior to the old leader in whose cabinet he had been minister of social affairs. He had joined Messali **Hadj**'s PPA at a young age and after the Second World War he had become secretary general of the MTLD.

He belonged to the faction which broke with **Hadj** and then supported the **FLN**, which sent him to Tunis to join the GPRA. In the meantime factions had also emerged in the GPRA; Ben Khedda was elected president because he had remained neutral and was acceptable to all.[24]

The negotiations were extremely tough. While the French did not yet recognize the GPRA, they nevertheless tried to get concessions from it which concerned French control of the oil in the Sahara and of military bases and guarantees of the rights of the white settlers. At one stage the idea of a partition of Algeria was even mooted, saving a coastal strip for the settlers. Finally de Gaulle asked his negotiators to finish their business as soon as possible. He feared that his own control of the situation not only in Algeria but even in Paris was greatly endangered.[25] The OAS was on the rampage not only in Algeria; it had unleashed violent unrest in Paris in February 1962. De Gaulle was frantic in his efforts to regain the initiative, even if that meant making concessions to the GPRA. It was a tragic irony that the guarantees of the rights of the settlers which the French negotiators salvaged in this tense last round were at the same time undermined by the murderous campaigns of the OAS aided by those same settlers in Algeria.

On March 18, 1962, the GPRA were able to sign the Evian accords with France. After France had officially recognized independent Algeria, the GPRA headed by Ben Khedda arrived in Algiers on July 3, 1962. But by now the struggle for power was in full swing. The civilian GPRA was afraid of **Boumedienne** who obviously planned to establish a military dictatorship with the help of his troops which could now enter Algeria, having experienced no losses during the war. The GPRA had tried to relieve **Boumedienne** of his command; he defied this order and joined **Ben Bella** in a 'Political Bureau' which resolved to overthrow the GPRA. In September 1962 **Boumedienne** and his troops entered Algiers and Ben Khedda resigned so as to avoid a civil war among the Algerian nationalists.[26]

In the chaotic summer of 1962 the various factions of the **FLN** attacked each other and all of them persecuted those Algerians who had collaborated with the French and had not fled. Tens of thousands of the so-called *harkis* were murdered.[27] More than one million European settlers fled from Algeria to France during those months. The GPRA which had signed the Evian accords had no power to enforce them. The sudden exodus of the Europeans left Algeria almost entirely without trained administrators, doctors and lawyers. In France these refugees were called *pieds noirs* (black feet), a nickname of uncertain origin. The French government tried to resettle them, for instance, in Corsica, where those who had grown wine in Algeria could take up the same activities. This settlement, however, was resented by the local population, the more so as the new settlers were supported with government subsidies which the local people had never received.

In September 1962 a constituent assembly had been elected with **Abbas** as its president. The same assembly installed **Ben Bella** as prime minister. **Boumedienne** became defence minister but it soon emerged that he had higher ambitions. **Abbas** soon resigned but later on agreed to serve as prime minister when **Ben Bella** became president under the new constitution. However, **Abbas** also resigned from that post in August 1963. **Ben Bella**, a charismatic leader, was singularly inept as far as creating stable political alliances was concerned. He was left by almost all of his old comrades while **Boumedienne** could rely on his army and actually had no further use for the **FLN** which soon became a mere shadow of its former heroic stature. On June 19, 1965 **Boumedienne** staged a coup, overthrew **Ben Bella** and sent him to prison were he remained until 1980.[28]

Boumedienne established a military dictatorship which survived him when he died in 1978. None of the old **FLN** politicians were in his government except for Abdelaziz Bouteflika who served as his foreign minister for many years and was destined to become Algeria's president in 1999. The other famous nationalists faded away. Messali **Hadj** spent his life in exile and returned to Algeria only to be buried there in 1974 when he was mourned by many of his old followers. Ferhat **Abbas** lived in retirement in Algeria where he died in 1985. He published a perceptive account of the Algerian war in 1980 (*Autopsie d'une guerre*), but the younger generation hardly remembered him.[29] The long period of dictatorial rule had produced a national amnesia as far as Algeria's history was concerned. Just like General Zia-ul Haque of Pakistan, **Boumedienne** had stressed Islam rather than republican secularism in order to legitimize his government. It was an irony of fate that his successors were challenged by a younger generation which turned to Islam in fighting against military dictatorship.

The violent separation of Algeria from France left a mark on French intellectual life. The French had always believed in the universal value of French civilization. It was difficult for the French intellectuals who sympathized with Algerian nationalism to accept the integral rebuff of such French claims by radical Algerians. Debates on Algeria consequently became much more intense in France. The British had no such deep philosophical problem with their decolonization. Even the experience of violent resistance in Kenya did not represent the serious intellectual challenge to the British that Algeria had been to the French.

KENYA: THE END OF A LANDLORD REGIME

Kenya's land is for the most part dry savannah, but in the heart of the country around Mount Kenya there are fertile highlands occupied by the Kikuyu, a Bantu people who regard Mount Kenya (Kirinyiga) as their holy mountain. It is 5,100 m high and almost rivals the famous Kilimanjaro. The highlands around Mount Kenya are at an altitude of around 2,000 m. Although close to the equator, they have a temperate climate and were therefore ideally suited to European settlers. Initially the Kikuyu were very hospitable and gave land to newcomers. Captain F. D. Lugard, who passed through this area on his way to Uganda in 1890, praised the Kikuyu and their hospitality. But he was soon followed by European adventurers who took advantage of this hospitality. When Lugard returned to their habitat on his way to the coast two years later, he found that the attitudes of the Kikuyu had changed. They now distrusted strangers and obviously had good reason to do so. Events during subsequent years would confirm their worst fears.

The British East Africa Company, on whose behalf Lugard had visited this region, soon propagated the idea of a railway connection from Mombasa via Nairobi to Lake Victoria. The construction was begun on behalf of the British government in 1895 after Kenya had become a British protectorate. In 1901 the railway reached Kisumu on the shore of Lake Victoria.[30] The railway was built by Indian construction workers most of whom returned home. However, they were followed by Indian railway staff and traders who remained permanently in Kenya and soon became fairly affluent. They also became interested in the fertile highlands. The British legislation which reserved the highlands for white settlers was aimed mainly at the Indians who were debarred from acquiring land there. As an initial step the coveted land was defined as Crown land and then areas for the white settlers were demarcated by the government. The Kikuyu were relegated to small native reserves in an area which they had earlier considered to be their communal domaine. The settlers looked down upon native agriculture which appeared very primitive to them, but they were dependent on African labour. In this way there developed a symbiosis between settlers and Kikuyu labourers which was extremely profitable for the settlers. When Kenya became a Crown colony in 1905, the rights and privileges of the settlers were further enhanced. They now even aimed at political power and would have liked to follow the model of the Union of South Africa.

The Great Depression of the 1930s hit the settlers hard because of the steep fall in the prices of their produce. There arose a controversy among them about the desirability of a maize control act which would restrict the area of maize culitvation so as to shore up its price. Some settlers cultivated only maize and would have welcomed such an act. Others cultivated various other crops such as wheat or pyrethrum, a plant used as insecticide. They were interested in low maize prices, because this is what their African labourers consumed and they did not want to pay them higher wages. The act was not passed and the settlers left the cultivation of maize mostly to African tenants. Those tenants effectively supported them through the lean years of the depression. When prices rose again during and after the Second World War, the settlers wanted to get rid of these tenants, calling them 'squatters'.[31] In the meantime the native reserves adjacent to the lands of the settlers had become overpopulated and the Kikuyu needed more land, which led to increased conflicts with the settlers.

When the first official census was conducted in Kenya in 1948, there was a total African population of 5.2 million. Among the non-African population there were 160,000 Indians and only 42,000 Europeans. Only about one-third of these Europeans were farmers. Compared to more than one million European settlers in Algeria, this seemed to be an almost negligible figure. But in Kenya the European farmers controlled the best land which was in short supply and they were surrounded by the Kikuyu who felt cheated by the white settlers.

Like the Ibo of Nigeria, the Kikuyu had an acephalous type of social organization, i.e. they had no chieftains but respected the elders of family groups. Moving up the ladder of age grades was the natural path to leadership among the

Kikuyu, but it was always a collective leadership. In facing the settlers, the Kikuyu had no legitimate spokesman who could articulate their interests. They got such a spokesman when Jomo **Kenyatta** returned to Kenya in 1946 after spending a long time abroad. He was about 50 years old in 1946 and thus deserved the respect of an elder. **Kenyatta** had studied anthropology with Bronislaw Malinowski in London and had completed an MA thesis on the Kikuyu. It was published in 1938 with the evocative title *Facing Mt. Kenya.*[32] The title page showed Kenyatta dressed as a Kikuyu warrior holding a spear. This thesis was more than an academic treatise, it was the manifesto of a modern traditionalist who wanted to reconstruct the solidarity of his people and defend their rights in land and their customary law. **Kenyatta** also showed a knowledge of magic in this thesis which he learned from his grandfather, a medicine man, whom he had accompanied on his tours as a young boy.

Kenyatta was a charismatic leader and his attempts at reminding the Kikuyu of their traditions was well received by them. Actually the resistance of the Kikuyu against the settlers had already begun in the early 1940s, but the British attributed it to **Kenyatta**'s influence. When the Mau Mau campaign was its height, he was arrested and imprisoned. However, the British could never prove his guilt.[33] **Kenyatta** even pleaded that he did not know what Mau Mau was supposed to mean. This was probably true, because the term had been given currency by the police. It is alleged that once, on tracking down Kikuyu rebels, a police patrol had heard the call 'Mau Mau', imitating the leopard's voice, probably used in order to warn others. The police considered it to be the slogan of the rebels and this is how the movement acquired its name. There have been many attempts at explaining the meaning of 'Mau Mau', but there is general agreement that those who participated in this movement did not use the term, nor was it mentioned in the secret oaths which they took. They referred to their movement as 'Land Freedom Army'. The initiation ceremonies of the rebels essentially repeated those of the traditional Kikuyu ritual.[34] Perhaps there were some elaborations such as those of Christian baptism by the anabaptists, some of whom practised complete submersion. Just like the anabaptists, the rebels also composed new hymns for the Church. Some of these were set to the tune of the British national anthem. Since hardly any British knew the Kikuyu language, they could call for the repatriation of the British in these hymns or praise 'King' **Kenyatta**. Any British listening to these hymns were led to believe that the Kikuyu had become very pious.[35]

The hard core of the rebels hid in the Aberdare Mountains in the centre of the 'white highlands'. They could attack the isolated farms of the settlers from this hideout at night. Actually throughout the years of the rebellion very few white settlers were murdered, but many thousands of Kikuyu 'traitors' were killed. The colonial government reacted to the rebellion by proclaiming a state of emergency in 1952 and then lauching 'Operation Anvil' in the course of which 24,000 suspects were arrested and put into concentration camps.[36] Some of them stayed in those camps for six years, while others were released and 're-educated'. The Kikuyu had lived in single homesteads rather than in villages. They were now re-settled in large villages which could be controlled by the police. In this way the rebels were isolated and had no access to sympathizers among the population. The same methods were used during the emergency in Malaya.

Kenyatta was arrested in 1952. His trial remained inconclusive but he was nevertheless sentenced to seven years of imprisonment in April 1953. The political activities of the African majority were therefore paralyzed. In 1955 the British prohibited all African political organizations. The government then launched an experiment of multiracial representation with parity among the three racial groups: whites, Indians and Africans. This was similar to the parity of representation of Europeans and Algerians introduced by the French in Algeria in 1947. This construction, which was an insult to the majority, did not work.

After the Kikuyu politicians had been removed from the scene, the Luo politicians took over. The Luo are the second largest people of Kenya; they are not Bantus but Nilotes. Their region of settlement is to the west of the Kikuyu area; they had no territorial conflicts with the Kikuyu and were on good terms with them. Their leaders Tom **Mboya** and Oginga Odinga campaigned for the release of **Kenyatta** and for independence. As mentioned earlier, **Mboya** presided over the **All-African People's Conference** convened by **Nkrumah** in Accra in 1958. **Mboya** was a trade union leader with his home base among the workers of Nairobi. He had to be cautious in his political moves so as not to displease **Kenyatta** who was still in jail. In 1960 **Mboya** represented Kenya at the constitutional conference held in London which resulted in a very limited constitutional advance. There would be no African prime minister as yet. The British governor remained the head of government, but he had four African ministers in his cabinet. The white settlers were appalled at this concession, but the African nationalists led by **Mboya** refused to serve as ministers. Macmillan's 'wind of change' speech had obviously emboldened **Mboya** to hold out for more concessions.[37]

After this constitutional reform, the government lifted the prohibition of political parties and two new parties were formed, the **Kenya African National Union (KANU)** and the **Kenya African Democratic Union (KADU)**. KANU was the party of the Kikuyu and the Luo, while **KADU** was supported by smaller peoples (Massai, Kalenjin, Giriama, etc.) **KANU** was, of course, **Kenyatta**'s party; it remained handicapped by his absence. Nobody in this party dared to make any commitments without **Kenyatta**'s blessings. The ambitious young **Mboya** had to watch his step so as not to arouse envy and distrust. He nevertheless managed to organize a good election campaign. The elections were held between January and March 1961. **KANU** obtained 67 per cent of the vote but only 19 of the total 53 seats; **KADU** got 16 per cent of the vote but 11 seats. The remaining 20 seats were reserved for the non-African minorities which were vastly over-represented in this way. According to the census of 1962 there was a total of 8.6 million inhabitants of which 177,000 were Asians (Indians), 56,000 Europeans and 34,000 Arabs. Compared to the figures of the 1948 census, it is surprising to note that the number of Europeans had increased by 33 per cent in 14 years in spite of the Mau Mau rebellion.

KANU and **KADU** now determined the further political development of Kenya. Whereas **KANU** represented the densely populated regions of central Kenya, **KADU** was strong in the thinly populated savannah and the coastal region. The allocation of constituencies had favoured the thinly populated areas. This is why **KADU** had obtained 11 seats. It was led by Ronald **Ngala**, a Giriama from the coast, who joined the government, while the **KANU** refused to do so. **Ngala** became 'leader of government business' like **Nkrumah** in Ghana four years earlier. After the elections, the British governor should have released **Kenyatta**, but he failed to do so. He also received no instructions from London to this effect, because the British government felt that the 'man on the spot' would be able to judge the security risk of such a release.[38] Actually, **Kenyatta** was not a rabble-rouser. He had the mind of a conservative Kikuyu elder. In his messages to his followers he had always stressed self-discipline and hard work. In fact, some of these followers would be disappointed by him after independence. He did not drive out the settlers so as to reward the Mau Mau rebels. When he was set free in August 1961, **Kenyatta** was made president of **KANU**. He then entered into a coalition with **KADU** and joined the government. In May 1963 new elections were held and **KANU** captured two-thirds of the seats in the legislature. **Kenyatta** then became Kenya's first prime minister in June 1963; at the end of that year Kenya attained independence.

In January 1964 **Kenyatta**'s government, like that of other East African countries, was shocked by a mutiny of the African troops which had to be suppressed with British aid. These mutinies were caused by the same frustration which had been experienced by all African soldiers after independence. Their country was free, but they were still commanded by the same British officers as before. The young African governments had not given any thought to this problem, taking their small armies for granted. **Nyerere**, who was the first African head of government to experience such a mutiny, actually had to go into hiding for some time until the British had disarmed the mutineers. He was very much ashamed of the fact that he owed his rescue to the British. The governments of Kenya and Uganda, however, were already forewarned and did not mind asking for British help when their soldiers mutinied. The government of Kenya faced more serious problems at that time. It was handicapped by the federal character of Kenya's constitution. **KADU** had insisted on the regional autonomy of the area which it controlled. This problem was solved when the **KADU** politicians dissolved their party, joined **KANU** and agreed to a change in the constitution. Thus, one year after its independence Kenya became a unitary republic and a one-party state. **Kenyatta** became president of Kenya and held this post until he died in the summer of 1978.

A HALFWAY HOUSE: THE FEDERATION OF RHODESIA AND NYASALAND

The other stronghold of white settlers among the British colonies in Africa was Rhodesia. It was named after the great British imperialist, Cecil Rhodes, who wished to subject Africa from the Cape to Cairo to British rule. He had founded the British South Africa Company and had tricked the chieftain of the Ndebele (Matabele), Lobenguela, into granting him mining concessions and other privileges in what was to be Rhodesia. The Ndebele were herdsmen and warriors who had been driven out of South Africa and then lorded it over the Shona settled around the Zambesi river. Like the Fulbe of West Africa, the Ndebele had established themselves as rulers over other Africans. Since they were bold warriors, the British had to handle them with care. Lobenguela was a shrewd man and saw through the game which the British played with him. He once asked a British visitor whether he had ever watched a chameleon stalking its prey, explaining to him that when the chameleon wishes to catch a fly it moves at first very cautiously, stopping on and off until it is close enough to the fly. Then at the right moment it snatches the fly at lightning speed with its tongue. Lobenguela added, 'The British are the chamaeleon, I am the fly'.[39] But when the British could no longer trick Lobenguela, there was a showdown. His warriors were armed only with bows and arrows and they were mowed down by British guns. In 1889 Rhodes had received the Royal Charter for his company. After he had defeated the Ndebele in 1893 he consolidated his control over the country which he had captured and which was soon to be called Rhodesia.

The two halves of Rhodesia to the north and the south of the Zambesi river were very different from each other. Northern Rhodesia was a dry and thinly populated country which attracted only a few white settlers and became important to the colonial rulers only when its copper mines were opened up. The European inhabitants of northern Rhodesia were miners, engine drivers and mechanics. A white labour aristocracy entrenched itself in this country which was very different in character from the white farmers of southern Rhodesia, but, of course, all these whites felt far superior to the black population of Rhodesia. The constitutional development of northern and southern Rhodesia followed different paths. Northern Rhodesia became a Crown colony in 1924. Southern Rhodesia had in a referendum of 1923 rejected the option to join the Union of South Africa; it then obtained a special constitutional status.[40] The vote in the referendum had been restricted more or less to the white settlers of southern Rhodesia, most of whom were British and did not like the Boers who dominated the Union of South Africa. According to estimates of 1953 northern and southern Rhodesia had an African population of about 2 million each, but whereas northern Rhodesia had only 50,000 whites, Southern Rhodesia had 160,000.

Although southern Rhodesia had an 'advanced' democratic constitution, the franchise was restricted by property qualifications. In 1953 there were 47,000 white registered voters as against 1,000 Asians and coloured people and only 400 black Africans. The social organizations of the Africans were practically destroyed. After the defeat of the Ndebele the British had not tried to install 'native authorities' here as they had done elsewhere in Africa. The white settlers could ignore the Africans while the colonial government's announcements in favour of 'native interests' remained on paper only. African nationalists had no scope for political activities here. They were brutally suppressed by the government. There were no 'white highlands' in Rhodesia, but the black peasants had also been deprived of their land by special legislation. They had been pushed to the dry periphery encircling the white settlements which were concentrated in the central plateau region. The peripheral African villages later became strongholds of guerrilla warfare.

Northern Rhodesia had no constitution at all. The blacks were considered to be British protected persons and had no right to vote. The whites were in a precarious position and would have liked to join southern Rhodesia. Roy Welensky, the leader of the North Rhodesian whites, was an enthusiatic advocate of this Rhodesian amalgamation. He was born in 1907 in Rhodesia, the son of a Jewish father from Poland and a Boer mother. He had been an engine driver on the local railways and had earned fame as a boxer. He was the founder of the local Labour Party. As he was a Rhodesian and not a proconsul sent to Africa from London, he would not take orders, nor could he be recalled or replaced. At the time of the 'wind of change', he became increasingly troublesome for the British government.

When Welensky had visited London after the Second World War, he had tried to convert his friends in the Labour Party to his plan of a consolidated Rhodesia. However, they told him that the British government was pledged to protect native interests and would never condone his plan. On the other hand, there would be no objection to a federation, provided it also included the neighbouring British protectorate of Nyasaland. With about 2.5 million black Africans and only 4,300 whites, Nyasaland was not an attractive prospect as far as Welensky was concerned, but he followed the advice given to him in London and became an ardent federalist.[41] The **Federation of Rhodesia and Nyasaland** was formed in 1953. Each of the three states had its own government and its own British governor which did not make life easy for the prime minister of the federation. The first federal prime minister held this post for only a short time and was then followed by Welensky in 1956.

Welensky was only two years in office when his nemesis appeared in the form of Dr Hastings Kamuzu **Banda**. He had studied medicine in the USA and then practised as a physician in London from 1945 to 1953. He had then settled in Kumasi (Ghana) where he could watch **Nkrumah**'s rise from close quarters. In 1958 he followed the call of his countrymen in Nyasaland and returned home. He became the president of the Nyasaland African Congress (NAC) and organized a campaign for Nyasaland's exit from the federation and the immediate attainment of independence. There were riots in Nyasaland in 1959 and **Banda** was arrested and imprisoned. Welensky would have liked to see him remain in prison, but when Macmillan visited the federation on his 'wind of change' tour of 1960, **Banda**'s continued imprisonment was an embarrassment to him. He avoided discussing this issue with Welensky, but soon after Macmillan's return, **Banda**'s release was ordered by the British government. This was a further blow to Welensky who had not been cheered by Macmillan's visit and his famous speech. Macmillan actually undermined Welensky's position gradually, while paying lipservice to the federation. Once when Welensky visited London, Macmillan sympathized greatly with him. Macmillan knew that he would have to sacrifice the federation on the altar of African nationalism, but he wanted to prevent Welensky from rocking the boat by appealing to the British public.

After Macmillan's tour of 1960, the three components of the federation were drifting apart, but they still had to live together for another three years. In southern Rhodesia, Joshua **Nkomo**, who led a union of railway workers, had initiated unrest in 1955 which had been suppressed. But while the Africans remained under control, the whites started to quarrel among themselves. The United Federal Party, which supported Welensky and the federation, came under attack from the opposition led by Winston Field which rejected the constitutional reform for southern Rhodesia of 1961. In northern Rhodesia the African nationalists led by Kenneth **Kaunda** were making headway. After boycotting the elections of 1959, the nationalists had formed the United National Independence Party presided over by **Kaunda** after he had been released from prison in 1960. As northern Rhodesia was under direct British colonial rule, the nationalists there could not be persecuted as brutally as in southern Rhodesia. Welensky followed **Kaunda**'s career with rising anger and when **Kaunda** attended the **Belgrade Conference** of 1961, he said disparagingly that this 'new Gandhi' had joined a pro-communist movement. **Banda** had already been a thorn in his side and now he also had to put up with **Kaunda**. He felt that the federation was a lost cause and that he could not expect much from the British government.

In February 1962 the Commonwealth minister, Duncan Sandys, visited the federation. At a dinner with Welensky and the govenrnor, Lord Alport, Sandys spoke freely about the political atmosphere in London and said, 'We British have lost the will to rule'. At this Welensky got a severe headache and Lord Alport went to the toilet and vomitted.[42] But it was not only Sandys' remark that shocked Welensky; he suspected that Sandys had already arrived at a secret agreement with **Banda** which could only mean the end of the federation.

The white settlers of southern Rhodesia now also became uneasy. They realized that Welensky was going to be let down by the British government and withdrew their support from his United Federal Party. Ian Smith emerged as the leader of the opposition. He had founded a new party, the Rhodesian Front, which defeated the United Federal Party in the elections of December 1962. **Kaunda** had in the meantime won elections in northern Rhodesia under its new constitution of 1962 and had formed a government. **Banda**'s Malawi Congress Party had scored an election success in August 1961 and was clamouring for the dissolution of the federation. Welensky was still reluctant to abandon the federation and reminded the British government of the responsibility which it had shouldered when establishing the federation in 1953. The British government was embarrassed by this appeal but nevertheless dissolved the federation in December 1963. This cleared the way for the African nationalists. Malawi attained independence in July 1964 and Zambia (northern Rhodesia) in October 1965.

This left southern Rhodesia in suspended animation. It had once been the foundation on which Welensky had constructed the federation; now its future was uncertain. It veered sharply to the right with Ian Smith replacing the moderate prime minister, Winston Field. Smith asked for independence which the British government could not grant as long as the black majority was deprived of its rights. He then boldly proclaimed the **Unilateral Declaration of Independence** in 1965 and thus openly defied the British goverment.

THE 'UNILATERAL INDEPENDENCE' OF SOUTHERN RHODESIA AND THE EMERGENCE OF ZIMBABWE

Ian Smith's action was unique in the history of decolonization, presenting the British government with a huge dilemma. The African nationalists would have applauded a British military intervention against the rebel government, but the Labour government of Prime Minister Harold Wilson refrained from this. Wilson would have faced an uproar in Great Britain if he had decided to fight against the 'kith and kin' of the British in Rhodesia.[43] Moreover, an intervention would have meant either the establishment of a British military government in Rhodesia or the immediate installation of an African government. Since the white minority had ruthlessly suppressed all African parties, there was nobody at hand for the kind of 'transfer of power' that the British had practised elsewhere.

Ian Smith was obviously aware of Wilson's predicament and was sure to get away with his rebellion. He was a determined leader whose stiff facial expression was due to wartime injuries; it suited his political style. He had imprisoned the African leaders who challenged him in 1964 and kept them in jail until 1974. The most prominent among them was Ndabangini **Sithole**, a Methodist clergyman who had founded the **Zimbabwe African National Union (ZANU)** in 1963, and Joshua **Nkomo** who had organized a trade union of black railway workers and then founded the **Zimbabwe African People's Union (ZAPU)** in 1962. The third prominent leader was Robert **Mugabe** who had first been associated with **Nkomo**, then joined **Sithole** and had also become the secretary general of **ZANU**. Both **Nkomo** and **Sithole** belonged to Lobenguela's people, the Ndebele, whereas **Mugabe** is a Shona. The Shona are in the majority in Zimbabwe; they feel animosity towards the Ndebele who once lorded it over them. Actually, tribal organization had disintegrated in Zimbabwe under colonial rule, but belonging to an ethnic majority was still an advantage in politics.

For about ten years, Ian Smith was able to rule his state without having to correct his political course. Being flanked by Portuguese Mozambique and the Union of South Africa, he could rely on like-minded neighbours. The Portuguese revolution of 1974 obviously alarmed Smith; he tried to take steps which would reduce international criticism of his antediluvian regime. **Nkomo**, **Mugabe** and **Sithole** were released in 1974. Instead of making common cause, they pursued different paths. **Nkomo** used Zambia as as base for **ZAPU**'s guerrilla warfare. He was supported by the Soviet Union. **Mugabe** relied on Chinese support in organizing **ZANU**'s guerrilla activities. **Sithole**, who had parted company with **Mugabe**, finally joined the moderate leader Bishop Abel **Muzorewa** who had founded the **African National Council (ANC)** in 1971. As Smith now tried to pose as a constitutionalist, he did not prohibit the **ANC** which was thus the only legal African party in southern Rhodesia. After their release **Nkomo** and **Mugabe** at first joined the **ANC** which they considered to be a convenient cover for their activities. However, **Muzorewa** disagreed with the guerrilla activities which they conducted from neighbouring states. **Nkomo** and **Mugabe** then formed the Patriotic Front (PF) which relied on armed struggled, whereas **Muzorewa** and **Sithole** signed an agreement with Smith in 1978 which provided for elections in 1979 which the **ANC** won. **Muzorewa** formed a government and **Sithole** joined his cabinet, as did Smith, serving as a minister without portfolio. However, this government received no international recognition and was regarded as a puppet regime. **Muzorewa** was even denied the right to address the **United Nations** Security Council after **Nkomo** and **Mugabe** had been invited to present their case. **Muzorewa**'s government was also ineffective in providing security at home beyond the immediate precincts of the capital. Although the guerrillas had taken over the countryside and many white settlers fled, the army was still controlled by the white minority and continued to fight the guerrillas. The legitimacy of **Muzorewa**'s government was contested by the other nationalist leaders. Finally he agreed to hold elections in 1980 which **Mugabe** and his **ZANU-PF** won with such an overwhelming majority that the political influence of all the others dwindled to insignificance.[44] But they did not wish to take their defeat lying down. Conflicts eventually reached the level of a civil war which erupted in the 1980s. The war ended when **Nkomo** and **Mugabe** signed a national unity accord on December 22, 1987. Henceforth, this day was celebrated as National Unity Day and **Mugabe** was able to continue to rule Zimbabwe undisturbed. While at first he did not take steps to drive out the white settlers, he did so in due course and many of them migrated to Zambia.

NAMIBIA'S LONG MARCH TO FREEDOM

South-West Africa, which is now called Namibia, was a German colony until the end of the First World War when it was handed over to the Union of South Africa as a mandate territory. As mentioned earlier, General Smuts, who had designed the mandate system, had graded Namibia as Class C which meant that it was not destined to achieve independence and could, therefore, be annexed by South Africa. The German farmers who had settled there before the war were granted South African citizenship in 1924. This also protected their property rights and, except for the Nazis among them who hoped for a restoration of German rule, these settlers were comfortable with their new status. The 1951 census recorded a white population of about 50,000 and a black population of around 370,000.

Compared to other colonies with white settlers the whites represented a fairly high percentage of the total population – about 12 per cent.

After the Second World War, the **United Nations** succeeded the **League of Nations** and the mandate territories were now called trusteeship territorities. General Smuts, head of government of the Union of South Africa, asked the **United Nations** in 1946 to agree to the outright annexation of South-West Africa, but the **United Nations** refused. Subsequently there were frequent tensions between South Africa and the **UN**, because discussions about South-West Africa invariably also touched on the problem of race relations in South Africa. Finally South Africa defied the **UN**; it no longer submitted the annual reports on South-West Africa which it had earlier sent to the **League of Nations**. When the Nationalist Party came to power, it went one step further and passed the South-West Africa Affairs (Amendment) Act of 1949 which practically converted this territory into a province of South Africa. The white settlers of this territory welcomed this act as it secured their representation in the parliament of the Union of South Africa, a situation that could be compared to the position of Algeria in the French Republic at that time.

It goes without saying that under South African administration no African national movement could arise in Namibia, which is why Sam **Nujoma** was forced to form the **South-West African People's Organization (SWAPO)** in exile in Tanzania in 1960. It scored its first diplomatic success when the General Assembly of the **United Nations** revoked South Africa's mandate in 1966. The Union of South Africa ignored this resolution, but **SWAPO** now began guerrilla attacks with the support of neighbouring African governments. Such attacks remained mere irritations until 1975 when Angola and Mozambique became free and Cuban troops clashed with South African troops in Angola. The whole area now became a fierce battleground in the Cold War. Namibia suddenly became a focal point of international attention. Several Western nations got together and tried to solve the Namibian problem. This finally led to Resolution 435 of the **UN** Security Council in April 1978, which was called the **UN** Plan for Namibia. Initially South Africa agreed to this plan which stipulated that all hostilities should cease and free elections should be held in Namibia. But then the South African government decided to go ahead with such elections under its own supervision in December 1978. These elections were boycotted by **SWAPO**. Hostilities were resumed and continued for another decade before a solution could be found.

The Cuban presence in Angola was of crucial importance for Namibia.[45] Burdened by its participation in the civil war in Angola, South Africa finally agreed to withdraw its troops if Cuba would do the same. An agreement to this effect was signed in December 1988. Subsequently the **UN** Plan for Namibia was also implemented. Free elections were held in 1989 and **SWAPO** obtained an absolute majority. Sam **Nujoma** became president of Namibia. He had agreed not to let his armed guerrillas enter Nambia, but in spite of this 2,000 troops of the People's Liberation Army of Namibia crossed the Angolan border and entrenched themselves in northern Namibia. There was intense fighting with South African troops, but finally the situation was resolved. A constitution drafted by Namibia's Constituent Assembly was adopted in February 1990. Formal independence was achieved on March 21, 1990. **Nujoma** was re-elected twice in subsequent years. He had had to wait three decades from the time he founded **SWAPO** in 1960 to the achievement of independence in 1990.

INDIAN LABOUR AND THE SUGAR COLONIES: MAURITIUS, GUYANA AND FIJI

SUGAR AND COLONIALISM

The cultivation of sugar was one of the earliest and most powerful motives for European expansion overseas. Of course, the quest for spices and gold were similarly strong motives. Spices and gold could be collected or extorted, but sugar had to be cultivated and this required an intervention in the process of production. Sugarcane is a demanding crop which requires plenty of water and a warm climate. It has been grown in India since ancient times. Alexander the Great is supposed to have brought it to Europe. At a later time the crusaders were also credited with this transfer. Similarly the Muslim rulers of southern Spain promoted its cultivation, but the Iberian climate was not warm enough and the cane grown there did not yield enough sugar. It was only when the Portuguese colonized Madeira that European sugar production really took off. The demand for sugar in Europe increased rapidly long before the combination of Chinese tea and American sugar affected the habits of European consumers in the eighteenth century.[1] Madeira owed a great deal to the managerial capacities of Prince Henry the Navigator who controlled the island as Administrator of the Order of Christ. Small plantations with limited numbers of African slaves produced increasing amounts of sugar on Madeira in the fifteenth century. The term 'plantation' was not current at that time. The sugar estates were named after their most important item, the sugar mill, called *engenho* in Portuguese and *ingenio* in Spanish. The 'engine' crushing the cane was much improved during the fifteenth century. Earlier sugar mills were operated with millstones like those used for pressing olives. The improved mill worked with rotating metal cylinders. These were in evidence on Madeira as well as on the Canary Islands where the Spanish copied what the Portuguese had done on Madeira. These European Atlantic islands became the springboards for the colonization of Brazil and the Caribbean. Technicians from Madeira and the Canary Islands were in great demand in those colonies to which they transferred European sugar technology.[2]

Columbus, who had lived on Madeira for some time, was convinced of the importance of sugar cultivation and took some plants to Hispaniola, the Caribbean island on which he first landed when he arrived in America. Although it took some time before sugar was cultivated there, Emperor Charles V even provided royal credit for the establishment of *ingenios* on Hispaniola.[3] At the same time the Portuguese expanded sugar production in Brazil. Since the indigenous population was decimated as a result of their contact with the Europeans who brought their diseases to the New World, the Europeans had to import slaves from Africa in increasing numbers to keep up with the growing demand for labour. The productivity of slave labour was limited; it took about three slaves to produce 1,000 kg of sugar per year. The planters were trying to introduce new methods for disciplining their labourforce and speeding up the work rate. They organized the slaves in gangs, 'driven' by a supervisor. It is said that this method was first introduced on a large scale on Barbados, a small Caribbean island which had come under British rule in the early seventeenth century.[4] Sugar transformed this small island very rapidly, the changes described by some historians as a 'sugar revolution'. One aspect of this 'revolution' was the decline of the white and the rapid increase of the black population. In 1650 there were about 30,000 white settlers on Barbados and 12,000 black slaves; by 1690 only 17,000 whites were left while the black population amounted to 48,000.[5] This was due to the con-solidation of the plantations which were restructured to achieve economies of scale. By the end of the seventeenth century Barbados was the most prosperous European sugar colony and became the wealthiest British colony of this time, far surpassing those in North America. In due course it was overtaken by other islands as sugar production spread from island to island.

From the eighteenth to the twentieth century sugar cultivation was practised in many countries, but the sugar industry also had its ups and downs. In the late nineteenth century, the market for cane sugar was greatly affected by the pro-duction of beet sugar in Europe. It recovered in the twentieth century, but then sugar prices declined from the 1920s. The Great Depression hit the sugar industry very hard. Producers tried to depress wages and thus caused labour unrest. There were attempts at introducing an international export quota system in the 1930s, but some governments adopted measures which were not very helpful in this context. At the very time when nine sugar-producing countries arrived at the Chadbourne Agreement of 1931, the British introduced a protective tariff on sugar imported into India which greatly stimulated sugar production in that colony, which had until then imported refined sugar mostly from the Netherlands Indies. By 1937 India had achieved full import substitution of refined sugar and the Indian producers were keen on getting an export quota. However, when the official International Sugar Agreement was signed in that year, India was denied such a quota. A heated debate between the Secretary of State for India and the Colonial Secretary had preceded this decision.[6] As yet, India's growing production of refined sugar had not touched imperial interests, but giving an export quota to India would have affected those British colonies whose economies depended almost entirely on the export of sugar, such as those colonies discussed below.

Mauritius, Guyana and Fiji were latecomers to sugar production in comparison to Barbados mentioned earlier. They became prominent only in the nineteenth century. They then shared a common feature: the massive immigration of Indian labour as indentured servants after the abolition of slavery. Mauritius was a French colony that had come under British rule in 1810. It quickly emancipated its slaves and its planters then gladly imported thousands of Indian 'coolies'.[7] The Indian term 'cooly' means a hired labourer, it is thus descriptive, not offensive, but in many countries it acquired a derogatory connotation. Guyana did have a substantial black slave population which amounted to 60,000 in 1803. After emancipation many ex-slaves left the sugar estates and cultivated land elsewhere or flocked to the urban centres. Between 1840 and 1880 about 120,000 Indian coolies entered Guyana.[8] Fiji, far off in the Pacific, was ceded to the British by a native chief in 1874. It so happened that its first British governor, Arthur Gordon, had served as Governor of Trinidad and of Mauritius before he came to Fiji.[9] He was a strong supporter of the recruitment of Indian labour, the more so as Fiji's native population was not available for work in the sugar plantations which Gordon sponsored in a big way.

Whereas the white settlers in African colonies remained minorities which nevertheless had a great deal of political weight, the Indians who had come as indentured servants to the sugar colonies were more or less in a majority in Mauritius, Guyana and Fiji, but found it difficult to gain political influence in keeping with their numbers. This aggravated the process of decolonization as the British were not at all interested in handing over those colonies to local Indian political leaders. On the contrary, they tried to use constitutional devices such as communal electorates or proportional representation in order to prevent the emergence of Indian majority rule. In this way they exacerbated ethnic conflicts which in some instances took an ugly turn. Political leaders had to learn the art of coalition making so as to defuse such conflicts. However, they could only succeed if the social setting or external interference did not frustrate their efforts. In this respect the cases discussed below provide a study in contrast.

THE EMERGENCE OF INDIAN MAJORITY RULE IN MAURITIUS

Mauritius was first colonized by the Dutch who named it after their Prince Maurice and controlled the island from 1638 to 1710.[10] The cutting of ebony wood was the most important activity of these first colonial rulers. The French East India Company then captured the island and held it from 1735 to 1767. The French Admiral Bertrand Mahé de Labourdonnais made Mauritius his stronghold in the Indian Ocean. As its governor from 1735 to 1746 he greatly improved its economic position. The first sugar factory was built at that time. From 1767 to 1790 Mauritius was under French royal administration, after which it was controlled by the French revolutionary government from 1790 to 1803. At the end of the period of royal government Mauritius had 7,000 free inhabitants and 36,000 slaves. There were no indigenous people living there. Under the revolutionary government these numbers increased to 10,000 and 60,000 respectively.[11] This was an anomalous situation as the French revolutionaries insisted on the emancipation of the slaves. The resistance of the local planters to this policy was successful and General Decaen, who was governor during the Napoleonic period, then restored the old order.

In their global campaign against Napoleon, the British also conquered Mauritius. Under their rule the abolition of slavery was pursued vigorously. The French planters received compensation and no longer resisted. Almost all emancipated slaves left the sugar plantations, but the planters were able to replace them with Indian coolies. In 1838, soon after the last slaves had been emancipated, there were already 24,000 Indians working in the plantations. By 1870 their numbers had risen to 216,000.[12] This was due to the sugar boom fuelled by increasing British demand. The annual British per capita consumption of sugar had doubled from about 8 to 16 kg between 1820 and 1860. Moreover, the population of Great Britain had increased during that period. Sugar production on Mauritius had grown by leaps and bounds from 11,000 tonnes in 1823 to 121,000 tonnes in 1860.[13]

The exploitation of the Indian coolies was severe and most of them refused to renew their contracts after the initial five years were over. They tried to make a living elsewhere on the island and were then prosecuted for vagrancy by the authorities. In the late nineteenth century the sugar boom collapsed as European beet sugar was competing with cane sugar. The London sugar price was halved between 1883 and 1887.[14] This affected the demand for indentured labour. The consolidation of plantations meant their numbers declined. The exploitation of the 'coolies' became even more severe. Mahatma **Gandhi** was shocked when he witnessed their miserable existence during a visit to Mauritius in 1901. He inspired a young Indian lawyer, Manilal Doctor, to go to Mauritius in 1907. This young man became the first political leader of the local Indians. He joined the Mauritian liberal party, L'Action Liberale, which had been founded in 1905.[15] In Great Britain the Liberal Party had won the elections of 1906 and under its auspices a Royal Commission was sent to Mauritius to enquire into the conditions of Indian labour. It recommended that the system of indenture should end, but it took a long time before this recommendation was implemented. Indenture was finally abolished in 1917.

Political life in Mauritius was very restricted. The franchise was limited to a few thousand rich people, mostly French, who dominated the Mauritian economy. Under such conditions trade unions could not grow and it took the upheaval caused by the Great Depression to make some progress in the organization of labour. The steep fall in the price of sugar triggered a strike in the sugar plantations in 1937. The strike was spearheaded by the increasing number of small cane growers who were exploited in a dual capacity by the sugar mills controlled by the big estate owners. These small cane growers, often ex-indentured servants, culti-vated cane on small plots. They sold their cane to the mills and also worked as casual labourers on the sugar estates.[16] They were thus at the mercy of the owners of mills and the estates. The labourers resident on the estates were comparatively better off and did not join the strike. Nevertheless the colonial authorities felt compelled to introduce reforms which were resented by the sugar oligarchy.

The sugar strike of 1937 was followed by a strike of the dock workers in 1938. Seewoosagur **Ramgoolam**, a medical doctor, had returned from London in 1935 and joined others in founding the Mauritian Labour Party (MLP).[17] Its first president was Dr Maurice Curé, a Creole (i.e. of mixed Afro/European parentage), but **Ramgoolam** soon became its most prominent leader.[18] His rivals in the Indian community were the brothers Basodeo and Sookdeo Bissoondoyal.[19] Basodeo had returned from studying in India in 1939. Inspired by the ideas of Mahatma **Gandhi** he founded the Jan Andolan (People's Struggle) Movement which was mainly aimed at the cultural and religious revival of the Hindus of Mauritius. This movement supported the MLP in its quest for constitutional reform which was finally granted in 1947. The first elections under the new constitution were held in 1948. The MLP won 12 seats in the new legislative council, but the Parti Mauricien of the French planters, which had captured only 7 elected seats, held the reins of power as it was supported by the 12 nominated and the 3 official members of that council. The next elections of 1953 showed gains for the MLP, but since the governor again nominated conservative members, the MLP remained in opposition and campaigned for further reforms. The British were ready to grant these reforms in 1956 but wanted to introduce proportional representation as the majority electoral system favoured the MLP. After vigorous protests, proportional representation was not introduced and in the elections of 1959 the MLP won 24 of a total of 40 seats.[20] The brothers Bissoondoyal had in the meantime founded the Independent Forward Bloc (IFB), inspired by Subhas Chandra Bose who had called his party Forward Bloc after he had been thrown out of the Indian National Congress in 1939. They were critical of the MLP which had betrayed the common man, according to them. The IFB got 6 seats in 1959 while the Muslim Committee of Action (MCA) won 5 seats. The Parti Mauricien had changed its name to Parti Mauricien Social Démocrate (PMSD) and had won 3 seats; the remaining 2 seats were won by independent candidates.

The political profile of Mauritius had emerged very clearly in the election of 1959, but during the run up to independence two more elections were imposed on the Mauritians by the parting colonial rulers. During this process the fear of Indian majority rule seems to have become more pronounced. This favoured the PMSD which originally represented the interests of the small minority of French planters but which now tried to attract the votes of the Creoles. At a constitutional conference held in London in 1961 it was decided that Mauritius should take a further step towards independence. The PMSD had objected to this and had withdrawn from the conference. In 1962 **Ramgoolam** was made chief minister and in 1963 new elections were held. The MLP suffered a surprising setback and won only 19 seats, whereas the PMSD captured 8 seats, the IFB got 7 and the MCA 4 seats; the independent candidates retained 2 seats. At the next constitutional conference of 1965 the British government extracted the concession of separating the Chagos Islands, which were then called British Indian Ocean Territory, from Mauritius. An important military base was located on Diego Garcia, which the USA could use as a stationary aircraft carrier at the very centre of the Indian

Ocean. **Ramgoolam** was obviously willing to pay this price for a further step towards genuine independence. Another election was due on the eve of independence. Since the last round, however, the MLP, IFB and MCA had formed an alliance called the 'Independence Party', which won 39 seats in an enlarged legislative council in 1967, while the PMSD got 23. The 'Independence Party' was mostly supported by the Indian vote, whereas those who resented Indian majority rule rallied behind the PMSD. Independence Day was celebrated on March 12, 1968.

The party structure as it had emerged at that time seemed to indicate an ethnic confrontation, but then there was a very surprising turn of events soon after independence had been attained. The IFB with its 11 seats left **Ramgoolam**'s government in 1969; he retained only 28 seats and was thus forced to enter into a coalition with the PMSD. This had the effect of blurring the lines of ethnic conflict. **Ramgoolam** had to respect the interests of the planters and could not move ahead with plans for the nationalization of the sugar industry. Meanwhile, the more conservative members of the PSMD could not tolerate the idea of working with the enemy. The party split and the conservative half formed the Union Démocratique Mauricienne (UDM).

The situation became even more complicated when a new left-wing group, the Mouvement Militant Mauricien (MMM) emerged under the leadership of Paul Bérenger, a young French-Mauritian who had returned from France after participating in the 1968 student revolt. The MMM posed as a Marxist-Leninist party and filled the gap left by **Ramgoolam**'s shift to the right. In the 1976 elections the MMM scored an enormous success, capturing 34 out of 70 seats against **Ramgoolam**'s Independence Party with 28 and the PMSD with only 8 seats. As there was a clear class conflict between MMM and PMSD, they could not form a coalition and **Ramgoolam**'s government continued. But it no longer represented a unified Indian majority. Of the 34 seats of the MMM, 17 were held by Hindus, 7 by Muslims, 9 by Creoles and 1 by a Chinese. In subsequent years, election results became even more variegated.[21] The Indian majority undoubtedly dominated Mauritian politics, but not in terms of a monolithic ethnic party, which augured well for Mauritian democracy.

The Seychelles, which had once belonged to Mauritius, only achieved their independence in 1976. Unlike Mauritius, whose volcanic soil is suitable for the cultivation of sugar, the granite of the Seychelles offers no such benefits. The islands were mostly known for their coconuts. Mahé de Labourdonnais established French rule on the Seychelles and the main island of the archipelago is named after him. The British annexed it in 1814 and it was made a separate Crown colony only in 1903. Political life developed rather late in this colony. The first political parties were founded in 1964 with Albert René leading the Seychelles People's United Party (SPUP) and James Mancham the Seychelles Democratic Party (SDP). The SDP, which represented planters and merchants, won the elections of 1966 and 1970. At the time of independence the SDP and SPUP formed a coalition. James Mancham became prime minister, but Albert René overthrew him in 1977. He ruled the country for many years as a one-party state, only returning to a multi-party system in 1991.

CONTRIVED STAGNATION AND ETHNIC CONFLICT IN GUYANA

The Carib and Arawak indians who lived in this country called it 'Guiana' (Land of many waters). The Dutch were the first Europeans to establish a permanent colony here. In 1616 they built a fort near the confluence of the Essequibo, Mazaruni and Cuyuni rivers, about 100 km from the coast. They gave the poetic name 'Kijk-over-al' (Look over all) to this fort, which in the twentieth century became the title of Guyana's most important literary journal. The Dutch controlled the country from this strategic location on behalf of the Dutch West Indies Company, founded in 1621, until they shifted their headquarters to Flag Island at the mouth of the Essequibo in 1738 where they were closer to the rapidly expanding sugar plantations. African slaves were imported in large numbers to work on these plantations. In 1763 a slave called Cuffy led a remarkable slave rebellion for which he was remembered as Guyana's national hero in later times. The European wars of the late eighteenth century also affected Guyana which briefly became a republic in 1795, following the example set by the French Revolution. The British then seized Guyana but had to return it to the Dutch in 1802, only to regain it some time later. They abolished slavery, but the emancipated slaves had to stay on under a new status euphemistically called 'apprenticeship'. It would, therefore, be more correct to speak of the end of slavery only after the end of the period of apprenticeship in 1838. At that time most slaves left the plantations. Some of them got together and purchased sugar estates, while others founded a village of their own and called it 'Queenstown'. This cooperative village movement of the 1840s was cited later on when Guyana became a 'Cooperative Republic' in 1970.[22]

In order to replace slave labour, the British imported Indian labourers as indentured servants. The first of them arrived in 1838, but with the sugar boom of the 1850s their numbers increased very rapidly. In 1861 23,000 Indians worked on the sugar estates; by 1871 there were 50,000.[23] Unlike slaves, the indentured Indians were not bound to work on the plantations indefinitely. Their contracts terminated after five years and they were entitled to a return passage to India. The planters were eager to retain these workers and to save the money for their passage. They offered them small plots on their estates and encouraged them to grow rice.[24] In this way they would supply food grain to the plantations and also be available for casual labour in the busy seasons. Many Indians would have preferred to settle on land of their own where they would no longer be under the control of the planters. The colonial government, however, in league with the planters prevented this. Land titles were not properly registered and therefore highly insecure. Big companies could acquire land for nominal amounts, but 'coolies' could not risk their savings on land for which they were unable to obtain a secure title. Moreover, a law was passed in 1853 which prohibited the sale of plots of less than 100 acres; it also ruled out sales to groups of buyers. In this way a regime of contrived stagnation was introduced in Guyana.[25] Indian cultivators could only survive as tenants at the will of the planters. This did not encourage intensive cultivation. Yields were low and the returns of agriculture were meagre. This was not helped by the lack of irrigation and/or drainage. The planters who controlled the land would of course ensure that their sugarcane got enough water, but they left their rice-growing tenants to fend for themselves. Moreover, they used the instruments of rent and usurious credit to extract whatever surplus these tenants could gain from their work.[26] Nevertheless, rice cultivation spread very rapidly. In 1891 it covered 4,000 acres; by 1911 it had risen to 40,000 acres.[27] During those 20 years the number of Indians working on the plantations had dropped from 72,000 to 61,000, while the total Indian population of Guyana had increased from 105,000 to 126,000. Rice cultivation continued to expand in subsequent years. By 1931 the land under rice exceeded that under sugarcane.

In the meantime, the sugar industry had undergone a process of consolidation. In 1838 there had been 306 estates of which only 46 were left in 1904. In 1900 the big company BookerMcConnell started operating in Guyana. It introduced large-scale mechanization and by 1950 it controlled 90 per cent of Guyana's sugar production.[28] Similarly, the only other industry in Guyana, the mining of bauxite, was controlled by two foreign companies which had been permitted to acquire vast tracts of land. Work in the bauxite mines was monopolized by the Afro-Guyanese who kept out the Indians – if necessary by force.[29] The Afro-Guyanese were also ahead of the Indians in terms of urban professions; the Indo-Guyanese had remained agriculturists with only a few traders among them who had profited from the rice business. The regime of contrived stagnation kept a lid on further development. It continued even after independence as the government could not overcome the colonial legacy in a short time, although one may argue that there was little effort to do so.

Political development was slow under colonial rule. There were small steps towards constitutional reform in 1891, 1909 and 1927, but they concerned only the small class which could meet the rigid property qualifications. In 1928 Guyana became a Crown colony which meant that the powers of the governor were enhanced. The colonial government was faced with violent unrest when the impact of the Great Depression hit the country. Sugar prices and rice prices were equally affected. There was a strike in 1935 and the Man-Power Citizens Association (MPCA) was founded in that year. It was mostly led by Indians and soon claimed about 10,000 members.[30] It pursued a more radical line than the moderate East Indian Association which represented the interests of the small Indian middle class. The ground was thus prepared for future political agitation. Dr Cheddi **Jagan**, an Indo-Guyanese, who had completed his studies in the USA in 1942, became treasurer of the MPCA in 1945. In 1950 he joined with a young Afro-Guyanese lawyer, Forbes **Burnham**, to establish the People's Progressive

Party (PPP). **Burnham** was made president and **Jagan** vice-president of the new party. This seemed to augur well for inter-ethnic political cooperation, but unfortunately the friendship between **Burnham** and **Jagan** did not last and soon turned into a bitter rivalry.

In 1953 the British introduced universal suffrage in Guyana and held an election which the PPP won resoundingly. **Jagan** became chief minister, but he projected a radical image as a Marxist who was completely opposed to foreign capitalists. The Cold War was already in full swing. The British found **Jagan**'s political views unacceptable. They sent troops to Guyana, deposed him and then arrested him. After this **Burnham** broke off his alliance with **Jagan** and posed as a more moderate alternative to **Jagan**'s leadership. In 1955 the PPP split into two factions, one led by **Jagan** and one by **Burnham**. However, when there were new elections in 1957, **Jagan** won again. **Burnham** started his own party, the People's National Congress (PNC). In 1960 a third party was added to this spectrum: the United Force (UF), which represented the more conservative elements of Guyanese society and was backed by the Catholic Church and the small Portuguese community. In the elections of 1961 which preceded the granting of full internal autonomy to Guyana, the PPP won 20 seats, the PNC 11 and the UF 4 in the legislative assembly. **Jagan** became prime minister and held this office until 1964.

The Afro-Guyanese called **Jagan**'s administration a 'rice government', because he paid special attention to the improvement of rice cultivation.[31] Actually this was the right thing to do in view of the fact that sugar and bauxite were now almost completely under foreign control. But, of course, rice was grown by the Indians and therefore this emphasis on rice could be interpreted as a bias in favour of **Jagan**'s own community. Ethnic conflict was actively promoted by the CIA which wanted to get rid of **Jagan** who it saw as too close to Castro and other communist leaders. Racial violence rocked Guyana repeatedly in the 1960s. The British announced that they would grant complete independence to Guyana in 1966 but insisted on another election before that. For this election to be held in 1964 they imposed the system of proportional representation on Guyana. In this way they hoped to circumscribe the Indian vote. As pointed out earlier, the British had also wanted to impose proportional representation on Mauritius in 1956, but this move had been stymied by **Ramgoolam**. In Guyana **Jagan** was not so successful and had to suffer the consequences. The population of Guyana at that time consisted of 320,000 Indo-Guyanese, 200,000 Afro-Guyanese and 120,000 members of other ethnic communities.[32] The PPP won the largest number of votes but did not attain an absolute majority. The PNC and UF teamed up and **Burnham** became prime minister and led his country to independence. He managed to hold on to this office by any means possible – he rigged elections, got vocal political opponents murdered and tightly controlled the small Guyanese army, manned almost exclusively by Afro-Guyanese, in his capacity as defence minister.[33] He was thus guarded against the danger of a military coup to which so many of his colleagues in other countries succumbed.

Whereas **Burnham** had earlier projected the image of a moderate leader, he turned more and more radical after coming to power. In 1970 he converted Guyana into a 'Cooperative Republic', inaugurated on the day devoted to the memory of Cuffy's slave revolt of 1763. He nationalized the sugar and the bauxite industries and thus controlled a great deal of patronage for his community. Otherwise he did very little for the economic development of Guyana. **Burnham** pretended to represent the working class, but actually his 'transition to socialism' only benefited a black elite of lawyers, teachers and professionals.[34] He died in 1985 and was succeeded by another PNC stalwart, Desmond Hoyte, who proved to be less authoritarian than **Burnham**. Finally **Jagan** had a triumph late in his life when the PPP won the elections of 1992 and he became president. He died in 1997. His American wife, Janet, succeeded him and won the elections of that year. She resigned in 1999 for reasons of health, leaving the office of president to her young finance minister, Bharat Jagdeo, another Indo-Guyanese, who won the elections of 2001. The PNC did not, however, accept the continued rule of the PPP; there was a recurrence of race riots. The legacy of the fateful split of 1955 was hard to overcome.

IMPOSED INDEPENDENCE AND INDIAN EXODUS: THE CASE OF DUTCH GUYANA (SURINAME)

Guyana's neighbours, Dutch Guyana (Suriname) and French Guyana had a rather different fate. French Guyana has remained a colony or rather an overseas department of France, while Suriname attained independence almost a decade after Guyana. It also had substantial sugar plantations in earlier years. African slaves were emancipated in 1873 and then left the plantations. They were replaced by indentured Indians. After the system of indenture was abolished, the Dutch imported Javanese from the Netherlands Indies. The last Javanese indentured labourers arrived as late as 1938.[35] According to the census returns of 1941 the population of Suriname consisted of a total of 184,000 people; there were 70,000 Creoles (Blacks), 49,000 Indians and 35,000 Javanese among them. Thus Suriname had a rather diverse multi-ethnic population and ethnic conflict could easily have erupted. Fortunately Suriname produced a great Afro-Surinamese statesman, Johan Adolf **Pengel**, who began his political career as a trade unionist and joined the National Party of Suriname (NPS) for which he won a seat in the small legislative assembly in 1949. In 1958 he became chief minister and in 1963 prime minister, a position which he held until 1969. He died in 1970. Under his leadership the NPS had formed a coalition with the Verenigde Hindostaanse Partij (VHP) led by Jagernath Lachmon, which remained in power from 1958 to 1967. **Pengel** and Lachmon got along very well together although **Pengel** was more interested in leading his country to independence whereas Lachmon felt that Dutch rule was better for the minority which he represented.[36]

The constitutional framework within which **Pengel** had to work was the Charter of the Kingdom of the Netherlands of 1954 under which Suriname and the Dutch

Antilles were autonomous parts of the kingdom, only defence and foreign policy remaining prerogatives of the central government.[37] The Dutch felt that they were providing a model of decolonization in this way, but in due course problems arose which upset the 'model'. Differences of opinion with Suriname over the conduct of foreign policy arose in 1960.

Pengel and his young nationalist followers were affected by the 'wind of change' which swept through Africa and the Caribbean at that time, but they could not express their sympathies with the emerging new nations as long as the Dutch controlled foreign policy. **Pengel** demanded a Round Table Conference to reconsider the terms of the Charter. This conference was held at The Hague in May 1961, but it did not result in agreement. The Netherlands Antilles were not interested in independence and have remained with the Netherlands ever since. **Pengel**'s Indian coalition partners also had second thoughts about it. Soon **Pengel** also forgot about his quest for independence as he was alarmed at the course of events in British Guyana.[38] In 1969 his government fell as a result of strikes and a conflict with his Indian coalition partner. The Dutch were not sorry to see **Pengel**'s demise, but almost at the same time they were faced with an event which changed their approach to their 'model decolonization'. There was violent labour unrest in Curacao (Netherlands Antilles) in 1969. The local government asked for Dutch troops to restore law and order. This was perfectly legitimate under the Charter, but the Dutch action was perceived as an anachronistic colonial adventure throughout the world. Since the link with Suriname and the Antilles was a burden rather than an asset to the Dutch, they now wanted to cut their losses.[39] However, the Charter did not permit the imposition of independence on unwilling partners. The Dutch were glad when a new government in Suriname once more embarked on a quest for independence. The Indian party, which was in opposition at that time, wanted to postpone independence, but the Dutch government practically imposed independence on Suriname in 1975. This led to a sudden exodus of a large part of the population, particularly of Indians who wanted to make use of their right to settle in the Netherlands before it was too late. In 1970 there were about 29,000 Surinamese in the Netherlands; by 1980 there were about 178,000. The Dutch government did not want to violate the Charter by restricting immigration.[40]

Independent Suriname benefited from generous Dutch financial aid. Even the new army was paid to a large extent by the Dutch. It was a travesty that this payment was continued even after the army had overthrown the democratic government in 1980.[41] In 1975 the transfer of power had been harmonious. Dr Johan **Ferrier**, an educationist who had served as a civil servant in the Netherlands and had then been appointed as the first indigenous governor of Suriname in 1968, became independent Suriname's first president.[42] The military dictator, Lt. Colonel Desire Bouterse, who replaced him in 1980, opted for a socialist policy; this strained relations with the Netherlands as well as with the USA. Suriname heavily depended for its export earnings on bauxite mining which was under the control of the big foreign company ALCOA. Under international pressure, Bouterse permitted the restoration of democracy. But he kept the government under control and when it displeased him, he overthrew it in another coup in 1990 and ousted President Ramsewak Shankar, an Indo-Surinamese. Suriname had avoided ethnic conflict, but it shared the fate of the many countries which were frequently subjected to the dictatorship of their otherwise rather insignificant military.

In terms of per capita income, Guyana and Suriname had always rated far below the Netherland Antilles or the remaining British and French dependencies.[43] This was true both before and after independence, when their position did not improve at all.

DELAYED DECOLONIZATION AND ABORTED DEMOCRACY IN FIJI

Fiji became a British colony in an unprecedented manner. It was ceded to the British by a native chief. This was not one of the usual 'unequal treaties' imposed by the British on unwilling 'natives'. The Fijians took the initiative because they hoped to benefit from British protection. They gave away their country in a formal ceremony and even celebrated the day of cession every year.[44] The first British governor, Arthur Gordon, who came to Fiji after this cession in 1874 had been governor of Mauritius until earlier that year. He had also served as governor of Trinidad. In both places he had encouraged the importation of Indian indentured labour. He knew that sugar cultivation depended on this labour and he felt that Fiji was eminently suited for the production of sugar. After his experience in the other colonies he had become a critic of the system of indenture and would have preferred to recruit free Indian labour. In Fiji, however, he fell back on indentured labour and made a contract with the Australian Colonial Sugar Refining Company (ACSRC), which obtained an exclusive right to buy Fijian sugar. It also gained access to nearly one-fifth of Fiji's land which Gordon sold to the ACSRC before he imposed a new land system which reserved the rest of the land for the tribal *mataqalis* (kin groups). This land was supposed to be inalienable and it belonged to the kin group as a whole, not to individual cultivators. Land distribution was in the hands of the chiefs whose powers were enhanced under Gordon's dispensation.[45] Indian labour had to fit in with this system, which in a way resembled Guyana's system of contrived stagnation. All land was locked up and Indians could only work as tenants of the omnipotent ACSRC once the indenture system was abolished in 1919 and the Indians stayed on as 'free' labour.

The Indians who had come to Fiji had hardly any national consciousness as Indians when they arrived there. They coined a new term for their collective identity: *girmityas*. Their indenture contracts were presented to them as an 'agreement' which became *girmit* in Hindi; a *girmitya* was thus a man bound by such an agreement.[46] For a long time they had no leaders until some Indian traders and professionals settled in Fiji. Some of them were in touch with Mahatma **Gandhi** who took an interest in the fate of Indian workers abroad. The British had enhanced the powers of the native chiefs and were in no hurry to grant any political rights to the Indians. In 1921 when elections to a local council were introduced, they imposed communal representation on Fiji although the Indian leaders had asked for a common roll. The ethnic cleavage was thus given a constitutional status. This was of crucial importance for the further political development of Fiji. Indian solidarity was demonstrated in a major strike of the sugar workers in 1943, which lasted for a whole season and greatly affected sugar production. The British then crushed the strike after declaring sugar an essential commodity for the war effort. Since the Indians had shown their strength and as they nearly outnumbered the native Fijians after the war, the British were even more concerned to keep them in check.

The native Fijians were actually afraid of decolonization and still looked upon the British as their protectors. This is why decolonization was delayed in spite of – or rather because of – the insistent demands of the Fiji Indians. Finally in April 1970 a conference was convened by the British and it was decided that Fiji should become independent in October 1970. For this purpose a complicated constitution was contrived which would guard the natives against Indian majority rule. The native Fijians and the Indians would get 22 seats each so as to achieve ethnic parity. Of those 22 reserved seats only 12 would be filled by the respective communal electorate, while 10 were designated as 'national' seats.[47] This implied that they had to be filled by the ethnic community for which they had been reserved, but that the whole national electorate would be entitled to vote for the respective candidates. Thus a labour party mainly supported by Indians could mobilize voters who would vote for a native Fijian labour candidate for a 'national' seat reserved for his ethnic community. This did not happen immediately. From 1970 to 1987 the conservative Alliance Party, headed by Ratu Sir Kamisese Mara, ruled Fiji. He belonged to the tribal aristocracy which had been nurtured by the British. The senate which consisted entirely of nominated chiefs would naturally support Mara's government.

In the elections of 1987 the Labour Party, which mainly represented Indians but had also gained some adherents among the native Fijians, routed Mara's party. The Indians did not dare to claim the office of prime minister as they were afraid that the native Fijians would resent this. They supported Dr Timoci Bavadra, a native Fijian, as prime minister, but even this did not remove the misgivings of the conservative Fijians. Colonel Sitiveni Rabuka launched a military coup, removed the civilian government and ruled the country as a military dictator.[48] Just as in Guyana, the Indians were not represented in the small Fijian army of which 8,000 men had served abroad during the Second World War. Rabuka's coup shattered the confidence of the Indians; about 12,000 of them left Fiji and this shifted the demographic balance in favour of the native Fijians. There was a great deal of international resentment and finally Rabuka relented and introduced a new constitution which was even more complicated than the old one. There were five electoral rolls for a total of 71 seats; 23 seats were reserved for native Fijians, 19 for Indians, 4 for other small communities and 23 seats were open to all electorates. Rabuka was stunned when the National Federal Party which he supported was wiped out in the elections held under the new constitution in 1999.[49] The Labour Party had gained an absolute majority; it was supported by 58 of the 71 elected members. For the first time, an Indian, Mahendra Chaudhry, became prime minister of Fiji. But he held this office for only about a year when another coup was staged, this time by a civilian, George Speight, who kidnapped Chaudhry and several of his ministers and held them as hostages for some time. Mara, who was president of Fiji, took charge of the government, but he soon resigned and handed over power to the military commander, Frank Bainimarame, who installed a native Fijian, Leisenia Qarase, as prime minister of Fiji.[50] Mahendra Chaudhry was set free and Speight imprisoned, but democracy had been aborted.

THE COMMONWEALTH CARIBBEAN: FROM EXPLOITATION TO DEPENDENCY

COLONIES OF EXPLOITATION

The Caribbean islands were among the oldest colonies of the European powers and the decolonization of most of them was rather belated. In fact, some of them have remained colonies even until today, often with the status of overseas departments of the respective metropolitan countries. Others, such as Haiti, the Dominican Republic and Cuba had achieved their independence in the nineteenth century, and are, therefore, not discussed in the present text. Decolonization in the period after 1947 encompassed only the British Caribbean islands which are referred to as the Commonwealth Caribbean. From the Bahamas in the north to Trinidad in the south the Commonwealth Caribbean extends over a distance of about 2,500 kms. Jamaica is located to the west of this Bahama–Trinidad axis. Even further to the west is Belize (British Honduras) on the mainland of Central America, which is regarded as part of the Commonwealth Caribbean.

The term 'Caribbean' is derived from the name of the American Indian tribe which Columbus encountered when he first discovered these islands. It seems that the tribe's name was actually 'Galibi', but the Spaniards transliterated it as 'Carib' and also asserted that these people were 'cannibals'. The Caribs came from the South American mainland and lorded it over the Arawaks who had migrated to the islands before them and had introduced settled agriculture. The Caribs were seafarers and warriors and put up some resistance to the early European settlers. Like other American Indian tribes, however, they were soon decimated by the diseases which the Europeans spread in America. At any rate, they were not available as agricultural labourers. The early European settlements were few and far between. Some of the early settlers were not actually interested in farming and earned a living by other means. The most notorious among them were the 'buccaneers'.[1] This term is derived from the American Indian word 'boucan' which refers to meat slowly dried over an open fire which can then be stored for a long time. The original buccaneers specialized in preparing such meat and selling it to the owners of ships who needed food for their crew. From this rather harmless activity it was only one further step to enter the ship and take it over. The buccaneer became a pirate and if he operated under a licence of the colonial authorities he became a respectable 'privateer'. Henry Morgan (1635–1688) who began his career as a pirate became so respectable that he finally attained the office of lieutenant governor of Jamaica.

While the seventeenth century was the age of the 'buccaneer', the eighteenth century saw the rise of the plantation owner who imported African slaves and produced sugar in ever increasing quantities. The Caribbean islands had never been quite suitable as settlement colonies; now they were turned into exploitation colonies.[2] They remained profitable as long as slaves were cheap, their supply assured and sugar fetched a good price in Europe. As has been mentioned earlier, Barbados set the pace in the seventeenth century and then sugar production spread from one Caribbeean island to the other.

Like other British colonies in America, the island colonies had governors and assemblies. The few seats in these small assemblies were, of course, filled by the planters who often proved to be very recalcitrant when their interests were at stake. The demise of this kind of restricted democracy was hastened by an event which is still remembered throughout the Caribbean: the Morant Bay Rebellion on Jamaica in 1865. The fatal course of events was triggered by the protest of two citizens, William Gordon and Paul Bogle, both Baptists, against the established church authorities and the governor. They were imprisoned and a large crowd gathered in front of the jail to protest against this. Since the crowd did not disperse it was fired at and some people were killed. This started the rebellion which the governor suppressed with great cruelty. Gordon and Bogle were hanged and 100 years later they were declared to be 'national heroes' by the Jamaican government. In 1865 the Jamaican assembly was so scared by this rebellion that it dissolved itself and left all power in the hands of the governor.[3] Crown colony government was then imposed on most other islands, which impeded the development of democratic institutions.

After the abolition of slavery, the recruitment of indentured servants from India was also practised in the Caribbean islands but it mostly concerned Trinidad. A total of about half a million indentured Indians arrived in the Caribbean region between 1838 and 1917, but whereas 238,000 went to Guyana, only 145,000 came to Trinidad and 21,000 to Jamaica.[4] In Guyana most of the former slaves had left the plantations, but on the islands they had hardly any other option but to stay on and perform as free labour what they had done as slaves before. The plantation economy covered the Caribbean like a wet blanket and smothered all other economic activities. The conditions of free labour were to some extent worse than those of the slaves. A slave had to be fed by his master to stay alive. Free labour could be left to its own devices whenever economic recessions hit the plantations. In fact, many black workers left the islands and migrated to the mainland. However, when the Great Depression hit the whole region in the 1930s, many migrants returned to their island homes and swelled the ranks of the unemployed there.[5] This enhanced the waves of unrest which swept the Caribbean in those years. Strikes and riots erupted without any coordination, affecting various islands at different times. The British government was taken aback by these troubles. It had been too complacent about imperial affairs. There were vigorous debates in parliament and in the daily press. Finally a Royal Commission was dispatched to the West Indies to report on labour problems and recommend improvements. This commission (Moyne Commission) visited many islands and reported on them in detail.[6] When it submitted its report in 1940, however, the government felt that it was inopportune to publish it during the war and it only saw the light of day in 1945. In the meantime some of its recommendations did lead to a change of government policy. The registration of trade unions and political parties was permitted. Presumably it was felt that political articulation and collective bargaining was to be preferred to violent riots. This provided an opportunity for charismatic leaders who could give expression to the sufferings and the fury of the exploited masses.

TRADE UNIONS, POLITICAL PARTIES AND THE RISE OF CHARISMATIC LEADERS

Trade unions of plantation labour emerged at a comparatively late stage in the Caribbean. Earlier there had been some welfare societies which fostered mutual aid among the poor. Such societies were able in due course to emerge as quasi-trade unions as the colonial authorities had outlawed such unions. An early friendly society was established by a black intellectual, Arlington Newton, on Barbados in 1916. He called it the Ulotrichian Universal Union. As 'ulotrichous' means woolly-haired, the name indicated its black membership. Similar societies were established elsewhere in the Caribbean. They were in touch with Marcus **Garvey** of Jamaica, the founder of the United Negro Improvement Association. Newton visited many Caribbean islands and on Antigua he found enthusiastic supporters in the brothers Robert and James Brown who had made money in the USA and settled down as merchants in St Johns, the capital of Antigua, where they had an Ulotrichian Universal Union Friendly Society registered in 1917. This organization became a quasi-trade union and supported the first serious strike of black plantation workers in 1918.[7] Antigua was often affected by droughts and experienced a bad one in 1918. As a result the cane was very light and the planters imposed the rule that the cane cut should be paid by weight whereas earlier it had been paid according to the measurement of the field harvested by the workers. This resulted in a reduction in canecutters' wages at the very time when prices of food and all other essential goods had risen under the impact of wartime inflation. The workers not only went on strike but also burnt the cane in many places. When the leaders were arrested, there was a riot in the streets of St Johns and some black people were shot by the white police. This spoiled race relations between the planters and their 'ulotrichous' workers. Similar sporadic riots also happened on other islands, but as long as the colonial rulers suppressed them vigorously and did not permit the registration of trade unions, no organized working-class movement could arise. This only changed under the impact of the Great Depression as mentioned above. The local leaders who then entered the field could start parties and trade unions which were more effective than those founded by the pioneers of the Ulotrichian Union.

The most impressive leaders of this new era were the cousins Alexander **Bustamante** and Norman **Manley** of Jamaica. They both had Irish fathers and

Afro-Caribbean mothers and looked like British gentlemen. **Bustamante** was senior to **Manley** by nine years. He was already 50 years old when he returned to Jamaica in 1934 in the midst of the Great Depression. He took an active interest in organizing labour and founded the Bustamante Industrial Trade Union in 1939 and soon thereafter the Jamaican Labour Party (JLP), whereas his cousin **Manley** founded the People's National Party (PNP) and remained its president from 1938 to 1967. Both cousins were very strong personalities and became political rivals, taking turns in heading the government of Jamaica in subsequent years. The PNP projected a socialist image whereas the JLP was more conservative and addressed the concrete interests of the workers in higher wages and better living conditions. Although **Bustamante** was a conservative labour leader, the British locked him up from 1940 to 1942 as they did not want to risk labour unrest during the war. However, when universal suffrage was introduced in 1944, **Bustamante** won the elections of that year and repeated this performance in 1953 when he was appointed chief minister of Jamaica.[8] However, in the next elections of 1955, **Manley** defeated him and became premier under a new constitution.

At this stage the idea of a **West Indies Federation** was once more resurrected. It had been mooted several times before, but without success. The British now thought of it as the best means of a joint decolonization of the Caribbean. **Manley** became an enthusiastic supporter of this federation. He shared this enthusiasm with his colleague Dr Eric **Williams** of Trinidad who was another charismatic leader of great stature. **Williams** was a historian whose great book *Capitalism and Slavery* (1944) had earned him academic as well as political fame. He had taught at Howard University in the USA and returned to Trinidad only in 1955. He founded the People's National Movement (PNM), won the elections of 1956 and then headed the government of his country until he died in 1981. He had a vision of a great future for the Caribbean and therefore welcomed the idea of a **West Indies Federation**.

Jamaica and Trindad were not the only islands which provided platforms for the rise of charismatic leaders. Antigua's Vere **Bird** was one of the most colourful characters of the Caribbean. Unlike the highly educated **Williams**, Vere **Bird** had no formal education and grew up in poverty. In 1951 he outdid the famous strike of 1918 and led the workers in a year-long strike which dealt a serious blow to the planters. He had formed the powerful Antigua Trades and Labour Union and the Antigua Labour Party which served as his support base for many decades. Grenada's Eric **Gairy** was initially also a labour leader who emerged as the national leader of his island nation. He had worked on the Dutch island Aruba from 1943 to 1948 and had organized the oil workers there. Returning to Grenada in 1948 he campaigned for higher wages for the plantation workers. His activities finally led to the riots of 1951. He founded Grenada's trade union and the Grenada United Labour Party which he headed for many decades. When we review the processes by which the different islands achieved independence, we shall meet these leaders again. At this stage they are introduced in order to provide a glimpse of the political atmosphere of the Caribbean in the crucial period from the years of the Great Depression to the post-war era. These were formative years not only for politics and labour relations but also for cultural movements and creative literature.

A very important cultural movement was led by Marcus **Garvey** who wished to awaken the pride of the black people in their African heritage. They had been 'deculturized' as slaves and either tended to look upon the British as role models or lived on in sullen indifference. In order to provide a definite focus to this African heritage and suffuse it with a Christian message, **Garvey** praised Ethiopia and saw a new age dawning when Prince Ras Tafari was crowned as Haile Selassie II. In contrast, the Caribbean was described by **Garvey** as a new Babylon which had to be overcome. These were the roots of **Rastafarianism** which became a strong social and cultural movement among coloured and black people.[9] Bob Marley was one of its most famous proponents. He became the protagonist of a new style of Caribbean music: reggae. The Rastafari made a strong claim for the voluntary repatriation to Africa, to be sponsored by the nations which had been responsible for the slave trade. These ideas had to be taken seriously by political leaders. In 1961 an official 'Mission to Africa' from Jamaica toured several African countries and submitted a report to Norman **Manley**.[10] The members of this mission were welcomed by Kwame **Nkrumah** and other African heads of government who encouraged the idea of repatriation. Except for a few isolated cases, however, this initiative was not followed up. Only the moving songs of the reggae musicians reflected the unfulfilled desire for a return to 'Mama Africa'.[11]

THE FATE OF THE WEST INDIES FEDERATION

Caribbean society would probably have benefited from the success of a **West Indies Federation**, because many of the islands are so small that they hardly provide the critical mass for political and economic development. This is why the luminaries of the Caribbean such as **Manley** and **Williams** as well as the great Caribbean economist, W. Arthur Lewis, were supporters of this federation. It was actually a rare instance of an enthusiastic reception for a British-sponsored federation by leading politicians and intellectuals. The British were quite ignorant of federalism as their own unwritten constitution is a very unitary one. But they had discovered federalism as a convenient mechanism of the devolution of power in the process of gradual decolonization. Nationalists of the respective countries were generally not in favour of this device which they regarded as a strategy opposed to their aspirations. The leaders of the Indian freedom movement were against the imposition of a federal structure as enshrined in the Government of India Act of 1935. The Malays were also not happy with British federal designs, and black nationalists saw the Federation of Rhodesia and Nyasaland as a sinister device for the preservation of white minority rule. No such problems affected the **West Indies Federation**. On the contrary, it was seen as a welcome step towards joint independence in the near future.

The idea of a **West Indies Federation** had first been mooted in 1945 by the British government. In 1947 a conference was held in Montego Bay, Jamaica, which was attended by political leaders from all the Caribbean islands under British rule. It took years to frame a constitution which was then confederal rather than federal. The federation was inaugurated with high hopes in 1958. Unfortunately none of the famous Caribbean politicians like **Manley** or **Williams** were willing to become prime minister of the federation although they were its enthusiastic supporters.[12] They probably feared that they would be deprived of their political home base once they opted for this post. It was thus left to the less prominent premier of Barbados, Grantley **Adams**, to become the first and only prime minister of the federation. He was a senior politician who had been president of the Barbados Labour Party since 1939 and was nearly 70 years old when he assumed his high office. He had to move to Port of Spain, the capital of Trinidad, which was also made the capital of the federation. W. Arthur Lewis was economic adviser to **Adams** and obviously took up this post with optimism. However, as the federation was not even a customs union, there were hardly any joint economic activities which could be conducted at the level of the federation. At the most Lewis could hope that from his new position he could have some influence on the individual member states. However, the economic aspects of the federation proved to be its real stumbling block. Jamaica did not like the idea of a customs union. Moreover, some Jamaican politicians were afraid that Jamaica would have to foot the bill of development expenditure for the poorer islands. Trinidad, on the other hand, was against the free mobility of labour, because its government was afraid that its budding industry might attract too many immigrants from the other islands. The period of the late 1950s was one which saw rapid economic growth for many Caribbean islands; in leaner years the mutual fears and jealousies would probably have surfaced even earlier. Later attempts at fostering economic cooperation by establishing first a Caribbean Free Trade Area (CARIFTA) and then a Caribbean Common Market (CARICOM) had for the most part only symbolic value. The small Caribbean states directed their trade to the outside world and not towards each other.

The demise of the federation was precipitated by Jamaica in 1961. **Bustamante** as leader of the opposition opposed the federation. Perhaps he also saw in his campaign against the federation an opportunity to dislodge his cousin **Manley**, who had defeated him in 1955. **Manley** boldly agreed to hold a referendum on this issue in 1961; he perhaps thought that nobody would really want to destroy the federation. But the Jamaican electorate voted against it. The margin was small and the turnout of voters low, but the fate of the federation was sealed – and with it that of **Manley**'s government. After winning the referendum, **Bustamante** challenged **Manley** at the polls in 1962 and defeated him. Thus **Bustamante** could lead his country to independence which Jamaica achieved together with Trinidad in that year. The other members of the federation were left behind and achieved their independence much later. Lewis took pity on them and wrote about their 'agony'. At least the University of the West Indies, of which he was the vice-chancellor, continued to prosper and very soon extended its reach out from its main campus at Kingston, Jamaica, to Trinidad and then to Barbados.

'INDUSTRIALIZATION BY INVITATION': DEVELOPMENT OR DEPENDENCY?

W. Arthur Lewis was born in St Lucia in 1915, earned a scholarship to study at the London School of Economics in 1932 and did his doctorate there in the field of industrial economics. In 1979 he was awarded the Nobel Prize. He was a social democrat and took an early interest in the Caribbean labour movements. His first book was on *Labour in the West Indies. The Birth of a Workers' Movement* (1939). He then emerged as a leading development economist. Faced with the hidebound plantation economy of the Caribbean, he thought of improving productivity both in agriculture and in industry. He also stressed the importance of education. He approved of some of the ideas of the Latin American economist Raoul Prebisch, who had recommended import-substituting industrialization to Latin American countries, but Lewis knew that this would not work for the Caribbean. The islands had very small home markets and could only hope for export-led growth by both improving their agricultural production and concentrating on manufactures which would benefit from low wages. In this context Lewis developed his theory of industrial growth based on an unlimited supply of labour. He saw the economy divided into a traditional and a modern sector. In this dual economy the modern, industrial sector could draw on a reservoir of cheap labour provided by the traditional sector. On the other hand, the productivity of the traditional sector would be enhanced after it had been relieved of underemployed labour. Low wages would prevail only in the short term, but when they began to rise the country would also be able to climb up the ladder of industrial production. Other economists took up his ideas and 'refined' them but also lost sight of his comprehensive approach to development. The catchy formula of 'industrialization by invitation', which he himself did not use but which was introduced by others as a convenient shorthand for his policy recommendations, also failed to do justice to his ideas.[13] Although Lewis did not use this formula, it actually described fairly well what the Caribbean governments did in the 1950s and 1960s.

There were two major problems with this policy. First of all, the transnational corporations which gladly followed the invitation to exploit cheap labour in the Caribbean were as little interested in fostering economic development as the planters had been before them. Their industrial activities rarely had any linkage effects and they did not train skilled labour. Moreover, the entrepreneurial decisions of the corporations were made elsewhere and the Caribbean governments could not influence them. In fact, the Commonwealth Caribbean was dependent on external control to a very great extent.[14] The second problem was that the supply of labour from the unlimited reservoir of the traditional sector did not flow in such a way as to be available 'just in time' to be absorbed by the industrial sector. The attraction of the urban centres proved to be stronger and led to urban unemployment which often assumed threatening proportions. In 1970 Trinidad experienced a wave of urban unrest. **Williams** weathered the storm by declaring an emergency and suppressing the unruly elements with an iron fist.[15] A few years later the oil price hike provided a windfall for Trinidad, allowing **Williams** to rule his country undisturbed until the end of his days. The increase in Trinidad's national income was dramatic. Before 1970 Trinidad and Jamaica had been more or less on the same level. In 1973 Trinidad's national income amounted to 454 million US dollars; four years later it had reached 3,000 million US dollars.[16] In per capita terms (in constant US dollars, 1960–1998), Trinidad stood at 2,763 in 1970 and 4,615 in 1980. In the same decade Jamaica's per capita income had decreased from 1,803 to 1,458.[17]

The Caribbean was subjected to the ebb and flow of the world market. In the 1950s, when many islands of the Commonwealth Caribbean achieved internal autonomy, economic conditions were very good and seemed to herald a bright future. Jamaica, for instance, achieved an annual growth of 6.5 per cent (GDP per capita), and other islands also did very well. Of course, at that time Jamaica profited from bauxite mining in which foreign companies invested a great deal. But this bonanza did not last long. In the 1960s growth rates receded and the effects of dependency became more and more obvious.[18] **Bustamante**'s government did not take any action about it, and was therefore challenged by the PNP, now led by Norman **Manley**'s son, Michael. **Bustamante** had retired and his JLP was defeated in the elections of 1972. Michael Manley now tried to redress the social imbalance created by the foreign-dominated export economy. He wanted to introduce a bauxite production levy and asked for a share for the Jamaican government in the equity of the foreign corporations. In this way he wanted to correct two major features of the regime of dependency: the meagre contribution of the foreign companies to national taxation and the complete lack of local control over economic decision making. He was taught a bitter lesson. The transnational companies rejected his measures and withdrew some of their capital. Jamaican growth rates turned negative, dropping to –1.7 per cent per annum in the 1970s.[19]

Jamaica's decline was an object lesson for Trinidad, where **Williams** chose not to interfere with the oil companies operating in his country and witnessed a steep increase of per capita income from US $790 in 1970 to 2,620 in 1977. Of course, income distribution was skewed and poverty remained a problem, but with an enormous increase in national income there were bound to be spill-over effects. Nevertheless, Trinidad remained subjected to the phenomenon of dependency – although at a more comfortable level. However, the oil wealth did not lead to the growth and diversification of manufacturing.[20] Actually the contribution of this sector to the economy receded. This also meant a decline in opportunities for skilled labour. Another similar example was the progress of dependent development on Antigua which attracted a booming tourist industry.[21] The hotel owners were mostly foreigners, but they gave jobs to the locals. These jobs did not provide for an upgrade and diversification of skills. Any change in foreign demand for vacations in the sun could badly affect the economy of Antigua. No doubt, these various patterns of dependency are still preferable to exploitation by sugar planters. To that extent decolonization has benefited the Caribbean islands, but for many of them it took a long time to come.

THE STAGGERED PROCESS OF ISOLATED DECOLONIZATION

Islands accentuate isolation. After the demise of the **West Indies Federation** the chance of joint decolonization was gone. The many Caribbean islands now 'staggered' towards their decolonization at their own pace. It took 21 years from 1962, when Jamaica and Trinidad had become independent, to 1983 when St Kitts and Nevis achieved that goal. Barbados, which became independent in 1966, was one of the 'progressive' islands in this respect. It had long been praised as a 'Little England' and offered excellent chances of higher education. Its labour movement was also long established; in Grantley **Adams** it had produced the first prime minister of the **West Indies Federation**. When **Adams** assumed this high office, his erstwhile political comrade and subsequent opponent, Errol Walton **Barrows**, could make his mark on Barbados politics. **Barrows** had served in the Royal Air Force during the war, then taken a law degree in London and returned to Barbados in 1950. He first joined the Barbados Labour Party (BLP) led by **Adams** in 1951, but then broke away and founded the Democratic Labour Party (DLP) in 1955. When Barbados was granted internal autonomy in 1961, **Barrows** became premier and subsequently led his country to independence in 1966, becoming its first prime minister. He retained this office for a decade. In 1976 the DLP was defeated by the BLP. **Barrows** went abroad and returned to Barbados at the end of his life when he once more served it as prime minister from 1985 to 1987. With its stable two-party system, Barbados presented itself as a haven of political stability.

The next in line were the Bahamas which attained independence in 1973. The Bahamas profited from their proximity to the USA, first during the American Civil War and then again during prohibition. After a long slump in the 1930s and early 1940s, they later prospered as a military base. When Cuba was closed to US tourists in 1961, a new boom began for the Bahamas which also attracted financial services. Typically, the man who led the Bahamas to independence, Lynden **Pindling**, was not a labour leader but an astute lawyer. He had studied law in London and then practised it in the Bahamas where he joined the Progressive Liberal Party (PLP) in 1953, at the age of only 23. Within a decade he had risen to the position of leader of his party, which he held until 1997. In 1967 he won the elections and became the first black premier of the Bahamas. His followers called him 'Black Moses'. After a constitutional change, he could adopt the title of prime minister in 1969. He then led his country to independence in 1973 and won subsequent elections in 1977, 1982 and 1987. With the PLP so solidly entrenched, the Bahamas practically became a one-party state. It was alleged that **Pindling** indulged in corrupt practices, but he also enriched his nation by his astute politics. The Bahamas could boast a per capita income in the 1980s which, at US $7,600, was very high compared to that of Jamaica ($1,047) or Trinidad ($2,837). The prosperity of the Bahamas was only surpassed by Bermuda which remained a British colony, having achieved internal autonomy in 1968. It must be said to **Pindling**'s credit that when his opponents won the elections of 1997, he took his defeat gracefully and quietly retired as the longest-serving head of government of the British Commonwealth.

The Bahamas were followed by Grenada which became independent in 1974. This small island with a population of about 100,000 had also produced one of the most flamboyant and charismatic labour leaders of the Caribbean: Eric **Gairy**. After finishing school and holding a clerical job in Grenada, he left for Aruba in the Dutch Antilles where he worked for an oil company and gained his first experience as a labour leader. On returning to Grenada in 1948 he soon emerged as a labour leader, organizing a strike in 1951 which culminated in a violent riot. He founded a trade union and the Grenada United Labour Party at that time. His methods, however, were not above reproach. In 1961, when he was both chief minister and finance minister, he was suspended by the British and accused of indulging in 'squandermania'. But he bounced back and led his country to independence in 1974, staying on as prime minister until 1979 when he was overthrown by Maurice Bishop, a radical lawyer and friend of Fidel Castro.[22] Bishop's reign was brief as he was in turn overthrown and murdered by the tiny army of Grenada. The USA then intervened in 1983, fearing the emergence of another Cuba. **Gairy** returned in 1984 but was defeated at the polls and could not return to power. 'Gairyism', as his style of politics was called in Grenada, had come to an end.

Dominica, another small island like Grenada, followed suit in 1978. It had been granted associated statehood in 1967. Only defence and external affairs remained under the control of the British government. However, it took 11 years before Dominica achieved complete independence under a republican constitution. It was led to independence by prime minister Patrick John, leader of the Dominica Labour Party. Prior to independence John had gained some notoriety as premier when he persecuted young members of the Rastafarian movement under the 'Dread Act' which made the wearing of dreadlocks a criminal offence. He obviously felt that these young people wanted to subvert his government. After independence John was soon accused of corruption. It was alleged that he had intended to sell one-eighth of the island to a US developer. He was forced to resign and was succeeded by the first female prime minister of the Caribbean, Eugenia Charles. John made two attempts to overthrow her government by coup, but he failed and was tried and imprisoned. Eugenia Charles was staunchly pro-USA and actually 'invited' President Reagan to intervene in Grenada in 1983. She continued in office until 1995.

St Lucia, which attained independence in 1979, also witnessed a fierce struggle for political leadership between the United Workers Party led by John **Compton** and the St Lucia Labour Party (SLP) led by Allan Louisy. **Compton** was a conservative somewhat like **Bustamante** of Jamaica. Louisy, who had served as a judge before entering politics, was also rather conservative, but he was in league with 'progressives' and espoused the cause of disgruntled civil servants who demanded higher salaries. An election held only a few months after independence led to a resounding defeat of the United Workers Party. Louisy became prime minister faced by **Compton** as a formidable leader of the opposition. Louisy's government befriended the revolutionary government of Maurice Bishop in Grenada. Due to a split in Louisy's party, he had to resign in 1981 and leave his post to a close associate, Winston Cenac, who was defeated in 1982 by **Compton** who then served a long second term until 1997.

St Vincent and the Grenadines had a very peculiar political history in the run-up to independence. Two prominent leaders, Milton Cato and James Mitchell, played a game of musical chairs. Cato was the premier from 1967 to 1972, then Mitchell, an independent, formed a coalition with the People's Political Party (PPP) and replaced Cato. This coalition collapsed in 1974 and Cato came back, leading a coalition of the PPP with his St Vincent Labour Party which remained in office until 1984. Cato thus led his country to independence in 1979. In 1984 Mitchell won the elections and headed the government until 2000.

Belize (British Honduras) was the next to achieve full independence in 1981 under the leadership of George **Price**. He was a clergyman who had joined politics as co-founder of the People's United Party (PUP). From 1958 to 1962 he was mayor of Belize City and while still holding this office he became first minister under a reformed colonial constitution in 1961. In 1964 he became premier and stayed on as prime minister of independent Belize until 1984. When the PUP lost the elections in that year, his long period of office seemed to have come to an end, but he returned to serve a second term from 1989 to 1993.

Together with Belize, Antigua also attained independence in 1981. It was led, of course, by Vere **Bird**, the charismatic labour leader, who has been mentioned earlier. He had founded the Antigua Trades and Labour Union in 1939. The Antigua Labour Party (ALP) became the political arm of the union and won all seats open to election in 1946. At that time it was still outnumbered by the nominated seats. The ALP did equally well in subsequent elections and in 1956 **Bird** became chief minister.[23] In 1967 he could further consolidate his position as premier of the associated state which had full internal autonomy. But whereas he had campaigned for democracy before, he now became an autocrat and victimized the opposition, the Progressive Labour Movement (PLM) led by his former associate George Walter. The PLM also had its own union, the Antigua Workers Union. The split in the political elite produced a two-party system. Both parties indulged in recriminations. **Bird** and his family were accused of corruption, but he was nevertheless able to hold on to power until he finally retired in 1994.

St Kitts and Nevis formed the rearguard of the Caribbean's march to independence. This group of two tiny islands had a special problem: Nevis wished to be separated from St Kitts. Some other Caribbean islands also had 'satellites', such as Trinidad and Tobago, Antigua and Barbuda, St Vincent and the Grenadines, but none of these satellites had ever raised such strong objections to the continued attachment to its larger partner as Nevis had done. Nevis is proud of its past; Alexander Hamilton, George Washington's finance minister was born here. Until 1882 Nevis had been a separate colony which was then attached to St Kitts for administrative convenience. Parties and movements on Nevis had again and again insisted on an independent identity. Therefore a clause had been inserted into the constitution of 1983 which provided that Nevis could secede at any time if it wished to do so. In spite of this, the Federation of St Kitts and Nevis has so far survived. This has been due mainly to the fact that the Nevis Reformation Party (NRP) has become the crucial coalition partner in the governments of St Kitts and Nevis since 1980. Prior to this, the Nevis secession movement had delayed the achievement of independence. The old Labour Party of St Kitts and Nevis had dominated politics since 1952. In 1967 its leader, Robert Bradshaw, had become premier of an autonomous state and retained this position until his death in 1978. His successor Paul Southwell then died in 1979. This left the field open for new talents. Dr Kennedy **Simmonds**, a co-founder of the People's Action Movement (PAM) in 1965, had several times stood for elections unsuccessfully but finally captured Bradshaw's seat in a by-election in 1979. In 1980 the PAM then won 3 seats, the NRF 2 and the Labour Party 4. **Simmonds** formed a coalition government with the NRF, led his country to independence and retained his post until 1995. He was probably one of the most highly qualified politicians of the Caribbean.

Not all countries of the region were equally well served by their leaders. Even though these leaders represented a wide spectrum of political ideologies, they often shared the same bad habits of autocratic behaviour and corrupt practices. There was everywhere a wide gap between the 'political directorate' and the masses. A weak bourgeoisie and a fragmented working class did not provide a stable support to state power.[24]

A DIEHARD EMPIRE: PORTUGAL IN ASIA AND AFRICA

THE FIRST AND THE LAST IMPERIALISTS

The Portuguese were the pioneers of European expansion. Prince Henry the Navigator trained a generation of competent seafarers in his nautical school at Sagres and also managed to raise funds for his maritime expeditions. As Administrator of the Order of Christ he organized a state within the Portuguese state which controlled the plantation economy of Madeira and other profitable enterprises. When he died in 1460 he left an invaluable heritage of practical knowledge and entrepreneurial skills. His royal relative, King Affonso, the 'African', amassed the gold of the west African coast and issued the *cruzado*, a gold coin, which was envied by all European monarchs. Although Portugal was dwarfed in size by its neighbours, it nevertheless emerged as a leading nation and set the pace for European imperialism.

The Portuguese kings not only established the *junta dos mathematicos*, which provided the Portuguese captains with detailed maps and tables, they also operated a worldwide intelligence service. The instructions that King Manuel gave to Albuquerque and other seafarers in his service were replete with very detailed information with regard to strategically important places which they should capture so as to control the entire Indian Ocean. When other European powers followed this lead, Portugal was soon left behind, because its capital and its human resources could not match those of the Spanish, the Dutch, the French and the British. Except for Brazil, Portugal did not initially acquire much overseas territory but rather established a far-flung network of fortified trading stations. It also spawned small coastal settlements of *casados* (married men) whose habits blended with those of the societies which hosted them. The influence of these *casados* survived the Portuguese seaborne empire when it lost its significance.[1] For a long time the Portuguese also benefited from the relationship with their oldest allies, the British.

Initially ports such as Goa in India, Malacca in Malaya or Macao in China were Portugal's most important possessions, all acquired in the early sixteenth century. These ports had very profitable relations with their respective hinterlands, but the Portuguese did not use them as bridgeheads for further expansion. The acquisition of large territories in Africa was left to a later phase of Portuguese imperialism, after the seaborne empire had already declined. Early contacts with some African colonies, however, enabled the Portuguese to participate in the **Scramble for**

Africa in a manner quite out of proportion to its actual position in the concert of European powers. It then happened that Portugal also managed to cling to its colonial possessions for much longer than other European powers. When Harold Macmillan proclaimed the 'wind of change' blowing through Africa, the Portuguese ignored it – and managed to get away with this for quite some time. This was due to a very peculiar political development in Portugal which was linked to the amazing career of Antonio de Oliveira Salazar (1889–1970).

Salazar first intended to become a Catholic clergyman but then changed his course of studies to economics at Coimbra University where he subsequently became a professor of economics with a specialization in public finance. After a series of incompetent and corrupt governments in the period after the First World War, a military coup of 1926 ushered in a long period of dictatorship. General Antonio Carmona who had seized power in 1926 was elected president of Portugal and remained in this office until 1951. He found a competent manager of the national economy in Salazar who first became finance minister in 1928 and then prime minister in 1932. Salazar continued in his post beyond Carmona's presidency and determined the fate of his 'Estado Novo' (New State). Being a fascist himself, Salazar was on good terms with the fascist dictators of his time, but he also managed to be on good terms with Portugal's old allies, the British, whom he permitted to maintain a military base on the Azores. He also extended this permission to the USA. In 1949 Portugal joined the North Atlantic Treaty Organization (NATO). Salazar obviously hoped that under this umbrella he could preserve the integrity of the Portuguese colonial empire. Actually the colonies were redefined as overseas provinces (*provincias ultramarinas*) in 1951; they were thus integral parts of the Estado Novo. Before Salazar's time, there had been relatively few Portuguese settlers in the African 'overseas provinces'. Salazar then actually urged the Portuguese to go there, but his propaganda met with limited success. Nevertheless, thousands of Portuguese went to Africa, probably glad to escape Salazar's austere and restrictive regime at home. Most of them were poor and uneducated but felt much superior to the black people. This increased social tensions enormously and anti-colonial movements gained added momentum. But 'decolonization' did not exist in Salazar's vocabulary; as long as he was in charge, no changes to Portuguese policies could be expected. Salazar was as adamant in his imperialism as Churchill had been, but whereas Great Britain was practically bankrupt at the end of the Second World War and could hardly afford to maintain an empire, Portugal had profited from the war without incurring much defence expenditure. Salazar could thus afford to stick to his reactionary policy.

Salazar suffered a stroke in 1968 and was succeeded by Marcello Caetano. Caetano was a liberal economist who seemed to reflect the new orientation of Portuguese capitalists who looked to Europe rather than to Africa. But he could not get out of the political straightjacket bequeathed to him by Salazar. He did try to make a new beginning, but could not get very far. Unlike Salazar, who had never been to Africa, Caetano visited the African 'overseas provinces' and tried to appease them by renaming them estados (states). In 1970, he commissioned

General Antonio de Spinola, governor general of Guinea-Bissau, to write a paper for him on the future of Africa.[2] Spinola's plans were similar to those of General de Gaulle in 1958. He envisioned a kind of Portuguese union with a high degree of autonomy for the African states belonging to it. Caetano sympathized with this approach, but in 1972 he clashed with Spinola which proved to be a point of no return. Spinola was haunted by the spectre of Goa and wanted to avoid a similar military defeat in Guinea-Bissau at the hands of a highly disciplined and effective guerrilla army. Actually such a defeat would have been worse than that of the Portuguese in Goa, because India was after all a very powerful adversary whereas in Guinea-Bissau the Portuguese armed forces outnumbered the indigenous guerrillas. To be defeated by them was a potential nightmare for Spinola who had so far been the most successful commander in Portugal's colonial wars. He had, therefore, approached **Senghor** who was willing to broker an agreement with the national movement of Guinea-Bissau. Caetano had vetoed this, arguing that he would prefer defeat in Guinea-Bissau to negotiations with 'terrorists' which would jeopardize Portugal's position in Angola and Mozambique.[3] Spinola was taken aback, because it was he who would have to face defeat in Guinea-Bissau. So far he had operated on the same wavelength as Caetano, but now this relationship broke down. When Caetano asked Spinola to serve as his colonial minister in 1973 the general turned down his offer.

While this rift at the highest level foreshadowed the course of future events, there was a groundswell of unrest among young Portuguese army officers which was initially unrelated to the rift. The colonial wars had made an enormous demand on Portuguese military manpower. Throughout the 12 years of conflict Portugal had constantly had about 70,000 Portuguese and 30,000 African troops in the field. This had forced the Portuguese defence minister not only to recruit more and more conscripts, but also to commission conscript officers who were not graduates of the Portuguese military academy. When he then decreed that these 'upstarts' would have the same career prospects as professional officers, he alienated the young officers who were proud products of that academy.[4] It was a typical case of 'relative deprivation', a term coined by Ted Gurr in his book *Why men rebel*.[5] As Gurr has argued, it is not the poor and underprivileged who tend to rebel, but the better off who face the threat of social decline. These young professional officers, most of whom had served in Africa, knew very well that the cause of their impending social decline was the colonial war. Their conviction that it must be stopped was not so much due to moral qualms, but to fears about their own future. The **Movimento das Forcas Armadas (MFA)** started by these young officers then converged with high-level dissensions on what to do about Africa.

The crunch came when Spinola published his book *Portugal e o Futura* (Portugal and the Future) in February 1974. He pleaded for an immediate end to the colonial wars which claimed 50 per cent of the budget and innumerable lives – and could not be won. The solution which he advocated was still of the 'federal' type which he had proposed earlier. In fact, there was nothing much new in the book. Caetano had read most of this in the paper which Spinola had written for him in 1970. He received an advance copy of the book before its publication.[6] The chief of the army staff, General Costa Gomes, had also read it and endorsed it. When reading his copy, Caetano may not have been very enthusiastic about its contents, but he did nothing to stop its publication. The book circulated with lightning speed. It was more the timing of its publication than the details of its contents which proved to be 'revolutionary'. It certainly precipitated the **MFA** coup. Caetano had asked Costa Gomes and Spinola to publicly demonstrate their loyalty to his regime. As they failed to do so, he sacked them. When he was cornered by the young officers, Caetano handed over power to Spinola. This general would not have been the officers' choice, but in the interest of a smooth transfer of power, they accepted him. Spinola was a gradualist as far as the process of decolonization was concerned, whereas the **MFA** officers were in a hurry to rid themselves of the colonial burden.

Spinola's provisional government did not last long. He did not really sympathize with the young officers and with the socialist and communist politicians who returned home from exile. He was a conservative rather than a revolutionary, whose intention had been to reform Caetano's regime, not to overthrow it. His plans for Africa were anachronistic, but the young officers had no idea how to deal with Africa either. It was left to Mario Soares as foreign minister of the 'revolutionary' government to deal with the leaders of the African national movements. It was they who really forced the pace of the Portuguese government. Finally, in July 1974, the so-called Constitutional Law 7/74 was promulgated which stated unequivocally that independence would be granted to the African colonies.[7] This implied Spinola's capitulation; his 'federal' ideas were crushed, but strangely enough he then experienced a sudden revival of his popularity. One could say that he had advanced from the position that de Gaulle had held in 1958 to that which de Gaulle adopted at the end of 1959 within a few months during 1974. However, Spinola was not really convinced about the new stance he had to adopt. By now he had outlived his usefulness and the decline of his authority proceeded very rapidly. In the final phase of his presidency he took erratic initiatives, among them a secret meeting with Mobutu on Sal Island, Cabo Verde, in mid-September 1974.[8] It seems that, like **Senghor** in 1972, he now wanted to use Mobutu as a mediator, but he probably also saw in him an ally against the leftists in Angola. A few days before his fall, his fertile brain gave birth to a chimera. He spoke of a federation of Angola, Brazil and Portugal – a Lusophone triangle spanning the Atlantic. He had obviously lost touch with reality.

Spinola had served his nation well by 'moderating' a revolutionary transition which was achieved almost without violence. But he had done this in spite of himself – and in the final period of his government this became increasingly obvious. He was succeeded by General Costa Gomes who then presided over a series of governments which drifted to the left. In July 1975 a Marxist government was brought down and replaced by a more moderate one. On November 25, 1975 there was another attempt at a coup by young leftist officers, but it did not succeed and thus marked the end of the Marxist trend of the Portuguese revolution. Moderate socialists now took over and in April 1976 Mario Soares formed the first 'post-revolutionary' government and successfully led Portugal to its admission as member of the European Economic Community in 1977. By that time the process of decolonization had been completed – with the exception of Macao.

Decolonization under a sequence of 'revolutionary' governments had been a somewhat chaotic affair, the more so as there were no 'leaders of government business' in Portuguese colonies who had been groomed for the 'transfer of power'. There were in addition very few black educated leaders in Portuguese Africa. Moreover, the two most highly educated among them, Professor Eduardo **Mondlane** of Mozambique and Dr Amilcar **Cabral** of Guinea-Bissau were both lost due to assassinations in 1969 and 1973 respectively. Under such conditions, the Portuguese decolonization was in some ways similar to the departure of the Belgians from the Congo 14 years earlier. As the subsequent reports on the fates of the individual colonies will show, the years of brutal repression followed by sudden decolonization resulted in civil wars, external intervention and general misery.

THE INDIAN LIBERATION OF GOA IN 1961

The first instance of Portuguese 'decolonization' was not the result of any desire to make a hasty departure. The Portuguese were simply defeated by the Indian army and their man on the spot was wise enough not to fight a hopeless battle against a regular army which far outnumbered his troops. Jawaharlal **Nehru** had hesitated for a long time to use force against the Portuguese. He had rather opted for a state of economic siege which would compel them to negotiate a withdrawal. Unfortunately for **Nehru**, the Portuguese found rich manganese ore deposits in Goa which could be exported at an enormous profit, particularly to Germany and Japan. Therefore they could afford to import food for the people of Goa from distant Africa and forget about the Indian 'siege'. Moreover, the importation of all kinds of luxury goods for which there was great demand in India gave rise to a great deal of smuggling. The anti-colonial movement in Goa was subjected to brutal repression. The Portuguese recruited many policemen and paid them well. In this way they were able to maintain their rule and Salazar did not need to budge an inch. Finally it was not **Nehru** himself, but his more radical friend Krishna Menon, the defence minister, who planned the liberation of Goa by the Indian army.

The year 1961 was a time of dramatic events in Portugal. In February a revolt broke out in Luanda, Angola, which precipitated a debate in the **UN** Security Council. President Kennedy's government seemed to be interested in a regime change in Portugal. The USA found a receptive partner in the Portuguese defence minister and chief of the army, Botelho Moniz, who staged a coup against Salazar in April. One of his chief supporters was Colonel Francisco da Costa Gomes who later on became president of Portugal in 1975. The coup, however, was aborted and Salazar emerged victorious from this challenge. He had an inkling about what was brewing in Goa and warned the **UN** Security Council in September 1961 about India's intentions. He also appealed to Portugal's old allies, the British, who told him that they would not support him against India, a member of the Commonwealth. In September 1961, the non-aligned nations met at the **Belgrade Conference**. After this conference, Kenneth **Kaunda**, the future president of Zambia, visited India and gave a speech which must have affected **Nehru** very much. **Kaunda** appealed to him to free Goa and thus send a signal for African nationalists, rather than waiting for them to throw the Portuguese out and then obtain Goa for India without firing a shot. **Nehru**, who took pride in his credentials as a leader of the Third World, could not ignore this plea. Nevertheless he still seemed to be slow in taking a decision. When he visited President Kennedy in November 1961 he did not say a word about Goa. Kennedy was annoyed when **Nehru** acted one month later without having given him any warning.[9]

For the Indians the liberation of Goa was a risky gamble. After all, the Portuguese had a full-scale NATO arsenal at their disposal in Goa and it was not a foregone conclusion that the NATO allies would not help them when faced with an attack. Similarly, Pakistan could have intervened and military precautions had to be taken for that eventuality. With the benefit of hindsight one can say that it was a walkover with hardly a shot fired and only a few bridges blown up by the Portuguese just to show that they were doing something. Salazar, of course, took it as a humiliating defeat. Moreover, it demonstrated to him that he could not expect any help in defending Portugal's 'overseas provinces'. Vindictively, he did not release the Goan nationalists, whom he had transferred to prisons in Portugal, for many years, although India had repatriated all Portuguese prisoners of war within a short time.

The blow dealt by India to Portuguese colonialism was somewhat of an embarrassment for China. It should have liberated Macao just as India had done with Goa. It also claimed to support African liberation movements and should have set a good example for them. But Macao, just like Hong Kong, provided China with a window to the outside world which was very useful when an embargo by the Western powers deprived China of the access to important materials which could not be sent to its ports. As described below, China even refused the Portuguese offer of returning Macao in 1974. Its own interests were more important to China than its reputation among African nationalists.

Another Asian leader who was embarrassed by the liberation of Goa was **Sukarno** who had so far not been able to wrest Irian Jaya (West Irian) from the Dutch. **Sukarno** had always envied **Nehru** whose success in Goa was a bitter pill for him to swallow. Moreover, he could not hope to do anything about Irian Jaya in the near future. Goa was on Indian territory, but taking Irian Jaya would require a major naval operation. When a journalist asked **Sukarno** what he was going to do about it, he gave the scurrilous reply that he had already appointed a governor of Irian Jaya and the man was on the spot, but for security reasons his whereabouts could not be revealed.

The most lasting effect of the liberation of Goa was on the Portuguese military leadership. From now on they were haunted by the spectre of Goa, a premonition of inevitable defeat. As mentioned earlier, General Spinola was deeply influenced by this thought. The course of events which led to the Portuguese revolution of 1974 started in Goa in 1961, but in a more immediate way it started in Guinea-Bissau in 1963 when the nationalists led by Amilcar **Cabral** managed to liberate large parts of this colony.

THE REVOLUTION IN GUINEA-BISSAU

Dr Amilcar **Cabral** was the most brilliant revolutionary leader of Portuguese Africa. He was a good military strategist but also an accomplished diplomat.[10] **Cabral** was an agronomist who had studied in Lisbon and had then served in the colonial government of Guinea-Bissau from 1952 to 1954. His work among the peasants permitted him to get an insight into their problems and to establish contacts in the villages which helped him when he became a guerrilla leader. In 1956 he founded with a few comrades the **Partido Africano para a Independencia da Guinea e Cabo Verde (PAIGC)**.[11] As the name of the party indicates it also aimed at freeing Cabo Verde, another Portuguese colony. The Cabo Verde islands are located about 650 km to the west of the African coast. They have a Creole population with little affinity with Africa. **Cabral**'s parents were from Cabo Verde, but he had been born in Guinea-Bissau. It was only natural for him that he should fight for the independence of both colonies, but his 'battlefield' was Guinea-Bissau.

PAIGC was initially a secret organization which was not in the political limelight. It 'surfaced' at the time of a dock strike in 1959 which it helped to organize. It was then forced to operate from abroad and took refuge in neighbouring Guinea where Sekou **Touré** supported it. From there, **Cabral** launched a very successful guerrilla offensive in January 1963. He kept strict discipline among his men and told them that they were 'militants' not 'militarists'.[12] Armed action had to be subordinated to the political aims which were defined by **Cabral**. By 1964 his 'militants' had liberated large parts of Guinea-Bissau and the Portuguese brigadier in charge of the colonial troops there reported to Lisbon that the war was lost. **Cabral**'s success was due to his superior leadership, his close contacts with the rural population and the backing of Sekou **Touré** whose ideas were very similar to his. But **Cabral**'s quick progress in liberating large tracts of Guinea-Bissau was also facilitated by the weakness of the Portuguese administration in this poor colony which had never attracted much attention in Lisbon.

In the late 1960s, **Cabral** received essential military aid from Cuba. He had met Che Guevara in Conakry in January 1965 and had then visited Cuba in January 1966.[13] Castro admired him and took him on a trip to the mountains. It seems he walked with him down memory lane, following the tracks of his own revolutionary warfare. **Cabral** asked him for military experts who could train his men, particularly in handling the artillery. He wished to keep the Cuban presence a secret and asked for black Cubans whose identity could be concealed. Castro selected Victor Dreke, a very able black *commandante* who had been with him in the Sierra Madre.[14] Dreke had also accompanied Che Guevara to the Congo in 1965 where a small Cuban detachment helped the rebels led by Laurent Kabila in their fight against **Tshombe**. This had been a frustrating affair, but Dreke had impressed Guevara in those days and he had praised him a great deal.[15] Dreke arrived in Africa once more in January 1967 and became **Cabral**'s trusted adviser. The Cubans respected **Cabral**'s wish and did not mention their help either at that time or in later years. In addition to military men Cuba also sent medical doctors to Guinea-Bissau. This was the only help which **Cabral** openly acknowledged.

The Portuguese government was alarmed by **Cabral**'s successful campaigns. Hence in 1968 Brigadier de Spinola was sent to Guinea-Bissau as governor general and military commander and he stayed there until 1973. He was surrounded by young officers who later became leading members of the **MFA**. Spinola's approach to the colonial question was different from that of his predecessors. He developed his 'federal' ideas for an equal partnership of Portugal with its colonies while he was on duty in Guinea-Bissau. He also sponsored quasi-democratic institutions which he called 'People's Congress'. However, he was not averse to rash military actions, launching a clandestine commando operation ('Operation Green Sea') to capture **Cabral**'s headquarters in neighbouring Guinea in December 1970. The commandos were supposed to assassinate Sekou **Touré** and **Cabral**. The operation was a complete failure and as it could no longer be kept a secret, it proved to be a diplomatic disaster for Portugal.

While Spinola had earlier been successful in colonial warfare, his tenure in Guinea-Bissau was not to be a feather in his cap. The **PAIGC** guerrillas made increasing advances. Even the assassination of **Cabral** in Conakry in January 1973 did not stop them. They had been so well organized by him that they continued the fight as if he were still leading them. In March 1973 the **PAIGC** guerrillas started using Soviet ground-to-air missiles and eliminated Portuguese air power. Since the Portuguese controlled hardly any of the land any longer, their airforce had been the only weapon left to them. Soon they controlled only the capital, Bissau, whereas the **PAICG** ruled in the countryside. Spinola did not witness his final defeat; he left Guinea-Bissau in August 1973. In September the **PAIGC** proclaimed the independence of Guinea-Bissau. The state was then recognized by 80 nations within a very short time. After the Portuguese revolution in April 1974 the **MFA** officers in Guinea-Bissau arrested the Portuguese governor and sent him back to Lisbon. Spinola then dispatched Brigadier Carlos Fabiao who was known as his 'right arm' to Bissau. Fabiao soon disappointed him, as he was a realist and could see that there was no chance of rescuing this colony for Spinola's federal scheme. Fabiao worked with the **MFA** officers and the leaders of **PAIGC** in the interest of a peaceful 'transfer of power'. The **PAIGC** had applied to the **UN** for admission and the Portuguese had to expect a heated debate in the General Assembly which would show the Portuguese 'revolutionary' government in a very bad light. Hurried talks were held in Algiers and on September 1974, one year after its 'unilateral declaration' of independence, Guinea-Bissau was granted its independence by the Portuguese government. Amilcar **Cabral**'s half-brother, Luis Cabral was its first president. The attainment of independence by Guinea-Bissau was not without its dark side. Many of those who had collaborated with the Portuguese were massacred just like the *harkis* of Algeria.

There was some unfinished business as far as Cabo Verde was concerned. Spinola wanted to hang on to those islands which he compared to Madeira and the Azores. He also hinted at their value for the defence of the Western powers in the Atlantic. But **PAIGC** had insisted that Cabo Verde should attain independence as soon as possible although the issue was not to be joined with the independence of Guinea-Bissau. After the fall of Spinola in September 1974 some interim arrangements were made and on July 5, 1975, Cabo Verde became independent with a **PAIGC** government led by Aristides Pereira as president and Pedro Pires as prime minister.

SAO TOMÉ AND PRINCIPE

Just like Cabo Verde, Sao Tomé and Principe was an island colony at a considerable distance from the African mainland. The Portuguese had founded the town of Sao Tomé in 1485 after they had reached the Gulf of Guinea in their quest for a passage to India around Africa. Initially they established sugar plantations on the two islands and imported slaves from the mainland. A slave revolt in 1530 frightened the Portuguese plantation owners. Moreover, sugar cultivation was no longer as profitable as it used to be. In later times coffee and cocoa gave the islands a new chance as plantation colonies. After slavery was abolished in 1875, the Portuguese plantation owners operated a cruel system of forced labour. In 1953 there was a revolt of plantation labourers which was brutally suppressed by Portuguese troops. About 1,000 labourers are supposed to have been shot at that time. A freedom movement had no chance under such conditions. After the Portuguese revolution of 1974, black troops mutinied in Sao Tomé. The Portuguese fled and left the islands stranded without capital and skilled manpower. A transitional government was formed in December 1974 and in July 1975 Sao Tomé and Principe attained independence. With about 100,000 inhabitants this was the smallest state of Africa. President Manuel Pinto da Costa initially tried to steer a moderate course, but he then increasingly depended on Angola and its communist allies. Opposition leaders had taken refuge in nearby Gabon and there were fears that they planned an invasion so as to change the regime on the islands. Although Angola sent troops in 1978 to guard against an invasion, nothing happened and Sao Tomé and Principe continued as a kind of ward of Angola until the collapse of the Soviet Union provided new options to its government.

ANGOLA AND MOZAMBIQUE: A STUDY IN CONTRAST

The freedom struggle of the two major Portuguese colonies in Africa progressed almost on parallel lines, but whereas in Mozambique the **Frente da Libertacao de Mocambique (FRELIMO)** was not challenged by important rival movements, Angola became a hotbed of rivalries which finally led to a bloody civil war. Paradoxically the rather quiet evolution of **FRELIMO** was due to the towering personality of an absent president, Eduardo **Mondlane**.[16] After a career as a professor in the USA, he had joined the **UN** Trusteeship Council as a permanent official. Having been elected as president of **FRELIMO** in Dar-es-Salaam in 1962, he returned to his post at the **UN**. His was a name to conjure with, but as he worked at a distance he did not get involved in petty intrigues. At the same time nobody would dare to challenge him. When Samora **Machel** emerged as the efficient field commander of the freedom fighters in 1966, he had **Mondlane**'s backing and could make a mark in his own way. When **Mondlane** was assassinated in Dar-es-Salaam in 1969, **Machel** succeeded him. Compared to the learned **Mondlane** with his international credentials, **Machel**, who had worked as a male nurse, had a very humble background, but he was an intelligent and highly successful guerrilla fighter. Having established his credentials when **Mondlane** was still alive, he could easily carry on after the death of the revered leader. **FRELIMO** was rather ineffective before 1970 and it owed much to **Nyerere** who supported it throughout. He probably also saw to it that **Machel** was not challenged by rivals.

In contrast, Angola was a veritable hornet's nest characterized by ethnic rivalries enhanced by the personalities of leaders who not only belonged to different ethnic groups but also represented conflicting ideologies and relied on alliances with foreign powers which in turn pursued their own interests when supporting them. Initially, Holden **Roberto** was the most powerful freedom fighter. He belonged to the Bakongo who straddle the border between Angola and the Congo. His wife being a sister-in-law of Mobutu, he had strong support from that side.[17] Moreover, he was a member of the Bakongo nobility and this strengthened his ethnic support base. His first political organization was aimed at his regional clientele, but finally he founded the **Frente Nacional para a Libertacao de Angola (FNLA)** in 1962. He had attended the **All-African People's Conference** in Accra in 1958 and this had converted him from 'tribalism' to a quest for African national solidarity. In fact, he adopted this larger vision perhaps also because, in purely ethnic terms, he had a major handicap. The Bakongo make up only about 15 per cent of the population of Angola. They are outnumbered by their southern neighbours, the Mbundu, who comprise 25 per cent and the Ovimbundu who are Angola's largest ethnic group at about 37 per cent.

The Mbundu live in the centre of Angola as well as on the coast, including the capital, Luanda. The capital also harboured a considerable urban intelligentsia. Dr Agostinho **Neto**, a Mbundu urban intellectual, was a natural leader of these people. As a Marxist, however, he looked beyond ethnic affiliations and saw the Angolan freedom movement in the wider perspective of African emancipation. He had studied in Lisbon, his wife was Portuguese and he had gained some fame as a Portuguese poet. He knew Mario Soares from his student days when they were both engaged in anti-Salazar activities. Back in Luanda he practised as a medical doctor but was arrested in 1960 and put in prison in Lisbon. He made a daring escape and then joined the headquarters of the **Movimento Popular para a Libertacao Angola (MPLA)** in Kinshasa, Congo, in 1962. The **MPLA** claimed to have been founded in 1956 and to have organized an attack on the central prison of Luanda in 1961. These claims were obviously made at a later stage for propaganda reasons. The revolt in Luanda of 1961 was the only action by urban guerrillas in Africa. It could be used to establish the fame of the **MPLA**, but the revolt was also a setback because, after its brutal repression, the **MPLA** could only work in exile. Its leadership was in disarray, but when **Neto** joined it, he got himself elected president of the **MPLA** in 1962 and from then on he guided its actions.[18]

In the meantime another colourful figure had appeared on the scene: Jonas **Savimbi**. He was an Ovimbundu and thus had potentially the largest political base in Angola. Having studied in Portugal and Switzerland, he first joined **Roberto** and became secretary general of the Union of the Peoples of Angola, **Roberto**'s first political organization which was then transformed into the **FNLA** in 1962. **Roberto** also established an Angolan government in exile and **Savimbi** became its foreign minister and met many African leaders. In 1964 he resigned from that government and parted company with **Roberto**.[19] He claimed to be a Maoist and spent some time in China learning the methods of Mao's warfare. At that time he also tried to establish contact with the **MPLA**. Finally he founded a movement of his own in 1966, the **Uniao Nacional para a Independencia Total de Angola (UNITA)**. At this time **Roberto** still led the largest number of guerrillas who killed **MPLA** guerrillas whenever they encountered them. **Savimbi**'s followers were a small group to begin with. He was both a charismatic leader and a clever opportunist. Thus he managed to attract both men and money and became more powerful as the years went by. From 1972 to 1974 he actually collaborated with the Portuguese only to emerge once more as a freedom fighter when he felt that this would be to his advantage.

Until the Portuguese revolution of April 1974, the rival movements could not do much in Angola. There then followed frantic activities which were influenced by the twists and turns of Spinola's *junta* of senior officers and of the young officers of the **MFA** who monitored the initiatives taken by the *junta*. Civilians like Mario Soares, who had become the new foreign minister of Portugal, had great difficulties in steering a course of their own. Spinola at first dispatched a new governor general to Angola who had some time earlier held this post under Salazar. The **MFA** officers in Angola clashed with him and demanded his recall in July 1974. At this stage Spinola took a very surprising decision. He sent to Angola Admiral Antonio Rosa Coutinho who was going to hold both the top civilian and the top military positions.[20] Rosa Coutinho was a member of Spinola's *junta*, but he was a Marxist and was himself surprised at his new appointment. This was, of course, a boon to the **MPLA**. Rosa Coutinho could have done for **Neto** what Governor Arden-Clark had done for **Nkrumah** or Governor Turnbull for **Nyerere** if there had been some kind of constitutional infrastructure in place in Angola at that time. He did try his best to help **Neto**, but this only incensed **Neto**'s rivals. When Spinola had his secret meeting with Mobutu on Sal Island, Cabo Verde, he did not inform Rosa Coutinho who then clashed with Spinola when he met him in Lisbon. He must have been relieved when Spinola fell soon after. However, the immediate consequence of Spinola's fall was a wave of unrest among the Portuguese settlers in Angola, of whom there were still about 300,000. To them Spinola's presidency had appeared to be a guarantee of their safety. Now the extreme elements among them wanted to stage a violent coup which Rosa Coutinho managed to put down. The **MPLA** was riven by factions, but finally **Neto** was victorious. He continued to be supported by Rosa Coutinho who became the high commissioner for Angola, a change which indicated progress towards independence. Rosa Coutinho's final work in Angola was to broker an agreement between the three rival movements so that they would aim at forming a national coalition government. The decisive conference was held at Alvor, Portugal, in January 1975.[21] Rosa Coutinho was not a member of the Portuguese delegation; **Roberto** and **Savimbi** felt that he was too committed to the **MPLA** and had urged the Portuguese government to remove him from his post.

The leader of the Portuguese delegation was Ernesto Melo Antunes, the chief planner of Portuguese decolonization policy. A major of the artillery in 1974, he had been the leading intellectual light of the **MFA** and had drafted its programme which was summarized as 'democratize, decolonize, develop'. He had grown up as the son of a military officer in Angola and had a deep affection for that country. He was close to Mario Soares and the socialists but critical of the **MFA** left-wingers. The Alvora conference was of great importance to him. He was glad that he could set a timetable for Angola's independence and arrange for an interim government composed of three 'rotating' presidents, **Neto**, **Roberto** and **Savimbi**. He later on remarked that he should also have insisted on the merger of the three guerrilla armies into one national army so as to prevent a civil war. In fact, this civil war started almost immediately after the three leaders had returned from Alvora. In the 'hot summer' of 1975 when Portugal was also close to civil war, Melo Antunes succeeded Soares as foreign minister and made air dashes to Angola without being able to salvage the situation there. He was more successful at home where he drafted the 'Document of the Nine', an open letter to President Costa Gomes warning him against the drift of Portuguese politics to the radical left. This drift was stopped when Portugal was at the edge of an abyss.

With Portugal being incapacitated by internal troubles, President **Kenyatta** of Kenya tried to stop the civil war in Angola by inviting the rival leaders to Nakuru in Kenya.[22] The Portuguese were not invited, but the meeting proved to be futile. The 'battle of Luanda' started on July 9, 1975, and ended with the **MPLA** driving the **FNLA** out of the capital. As the date of independence, fixed for November 11, 1975, drew nearer, the struggle for power became more intense. **Roberto** and **Savimbi** conspired with the Union of South Africa which actually sent troops to Angola in order to capture Luanda before November 11.[23] The South African initiative was backed by the USA. It caused a great deal of dissent among the officers of the US administration, some of whom doubted the wisdom of this covert operation. But Henry Kissinger, who felt that the USA had lost its prestige in the Vietnam War, was bent on saving Angola from a Marxist regime. He did not even think of Cuba in this context, but it soon turned out that Castro was destined to save the **MPLA** regime, forcing a reluctant Soviet Union to support his initiative.

In August 1975 **Neto** had asked Castro for help. At the same time Rosa Coutinho visited Havanna and talked to Castro at length. Rosa Coutinho was no longer in charge of Angola, he was now the head of the Portuguese navy, but still took an interest in Angola. While he was in command he could use the Portuguese troops to control unrest in Angola, but he knew that now they would not help **Neto** in the civil war. Castro informed Brezhnev about his intentions to send troops to Angola, but since Brezhnev did not respond, he did not act.[24] In August the **MPLA** still seemed to be victorious so there seemed to be no urgency. The South African invasion of Angola in October 1975 changed this situation dramatically. The South African troops advanced very swiftly. At that time there were only a few Cuban military advisers in Angola. When some of them were killed by the advancing South Africans, Castro took a quick decision without contacting the Soviet Union. He dispatched Cuban troops in old Cuban planes.[25] Some of them arrived just in time to help the **MPLA** to defend Luanda at the 'Battle of Death Road' at Quifangondo a few kilometres to the north of the capital. **Roberto** was impatient to capture Luanda and disregarded the advice of the South African military. He ordered an offensive and his soldiers were mowed down by the 'Stalin Organs' handled by the Cubans.[26] Winning this battle did not yet mean that the war against the South Africans was won. They could no longer prevent the transfer of power to **Neto** on November 11, but soon thereafter they attacked Luanda from the south on November 23 where another battle was fought at Ebo. In this battle the Cubans happened to be alone in fighting the South Africans. They won the battle which proved to be a turning point of the war.[27] Convinced by the success of the Cubans, the Soviet Union now supported them by airlifting more Cuban troops in Soviet planes. Until then the Cubans had had to rely on their old planes which could cross the Atlantic only with great difficulties. It was an irony of fate that in the west the Cubans were depicted as Soviet mercenaries whereas they had taken the initiative and forced the hand of the Soviet government. Castro respected Angolan national pride and did not boast about the Cuban victory. But on March 15, 1976, he met **Neto**, Sekou **Touré** and Luis Cabral in Conakry and issued a warning to the South Africans, hinting at an African war of liberation against them if they did not leave Angola immediately.[28] On March 27 the last South African troops left Angola.

In the meantime more Cuban troops arrived in Angola, until about 20,000 of them were stationed there. They valiantly defended Angola against both the South Africans and the rebel government of **Roberto** and **Savimbi**. It may sound cynical, but one could say that **Roberto**'s bravado and the brazen intervention of South Africa actually proved to be a blessing in disguise for the **MPLA**. With the military help of the Cubans and the income from oil revenues, the **MPLA** could shore up its fragile regime and sustain its Stalinist state which would otherwise have collapsed. The Cubans also saved **Neto**'s government when it was almost overthrown in a coup led by a former guerrilla commander, Nito Alves, in 1977.[29] During the next two decades some Cuban troops remained stationed in Angola and the South Africans tried repeatedly to invade Angola. As has been mentioned in the context of the independence of Namibia, an agreement was reached only in 1988 which provided for the simultaneous withdrawal of Cuban and South African troops.

Neto did not live to see the end of the civil war; he died in a hospital in Moscow in 1979. He was succeeded by José Eduardo dos Santos, a Russian-trained engineer. **Savimbi** remained an Ovimbundu warlord. In 1992 he agreed to participate in a presidential election, but when he narrowly lost it, he returned to the warpath. Controlling diamond mines in the heart of the Ovimbundu territory, he was not short of funds. In 2002 he was killed by government troops. **Roberto**, who had been on the payroll of the CIA, had outlived his usefulness and occasionally published peace proposals of an 'old man'.

Mozambique had achieved its independence before Angola on June 25, 1975. **FRELIMO** was the only party the Portuguese had to deal with. There were no serious rivals and no civil war. Nor was there ever any Cuban aid for **FRELIMO**. **Mondlane** and Che Guevara had clashed when they met in Dar-es-Salaam in 1965 and this had probably settled the matter once and for all.[30]

The profile of Mozambique is very different from that of Angola. It extends for more than 2,000 km along the southeast coast of Africa and its capital, Maputo, is at the extreme south of this coastline. There are a great number of ethnic groups, none of which outweighs the others in terms of population and political power. **FRELIMO** was able to recruit members of various groups. However, its main support came from the extreme south and the extreme north. The people of the central part of Mozambique did not yet emerge into the political limelight. They did so with a vengeance, however, when they later supported **RENAMO**. **FRELIMO**'s successes in guerrilla warfare were considerable in the days of the freedom struggle. The Portuguese revolution of 1974 then helped **FRELIMO** in a decisive way. The chief military leader of the **MFA**, Major Otelo Saraiva de Carvalho was born and brought up in Mozambique and took a personal interest in its decolonization. At the beginning of June 1974 he accompanied Soares to a meeting with **Machel** in Lusaka.[31] Soares made a friendly gesture when he met Machel; he embraced him cordially. He wanted to show that he sympathized with him, but this cordiality was also meant to compensate **Machel** for the terms of reference which Spinola had imposed on Soares. Carvalho wanted to make more concessions and stated this quite undiplomatically, embarrassing Soares in this process. This showed in a striking manner how politics worked in Portugal at that time. **Machel** must have taken note of this and realized that he had to bide his time. But at least it assured him that the Portuguese government was moving in the right direction. Further progress was made after the promulgation of Constitutional Law 7/74. Now Melo Antunes took charge of decolonizing Mozambique. He had joined the government as minister without portfolio and as he was also an **MFA** leader he could act much more confidently. He attended a meeting with **FRELIMO** in Dar-es-Salaam at the end of July 1974. This was a real breakthrough as he accepted the terms of **FRELIMO**. In a subsequent meeting at the same place only two weeks later he could finalize the details. There would be a transitional government under a Portuguese high commissioner. It was soon agreed that this would be Victor Crespo, a distinguished naval officer and prominent **MFA** leader, who had taken a great deal of interest in secret talks with **FRELIMO** leaders in Lisbon.[32] Serving under him, there would be an interim **FRELIMO** prime minister, Joaquin Chissano, a very able man and close associate of **Machel**. It is amazing that all this was achieved while Spinola was still in power, a tribute indeed to the great political skill of Melo Antunes.

The white settlers were taken aback by this quick agreement. They had trusted that they would be safe as long as Spinola was in power. There were still about 250,000 settlers in Mozambique at that time. Some of them staged a rebellion along the lines of the white settlers of Algeria, although this example should have shown them that they would not achieve their aims in this way. And just as in Algeria, there was soon an exodus of white settlers to the extent that Mozambique was then left without any skilled manpower. The colonial government had not given the black population any opportunities to get technical training.

Samora **Machel** became Mozambique's first president. The Portuguese prime minister, Vasco Gonsalves, attended the celebrations, accompanied by Otelo Saraiva de Carvalho.[33] In striking contrast with this transfer of power in Mozambique, the same procedure in Angola only about five months later was concluded with undignified haste. There were no prominent guests from Lisbon and the Portuguese high commissioner rushed to the frigate which was waiting for him in the port of Luanda after proclaiming Angola's independence. However, the dignified ceremony in Mozambique only disguised for a short time the financial problems which plagued its relations with Portugal. And then, only a few years later, the ravages of civil war hit the country which had been spared such a war before independence. **FRELIMO** in government was soon caught in a trap of its own making. **Machel** and his followers were radical secular nationalists who tried to recreate the society of Mozambique so as to correspond to their ideology. **Machel** proudly announced: 'We have killed the tribe to give birth to the nation'.[34] But this was wishful thinking. The tribes were still alive and kicking and dominated large parts of the countryside. Party control of vast rural provinces was more difficult to achieve than conducting guerrilla warfare in selected areas. In addition, **FRELIMO** boldly challenged its neighbours, South Africa and

Rhodesia, by harbouring the freedom fighters of the African National Congress and the **Zimbabwe African National Union (ZANU)**. In doing this, **FRELIMO** followed the same course as **Nyerere** had done when he had harboured its freedom fighters in Tanganyika for many years. But **Nyerere** did not have to fear fierce neighbours nor would the Portuguese have been able to attack him. **Machel** was in a much more vulnerable position in this respect.

Unlike the civil war in Angola, the war in Mozambique which began in 1982 was intially not conducted by rival leaders within the country, but by an organization called **RENAMO (Resistencia Nacional Mocambicana)** which was sponsored by the secret services of the Union of South Africa and of Southern Rhodesia. About a million people are supposed to have died in this war. In the beginning **RENAMO** had no particular aim; it was only told to destroy and kill. In due course, however, it acquired a territorial base in the central provinces of Mozambique. Its leader, Afonso Dhlakama, was born as the son of a Ndau chief.[35] The Ndau are an ethnic group living in the central part of Mozambique and are related to the Shona of Zimbabwe. Dhlakama proved to be an astute political entrepreneur. As long as he was financed from abroad, he behaved like a brutal warlord, but when his resources dwindled to insignificance and **FRELIMO** was also at the end of its tether, he converted **RENAMO** into a political party and pursued the 'parliamentary path'.[36] In this he was quite successful due to his political stronghold in the central provinces. He did not capture power in this way, but became the leader of the opposition and kept the peace, unlike **Savimbi** in Angola who fought until the bitter end. Samora **Machel** did not live to see this happen, having lost his life in a plane crash on South African territory in 1986.[37] There is circumstantial evidence that this was not merely an accident but that the plane was deliberately misdirected. **Machel** was succeeded as president by Joaquin Chissano who retained this office until 2004, defeating Dhlakama at the polls rather than on the battlefield.

THE REARGUARD: MACAO, 1999

The Portuguese colony of Macao near Hong Kong was one of the oldest footholds of Portugal in Asia. Portuguese seafarers had visited Macao frequently after 1513, but a permanent trading post was not established until 1557. The Portuguese remained there on Chinese sufferance. The Chinese authorities continued collecting taxes in Macao. The British victory over China in the Opium War had an ambivalent impact on Macao. On the one hand, Macao's importance declined due to the rise of Hong Kong, on the other hand the Portuguese were emboldened by the British imposition of 'unequal treaties' on China. In 1845 the Portuguese made Macao a 'free port' without consulting the Chinese authorities. The Chinese stopped collecting taxes in Macao and practically surrendered their sovereignty. In 1888 a treaty was drafted which gave the Portuguese the right to permanently reside in and administer Macao, but the treaty was never ratified by China. Actually the Portuguese remained in Macao on Chinese sufferance throughout, but this did not matter to them as long as China no longer exercised its sovereign rights in Macao.

When Mao seized power in China, he refrained from throwing the Portuguese out, because Macao provided him with a useful channel of trade. In 1966 Chinese workers rioted in Macao under the influence of the Cultural Revolution. Even Salazar's government was prepared to yield Macao to China at that time, because it wanted to avoid another Goa. But the Chinese government did not wish to take Macao back. The same Portuguese offer was repeated after the revolution of 1974 and again the Chinese asked the Portuguese to stay on. In 1979 diplomatic relations were established between Portugal and China and in 1987 a Joint Declaration was signed which stipulated that Macao would revert to China at midnight on December 19, 1999. Hong Kong provided a precedent for the 'one country, two systems' formula which was then also applied to Macao. Macao was similarly assured of a period of 50 years of economic autonomy.

Unlike the thriving economy of Hong Kong, Macao's economy was rather trifling. The leading sector of this economy was the gambling industry. The casinos of Macao attracted many visitors from Hong Kong and contributed about half of Macao's gross domestic product. It was a sad comment on the end of the Portuguese empire, that in its final stage the Portuguese had to act as protectors of gambling and prostitution. At least this was a more peaceful activity than the violent overseas expansion which characterized the early years of that empire.

THE PACIFIC ISLANDS: SMALL NATIONS AT SEA

The Pacific Ocean harbours innumerable islands, most of them settled by Polynesian seafarers who hopped from island to island using their unique outrigger boats. European colonial powers staked their claims on many islands and some of them changed hands several times. The British and the French finally controlled most of them and they still hold on to some island colonies. When the high tide of imperialism swept around the world, the Germans also claimed a share of these islands, which were then turned over to the Japanese under the mandate of the **League of Nations** after the First World War. The Japanese and the USA waged fierce battles over many strategically important islands during the Second World War. As discussed in the context of the development of **trusteeship** after that war, the USA saw to it that they kept many of these islands under control by special arrangement of a **UN** Trust Territory of the Pacific. When the need for keeping bases in the Pacific receded, some of these islands were granted independence, while others stopped short of independence. The Northern Marina Islands, for example, adopted a constitution in 1978 and then entered into a covenant with the USA in 1986 as Commonwealth of the Northern Marina Islands in political union with the USA. This status is slightly different from that of the neighbouring island of Guam, which has been a US colony since 1898 and has remained an unincorporated territory of the USA. After vanquishing the Japanese, the USA also took over a second line of islands which are now formally independent but are tied to the USA by special treaties. These new states will be discussed first, before we turn to the others which have a very different history of decolonization. Fiji, which has a peculiar history of its own, has already been discussed in the context of the sugar colonies and the role of Indian labour.

PALAU, MICRONESIA AND THE MARSHALL ISLANDS

Palau, a small island to the west of the Federated States of Micronesia, was originally supposed to join that federation but decided that it would rather remain separate. It had been a German colony from 1899 and then a Japanese mandate territory. The Japanese converted it into a fortress and it thus became a scene of fierce fighting during the Second World War. When the USA planned to grant independence to Micronesia, they thought that Palau would be a natural part of it. The people of Palau, however, voted against this in 1978; they were then blessed with their own constitution in 1980, but independence had to wait until a Compact of Free Association with the USA was ratified in 1993.[1] The USA retained about one-third of Palau as a base under this treaty and paid for this by means of a grant of 450 million US dollars to be disbursed over a period of 15 years.

The Federated States of Micronesia achieved their independence before Palau. These islands had also been German colonies since 1898; they had become Japanese mandate territories after the First World War and had been attached to the UN Trust Territory of the Pacific Islands after the Second World War. They adopted a constitution in 1979 and in 1986 they concluded a Compact of Free Association with the USA and became independent. But this independence is only a political formality. In economic terms Micronesia is overdependent on US aid which has amounted to 1.3 billion US dollars for the period from 1986 to 2001.[2] If one considers that the total population of Micronesia amounts to about 100,000, US aid per capita/per annum is about 866 US dollars. About the same rate also applies to the Marshall Islands, Micronesia's neighbours to the east.

The Marshall Islands consist of 30 atolls and 1,125 islands. Two of the atolls, Bikini and Enewetak, have acquired notoriety as they were the sites of atom bomb tests in the 1960s. The claims for compensation of people whose health has been affected by the tests are still pending. The steps to independence were the same here as in Micronesia: the constitution was adopted in 1979 and a Compact of Free Association concluded in 1986. In this case the Compact also included the further maintenance of the US Army Kwajalein Atoll Reagan Missile Test Site, which is of crucial importance to US military strategy.[3] The Kwajalein atoll is located at a distance of 6,000 km from the coast of China.

PAPUA NEW GUINEA

The huge island of New Guinea was colonized by various powers. The Dutch occupied the western half which is now part of Indonesia, the Germans got hold of the northeast including the adjacent islands in 1884, and the British also took over the southeast at that time. In 1906 British New Guinea was renamed Papua and turned over to newly independent Australia. After the First World War, Australia received the German northeast as a **mandate territory** under the **League of Nations**. The Japanese conquered a large part of Papua in the Second World War and built strong fortifications on the islands of New Ireland and New Britain. After that war, the Australians were entrusted by the UN with the whole territory which is now called Papua New Guinea. A legislature was established in 1951 but a national movement emerged only some years later. In 1967 Michael **Somare** founded the Pangu Party. He was from Rabaul and had attended a Japanese primary school during the Second World War. He later became a teacher, then a radio broadcaster and a civil servant. He left the civil service in 1968 to contest elections. His Pangu Party remained in opposition, but in 1972 **Somare** became chief minister. He then led his country to independence and became its first prime minister in 1975. He lost this position after a vote of no confidence in

1980 but from 1982 to 1985 he was once more prime minister. After another long period in the political wilderness he made a comeback in 2002.

In the meantime Papua New Guinea had to face a serious challenge from a secessionist movement on Bougainville Island. The rebels proclaimed a separate state called the North Solomon Islands. The rebellion dragged on for a long time and the government of Papua New Guinea received help from the Australians in fighting against the rebels. Australia had a stake in Bougainville Island where the Panguna Copper Mine, owned by Australians, had destroyed the environment of the island. For their mining rights the Australians paid royalties to the government of Papua New Guinea. These payments made up about one-third of its budget, but none of this was shared with the local people.

THE SOLOMON ISLANDS AND VANUATU

The Solomon Islands had been a British protectorate since 1896; in 1942 they were occupied by the Japanese who built a major military base in Guadalcanal. The USA conquered it after heavy fighting and then established their own huge base there. After the war the Solomon Islands reverted to the British, but the local people, many of whom had been employed by the Americans, had become pro-USA and resented British rule. The Americans left the islands in 1950 and the British suppressed the nationalist movement. However, in 1970 they introduced self-government and in 1978 they granted independence to the Solomon Islands.

The neighbouring islands called the New Hebrides and now Vanuatu had a more complex history. The 80 islands were coveted by several European nations and finally, in 1906, the British and the French established a condominium there with two flags and two currencies but no citizenship. The native Melanesians were stateless in terms of international law.[4] Since two-thirds of them were considered to be anglophone, the francophone portion was in a minority, which was a source of political conflict. The anglophone majority was led by Walter **Lini**, a former Anglican clergyman. Decolonization was difficult as the French and the British could not agree on a joint retreat for a long time. Moreover, French plantation owners and Catholic Melanesians supported a secessionist movement led by Jimmy Steven after independence had been attained by Vanuatu in 1980. The secessionists fought against the new government led by **Lini** in the so-called 'coconut war'. The British and the French sent troops to restore order, but the secessionists could not be suppressed and **Lini** asked for troops from Papua New Guinea. With this help he was able to vanquish the secessionists. He remained the prime minister of Vanuatu until 1991. Considering the turbulent times in which he governed his island state, he was certainly the most successful statesman of the South Pacific.

NAURU, TUVALU AND KIRIBATI

Tiny Nauru, the world's smallest republic, is one of the few phosphate islands of the Pacific. British prospectors had discovered phosphate on this island in 1899, but it became a German colony before it was occupied by the Australians during the First World War. After the war, Nauru was turned into a British **mandate territory** governed by Australia. The Japanese captured Nauru in 1942 and deported half of its population. The British returned after the war and granted independence to Nauru in 1968. In the meantime Nauru's phosphate had been exploited by the Australians for years. They had devastated most of the surface of the island. Claims for damages were made in 1989 and settled out of court in 1993, but the sum received was only a fraction of what it would have cost to restore the island.

The Gilbert and Ellice Islands to the east of Nauru had been a British protectorate since 1892 and a Crown colony since 1916. Constitutional reforms were introduced in the 1960s but the two groups of islands did not wish to stay together. In 1974 the Ellice Islanders voted for separation. They attained independence in 1978 and adopted their precolonial name: Tuvalu. The Gilbert Islanders attained independence a year later and then called their state Kiribati.

SAMOA AND TONGA

Samoa had come under Christian missionary influence in the early nineteenth century before it was subjected to colonial rule. The Germans, the British and the USA vied with each other for the control of Samoa. Western Samoa became a German colony which was captured by New Zealand during the First World War. New Zealand obtained a mandate of the **League of Nations** in 1921 and ruled Western Samoa until it attained independence in 1962, whereas Eastern Samoa preferred to continue under US rule.

The Independent State of Samoa, the official title of Western Samoa since 1995, is a constitutional monarchy of a very peculiar kind. There is universal suffrage but only the nobility is entitled to be elected to the assembly which elects the head of state who must be a member of a royal family.

The royal tradition is even stronger in Tonga. The kings of Tonga had earlier ruled a part of Fiji and the Samoas. The British imposed a protectorate on Tonga in 1896. From 1918 to 1965 Tonga was reigned by Queen Salote. The British restored full sovereignty to her son and successor in 1976. Tonga was an absolute rather than a constitutional monarchy. The Tonga Pro-Democracy Movement has challenged the monarchy, demanding more rights for the commoners.[5]

THE LEGACY OF COLONIAL RULE

THE TEMPLATE OF THE NATION STATE

The European template of the nation state was to a large extent adopted by the former colonies. After having been denied self-determination for a long time, the people of the colonies had come to look upon the nation state as the aim of their political aspirations. Colonial constitution making in the run-up to independence had confirmed them in striving for this aim. The people may have had only vague ideas of the nation state, but their leaders were very keen to attain it, the more so as it provided them with the levers of power. They took over the colonial state as a going concern and legitimized it as a nation state. The structure of the colonial state, however, was not uniform in all parts of the world.

In India, the British had inherited the structure of the Mughal state. Although the Great Mughal had lost his power, the successor states had for the most part faithfully preserved the main features of Mughal administration. But whereas in this administration all high officials had been military men, the British entrusted their administration to 'civil servants'. In general, the civil servant was an educated man and had to pass an examination before joining the service. He was freely transferable and his career was governed by strict rules controlled by the central administration. This service was a 'bourgeois' one; it had none of the 'feudal' features of earlier regimes.

In Africa, the colonial rulers could not superimpose their administration on a Mughal system; they introduced for the most part a completely new regime which overshadowed the existing structures of governance like a strange canopy. Expatriate civil servants were the bearers of this canopy. They saw to it that it provided a strong cover. As pointed out earlier, Mahmood Mamdani has written about the 'bifurcated state' in Africa.[1] In fact, the upper layer of this state was the colonial canopy which was an alien artefact, but which was nevertheless preserved by the national leaders after decolonization. The skills involved in preserving this legacy were due to the acquisition of colonial education. In the course of this education the leaders had also learned that a nation state requires a competent bureaucracy, a legislature, a judiciary and, of course, a modern army. In most cases, these elements of the nation state already existed when independence was achieved. Very often the leaders of the new nation states took these elements for granted and did not give much thought to their proper maintenance. They did not realize that their power depended on the judicious control of these elements. Some of them resorted to the arbitrary use of power and thereby undermined the stability of their states.

The nation state requires nation-building. This was not a unique experience of ex-colonial nation states. After Italy had achieved its political unification in the nineteenth century, a political leader had said: 'We have made Italy, now we have to make Italians'. Of course, the Italians did exist, but they were hardly conscious of being citizens of a new nation state and thought in terms of their regional identity. A long freedom struggle such as the one led by **Gandhi** in India contributed to the rise of national consciousness, the more so as Gandhi organized mass action and was not content with mere verbal propaganda. As a by-product of his campaigns he recruited many political workers who subsequently played a role in the Indian nation state. But for many other ex-colonies, the period of decolonization had been rather brief and nation-building could begin only after independence. Moreover, the national territory often had arbitrary boundaries. Since the idea of national sovereignty implies that this sovereignty is derived from a nation residing in a specific territory, it was not enough to encourage national consciousness in the capital; it had to assert itself throughout the whole territory. In this respect the colonial legacy was often not very helpful. In spite of the legacy of arbitrary boundaries, there have been very few serious secessionist movements after decolonization. This could be interpreted as evidence of successful nation-building, but in most cases it was due to the repressive power of the nation state geared to the preservation of the status quo.

The template of the nation state is also supported by the structure of international relations. The term 'international relations' itself indicates that such relations presuppose the existence of identifiable nations. Similarly the **United Nations** are constituted by such identifiable nations. The admission to membership of the **United Nations** has often played an important role in the process of decolonization. The **UN** as well as regional organizations like the **Organization of African Unity** are pleged to uphold the status quo in this respect.

In Europe the nation state has changed its features very rapidly in recent years due to the process of European integration. Many elements of national sovereignty have been transferred to the European Union. But at the time when most countries of Africa and Asia were decolonized, the European nation state was at the zenith of its power and prosperity. It soon became apparent that this was the end of an era rather than the beginning of a new one. This period terminated in the late 1960s.[2] The new nation states of Africa and Asia, however, tried to emulate the model of the nation state which seemed to be so eminently successful in Europe. In fact, they were stuck with an old model which they nevertheless preserved conscientiously.

THE CONSEQUENCES OF COLONIAL CONSTITUTION MAKING

Many African and Asian constitutions bear the stamp of the process of decolonization because they were framed with a view to facilitating the transfer of power. Since the devolution of power implied the prescription of administrative procedures, the colonial constitutional documents often contain a great deal of contigent detail, whereas 'normal' constitutions are restricted to statements of fundamental rights and basic principles. This led to such ironies as that of the Independence of India Act, which subsequently formed the basis of the Indian constitution; it is the longest act ever passed by the British parliament which is itself based on an unwritten constitution.

The formidable Independence of India Act and its impact on the Indian constitution is a typical example of the colonial constitutional legacy. Except for the insertion of fundamental rights, the constituent assembly which produced the Indian constitution added nothing of importance to the existing constitutional arrangement. Whenever the departments of government were asked for comments on the paragraphs debated in the constituent assembly, they invariably endorsed the status quo because they were working within the framework predetermined by the British.[3] In the course of the Indian freedom movement, Jawaharlal **Nehru** had frequently asserted that the constitution of independent India would be framed by a constituent assembly based on universal suffrage and unfettered by the constitutional arrangements made by the colonial rulers. This remained a dream; the actual constituent assembly was based on the limited franchise introduced by the British in the 1930s and it proved to be completely fettered by colonial precedent.

It is impossible to review all constitutions which owed their origin to the process of decolonization. A few examples must suffice which illustrate how crucial decisions made at the time of the transfer of power have influenced the further course of political development. A constitution is an agenda which regulates the transactions which are considered to be relevant in the political life of a nation. It must contain references to the structure of government which may sometimes be of cryptic brevity. Thus the Indian constitution contains the sentence: 'There shall be a prime minister'. This is meant to imply that the type of government will be a parliamentary one and that the conventions governing the powers of the Indian prime minister are the same as those of the British prime minister. But none of this is stated explicitly in the Indian constitution. There is nothing in the Indian constitution that would preclude the appointment of a prime minister of the present French type. Actually, **Jinnah**, who inherited the same constitutional framework for Pakistan as **Nehru** did for India, opted for what may be called a 'Gaullist' interpretation of this constitution, whereas **Nehru** followed the British precedent.

In the British sphere much of this informal constitutional agenda setting preceded the final act of decolonization. Introducing legislative assemblies and appointing the head of the largest party as 'Leader of Government Business' was a step towards parliamentary government. African politicians such as Kwame **Nkrumah** held this position before they became prime ministers in the next round of constitutional reform. Parliamentary democracy, which was the only form of government with which the British were familiar, had to be transferred gradually, because in its fully fledged form it would have left no room for the powers of a colonial governor. The introduction of incomplete parliamentary democracy, however, made those from whom its complete form was withheld even more eager to get the genuine article. Accordingly, most nationalists in British colonies never even considered other forms of government. As we shall see, when the British experimented with federalism in the process of decolonization, it was usually resented by nationalists who saw in it a devious ploy of the colonial rulers. Parliamentary democracy basically implies a unitary state and, therefore, federalism was seen as counterproductive in this context.

While the British style of agenda setting was more or less uniform, it was nevertheless adapted to local conditions. The British produced tailor-made constitutions for each colony. Some of them fitted better than others. In some places they made interesting experiments of doubtful value. Ceylon provides a striking example of this procedure. As mentioned earlier, the Donoughmore Constitution of 1931, which created a government working along the lines of the London County Council, had its drawbacks. It did not contribute to national interest aggregation but encouraged a kind of bargaining within the political elite. In the end this ensured a rather smooth transfer of power with no dramatic 'freedom struggle'. The real conflicts emerged later on when Ceylon 'graduated' to a parliamentary system and interest disaggregation rather than aggregation became a persistent problem.

The French type of agenda setting was very different from the British. The Cartesian mind of French politicians and administrators projected a uniform pattern of imperial governance. When the machine had to be put into reverse gear, i.e. decolonization, it was operated with the same mindset. This was clearly expressed in the **Loi cadre** which was applied to all French colonies in Africa in 1956. Under this law they were all blessed with universal suffrage, they had elected territorial councils and were parts of a **French Union**. The **Loi cadre** was a grand scheme, but it was bound to be a halfway house. It stimulated the demand for independence, but in Paris there was no plan for further agenda setting. This was also a result of the lack of stability of the Fourth Republic which was much more directly affected by the problems of decolonization, including the Algerian problem, than the British government ever was. It was left to General de Gaulle to cut the Gordian knot. His idea of agenda setting was not at all clear to begin with, but he soon took surprising initiatives. Initially he just built on the foundation of the **Loi cadre** and held a referendum on the new constitution of the **French Community** of 1958 which he expected to be universally endorsed. When he was defied by Guinea he hoped that this state would collapse, thus demonstrating what would happen to those who did not accept his agenda setting.

When Guinea did not collapse and the Algerian problem became worse, he finally cut the Gordian knot completely and announced the granting of independence to all African colonies in 1959, which was then achieved by most of them in 1960. De Gaulle's decision had an immediate impact on British agenda setting. But for the British it was not that easy to decolonize at the speed of the French. They had no **Loi cadre** supplemented by the constitution of 1958 and had to adopt a piecemeal approach.

In addition to the setting of the political agenda, the setting of the arena of political contests is of major importance. This means the delimiting of constituencies, the granting of the franchise, the election system, etc. Most constitutions contain no reference to these subjects at all. They are left to specific legislation passed by the respective parliaments. However, the best constitution may not work if the political arena is deliberately designed to distort the results of elections. Early US political practice has produced a term which graphically describes one aspect of arena setting: gerrymandering. It refers originally to the clever redrawing of the boundaries of a constituency in the district of Essex, Massachussetts, under the auspices of Governor Elbridge Gerry in 1812.[4] Since the constituency had the irregular shape of the spots of a salamander, it was portrayed like that animal in caricatures which circulated throughout the USA. The term was soon applied in a more general way to all kinds of political cheating in order to serve party interests. In trying to secure a social base for their rule, the colonial powers often resorted to such schemes. They limited the franchise in terms of property qualifications, favouring those on whose support they thought they could rely. They vetted the lists of voters and restricted the registration of trade unions and political parties. They introduced communal representation by specific electorates. Finally they channelled political activities into arenas which would not directly affect their central control of the respective colony. The scheme of 'provincial autonomy' introduced in India in the 1930s is of special relevance in this context. It will be discussed later as it was part of the federal scheme of the Government of India Act of 1935.

All these attempts at 'gerrymandering' in the most general sense of the term originally played a role in the usual game of 'divide and rule' which characterized all colonial empires. The results of this type of arena setting were, of course, still very much in evidence when decolonization became the order of the day. They could not be suddenly eradicated and sometimes they were even continued and improved upon so as to assure a smooth transfer of power, uninterrupted by oppositional forces. Special problems usually arose when the respective colony did not have a homogenous population but had been significantly affected by foreign immigration. This has been discussed earlier with regard to white settlers in Africa and Indian labour in the sugar colonies. One stratagem which the colonial rulers used in the field of complex constitution making was federalism, both in terms of arena setting within colonies and for the purpose of tying the colonies to the metropolitan power.

At the highest level, federal designs were supposed to transform imperialism into some kind of partnership. The model for this was the British Commonwealth of Nations which, in a rather attenuated form, has survived until the present day. Initially it was based on the dominion status of ex-colonies like Canada and Australia. This status was also conferred on India and Pakistan at the time of their being granted independence. The same applied to Ceylon a year later. India insisted on becoming a republic which would no longer recognize the British monarch as head of state represented by a governor general. A new formula was then found which enabled India and Pakistan to remain members of the Commonwealth as republics, while acknowledging the monarch as head of the Commonwealth. Ceylon later followed the same path when it became a republic and adopted the name Sri Lanka.

The **French Union** was originally based on a similar design, but it did not provide for such an elegant form of attenuation as the Commonwealth did. In fact, it contained a great deal of uniformity and centralization which was exemplified by the **Loi cadre**. As a consequence of this tendency the earlier quasi-federal structures of French West Africa with its governor general at Dakar and French Equatorial Africa with its governor general at Fort Lamy (N'Djamena) withered away to be replaced by more direct ties between Paris and the individual colonies. General de Gaulle's superimposition of the constitution of the Fifth Republic on the **Loi cadre** in 1958 at first seemed to produce a very strong tie which firmly attached the colonies to the **French Community**. But within a short time, de Gaulle had to abandon this construction and what was left of the **French Community** in 1960, after most French colonies had attained individual independence, was a mere shell. Actually this process contributed to the Balkanization of Africa which many African leaders such as Félix **Houphouet-Boigny** and Barthélemy **Boganda** had wished to avoid.

The Union which the Dutch had created in order to contain the rebellious Republic of Indonesia was doomed even earlier. The Republic of Indonesia owed its origin to the unilateral declaration of independence proclaimed by **Sukarno** in 1945 at the end of the Japanese interregnum. Finally the design of the Union only served as a transitory figleaf at the time of granting independence to the republic which soon scrapped the Union and asserted its control over the entire archipelago. Elsewhere the Union did survive as has been discussed in the context of the delayed independence of Suriname. In fact, with regard to Suriname the Union proved to be a heavy burden for the Netherlands.

Whereas the colonial rulers introduced many federal schemes, the ambitious federal plans of colonial nationalists were doomed. Most African nationalists had been inspired by Pan-Africanism and Kwame **Nkrumah** had advocated the creation of a United States of Africa. But all that the African leaders could finally produce was the **Organization of African Unity (OAU)**. Julius **Nyerere** later said of the OAU that it had become a trade union of African heads of government who jealously guarded their sovereign rights. The leaders of ex-colonies were caught in the cage of inherited constitutions and did not dare to transcend the limits imposed by those arrangements.

At an intermediate level, the British tried to use federal designs in regional contexts in the process of decolonization. The most successful one was the Union of India which has retained the federalism imposed by the colonial rulers until the present day. The Government of India Act of 1935, which contained this federal design, was a clever piece of constitutional engineering for the purposes of a centrally controlled 'devolution of power'. It consisted of two parts: one concerned the newly introduced feature of 'provincial autonomy', the other a federal centre in which the Indian princely states were supposed to act as a conservative counterweight to the British Indian provinces, which were for the most part dominated by the **Indian National Congress**. 'Provincial autonomy' actually worked and to some extent did serve the purpose of diverting the attention of Indian politicians to this arena, which had been set for them by the British. The major leaders such as **Gandhi**, **Nehru**, **Patel** *et al*. did not descend to this arena and formed a 'high command' which aimed at taking over power at the centre in due course. They were quite naturally anti-federalist, as they saw in this construction a device to thwart their national ambitions. It so happend that the federal part of this constitution did not come into operation, because the required assent of at least 50 per cent of the Indian princes was not forthcoming. As a consequence of this refusal, all powers of the federal centre were left in the hands of the viceroy who was now more powerful than ever before. This constellation led to a strange amalgamation of centralism and federalism in independent India. A powerful centre was transferred to the 'high command' which nevertheless did not abolish federalism, but weakened it by specific legislation which embodied the heritage of the interventionist British colonial state which had emerged during the Second World War. In independent India, federalism has contributed to the stability of the Indian Union by setting a variety of political arenas.

Similarly the Federation of Malaya, designed by the British, produced a rather stable political structure. The initial plan for a Malayan Union was scrapped very early on as it was rejected by the Malays. In 1948 the British introduced a new constitution for a Federation of Malaya which favoured the Malays and retained the powers of the sultans, one of whom would be the head of state. This rather unique construction has stood the test of time and is still working.

Another federation which was designed by the British for the purposes of decolonization was the West Indies Federation. It was inaugurated in 1956 and, had it worked, would have led to the simultaneous granting of independence to all islands of the British Caribbean by 1960. However, the whole scheme collapsed before it could take off. A more enduring federation established by the British was the state of Nigeria which has retained its federal character until the present day, but not without great difficulties and enormous sacrifices. These difficulties had their origin in the pecularities of the constitutional development of colonial Nigeria. Having set the arena in such a way that national interest aggregation could not be achieved and that the north would predominate, the British contributed to a violent power struggle which soon engulfed Nigeria.

A rather infamous British federal scheme was the Federation of Rhodesia and Nyasaland. The white settlers of northern Rhodesia were a small minority and looked to the more powerful settlers of southern Rhodesia as their main support in an uncertain future in which the black majority would play an important role. The not-so-hidden agenda of this construction – the preservation of the political power of the white settlers – was soon affected by the 'wind of change' which Harold Macmillan conjured up in Africa in 1960. This wind turned into a storm which swept away the federation in 1963. The subsequent Unilateral Declaration of Independence of Southern Rhodesia was the greatest blow to the British government in the field of decolonization.

Colonial constitution making has not been a success story everywhere, but much of the constitutional legacy has prevailed. It has certainly had a pervasive influence on the agenda setting and arena setting which determines political life.

EDUCATION AND THE COLONIZED MIND

Western education as a formal system of instruction has been one of the most important and enduring elements of the colonial legacy. In the early nineteenth century Lord Macaulay, as a member of the British-Indian government, had given the most striking expression to the formative impact of Western education. He had advocated the education of Indian gentlemen who would be Indian in blood only but English in every other respect. In supporting this recommendation, he poured scorn on Indian tradition and belittled Indian literature of which he knew hardly anything. Few other colonial rulers have dared to make such brazen statements but they probably shared Macaulay's views. Actually, the attempts at educating such gentlemen were rather successful and in later years many British were alarmed when they met Indians who spoke better English than they themselves did and knew their Shakespeare by heart. **Gandhi** reports in his autobiography how he behaved in London when he arrived there as a student. With the benefit of hindsight he criticized this behaviour as so many instances of vanity, but if one takes note of the details of his behaviour, they fall into a pattern. He simply tried hard to become an English gentleman.[5] British society was both class conscious and fairly open. If one behaved like a gentleman one could get along very well. **Gandhi** soon abandoned this mimicry, but others made their career in this way.

Education was, of course, more than social mimicry; it consisted of the acquisition of a great deal of knowledge. Both the British and the French had a rather clear idea about what young people should be taught. For each subject there was a prescribed curriculum and a detailed syllabus. This was formal enough at home but even more standardized in the colonies. The formal approach to education did not encourage independent thinking, but it created a universe of discourse. Every man educated in this way had read the same texts and could refer to them in discussions with people of his kind in London or Paris, Dakar or Accra, Calcutta or Saigon. From the point of view of maintaining colonial rule, it seemed to be counterproductive that many prescribed texts contained 'subversive' ideas.

Who could read John Stuart Mill's *On Liberty* and not notice that liberty was denied to him if he was a colonial subject? The colonial rulers were not afraid of this impact of education. They were convinced that the discourse in English or French did not affect the masses. It was typical that some of **Gandhi**'s writings were proscribed when he published them in his mother tongue, Gujarati, while their publication in English was tolerated.[6]

Colonial education was mostly education of the elite, not the masses. It was also to a large extent 'liberal' education and not medical or technical education. The colonial rulers needed educated scribes for the lower ranks of their administration. In India there was also a great demand for lawyers. The British had introduced their legal system in India which yielded a handsome revenue to the government due to high court fees. They recruited judges from the ranks of successful lawyers, and the post of High Court judge was about the highest position to which an educated Indian could aspire.[7] In most other colonies the jurisdiction was left to 'native authorities' and there was no need for lawyers.

There were occasional attempts at challenging the monopoly of colonial education. The Indian freedom movement has produced some remarkable examples of such challenges. At the time of the protest against the partition of Bengal in 1905 some national educational institutions were founded. The great poet, Rabindranath Tagore, played an important role in this movement. In northern India the Gurukul Kangri adopted Sanskrit as a medium of instruction which, combined with instruction in traditional knowledge with strict discipline, was admired even by its British visitors. Mahatma **Gandhi** combined a new system of elementary education with village reconstruction. In the long run, however, all these initiatives failed because they were not recognized by the state authorities and their certificates were no passports to ordinary careers. Even in independent India this did not change; the authorities recognized only the certificates and degrees of the institutions inherited from the colonial state. Curriculum and syllabus continued to reflect colonial standards and English remained the medium of instruction for higher education. Nationalist politicians often showed a strange ambivalence in this respect. They publicly recommended Indian languages as the media of instruction but sent their own children to English-language schools so as to assure them of a good career.

The legacy of colonial education ensured the reproduction of colonized minds. It could be presumed that with the passage of time the colonial past would be forgotten, which did happen to some extent, but it hardly affected formal education. On the contrary, since the system of education was no longer associated with colonial rulers, it ceased to be a target of nationalist resistance. As educational institutions are usually extremely conservative, they faithfully preserved the colonial legacy. For the educated elite this often meant that it would look at its own environment from the perspective of its earlier colonial rulers, the more so as these rulers had always been proud of the universal validity of their knowledge. The nation state and the legacy of colonial education thus supported each other.

LEGAL SYSTEMS AND BUREAUCRACIES

The judges and lawyers who maintained the legal system and the bureaucrats who controlled the administration were, of course, all products of this system of education. Many of them had even spent some time in the former metropolitan country acquiring a foreign degree. Actually the legal and the administrative systems were taken over by nationalists without any criticism. They had protested against foreign rule, but not against its supposedly neutral manifestations such as laws on the statute book and the organization of state administration. Some nationalist politicians clearly acknowledged the value of this part of the colonial legacy. The Indian home minister, Vallabhbhai Patel, when speaking in the Constituent Assembly, called the Indian bureaucracy bequeathed to him by the British a 'ring of service' which was required to keep the country together. Neither in India nor in most other ex-colonies had there been a revolution which would have swept away all institutions. There is, of course, no doubt that the maintenance of 'law and order' contributed to political stability of which the ex-colonies were in great need. However, many urgent reforms were postponed indefinitely as they might upset this stability.

Even countries which were left with a very meagre colonial legacy in this respect did not jettison it but tried hard to make up for their deficiencies by following the pattern preserved elsewhere. Tanzania is a case in point; it had hardly any indigenous bureaucrats and judges when it attained independence and turned to Ghana and Nigeria with a request to send some of their personnel to fill the vacancies left by the departure of the British. The canopy of the colonial state needed new bearers, which provided careers for educated people who eagerly took up this new task.

MILITARY ORGANIZATION

As with the legal and administrative systems, military organization was also accepted as a colonial legacy without much thought. An army was considered to be one of the fundamental attributes of national sovereignty and most national leaders took it for granted that the ex-colonial troops would now faithfully obey their command. In the early times of colonial expansion, European troops had played a role in subjecting the people of Africa and Asia, but soon the colonial rulers had recruited and trained indigenous soldiers who served them well. They were even made to fight for them in two world wars. The formidable Indian army had one million soldiers in the field during the First World War and two million during the Second World War.[8] African troops also participated in those wars. The King's African Rifles under British command and the Tirailleurs Sénégalaises under French command are impressive examples of this kind of service. The King's African Rifles were founded in 1902, encompassing some earlier indigenous batallions. They fought in the Boer War and in the two world wars. After independence they were distributed among the newly independent countries as the Tanganyika Rifles, the Uganda Rifles, etc. They were still commanded by British officers but this led to the mutinies of 1964 as the national leaders had given no thought to 'decolonizing' their troops.

The Tirailleurs Sénégalaises were initially recruited as irregular auxiliary troops of the French colonial army. Their name, which means 'sharpshooters', indicates what they were supposed to do. In due course people from other French African colonies joined the Tirailleurs. Initially their numbers were small, but during the First World War about 164,000 black soldiers were enlisted for service in Europe and elsewhere. During the Second World War about 200,000 black soldiers were enlisted by the French. Some of them became prisoners of war of the German army and were released in 1944. When they returned to Dakar they demanded the arrears of their pay. These unarmed soldiers were shot at by French troops and several of them died. Nevertheless, the Tirailleurs continued to serve the independent African government commanded by French officers as if nothing had happened. As mentioned earlier, the Force Publique of the Belgian Congo was less obedient and rebelled. Since most of the new African states which had been under French rule had defence treaties with the French, neocolonialism was well protected and the nationalist rulers were also safe from military coups for some time, except for poor **Olympio** in Togo whose tragic fate has been mentioned earlier.

Africa, with its many small states, has been an ideal breeding ground for military dictatorships. Most military coups could be traced to a perceived threat to the position of the army. A case in point was **Nkrumah**'s creation of the President's Own Guard Regiment, a kind of privileged praetorian guard, which could be used to put the army in its place.[9] Its very existence showed that **Nkrumah** did not trust his regular army. Another cause of military coups could be a kind of symbiotic relationship between politicians and army leaders such as that between Albert Margai and Brigadier David Lansana in Sierra Leone.[10] In rare cases military conspirators had ideological motives for participating in coups, such as the young majors who organized the Nigerian coup of 1966.[11] The military has sometimes claimed that it played a positive role in the development of its country but its record in this respect has hardly been better than that of civilian governments.[12]

In India the British had in earlier times also insisted on commissioning only British officers, as they did not trust an Indian army under the command of its own officers. In the Second World War they had to change the rules as there were simply not enough British officers for the expanded Indian army. About 8,000 Indian officers were commissioned during the war, enough for the officer corps of both the Indian and the Pakistani armies after demobilization and decolonization. In India a stable democratic government saw to it that the army remained a professional one with no political ambitions. In fact, the Indian government under **Nehru** had a rather distant relationship to its army. As a retired Indian officer once put it, the government's position with regard to the army was like that of a teetotaller who had inherited a brewery. Civilian control of the army was rigorously maintained. The defence minister was always a politician and military officers never held any positions in that ministry. In Pakistan, where there was no stable political structure, the army seized power in due course, although it had the same British tradition as the Indian one. There was, however, one common feature which distinguished the armies of South Asia from those elsewhere: military coups both in Pakistan and later on in Bangladesh were always led by the chief of staff and never by junior officers. The coups were institutional ones and not the result of revolutionary action such as that of the Free Officers in Egypt in 1952.

In Southeast Asia, where the Japanese interregnum was of crucial importance, military organization followed a different pattern. In Indonesia, the Japanese had trained about 6,000 Indonesian officers. After **Sukarno** had proclaimed the independent Republic of Indonesia in 1945, the revolutionary army elected its own chief, General Sudirman, a former teacher. The Indonesian army retained its revolutionary legacy and derived its claim to hold political power from this. In Vietnam the Japanese had governed with the intermediation of the Vichy French. They had thus hardly any chance of training military officers, but the Vietminh then established a revolutionary tradition of their own and finally defeated even the mighty USA. The military organization of the Vietminh was thus a very special one. The Burmese army was also a revolutionary one, although it had no credentials comparable to those of the Vietminh.

In most ex-colonial countries military organization has been, in its own limited ways, more efficient than civilian government. It usually had special privileges and could offer its soldiers and officers a better standard of living than that enjoyed by other people. It was therefore quick to defend its privileges when they were threatened. A clear chain of command and a military *esprit de corps* ensured that the army could act decisively in a political crisis. Whereas none of the major colonial powers had ever been challenged by its own army – with the exception of the French during the Algerian war – the governments of the ex-colonies have faced numerous challenges of this kind and several of their leaders have lost their lives at the hands of their military officers.

The ubiquitous military coup in ex-colonies could sometimes happen in rather grotesque circumstances. Suriname is a case in point; it did not have any army when the Dutch left it rather suddenly in 1975. The Dutch were so happy to be able to relinquish this charge that they readily agreed to pay for the maintenance of the small army which the government of Suriname insisted it should have. When this army then overthrew the government, the Dutch were bound by their earlier agreement to pay the military dictator and his troops. They were embarrassed by this turn of events but nevertheless honoured their commitment.

PUBLIC HEALTH AND POPULATION GROWTH

Another important aspect of the colonial legacy is the maintenance of a system of public health. The colonial rulers introduced such systems not necessarily for altruistic reasons. They knew that they themselves would be affected if their colonial subjects were ravaged by contagious diseases. Since the progress of modern medicine equipped them with the means to eradicate such diseases they often resorted to draconian measures to prevent the spread of diseases whether the people liked it or not. Some diseases could be controlled in this way. The Spanish influenza which raged throughout the world and killed more people than the First World War had done was not amenable to such measures. However, it showed how important it was to control epidemics if one had the means to do so.

The effect of the progress of public health was a decline in the death rate and this rather than high birth rates contributed to a dramatic increase in the populations of Africa and Asia in the course of the twentieth century. The colonial legacy of public health was maintained by most ex-colonies and they were supported in this by the World Health Organization. At the same time most newly independent countries experienced some improvement in the standard of living. Nowhere did this really come up to the expectations of the people who had thought that independence would completely transform their lives. Family planning was difficult to propagate among people who knew that they could only depend on their children in old age and that many of their children would die before them. It takes more than a generation before people realize that due to the spread of public health more children survive and fertility rates decline accordingly. In the meantime the rise in national income (in per capita terms) was reduced by population increase. But, of course, no government would contemplate neglecting public health and allowing its people to die in epidemics so as to reduce population pressure.

MIGRATION AND URBANIZATION

With the growth of population there was also an increasing trend for migration from the countryside to urban centres. This started under colonial rule but continued in post-colonial times. There were many patterns of migration. The migration of Indian labour to the sugar colonies has been described in detail earlier. The Indian exodus from Suriname to the Netherlands has also been mentioned. The main trend of migration, however, was from the rural hinterland to the cities of the same country. The extension of railway lines not only helped to transport cash crops to the ports but also brought rural people in search of employment to the cities. The bigger the city, the greater the variety of jobs, often casual ones, which were available to the migrant.

In India, the megacities of Bombay (Mumbai), Calcutta (Kolkata) and Madras (Chennai) attracted millions of people during colonial times and continued to do so after independence. The colonial legacy is most visible here, both in terms of town planning and architectural styles. In Africa, urbanization gathered momentum only in the last decades of colonial rule. Kinshasa (Leopoldville), the capital of the Belgian Congo, was a small town of 44,000 in 1939 but had grown to 451,000 by 1960. Whereas in India, despite the megacities, the total rate of urbanization remained rather moderate, in Africa some colonies were highly urbanized by 1960. This was particularly true of the Central African Republic (23 per cent), Congo-Brazzaville (32 per cent) and the Belgian Congo (22 per cent). Post-colonial urbanization followed this trend at a rapid rate. The data for 1994 show the following percentages of urbanization: Central African Republic (39), Congo-Brazzaville (59), Zaire (former Belgian Congo)(29).[13]

In colonial times there were usually rather tough vagrancy laws which protected the urban centres against being swamped by migrants. The post-colonial regimes, however, hesitated to use such laws against their own people. Migration subsequently led to the growth of slums and to the increase of pavement-dwellers in the centres of megacities. The contrast of Western-style buildings and bustling African or Asian slums characterized most ex-colonial urban centres.

LIFESTYLES AND SPORTS

The colonial legacy has also visibly influenced the lifestyles of many people. Western dress, at least for men belonging to the educated elite, has become the hallmark of social distinction. This makes the gulf between them and others even more obvious. Since the end of colonial rule the influence of the mass media has been perhaps even more pervasive than the trend set by colonial rulers. In sports, however, the pattern of preferences has clearly been determined in colonial times. Cricket, a very British sport, conquered the whole of South Asia, whereas football spread like wildfire in Africa. Of course, there are also football clubs in South Asia and Caribbean champions have won many cricket matches. In Africa, football was first associated with missionary schools and was a kind of elite sport, but after the Second World War and the increase of urbanization, it became a popular sport.[14] To some extent football clubs even contributed to national movements against the colonial rulers. Such clubs provided a convenient front for proscribed political associations. After independence, success in football matches served as symbols of national pride, a fact which was highlighted by leaders such as Kwame **Nkrumah**.

The enormous importance of the colonial legacy in sports is negatively attested by the fate of indigenous sports.[15] There are many such sports in Africa and Asia, but none of them have been able to rival cricket and football. The same is true of other sports where the universal attraction of the Olympic games has set the standard for the aspirations of Africans and Asians. The reason for the eclipse of indigenous games was probably that they were not as 'serious' as those bequeathed to the Africans and Asians by the colonial rulers. Indigenous games were played by people whose main aim was to have fun together. Colonial games were competitive and bound by firm rules. Within this framework one could aspire to championship in national or even international matches.

The colonial legacy not only affected styles of dress and the participation in sports but also food habits. The transfer of American corn, of potatoes, tomatoes and chillies, etc., to Africa and Asia have been the subject of many studies. The spread of bread has received less attention. In Africa and Asia the dough made from cereals was usually fried or roasted in a pan and not baked in an oven. Bakeries were introduced with the colonial rulers and stayed on after they left. There were good reasons for the popularity of bread. The indigenous preparations have to be eaten as fresh as possible, whereas bread can be stored and transported. In addition to the types of food, the style of eating was also affected by the colonial legacy. In Africa and most of Asia people normally eat with their fingers. In fact, the kind of food which is mostly made up of cooked cereals and vegetable sauces is tasty only when it is mixed with fingers rather than pushed around with fork and knife. But the use of cutlery was considered to be 'decent' by the colonial rulers and their standards have prevailed in many places long after their departure.

FROM COLONIALISM TO NEOCOLONIALISM?

COLONIAL ECONOMIC DEBATES

Colonial rulers and the colonized often engaged in debates about the economic consequences of colonialism. For the rulers this was mostly a cost/benefit analysis unless they maintained their colonies purely for enhancing their prestige or for strategic reasons. The Uganda Agreement provided an example of the discussion for the need of taxation to make a colony pay. First of all, the colonial rulers had to make sure that the colonized themselves paid for being colonized. Second, there was the quest for profitable export products and last, but not least, the interest in the colony as a captive market for the goods of the metropolis. If the colony did not pay, there was criticism in the metropolis. This was particularly so with regard to the British colonies, because the British controlled their empire as a careful accountant would do his firm.

The British praised the doctrine of free trade, but this was an obsession of their economists rather than their merchants who were often keen to make use of the protection of their government. Recent studies in economic history have shown that British traders were usually successful wherever they could rely on political support but did not do very well at all when they had to face free and open competition.[1] Economic debates, however, were conducted by economists and not by merchants. This was also true among the colonized, who took some time to respond. They first had to produce an educated elite who could confront the British economists on equal terms. As India had been colonized at an early stage, it was India that first produced intellectuals who could take issue with British economists. The career prospects of 'native' economists were dim in India, but there were learned Indian judges well read in British economic writings who could argue against the prevailing doctrines. Kashinath Trimbak Telang, a judge of the Bombay High Court, produced a remarkable paper on 'Free Trade and Protection from an Indian Point of View' in 1877.[2] He wrote this paper as a reaction to the contemporary British regulation of tariffs concerning cotton textiles. Having read Friedrich List, he knew about the protection of infant industries by suitable tariffs. He applied this theory to India and wrote: 'It is a mockery and a delusion to speak of liberty, when the native endeavouring to develop the resources of his country, can be undersold and commercially ruined by the unlimited competition of the foreigner'. India had always grown cotton, and there was cheap labour and a large home market, so India should be permitted to develop its industry by means of import substitution. The British textile industrialists did not like such arguments and they saw to it that the government of India did not change its tariff policy. British economists argued that protection always hurts the consumer and they pretended to be advocates of the poor Indian peasant. It is amazing that some Indian industries survived under colonial rule. For the Indian cotton textile industry this was only possible because it found a niche in supplying coarse and cheap cloth for the Indian masses. The Indian steel industry was able to survive only due to a special historical constellation. Jamshed Tata, who founded this industry, had made money in the textile industry. He was also a steel trader and knew about the demand for steel in India. However, he embarked on the risky venture of building a steel mill because of his patriotism rather than for commercial reasons. He managed to raise enough capital in India and to hire US engineers who could provide the expertise. The mill started production in 1907, four years after his death. His sons inherited this venture, which almost ended in bankruptcy, but for the advent of the First World War during which the British needed rails for constructing a railway in Mesopotamia.[3] The Tatas got a huge order and earned a handsome profit. After the war they expanded their production, but soon they faced the competition of cheap German and Belgian steel. It was then that the British abandoned their doctrine of free trade and imposed a protective tariff on steel with preferential rates for British steel. At the time of the Great Depression this tariff policy was extended to cotton textiles so as to keep cheap Japanese textiles out of the Indian market.[4]

The introduction of preferential tariffs for British goods led to market sharing between British and Indian producers. While market sharing may be useful in some contexts, the special kind induced by 'imperial preference' was not. It hurt the consumer as all protective tariffs do, but since it gave privileged access to the market for 'imperial' products, it prevented the indigenous industry from improving its position to such an extent that it would benefit the consumer in the long run. The Indian producers then looked forward to pure protectionism undiluted by 'imperial preferences'. Debates on British currency policy added to an increasing awareness among Indian industrialists that nationalism was their best bet. Import substitution behind tariff walls guaranteed by a national government was the ideal which they pursued. In this way socialists like Jawaharlal **Nehru** and Indian capitalists were able to find a common denominator. Both preferred a national interventionist state to a pseudo-liberal colonial state. This interventionist state was established by the colonial rulers themselves when they had to face the challenge of the Second World War. After the war, they bequeathed that interventionist state to **Nehru** who could never have realized his dream of a socialist state without the instruments which the British left to him.[5] He did not nationalize the enterprises of Indian capitalists but integrated them into a 'mixed economy'. These capitalists were glad that the state would invest in heavy industries while letting them make their profits in light industries that served the Indian consumers.

While **Nehru** insisted on industrialization, Mahatma **Gandhi** had different ideas about India's economic development. For him, agriculture and the work of artisans deserved more attention. He used to carry along his spinning wheel, demonstrating that everybody should earn his living by working with his hands. Heavy industry and the cramming of millions of people into cities was not **Gandhi**'s ideal. There were differences of opinion between him and **Nehru** in this respect. The interventionist state which **Nehru** had inherited from the British was regarded by **Gandhi** as an obstacle to development. When the Indian interim government continued to control food and scarce resources after the war was over, **Gandhi** objected. He compelled the government to cancel these controls. He was warned that prices would rise, but he argued that they would fall. When the controls were lifted and prices fell, he was jubilant and published food prices regularly in his journal.[6] In recommending this policy, **Gandhi** was ahead of Dr Ludwig Erhard who abolished these controls in Germany against the advice of the allied army of occupation in 1948. By that time **Gandhi** was dead and **Nehru**'s policies triumphed in India.

The Indian example is, of course, somewhat unique. Other colonies had almost no industries, entrepreneurs nor economists who could challenge the views of the colonial rulers. In such colonies the colonial rulers conducted economic debates only among themselves. They were opposed to import substitution because they wanted to retain the colonies as markets for metropolitan products. They recommended that colonies should continue doing what they had always done under colonial rule; they should supply raw materials. This is why the increase of agricultural production was the favourite subject of the colonial rulers. Some experts suggested huge projects of mechanized production on large farms. They did not realize that small peasant production was for very good reasons the norm in tropical agriculture. The risk of harvest failure at times of insufficient rainfall was spread among many people in this way; family labour was also utilized much better under such conditions. Since India attained independence soon after the war, it did not share the blessing of late colonial development projects, which proliferated in the 1950s. Africa, however, had the pleasure of being subjected to some experiments of doubtful value, which will be outlined in the subsequent section.

DEVELOPMENT PROJECTS IN THE LAST PHASE OF COLONIAL RULE

In France the idea of enhancing the economic value of the colonies (*mise en valeur*) had been debated after the First World War, when colonial exports had increased and colonial trading companies had earned handsome profits. However, the Great Depression subsequently affected the prices of colonial produce to such an extent that it almost seemed uneconomical to have colonies any longer. So far they had been maintained because they guaranteed privileged access to raw materials. If everybody could buy these materials cheaply, such privileges were no longer required. The Second World made these prices rise again and, therefore, development plans for the colonies were made during the war. The British parliament passed a Colonial Development and Welfare Act in 1940, which remained a mere gesture, because hardly any funds were available under the act. However, it was then amended in 1945 with somewhat more ambitious aims, but at that time Great Britain was almost broke. India had emerged as Great Britain's creditor after the war. Before achieving independence, India had to sign a moratorium, which restricted the access to its balances in the Bank of England. In 1948, British prospects improved. The devaluation of the pound had enhanced British competitiveness. Accordingly more funds could be made available for colonial development.

France had started a fund for the development of the colonies in 1946 (*Fonds d'Investissement pour le Developpement Economique et Sociale* = FIDES). French spending under this scheme, however, remained even more modest than the British expenditure on colonial development. FIDES did not invest any money in large agricultural projects, but it spent about half of the respective funds on the construction of roads, ports and railways; 20 per cent was devoted to the building of hospitals and schools, 12 per cent on agriculture, 7 per cent on research and the rest on sundries. Nearly half of the FIDES expenditure benefited West Africa.

It was a great innovation that the metropolitan powers included funds in their budgets to be spent on the colonies. The British did this with the main aim of enhancing the production of colonial raw materials, which they needed very urgently after the war. The process of decision making in the Colonial Office was of crucial importance in this respect.[7] Policy perspectives ranged from orthodox liberalism to technocratic megalomania. The head of the respective department in the Colonial Office, Sydney Caine, who had held this post since 1940, was an orthodox liberal. He did not believe in the industrialization of the colonies. His greatest critic was W. Arthur Lewis who acted as an economic adviser to the Colonial Office at that time. Even under the Labour government the bureaucrats of the Colonial Office tended to follow Caine's line, which did not lead to a very vigorous development policy. Individual colonies received relatively modest amounts to be spent almost in the same way as those sanctioned by FIDES. The British differed from the French, however, in occasionally supporting huge agricultural projects. A case in point is the Tanganyika groundnut project, which was to help Great Britain cope with the shortage of vegetable fat.

The groundnut plan, which ended in total disaster, was initially hatched by the British Director of Agriculture in Tanganyika and a manager of the United Africa Company (UAC), which belonged to the Unilever Corporation.[8] The predecessor of the director, who should have known better due to his earlier experience in that colony, was dispatched to prepare a feasibility report. He recommended an annual production of about 600,000 tonnes of groundnuts on more than 100 giant farms of 12,000 ha each. The British minister of agriculture was enthusiastic about the plan and it was decided to establish a government company, which would operate the scheme. The initial work, however, would be entrusted to the UAC. Peasant agriculture was, of course, excluded from this scheme; the huge government farms would deploy gigantic machines. It soon became apparent, however, that those machines would not work in Tanganyika. The soil was unsuitable and the rainfall too scarce. Nevertheless, the project was continued with an investment of a great deal of capital. The first harvest was a disappointment and the second one a catastrophe. Losses amounted to about 36 million pounds sterling. Tanganyika had only 6 million pounds sterling in its treasury at the time of independence. The young state would have benefited from even a fraction of the money wasted on the groundnut scheme.

This was not an isolated accident; more were soon to follow. The groundnut scheme had been administered by the Overseas Food Corporation. In 1948 another corporation was established for similar purposes. This was the Colonial Development Corporation (CDC) which would soon match the failure of the groundnut scheme with another disastrous venture involving the production of chicken and eggs in Gambia, the small British colony inside Senegal. Half a million chickens would be kept there and their eggs and meat were to be exported to Great Britain. Chicken feed was to be produced in a huge farm in Gambia. Once again the scheme failed because the machines were unsuitable and then there was a drought. Half of the chickens died; the eggs did not meet British standards. The director of the corporation resigned, but this was not the end of the story. The CDC continued to operate and made further mistakes. When the government totalled up the debts of the CDC, they amounted to 210 million pounds sterling. In the meantime the CDC had started making some profit and was therefore retained, but the profits were due to the fact that the CDC had given up its earlier business and only acted as a moneylender to colonial governments. There were no risks in this business, but it would not have been necessary to establish the CDC for this purpose.[9]

It is astounding that the British with their experience as colonial rulers could make such enormous mistakes. But, of course, as colonial rulers they had so far not made any productive investments; they had collected taxes and in some cases manipulated the colonial currency to their advantage but they had not taken any risks. Investments were made only by private companies, but even they were on a modest scale. The only exception was the large investments in the Indian railways, but they were financed with bonds for which the interest was paid by Indian taxpayers. The British were past masters in such types of arrangements but they failed miserably in their late colonial development policy. Sydney Caine was probably a wise man after all, but instead of defending his point of view by reference to orthodox liberalism, he should simply have said that colonial rulers are unfit for launching development projects.

The misadventures outlined above must be seen in the context of the economic situation in the years after the war. There was an initial euphoria about the prospects of the markets for raw materials, which was soon to turn to disappointment. The Second World War and subsequently the Korean War had driven up prices for raw materials, which then fell again when these wars were over. The fall in prices after the Korean War was even steeper, because the USA had hoarded raw materials during the conflict which it sold after the war was over. The fall in prices was made even worse because, during the interlude of high prices, production had been expanded and this had a severe adverse effect on the market. Such cycles are well known, but they had rather dramatic consequences in the 1950s. Looking back at those years one must conclude that the development projects of the last phase of colonial rule were, for the most part, disappointing. Education and health care were promising areas, but they received only minimal funds.

DEVELOPMENT PLANS OF FORMER COLONIES

The immediate sequel to the plans of the departing rulers were those plans which were launched by the newly independent nations. India was far ahead in this respect due to its early attainment of independence, but also because Jawaharlal **Nehru** had propagated development planning in the **Indian National Congress** as early as the 1930s. In the two years, 1938 and 1939, in which the INC had formed seven provincial governments, there was an urgent need to supply the provincial governments with a blueprint for productive investment. **Nehru** had chaired a National Planning Commission consisting of members of those governments and some experts who were not members of the INC. The war put a premature end to this exercise and **Nehru** was unable to submit the report of this commission until 1940, by which time it no longer had any practical consequences. The report made only qualitative suggestions; it was more or less a list of essential industries, which did not include any estimates of the capital needed for them.[10]

In 1944, when the end of the war was near, a group of Indian industrialists got together in Bombay and drafted a development plan for 15 years from 1947 to 1962. During this period the national product would be doubled if the plan could be implemented.[11] The planners also made detailed suggestions with regard to the capital required. India had large balances in the Bank of England by that time. The industrialists had also learned about Keynes's theory and his defence of deficit spending. Printing money would not cause inflation as long as there was no full employment, according to Keynes's view. In addition the planners felt that they could draw upon the savings of the Indian people and to some extent also on foreign investment. The plan also contained the idea of a 'mixed economy', in which the state invested in heavy industry while the private sector invested in the light industries that supplied goods to Indian consumers. The latter would be more profitable and require less capital than the heavy industry. Left-wing critics called this a 'fascist plan'. The INC leaders were still in prison when this plan was published, so they could neither criticize nor support it, but when they formed a government, it appeared that the official plans more or less parallelled the Bombay Plan of 1944. In 1950 Nehru inaugurated a Planning Commission by cabinet resolution. The prime minister would be the ex officio chairman. The plan documents would not be acts of the national legislature, but since the prime minister staked his political reputation on the implementation of the plan, it did have a great weight.

The first five-year plan (1952–1956) was a modest one and its target was reached without any major effort.[12] Moreover, the harvests were good in those years which made it easier to show good results. The five-years plans were modelled on those of the Soviet Union, but there was a fundamental difference due to the 'mixed economy'. The second plan was much more ambitious than the first and reflected **Nehru**'s idea of rapid industrialization. This plan required massive foreign aid. The same was true of the third plan whose completion **Nehru** did not witness as he died in May 1964. The targets of the second and the third plans could not be reached, but they did lead to a large increase in industrial production. While concentrating on industrialization, **Nehru** neglected agriculture, which at that time contributed half of the national product and employed about 70 per cent of the population. **Nehru** kept food prices at a low level in order to prevent the rise of wages for industrial workers. He also avoided any radical agrarian reform. The top layer of large landlords was expropriated, but the large number of rich peasants were not touched because **Nehru** needed their votes. The land revenue, a direct tax, had not been enhanced since the Great Depression and had almost dwindled to insignificance. Keeping agrarian prices low amounted to an indirect taxation, which did not touch the pockets of the voters directly. Agrarian production did rise during **Nehru**'s leadership, but only due to an extension of cultivation. This meant that marginal soils were cultivated which would not yield anything when rainfall decreased. Two years of drought struck India after 1965, which led to the collapse of the policy of low prices.[13]

Nehru's economic strategy was in tune with contemporary economic theory. He was very much impressed with W. W. Rostow's 'take-off into self-sustained growth'.[14] India would also reach that stage. Theories of 'unbalanced growth', which will be discussed later on, pointed in the same direction. Once a break-through was achieved in the industrial sector, sluggish agriculture would follow suit in due course. Trying it the other way round seemed to be impossible as agriculture was in the hands of millions of peasants, making state intervention very difficult in this sector. **Nehru**'s success in almost trebling industrial production during his period of office seemed to justify his approach.

In other former colonies there were tendencies to follow a similar path, but often the instruments of state intervention simply did not exist. Indonesia is a case in point. It made a belated attempt at launching a planned economy, which ended in complete disaster. **Sukarno** would have loved to excel **Nehru** in this field, but the state which he had inherited from the colonial rulers was not equipped for such ventures. There was hardly any 'national bourgeoisie' of the type existing in India. The Dutch and the resident Chinese dominated the Indonesian economy. The educated elite was small, as the Dutch had not done much for higher education in Indonesia. Moreover, the instruments of intervention, which Nehru had inherited from the British war economy, were missing in Indonesia where the Dutch had been replaced by the Japanese during the war. In the period of parliamentary democracy, which ended with the one and only election in 1955, no progress could be made in the field of economic management. It was only when **Sukarno** introduced 'guided democracy' that he could make some headway towards a planned economy, the more so as he had expropriated Dutch firms after 1957. A very ambitious eight-year plan was inaugurated in 1960, which was supposed to be a great leap forward. Since the Dutch had been driven away, however, there was a lack of qualified personnel. The instruments of intervention were also still missing. The plan only generated social tensions, which led to the abortive coup of 1965 and the subsequent persecution of Indonesian communists by the army.

Egypt's planned economy had a similar fate. Before **Nasser**, economic development had been entirely unplanned. **Nasser**, however, was a 'progressive' dictator who stressed 'Arab socialism' and wished to make up hastily for lost time. He created a planning authority in 1957 and inaugurated an ambitious ten-year plan in 1960, which aimed at an annual increase of the national product at a rate of 7.5 per cent. The introduction of a planned economy was accompanied by the nationalization of all industries, banks, insurance companies and of foreign trade. There was no 'mixed economy'. Beginning in 1962, peasants and artisans were forced to join cooperatives. These measures led to a flight of capital and to a flight of the peasants to urban areas. This kind of planned economy was a total failure, but it was maintained until **Nasser**'s death, when only his successor was able to revise the policy.

In Syria and Iraq, the Baath Party, which was also inspired by 'Arab socialism', introduced a planned economy. In Tunisia, **Bourguiba** could have tried to opt for a planned economy in 1954, but he initially pursued a rather conservative policy. In 1957 he then introduced legislation which enabled him to nationalize industries and embark on radical agrarian reform. In 1961 he proclaimed 'Tunisian socialism' and inaugurated a ten-year plan for the period 1962 to 1971. He closely followed the Egyptian precedent. In keeping with his new policy he even changed the name of his party from the Neo-Destour Party to the Socialist Destour Party (*Parti Socialist Destourien*). Algeria later followed the same course of economic policy and continued to pursue it for much longer than other countries.

In black Africa there was less scope for a planned economy. The former French colonies were more or less dependent on France, even after independence. In fact, neocolonialism was a very obvious trait in those colonies whose rulers not only maintained close economic links with France, but sometimes even asked for French military intervention to keep them in power. The former British colonies were either preoccupied with internal problems or had hardly any economic substance which would have enabled them to make ambitious plans. Tanganyika and Kenya, however, produced some modest plans. When **Nyerere** assumed office in 1962 he established a planning department under his immediate jurisdiction. His main emphasis was on village development. A three-year plan was started forthwith, but coordination was a problem. With disarming frankness **Nyerere** admitted: 'We have built schools in some villages although we lacked qualified teachers for them, sometimes roads were constructed which ended somewhere as we had neither the money nor the engineers to build the bridges across which these roads should lead'.[15] He promised that such mistakes would be avoided in the five-year plan which was to start in 1964. This plan contained an allocation of only 42 million pounds sterling for the industrialization of the country. **Nyerere** therefore gratefully acknowledged the decision of a private oil company to build a refinery in Dar-es-Salaam. His enthusiasm for African socialism did not prevent him from welcoming private investment.

In Kenya, Jomo **Kenyatta** wrote a preface for the country's first six-year plan (1964–1970) in which he stressed that the plan was not based on any ideology but on the experiences of all successful national economies of the world.[16] He gave first priority to the increase of agricultural production for export. Furthermore he highlighted the importance of higher education. There was also a reference to increasing employment, but except for a brief reference to import substitution there was no comment on industrialization, which was given high priority by all other planners. As distinct from **Kenyatta**'s preface, the plan document itself contained more detailed references to the generation of employment by industrialization, but there was also the admission that Kenya could not compete with others in the world market and had to look to its home market only. The processing of agrarian produce was mentioned as the only real chance of industrialization in the near future. The sum required for three years of plan expenditure was estimated at 42 million pounds sterling. Only half of this amount could be financed from the government budget; the other half had to be provided by foreign aid. The plan document admitted that the plan was 'ambitious'; in his preface **Kenyatta** had called it 'realistic'. He also refrained from any propaganda, which usually accompanied the inauguration of such plans.

A sorry example of a late attempt at economic planning was the National Economic Plan of Mozambique designed in 1978. In addition to health and education, the major emphasis of this plan was on industrialization and on state farms. In fact, 70 per cent of all plan investment in agriculture was concentrated on the state farms. The peasant economy was almost totally neglected. As mentioned earlier, **FRELIMO**, the party in power in Mozambique, fell into a trap of its own making and the ambitious plan only contributed to its problems.

All the plans of former colonies, whether ambitious or modest, pleaded for foreign aid. This was an appeal to the donors, who were initially to be found only among the Western industrial nations. This appeal was also addressed to those nations beyond the circle of the earlier colonial rulers, particularly the USA which was supposed to help the 'new' nations.

DEVELOPMENT AID AND ITS DONORS

The grand model of foreign aid after the Second World War was, of course, the Marshall Plan, which was, however, exclusively devoted to the reconstruction of Europe. This plan was in many respects unprecedented. In earlier times, victors would ask the vanquished for reparations rather than helping them to recover from the war. The Marshall Plan provided the Allies and the vanquished alike with aid approximating 2–3 per cent of the national product of the USA at that time. There was, of course, a political motive for this generosity. An impoverished Europe would have been an easy target for the Soviet Union. In March 1947 President Truman had announced the 'Truman Doctrine' of US support for free nations. Three months later, Secretary of State George Marshall, gave his famous speech at Harvard University in which he stressed that the reconstruction of a viable world economy was essential for the survival of democratic institutions and outlined his plan.[17] The relevant act was passed in April 1948. A few months earlier, in October 1947, the General Agreement on Trade and Tariffs (GATT) had already established the new rules of the game for a revival of international trade.

The Marshall Plan proved to be very successful, but it also had favourable preconditions. It financed the reconstruction of economies which possessed valuable human capital in spite of the heavy losses caused by the war. Moreover, there was a post-war boom, which prepared fertile ground for the successful absorption of Marshall Plan aid. In Germany, for instance, the boom was so strong that this aid only provided additional impetus to the German 'economic miracle'. The success of the Marshall Plan should have motivated US political leaders to follow it up with similar plans for Asia and Africa. This was not considered, however; rather they used the instruments of military pacts and military aid on those continents.

When **Nehru** visited the USA in 1949, he was deeply disappointed. He had not come to beg for aid, but he did mention the lack of capital which handicapped India. It had granted a moratorium to Great Britain in 1947 and the USA had helped to bring this about, so they were well informed about India's predicament. However, since **Nehru** did not commit himself to the West in the Cold War, which had just begun, there seemed to be no point in helping India. Even the very specific request for 2 million tonnes of wheat to ward off a famine in India was handled so tardily that the respective deliveries reached India about 18 months later. A generous gesture would have been very important at that time. While Roosevelt had been regarded as a friend of India, Truman did nothing to preserve this good will.

After a considerable delay, the USA did consent to provide development aid to the Third World, but the respective programme was very modest compared to the Marshall Plan. From 1950 to 1955 this aid amounted to about 0.32 per cent of the national product of the USA. In 1960 it briefly reached 0.56 per cent, but it subsequently declined. Nevertheless, in this early period US aid amounted to about half of all international development aid.[18] The countries which later formed the European Economic Community spent more on development aid in proportion to their national products than the USA. From 1950 to 1955 aid spending was 0.52 per cent; in 1960 it reached 0.64 per cent. The Soviet Bloc was not very active in this field in the early years, but by 1960 its contribution to international development aid amounted to 10 per cent of the total. It is difficult to gauge the share of this aid in the respective national products. Development aid consisted only to a small extent of grants; most of its was credit at low interest rates or free of interest. The period of repayment was usually very long.

Many donors regarded development aid first of all as a stimulus for promoting their exports. The developing countries needed investment goods for which they could not pay; the producers of such goods were happy to see the taxpayers of their countries providing funds to those countries, which they would then spend on their products. In Germany, the association of the producers of investment goods was among the first to lobby for aid to developing countries. In France, FIDES provided an appropriate channel. Moreover, by means of clever diplomacy the French managed to attach their former colonies to the European Economic Community as associated members. This meant that aid to these countries would also come from other European countries.

In order to be sure that aid would promote their own exports, some donors pursued a policy of 'tied aid'. The USA opted for this, because its investment goods were expensive. Germany did not insist on it, however, as it was confident that its investment goods were either cheaper or better than those of its competitors. But Germany did tie its aid to a political condition: countries recognizing East Germany (German Democratic Republic) would be debarred from receiving West German aid. This 'tie' was very effective. Even **Nehru**, who was greatly inclined to recognize the German Democratic Republic, did not do so, because he did not want to forfeit (West) German development aid.

In those early years of development aid, the donors did not think of admonishing the developing countries to liberalize their economies. The producers of investment goods were happy that those countries were good customers and refrained from teaching them lessons on the virtues of a liberal economy. The donors formed groups dealing jointly with important developing countries (e.g. the Aid India Consortium), but these groups only examined the general viability of the respective economy and coordinated the allocation of aid. They did not raise questions about the virtues of a planned economy and were usually not concerned with macroeconomic questions, concentrating instead on the financing of specific projects. This practically forced the developing countries to present 'attractive' projects. Sometimes these countries agreed to doubtful projects, which were liked by the donors who wanted to show off what they had sponsored.

Whenever development aid was not restricted to the mere financing of investment goods but also involved the sending of experts, special problems were bound to arise. After an initial period when the lack of capital appeared to be the only problem to be solved, there was an increasing awareness of the need for the transfer of know-how. It was rarely taken into consideration that this know-how had to be acquired in a particular context. Sometimes the expatriates who were sent abroad soon returned rather frustrated by the different context in which they were supposed to perform, or they created their own context and thus saw to it that they were practically irreplaceable. If they were withdrawn, the respective project would collapse. The salaries of these expatriates were very high and a great deal of the expenditure on aid was absorbed by them. This is why critics in the developing countries pleaded for capital aid rather than this type of aid, but the donors remained convinced that the transfer of know-how was essential.

In a later phase of development aid, there was another fundamental change in the philosophy of donors. They felt that the transfer of capital and know-how had undoubtedly contributed to economic growth, but it had not reduced poverty. Accordingly it was stated that the fight against poverty was the most important aim of development aid. But how could donors 'target' the poor so as to make aid effective? Hunting for 'target groups' became a major concern for innumerable non-governmental organizations (NGOs). Many NGOs had admirable motives and were enthusiastic about their work, but their expenditure on personnel was also high. The same problem that arose with regard to experts transferring know-how reasserted itself in this new context. To make matters worse, however, the people dispatched by the NGOs were rarely qualified technical experts and their programmes were often well intentioned but ill considered. As long as the developing countries did not have to foot the bill, they gladly hosted the NGOs. The elites of those countries often derived some benefits from this, such as receiving fees as advisors or renting premises to NGO staff, etc.

The programmes of the donors were rarely guided by the theories of development economists, who were sometimes quoted after the event in order to justify what had been done. On the other hand, the development economists were given food for thought (and career prospects) by the expanding field of development aid. Economics had been rather compartmentalized before development economics appeared on the scene. Under the influence of Keynes, economists had concentrated on the analysis of the national economy. The economics of international trade was practically a separate discipline. Development economics raised the question of how to deal with the economy of a country totally different from one's own 'national economy'.

THE THEORIES OF DEVELOPMENT ECONOMICS AND THE 'DEPENDISTAS'

Neoclassical economics, with its equilibrium models and its belief in the 'invisible hand' of the markets does not actually make allowance for 'development economics' as a discipline *sui generis*.[19] This has changed only in recent years when microeconomics, modern political economy and the economics of information have been integrated into development economics along neoclassical lines. In earlier years, economists would at the most agree that the application of neoclassical doctrine to developing countries might require some special effort. Development economists of this school found it disconcerting that they had to deal for the most part with state intervention in developing countries. According to them this kind of intervention only distorts the market and should be avoided. Nevertheless they did admit that there could be both 'market failure' and 'state failure'. Such a 'failure' would be considered a temporary aberration. The effectiveness of the 'invisible hand' was never doubted.

The central problem of this kind of development economics is that it must respect the 'invisible hand' but cannot rely on its working properly. If it did work properly one would only have to wait until it produced the most desirable development. It is revealing that in the 1950s the term applied to developing countries was 'underdeveloped countries'. This implied that these countries were on the right track but stood much further back. They would catch up with other countries in due course. The new term 'developing countries' directed attention to the process of development which could require active support. The 'invisible hand' of the market was replaced by the visible hand of the planner. This highlighted the problem of adequate information. The 'invisible hand' was supposed to act as if it had this information. Prices were the universal standard of such information. The working of the 'invisible hand' was the feedback by which prices would regulate the market. But economic coordination does not often respond to market forces and, therefore, it seemed to be preferable to entrust coordination to a planner. The planner, however, was tempted to opt for 'unbalanced growth' instead of waiting for the slow adjustment required by equilibrium models.[20] Instead of simulating feedback by means of a great amount of data, one would just make a bold decision and proceed in one direction, hoping that equilibrium would be restored in due course. It was like slapping the 'invisible hand' hard so that it would then do what it was supposed to do. This approach was tempting, because it encouraged planners to be proactive without actually leaving the secure foundation of neoclassical theory. Whatever the planners did, however, they could not compete with the 'invisible hand'. Despite this, the optimism of development planners prevailed until the 1960s. Thereafter this optimism evaporated and development economists tended to give up planning and recommend the liberalization of the market to the developing countries. In the meantime bilateral development aid had been replaced to a large extent by multilateral aid. The international organizations which had to supervise this aid were imbued with the neoclassical doctrine. This was particularly true of the International Monetary Fund, whereas the World Bank, which had been established in the context of the Marshall Plan, occasionally encouraged unorthodox experiments. It also adopted poverty alleviation as a special aim of development aid. This aim is in itself unorthodox because it requires intervention, which is anathema to the orthodox.

In the 1970s and 1980s a new problem confronted the development economists: the rapid increase in the indebtedness of developing countries. If these countries had to pay more in terms of debt service than they received as development aid, they were caught in a vicious circle. The spectre of neocolonialism raised its ugly head. The optimistic modernization theory which had prevailed in the period of rapid decolonization was suddenly eclipsed by a new pessimism. The economic aspect of modernization theory was reflected in W. W. Rostow's *Stages of Economic Growth*. Rostow's influential book was published in 1960 but it seemed to be out of date by 1970. A new formula had replaced Rostow's 'take-off into self-sustained growth'; now 'development towards underdevelopment' was widely proclaimed. It was a reversal of Rostow's theory; instead of the developing countries providing a role model for the 'Third World', their very development was deemed to be the cause of the underdevelopment of the 'Third World'.[21] This message was initially propagated by economists based in Latin America. They spoke of *dependencia* (dependency) as an inevitable feature of the growth of the capitalist world system. The theories propounded by this school were not new. They had their origin in the attempts at explaining the fate of the periphery of the world market at the time of the Great Depression. The lessons derived from the experience of the Great Depression were epitomized by the Prebisch-Singer thesis of 1950.[22] This thesis contradicted two basic assumptions of the economists of the nineteenth century: 1) that international trade always leads to a beneficial division of labour; 2) that industrial progress will lower the prices of industrial products whereas agricultural produce will become more expensive because population increases and the available land is scarce. The Argentinian economist, Raoul Prebisch, however, argued that 1) the international division of labour results in structural differences which privilege the centre of the world market while underprivileging the periphery, which nevertheless cannot opt out of international trade; and 2) that technological progress does not reduce the prices of industrial products whereas the prices of agricultural produce tend to fall and thus affect the terms of trade for agriculturists negatively. Prebisch had elaborated the structural differences between centre and periphery even earlier. He had argued that the centre is characterized by a homogeneous (well-integrated) structure of its economy and a diversification of its production, whereas the periphery has a heterogeneous economic structure, but its production is not diversified. In an extreme case a country on the periphery may concentrate on producing a single cash crop for export. Since the countries on the periphery depend on the import of industrial goods, industrial import substitution is their only chance of economic improvement. While Prebisch's contribution to the Prebisch-Singer thesis consisted of this structural analysis, Hans W. Singer had – initially without being in touch with Prebisch – worked on extensive data analysis concerning the terms of trade which confirmed Prebisch's analysis. Since Prebisch was associated with the Economic Commission for Latin America (ECLA), the thesis has also been called the ECLA thesis. The 'dependistas' then built their ideological scheme on this foundation. They argued that the structural differences observed by Prebisch reflected a necessary trend towards underdevelopment.

The Prebisch-Singer thesis was criticized by many economists who found fault with Singer's statistics. Indeed, the trend of the terms of trade looks different according to the choice of dates for the beginning and the end of the statistical analysis. The years of the Great Depression show very clearly that the prices of agricultural produce fell precipitously while those of industrial products fell much less and recovered more quickly. However, in 1950, just when Singer announced his results, the prices of raw materials increased rapidly. Thus, if one includes the 1950s in the time series one can easily controvert Singer's thesis. Moreover, Singer's critics had more modern tools of statistical analysis at their disposal than those Singer had used. Having discredited Singer's data, the critics thought that they had debunked the Prebisch-Singer thesis. It was a case of guilt by association from which Prebisch's structural analysis could not recover. If one combined

Prebisch's structural analysis with the theory of the 'invisible hand', one may be able to rehabilitate it, even in the eyes of neoclassical economists.

The 'invisible hand' can perform its task smoothly only in a homogenous (integrated) economy, a system in which the feedback will be undisturbed, but it can only touch a heterogeneous economy at the most from the outside, e.g. with regard to the demand for a specific export product in the world market. Within the heterogeneous economy, the 'invisible hand' cannot work because the lack of 'networking' precludes feedback. This networking depends on numerous institutional preconditions, which are often neglected by economists. It is only in recent years that 'property rights' and 'transaction costs' have re-introduced institutional conditions into the discourse of the economists.

The tragedy of black Africa illustrates the problems of heterogeneous economies, which often depend on the export of one commodity and which have achieved neither homogeneity nor diversification. Moreover, the production of agricultural produce in Africa, which mostly depends on small peasant households, can no longer compete in the world market with more efficient capitalist production of the same produce elsewhere. Wages are low in Africa, but so is the productivity of labour. Higher productivity on mechanized farms elsewhere ruins the African peasant.[23] This means that he is not exploited by neocolonialism but marginalized by the forces of the world market. The Balkanization of Africa during the course of colonization and decolonization has contributed to this 'underdevelopment'. There are hardly any 'national economies' of sufficient size. Moreover, the conscientious nationalists who headed the freedom movements have been replaced by parasitical elites or military dictators who treat the state as their patrimony. They do not hesitate to pocket development aid and if their dismal performance is criticized they blame 'neocolonialism'. This does not mean that the Africans have only themselves to blame for their sad fate. The atmosphere of world politics was conducive to this kind of 'underdevelopment' as Western powers often preferred 'reliable' dictators as political partners.

India had a different experience because it is a huge national economy, which managed to withdraw from the world market for a long time, largely relying on autocentric development. It paid for this in terms of reduced economic growth and a rapidly expanding public sector. During the period of autocentric development, however, it could attain a certain homogeneity (integration) and diversification of its economy.[24] Under colonial rule, India had been an open economy, completely dependent on developments in the world market. In the eastern part of India there were numerous economic enclaves (tea plantations, jute factories, coal mines) mostly geared to export production. In the western part of India there was an import substituting cotton textile industry. These two different economic regions were hardly in touch with each other. After independence, import substitution was pushed ahead, the home market grew and the diversification of industrial production increased. Of course, this autocentric economy was not equipped for competition in the world market, but when it did open up in the 1990s it was what Prebisch would have called a 'homogenous' and diversified national economy.

Of course, compared to highly industrialized countries, India still contains many backward regions and has not yet attained a complete integration of its economy, but it is certainly ahead of many other ex-colonies. India, like China and South Korea, generated a high 'forced' savings rate; it did this through nationalized banks in a protected economy. But India could afford this period of autocentric development also due to foreign aid. It had imported a great deal of investment goods and had this required immediate payment in foreign exchange, India would have had to increase its exports tremendously. Furthermore, it earned a great deal of foreign exchange by means of manpower export to the countries around the Persian Gulf. This was a source of income hardly available to other developing countries to the same extent.

The experience of the former colonies was thus highly differentiated. Not all of them were afraid of neocolonialism, but it was a phenomenon which was frequently discussed by the leaders of the Third World.

THE HIDDEN HAND OF NEOCOLONIALISM?

Kwame **Nkrumah** wrote: 'Neocolonialism is negative action playing possum'.[25] This figure of speech refers to the animal, which feigns death when attacked. 'Negative action' in **Nkrumah**'s terminology represents the sum of those forces tending to prolong colonial subjugation and exploitation. In other words, it was felt that a hidden hand was at work, which controlled the fate of the former colonies in spite of their being politically independent. Was this merely a case of paranoia? Or were the leaders who spoke of neocolonialism only interested in finding an excuse for their own failures? One may be able to identify this 'hidden hand' by referring once more to the 'invisible hand' of the market. As pointed out earlier, this 'invisible hand' can touch a heterogeneous economy (as characterized by Prebisch) only from the outside. Most post-colonial economies did remain heterogeneous and lacked diversification. To the extent that they were affected by the dynamics of the world market, they often suffered from negative effects such as the volatile prices of raw materials, increasing indebtedness, etc. To those affected in this way, the 'invisible hand' of the world market appeared to be the 'hidden hand' of neocolonialism. Moreover, a kind of police of the creditors has evolved out of the Bretton Woods institutions, which were originally created for very different purposes. Keynes, who was an expert in the field of monetary economics, had been very active at Bretton Woods. His aim was to create a mechanism which would prevent the kind of meltdown that had led to the Great Depression. Actually, the World Bank and the International Monetary Fund (IMF) did not quite achieve the aims envisioned at Bretton Woods, but institutions acquire a momentum of their own and find new tasks if the old ones become irrelevant. The IMF in particular has been very good at that and has emerged as stern tutor of indebted countries. It prescribes to everyone the same medicine – the 'structural adjustment programme'. This normally implies a devaluation of the currency so as to reduce imports and foster exports, a reduction of budget deficits and a balanced budget. All this is backed by what has been called the 'Washington Consensus' of neo-liberal experts. For those who come under the tutelage of the IMF, the 'hidden hand' of neocolonialism appears to show itself in a rather concrete and threatening form. The economists working for the IMF would, of course, reject the charge of neocolonialism. They only want to make sure that the world market functions smoothly. The old orthodox rule that the world market benefits all who participate in it because if it did not do so, the participants would withdraw from it, is still the basic article of their creed. As mentioned earlier, Raoul Prebisch had pointed out that the underprivileged periphery of the world market simply cannot opt out of it. Its fate is not one of exploitation but of marginalization. The dynamics of globalization aggravate this problem. One must either be a global player or a loser. Some losers may claim that the cards have been stacked against them and if they belong to the former colonies, they will call this neocolonialism.

The problem of neocolonialism must be traced to a deeper level. The processes of colonization and decolonization have spawned a multitude of 'nations' whose basic equipment was simply inadequate for a gainful participation in the world market.[26] The respective countries had been exploited for a long time and while some colonial rulers pretended that decolonization was meant to be a constructive 'transfer of power', it was nevertheless a hurried liquidation of assets which were no longer considered to be useful. The colonial powers were more interested in Europe than in the maintenance of their overseas 'empires'. The very late decolonization of the Portuguese empire shows this change of orientation most acutely. It was shrouded in a confused revolution, but whereas the Portuguese quickly found a new haven in Europe, their huge African colonies were mired in civil war and misery.

There has never been a concerted effort by the developed nations to help the developing nations to overcome the heterogeneity and the lack of diversification of their economies. The period of the Cold War was characterized by a preponderance of strategic interests. 'Making the world safe for democracy' was seen in terms of security interests rather than as a task of social and economic reconstruction. The subsequent period of increasing global economic competition has also not been the best time for such long-term constructive tasks. They will remain the challenge of the future.

III
SOURCES, NAMES AND TERMS

GUIDE TO SOURCES AND SECONDARY READING

This chapter introduces the reader to major source collections published by the respective governments and provides suggestions for secondary reading. The publication of source collections is sometimes politically motivated and wherever possible the motives will be briefly mentioned because they determine the scope of these publications. The suggestions for further reading will be brief. A repetition of titles mentioned in the notes to the text and in the section on historiography will be avoided as far as possible. After a reference to general surveys and readers, the subsequent sections of this chapter will follow the regional order of the material presented in Section II (pp. 41–274).

GENERAL SURVEYS AND READERS

There are many general introductions and surveys of this field. It is impossible to mention them all. The most useful reference work is by Muriel Chamberlain.[1] It is more or less a timetable of decolonization and also contains an annotated bibliography but no interpretative text. Her book includes a very extensive biographical section which not only lists national leaders but also has many entries concerning the officers of colonial administrations and of the metropolitan ministries in charge of the colonies. More recently John Springhall has provided a brief survey of the subject.[2] It is not a reference work but a textbook covering the whole field of European decolonization. This survey is comprehensive, but, of course, highly selective in dealing with its subject matter. Even more concise and selective is the survey by Raymond F. Betts.[3] It contains a series of essays on decolonization which are devoted to important aspects such as the rural/urban divide, colonial migration, the hegemonic impact of languages, etc. For a general survey of French decolonization in Africa, see Catherine Coquery-Vidrovitch, *Afrique noire: Permanences et ruptures*.[4]

The United Nations played an important role in the process of decolonization. Evan Luard, *A History of the United Nations, Vol. II: The Age of Decolonization, 1955–1965*, provides an essential survey of the decisions made by the UN in this crucial period.[5]

In addition to these surveys there are some recent anthologies containing collections of important articles. Prasenajit Duara edited a volume on decolonization which has three parts.[6] The first consists of historic statements by Sun Yat-Sen, Ho Chi Minh, Jawaharlal Nehru, Frantz Fanon, Jalal Ali Ahmad and

Kwame Nkrumah. The second part deals with imperialism and nationalism and the third with 'Regions and Themes' including among others articles on national divisions in Indo-China by Stein Tonneson and on labour movements in West Africa by Frederick Cooper. James D. Le Sueur has edited a massive decolonization reader which includes 22 substantial articles reprinted from important academic journals.[7] Together, these two volumes provide an impressive cross section of current research work.

BRITISH DOCUMENTS ON THE END OF EMPIRE

The publication of sources on the decolonization of the British empire has increased in recent years. They have a broad scope, covering metropolitan policies with regard to the empire in general. Whereas the regionally restricted publications will be discussed later on, the general publications will be mentioned here. In 1987 a project was inaugurated to publish *British Documents on the End of Empire* under the auspices of the British Academy and the Institute of Commonwealth Studies of the University of London. The project has three series: A, B, and C. Series A is devoted to five periods of British policy concerning decolonization under successive governments from 1945 to 1971. Series B contains documents on the decolonization of different countries with the exception of India and Burma which have been covered by earlier source publications. Series C consists of two volumes listing the archival sources available in the Public Records Office and other official archives. The volumes of Series B will be mentioned in the context of the specific countries to which they refer. The present section will deal only with Series A and C.

Series A begins with a volume on *Imperial Policy and Colonial Practice, 1925–1945*, edited by S. R. Ashton and S. E. Stockwell.[8] It has two parts: the first deals with political issues, the second with economic and social policies and colonial research. It outlines the preconditions for the subsequent phases of decolonization. The second volume, edited by R. Hyam, deals with *The Labour Government and the End of Empire, 1945–1951*.[9] It is subdivided into four parts, each covering various aspects of politics and economics as well as race relations. The third volume, edited by D. Goldsworthy, is devoted to *The Conservative Government and the End of Empire, 1951–1957*.[10] It is subdivided into three parts covering international relations, politics and administration and economic and social policies. The fourth volume, edited by R. Hyam and W. R. Louis, deals with the subsequent Conservative governments of Harold Macmillan and Alex Douglas-Home: *The Conservative Government and the End of Empire, 1957– 1964*.[11] Its two parts cover political and constitutional change, and economics and international relations.

The fifth volume, edited by S. R. Ashton and W. R. Louis, *East of Suez and the Commonwealth, 1964–1971*, is the final one of Series A.[12] It has three parts, starting with the defence reviews of the 1960s and the withdrawal from Aden and South Arabia. The second part portrays the development of the Commonwealth and the withdrawal from east of Suez. The third part ventures beyond its time limit and throws light on the remaining dependencies as well as on the Falkland Islands and Hong Kong. With their several parts the five volumes of Series A amount to 14 tomes – an impressive production, indeed. The two volumes of Series C, edited by A. Thurston and S. R. Ashton, are guides to the records.[13] The first volume deals with the files of the Colonial and Dominion Offices in the Public Records Office, and the second volume with those of the Cabinet, the Foreign Office and the Treasury, etc.

In addition to these recent publications of British sources there is an earlier publication of a selection of documents by A. J. Stockwell, *British Imperial Policy and Decolonization, 1938–1964*.[14]

Secondary Reading

In addition to the books by John Darwin and Robert Holland mentioned earlier, the more recent work of Frank Heinlein on *British Government Policy and Decolonisation, 1945–1963* may be useful for the reader.[15] Heinlein deals with the phases of British policy from the Attlee to the Macmillan governments. His book is thus a good companion to the themes of the *British Documents on the End of Empire* which the reader may consult before delving into the flood of published documents.

ASIA

India: Freedom Movement, Transfer of Power and Partition

Sources

The emancipation of British India was the first and largest instance of decolonization and gave rise to an enormous volume of official publications documenting all aspects of political decisions and their implementation. The first step was the British publication of 12 volumes on *The Transfer of Power*, edited by Nicholas Mansergh.[16] The editor approached his task from a liberal point of view. He was convinced that the British had intended to hand over power to the Indians and that the implementation of this programme was a success. The starting point of his documentation is revealing. It is the August Offer of 1940 by which the Viceroy invited the Indian leaders to join his executive council so as to form a kind of Indian national government during the war, a replica of the British war cabinet in which all parties were represented. Mansergh obviously saw this offer as a first move towards the transfer of power. If the Indian leaders had accepted this offer in 1940, the final transfer could have been smoother and partition could have been avoided. The British government, however, was not prepared to declare its war aims with regard to India and thus the Indian National Congress rejected the offer. The British had not intended to partition India. They were forced to do so in order to implement the transfer of power. Accordingly Mansergh documents in detail the various efforts made by the British to avoid partition. The documents he presents were almost all produced at the highest level, i.e. the correspondence between the Government of India and the home government and occasionally the correspondence of the Viceroy with the governors of Indian provinces. The actions of Indian leaders are documented only to the extent that they were reflected in such official correspondence. Except for the bias inherent in the type of sources presented, the editor has not projected a partisan account.

The publication of *The Transfer of Power* should have moved the Government of India to launch a parallel documentation of the freedom movement. This project had to wait for various reasons. Several Indian state governments actually published their own series based on the respective provincial archives. The Government of India commissioned the *History of the Freedom Movement* mentioned in the section on historiography. It also sponsored a huge edition of the *Collected Works of Mahatma Gandhi* in 90 volumes.[17] This publication not only contains Gandhi's works and his numerous newspaper articles but also his private correspondence. This is of particular relevance as it provides insights into his way of thinking and acting almost day by day. The Government of India then planned *Towards Freedom*, a publication which would literally dwarf *The Transfer of Power*. The starting point of this documentation was the formation of provincial governments by the Indian National Congress in 1937 under the Government of India Act of 1935. This was a date set by the British rather than by the leaders of the freedom movement. Gandhi's famous Salt March of 1930 would have been a more suitable starting point if the intention was to document the freedom struggle. Selecting 'provincial autonomy' as a starting point seemed to be a reply to Mansergh's choice of the August Offer of 1940. It indicated that the Indian National Congress was prepared to participate in responsible government but had to withdraw from it as the British failed to declare their war aims. The actual implementation of the *Towards Freedom* project was beset by many organizational problems. The first volume on the year 1937 was edited by P. N. Chopra who was employed by the Indian Council of Historical Research for this task. It was published in 1986.[18] In the meantime the authorities concerned had come to the conclusion that a single editor would not be able to cope with this project, so the volumes were farmed out to individual historians. Basudeb Chatterjee, a noted historian, was responsible for the year 1938 and produced a vast panorama of India in that year.[19] He did not hesitate to document the problems which the Indian National Congress faced 'in office'. He also dealt in detail with the princely states. The high standard which he set by editing this volume served as a benchmark for further work. Partha Sarathi Gupta had published two years earlier an equally impressive documentation of the years 1942 to 1944.[20] More volumes were in the pipeline: Sumit Sarkar worked on the year 1940 and K. N. Pannikar on 1946. Their manuscripts had been handed in before the BJP-dominated government (1998–2004) took over. It suspended the publication of these two volumes, supposedly because the editors were 'leftists'. The real reason was probably because the leaders of the BJP were concerned about the portayal of the historical role of their predecessors who had not supported the Indian National Congress in the freedom struggle in those crucial years. The further work on the ambitious project was delayed by this political contest.

Secondary Reading

H. Kulke and D. Rothermund's *A History of India*[21] contains a chapter on the Indian freedom movement and the partition of India. Judith Brown's *Modern India. The Origins of an Asian Democracy* also deals with India's decolonization.[22]

Pakistan

Sources

Since Pakistan was established by the leader of the Indian **Muslim League**, the sources concerning this party are of special importance. S. S. Pirzada has edited the respective documents in two volumes.[23]

The partition of India as seen from the Pakistani side was documented by M. M. Sadullah in four volumes.[24] The last volume contains reproductions of the maps delineating the border between India and Pakistan.

Secondary Reading

C. H. Philipps and D. Wainwright, *The Partition of India. Policies and Perspectives, 1935–1947.*[25]

Sri Lanka

Sources

Kingsley M. De Silva is the leading historian of Sri Lanka. He has edited the volume devoted to Sri Lanka in Series B of the *British Documents on the End of Empire.*[26]

Secondary Reading

The most comprehensive work on the history of Sri Lanka was also written by K. M. De Silva: *A History of Sri Lanka.*[27]

The Dutch and the Republic of Indonesia

Sources

In the winter of 1966/67 questions were asked in the parliament of the Netherlands about excesses of Dutch troops during the 'police actions' in Indonesia in 1948 and 1949. In response to these questions the government published a comprehensive selection from archival sources of the Council of Ministers as well as of several ministries and the army and navy. Material available at the Netherlands Indies Secretariat which was transferred to the Netherlands after 1950 was also included in these publications. The title of the 20-volume collection is *Officielle bescheiden betreffende de Nederlands-Indonesische betrekkeningen, 1945–1950*.[28]

Secondary Reading

History of Indonesia in the Twentieth Century by Bernhard Dahm contains a detailed analysis of the decolonization of Indonesia.[29]

The French and the War in Indo-China

Sources

Lt. Col. Gilbert Bodinier has edited two volumes of documents on the French Indo-China war on behalf of the Historical Service of the French Army.[30] A French journalist, Lucien Bodard, who had reported on the conflict, produced a history of the war in four volumes of which an abridged translation was published as *The Quicksand War*.[31]

Secondary Reading

A classic account of the war was written by Bernard Fall: *Street without Joy*.[32] See also J. Buttinger, *Vietnam: A Dragon Embattled. Vol. I: From Colonialism to Vietminh*,[33] and Jacque Dalloz, *La Guerre d'Indochine, 1945–1954*.[34]

The Liberation of Burma

Sources

While Nicholas Mansergh was still working on the *Transfer of Power in India*, Hugh Tinker edited the documents relating to the decolonization of Burma: *Burma. The Struggle for Independence*.[35] These two publications set the standard for the subsequent series of *British Documents on the End of Empire*.

Secondary Reading

J. F. Cady, *A History of Modern Burma*, provides a good survey of the period of decolonization in Burma.[36]

The Delayed Decolonization of Malaya

Sources

A. J. Stockwell and S. R. Ashton edited the volume on Malaya in Series B of *British Documents on the End of Empire*.[37] It covers the period from the fall of Singapore in 1942 to the independence of Malaya in 1957. Subsequently, another volume in this series was published which covers the creation of Malaysia.[38]

Secondary Reading

An important scholarly study of the communist insurrection was published by Anthony Short in 1975.[39] A revised edition of this book was published under the title *In Pursuit of Mountain Rats* (Singapore, 2000). For Singapore, see E. C. T. Chew and E. Lee (eds), *A History of Singapore*.[40]

The USA and the Philippines

Secondary Reading

The award-winning book by Theodore Friend, *Between Two Empires. The Ordeal of the Philippines, 1929–1946*, provides a good introduction to the history of the Philippines in the period of decolonization.[41] The peasant insurrection was studied by Bernard J. Kerkvliet: *The Huk Rebellion. A Study of Peasant Revolt in the Philippines*.[42]

The Termination of Japanese Rule in Korea and Taiwan

Secondary Reading

Murray Rubinstein, *Taiwan. A New History*;[43] Bruce Cumings, *Korea's Place in the Sun. A Modern History*,[44] D. L. McNamara, *The Colonial Origins of Korean Enterprise, 1910–1945*.[45]

Imperial Sunset: Hong Kong, 1997

Secondary Reading

C. Chang, *Politics of Hong Kong's Reversion to China*;[46] Yash P. Ghai, *Hong Kong's New Constitutional Order. The Resumption of Chinese Sovereignty and the Basic Law*;[47] Steve Tsang, *Modern History of Hong Kong, 1841–1998*.[48]

THE ARAB WORLD

Syria and Lebanon

Secondary Reading

Philipp K. Hitti, *Syria: A Short History*;[49] Philip S. Khoury, *Syria and the French Mandate. The Politics of Arab Nationalism*;[50] S. H. Longrigg, *Syria and Lebanon under French Mandate*;[51] John F. Devlin, *The Ba'th Party. A History from its Origins to 1966*;[52] M. Zamir, *The Formation of Modern Lebanon*.[53]

Iraq and Transjordania

Secondary Reading

Matthew Elliot, *Independent Iraq. The Monarchy and British Influence*;[54] Charles Tripp, *A History of Iraq*;[55] Mary C. Wilson *et al.*, *King Abdullah, Britain and the Making of Jordan*.[56]

Palestine and Israel

Secondary Reading

British policy at the time of the termination of the mandate is analysed by M. J. Cohen: *Palestine. Retreat from the Mandate*.[57] He followed this up with a study of *Palestine and the Great Powers, 1945–1948*.[58] See also Ritchie Ovendale, *Britain, the United States and the End of the Palestine Mandate, 1942–1948*.[59]

Egypt

Sources

John Kent has edited the volume on *Egypt and the Defence of the Middle East* in Series B of the *British Documents on the End of Empire*.[60]

Secondary Reading

P. J. Vatikiotis, *The History of Modern Egypt*;[61] Matthew F. Holland, *America and Egypt. From Roosevelt to Eisenhower*;[62] S. R. Ashton and J. Kent, *Egypt and the Defence of the Middle East*.[63]

Sudan

Sources

Douglas Johnson edited the volume on the Sudan in Series B of *British Documents on the End of Empire.*[64]

Secondary Reading

A unique problem of the Sudan was that it was jointly ruled by Egypt and Great Britain. M. W. Daly has devoted an important monograph to this condominium.[65] See also M. O. Beshir, *Revolution and Nationalism in the Sudan*[66] and Ann Mosley Lesch, *The Sudan. Contested National Identities.*[67]

Aden and Yemen

Secondary Reading

R. J. Gavin, *Aden under British Rule, 1839–1967.*[68]

Libya

Secondary Reading

Adrian Pelt, *Libyan Independence and the United Nations. A Case of Planned Decolonization;*[69] Majid Khadduri, *Modern Libya. A Study in Political Development.*[70]

Tunisia

Secondary Reading

Kenneth J. Perkins, *History of Modern Tunisia.*[71]

Morocco

Secondary Reading

C. R. Pennell, *Morocco since 1830. A History.*[72]

Mauritania

Secondary Reading

R. Adloff, *The Western Saharans: Background to Conflict* describes the rise of POLISARIO.[73] See also T. Hodges, *The Western Sahara. The Roots of a Desert*

War[74] and Toby Shelley, *Endgame in Western Sahara. What Future for Africa's Last Colony?*[75] Garba Diallo has discussed the relations between Arabs and Black Africans: *Mauritania. The Other Apartheid?*[76] See also G. Gerteiny, *Mauritania.*[77]

BLACK AFRICA

Ghana, Sierra Leone and Guinea

Sources

Richard Rathbone has edited the volume on Ghana in Series B of *British Documents on the End of Empire.*[78]

Secondary Reading

Richard Rathbone has also studied the tense relations of Nkrumah with the chiefs in Ghana.[79] Joe A. D. Alie of Sierra Leone has portrayed the history of his country.[80] Victor Du Bois has analysed the decline of the Guinean revolution.[81]

Senegal and the Ivory Coast

Secondary Reading

A. Ly, *Les Regroupements politiques au Sénégal (1956–1970);*[82] Guy P. Pfefferman, *Industrial Labour in the Republic of Senegal;*[83] Aristide R. Zolberg, *One-Party Government in the Ivory Coast.*[84]

Togo

Secondary Reading

Robert Cornevin, a leading French historian of Africa, has written several books on Togo, the most comprehensive one is *Le Togo. Des origines à nos jours.*[85]

Dahomey/Benin

Secondary Reading

R. Cornevin, *La republique populaire due Bénin. Des origines dahoméennes à nos jours.*[86] See also P. Manning, *Slavery, Colonialism and Economic Growth in Dahomey, 1640–1960.*[87]

Burkina Faso, Niger, Chad

Secondary Reading

F. Fugelstad, *A History of Niger.*[88] Mario Azevedo, *Roots of Violence. A History of War in Chad.*[89] Mario Azevedo and Emmanuel Nnandozie, *Chad. A Nation in Search of its Future.*[90]

Nigeria

Sources

Martin Lynn edited the volume on Nigeria in Series B of *British Documents on the End of Empire.*[91]

Secondary Reading

A good account of Nigeria's path to independence is given by Michael Crowder in *The Story of Nigeria.*[92]

Cameroon

Secondary Reading

Richard Joseph, *Radical Nationalism in Cameroon. The Origins of the UPC Rebellion,*[93] and by the same author, *Gaullist Africa. Cameroon under Ahmadu Ahidjo.*[94]

Central African Republic, Congo-Brazzaville, Gabon

Secondary Reading

Marc Aicardi de Saint-Paul, *Gabon. Development of a Nation.*[95]

Congo (Zaire)

Secondary Reading

Georges Nzongola-Ntalaja has portrayed the history of the Congo from the days of King Leopold to the regime of Laurent Kabila.[96] Ludo De Witte has given an account of the assassination of Lumumba.[97] See also Charles Didier Gondola, *The History of the Congo.*[98]

Tanzania

Secondary Reading

John Iliffe, *A Modern History of Tanganyika*, is a study of major importance.[99]

Uganda

Secondary Reading

S. R. Karugire, *A Political History of Uganda*,[100] and Kenneth Ingham, *The Making of Modern Uganda*,[101] serve as good introductions to the history of Uganda.

Rwanda and Burundi

Secondary Reading

There are two parallel studies of conflict and genocide in the two states: Gérard Prunier, *The Rwanda Crisis. History of a Genocide*,[102] and René Lemarchand, *Burundi. Ethnic Conflict and Genocide*.[103]

Somalia, Djibouti, Eritrea

Secondary Reading

I. M. Lewis, *A Modern History of the Somali. Nation and State in the Horn of Africa*.[104] Dan Connell, *Against all Odds. A Chronicle of the Eritrean Revolution*.[105] Ruth Iyob, *The Eritrean Struggle for Independence. Domination, Resistance, Nationalism*.[106]

Madagascar

Secondary Reading

Maureen Covell has studied the politics and economics of Madagascar.[107] See also Jacques Tronchon, *L'insurrection malegache de 1947. Essay d'interprétation historique*.[108]

Botswana, Lesotho and Swaziland

Secondary Reading

Antony Sillery, *Botswana. A Short Political History*.[109] Stephen Gill, *A Short History of Lesotho*.[110]

WHITE SETTLERS IN AFRICA: RESISTANCE TO DECOLONIZATION

Algeria

Sources

The Historical Service of the French Army has sponsored an extensive publication of official documents concerning the Algerian war, edited by Jean-Charles Jauffret with the assistance of military experts. The first volume covers the period from 1943 to 1946, the second the period from 1946 to 1954.[111] Since these volumes have so far only arrived at the beginning of the war, more volumes are expected in due course.

Secondary Reading

Benjamin Stora, the leading French expert on the history of the Algerian war, has published numerous works in French on this subject; a selection from his writings has been translated into English: *Algeria, 1830–2000. A Short History.*[112] A very thorough study based on archival sources of several countries has been published by Matthew Connelly: *A Diplomatic Revolution. Algeria's Fight for Independence and the Origins of the Post-Cold War Era.*[113] Connelly's main thesis is that the Algerians won their war not on the battlefield, but in the field of international diplomacy. He covers the history of the Algerian war and its aftermath in great detail.

Kenya

Secondary Reading

Kenya's colonial period was studied by George Bennett: *Kenya. A Political History.*[114] George Bennett and Carl Rosberg analysed the crucial elections in Kenya which preceded independence: *The Kenyatta Elections, 1960–1961.*[115] A detailed account of Kenya's decolonization and its aftermath was published by Bethwell A. Ogot and W. R. Ochieng (eds) *Decolonization and Independence in Kenya, 1940–1993.*[116]

Rhodesia and Nyasaland (Zambia, Zimbabwe and Malawi)

Secondary Reading

Andrew Sardanis has studied the emancipation of Zambia.[117] Robert Blake has shown his sympathies with the white settlers in *A History of Rhodesia.*[118] The background of the negotiations which preceded the independence of Zimbabwe is discussed in the volume edited by W. H. Morris-Jones: *From Rhodesia to*

Zimbabwe. Behind and Beyond Lancaster House.[119] See also Robert Rotberg, *The Rise of Nationalism in Central Africa. The Making of Malawi and Zambia.*[120]

Namibia

Secondary Reading

Peter H. Katjavivi has written a history of resistance in Namibia.[121] Individual life histories of people who have lived through the liberation struggle were recorded by Colin Leys and Susan Brown: *Histories of Namibia. Living Through the Liberation Struggle.*[122]

INDIAN LABOUR AND THE SUGAR COLONIES: MAURITIUS, GUYANA, FIJI

Mauritius

Secondary Reading

Richard Allen studied the labour migration to Mauritius: *Slaves, Freedmen and Indentured Labourers in Colonial Mauritius.*[123]

Guyana

Secondary Reading

Leo A. Despres, *Cultural Pluralism and Nationalist Politics in Guyana*;[124] Ralph R. Premdas, *Party Politics and Racial Division in Guyana.*[125]

Suriname

Secondary Reading

The book by the Dutch scholars Gert Oostindie and Inge Klinkers, *Decolonising the Caribbean*, contains a chapter on the independence of Suriname and the 'Caribbean Exodus'.[126]

Fiji

Secondary Reading

The most comprehensive recent study of Fiji is by John Kelly and Martha Kaplan: *Represented Communities. Fiji and World Decolonization.*[127] For an account of Fiji's history from an Indian point of view see B. V. Lal, *Broken Waves. A History of the Fiji Islands in the Twentieth Century.*[128]

THE COMMONWEALTH CARIBBEAN

Sources

S. R. Ashton and D. Killingray edited the volume on the West Indies in Series B of *British Documents on the End of Empire*.[129] It covers the period from 1948 to 1966 and deals especially with the failure of the West Indies Federation. It includes material on British Guyana and Belize (British Honduras).

Secondary Reading

Franklin W. Knight has portrayed the political development of the Caribbean in a comprehensive book: *The Caribbean. The Genesis of a Fragmented Nationalism*.[130]

PORTUGAL IN ASIA AND AFRICA

Sources

A historical commission of the Portuguese army has published a massive collection of sources pertaining to the military campaigns in Africa (1961–1974). From 1988 to 1998 a total of six volumes were published, some of these consisting of several parts.[131]

Secondary Reading

The best survey of the Portuguese withdrawal from Africa is by Norrie McQueen: *The Decolonization of Portuguese Africa*.[132] See also Patrick Chabal *et al.* (eds), *A History of Postcolonial Lusophone Africa*.[133] For Goa see Arthur Rubinoff, *India's Use of Force in Goa*.[134]

THE PACIFIC ISLANDS

There are very few monographs on the history of individual Pacific islands available as yet. The reader is therefore referred to *Pacific Islands. An Encyclopedia*, edited by Brij Lal and Kate Fortune.[135]

Papua New Guinea

Secondary Reading

John Dademo Waiko has given a good account of his country: *A Short History of Papua New Guinea*.[136]

Vanuatu

Secondary Reading

Kalkot Matas Kele-Kele *et al.*, *New Hebrides. The Road to Independence.*[137]

Tonga

Secondary Reading

Ian Campbell, *Island Kingdom. Tonga, Ancient and Modern.*[138]

BIOGRAPHIES OF AFRICAN, ASIAN AND CARIBBEAN LEADERS

The entries in this section refer only to leaders involved in the process of decolonization: nationalists of earlier colonial times have not been included.

Abbreviations: arr. = arrest, arrested and imprisoned; att. = attended; Ed. = educated at; indep. = independent; memb. = member of; PM = prime minister; Pres. = president; Publ. = publications; Sec. = secretary of party or trade union; U = university; return. = returned to.

$$\boxed{A}$$

ABBAS, FERHAT (1899–1985) Ed. U of Algiers (pharmacy), Pres. Algerian Muslim Students Union, served in French army in Second World War, arr. 1945 for political activities, founded *Union Democratique du Manifeste Algérien*, 1946, opposed rebellion of 1954 but supported **FLN** in 1956, Pres. Provisional Government of Algeria, 1958–1961, Pres. National Assembly of Algeria, 1962–1963, clashed with **Ben Bella** and resigned. Publ. *Le Jeune Algérien; Manifeste Algérien; Autopsie d'une guerre.*

ABDULLAH, KING OF TRANSJORDANIA (1882–1951) Ed. Harrow and Sandhurst (British military academy), Amir of Transjordan, 1921, King of Transjordania since 1946, assassinated in Jerusalem, 1951.

ABUL KALAM AZAD (1888–1958) Born in Mecca, ed. by his father, a Muslim *pir*. Return. India 1895. He had a mystical experience in 1909 and propagated his ideas in his Urdu journal, *Al Hilal*, the British expelled him from Calcutta and interned him in Ranchi during the First World War. He then met **Gandhi** and they cooperated in the **Khilafat** movement. Remained with **Gandhi** throughout, arr. several times in 1930s and 1940s, Pres. **Indian National Congress (INC)**, 1940–1946, Minister of Education in independent India, 1947–1957. Publ. *Tarjuman al-Quran* (Urdu translation of the Quran and commentary).

ADAMS, GRANTLEY HERBERT (1989–1971) Black politician, Barbados, Pres. Barbados Workers' Union, 1941–1954, and Pres. Barbados Labour Party (BLP) from 1939; PM Barbados before independence, first and only PM, *West Indies Federation*, 1958–1962.

AFLAQ, MICHEL (1910–1989) Ed. Sorbonne, Paris 1928–1932 (history), return. Syria 1932, founded **Baath Party** (*Harakat al-ba'th al-arabi* = Movement for Arab Rebirth) in 1943, first party congress 1947. Although he was a Greek Orthodox Christian, he stressed the importance of Islam for Arab solidarity, advocated non-Marxist socialism. Moved to Bagdad 1968 after Baath takeover. Publ. *Discours à la mémoire du Prophète arabe; L'idéologie du* *parti socialiste de la résurrection arabe. comment nous nous situons par rapport à la doctrine communiste* (Orient, Paris: 8/29).

AHIDJO, AHMADOU (1924–1989) Memb. Assembly of French mandate territory Eastern Cameroon 1947. Memb. Assembly of French Union 1954. PM of pre-independence government. Pres. Republic of Cameroon 1960, formed federation with British mandate territory, Pres. Federal Republic of Cameroon 1961, re-elected 1965, resigned 1982.

AHOMADEGBE, JUSTIN (1917–) Trained as a teacher in Dahomey; trade union leader, founded Union Démocratique Dahoméen, Vice-Pres. Dahomey 1964, Pres. 1965, 1972 (triumvirate with **Maga** and **Apithy**).

AL-AZHARI, ISMAIL (1898–1969) Ed. Gordon Memorial College, Khartoum, and American U, Beirut, teacher of mathematics and government servant, co-founder Graduates' General Congress, Khartoum 1938, Pres. National Unionist Party, 1952, PM Sudan 1954-1956, led Sudan to independence, then opposition leader, Pres. Sudan 1965-1969, overthrown by military coup, died in prison.

APITHY, SOUROU (1913–1989) Ed. Porto Novo, Dahomey, and France (political science), practised as an accountant, member of French Constituent Assembly 1946, later member of French parliament, att. founding of **Rassemblement Démocratique Africain** at Bamako, 1946, but 1948 he broke with it and took sides with **Senghor**, founded Parti Républicain Dahoméen (PRD), Mayor, Porto Novo, 1956, headed government, 1957–1959, vice-president of Dahomey, 1960, Pres. 1964 –1965, member of triumvirate (national government) with **Maga** and **Ahomadegbe**, 1970–1972, overthrown by the army.

APTIDON, HASSAN GOULED (1916–) PM Djibouti, 1977, Pres. 1977–1999, leader of Rassemblement Populaire pour le Progrès (RPP), retired voluntarily after five periods of office.

AUNG SAN (1915–1947) Ed. U Rangoon, leader of 'Dobama Asiayon' (We Burmans Association), led students strike 1936. During the Second World War he and several of his comrades were trained by the Japanese and entered Burma with them in 1942, heading the Burma Independence Army. In March 1945 he and his followers changed sides and joined the British against the Japanese. Their new organization, which included nationalists and communists, was called **Anti-Fascist People's Freedom League (AFPFL)**. Aung San became de facto PM in 1946 and was assassinated on July 19, 1947.

AWOLOWO, OBAFEMI (1909–1987) Ed. Wesley College, Ibadan, London (law). Sec. Nigerian Motor Transport Union, co-founder Trade Union Congress of Nigeria, 1943, organized Action Group of the Yoruba of Western Nigeria, which won elections in that region in 1951, first PM Western Region 1954, resigned 1959, contested federal elections and became leader of the opposition, arr. 1962–1966. Publ. *Path to Nigerian Freedom*.

AZIKIWE, NNAMDI (1904–1996) Ed. Howard and Lincoln U and U of Pennsylvania, taught in USA, return. West Africa (Gold Coast) 1934, to Nigeria 1937. Founded **National Council of Nigeria and the Cameroons (NCNC)** 1942, PM Eastern Region (Nigeria) 1954, Governor General of Nigeria 1960, first Pres. Nigeria 1963, overthrown by coup 1966.

B

BALEWA, ABUBAKAR TAFEWA (1912–1966) A leader of the Northern Peoples Congress (NPC) of Nigeria which he represented in the federal centre. Formed federal government as first PM of Nigeria 1957, heading a coalition of the NPC with the NCNC led by Azikiwe. Assassinated 1966.

BA MAW (1897–1977) Ed. Burma, India, France, England (law), defended **Saya San**; PM Burma, 1937–1939, arr. by British for protest against the war effort, Pres. Burma, 1943–1945, after Japanese had declared the independence of Burma. Fled with the Japanese to Japan and was arr. by the Americans as war criminal, released in 1946, return. Burma, founded a party of his own which did badly at the polls. Active as a political writer and commentator. Publ. *Breakthrough in Burma*, 1968.

BANDA, HASTINGS KAMUZU (1906–1997) Ed. U of Indiana, U of Chicago, U of Glasgow, U of Edinburgh (medicine), practised as physician first in Liverpool and London then at Kumasi (Gold Coast), return. Nyasaland 1958, Pres. Nyasaland African Congress, arr. 1959–1960. Banda's party, renamed Malawi Congress Party, won elections 1961. PM 1964, Pres. 1966–1993.

BANDARANAIKE, SOLOMON (1899–1959) Founder of Sinhala Mahasabha (SMS) 1937, representing the Sinhalese Buddhist element in the nationalist movement of Ceylon (Sri Lanka). Joined the **United National Party (UNP)** of D. S. **Senanayake** and became cabinet minister in 1947. Resigned 1951 and founded **Sri Lanka Freedom Party (SLFP)**. Before the 1956 elections he formed a broad national front (Mahajana Eksath Peramuna) with Buddhist groups, PM 1956–1959. Introduced legislation making Sinhalese official language, alienating Tamil minority. Shot by a Buddhist monk, September 26, 1959.

BAO DAI (1913–1997) Emperor of Annam (Vietnam), ed. Paris, ascended throne in 1932, collaborated with Vichy government and the Japanese, declared independence 1945, exiled after the end of the war, he returned to Vietnam in 1949, formed government of South Vietnam, 1950, recognized only by Western powers, overthrown in 1955, spent rest of his life in exile in Paris.

BARROWS, ERROL WALTON (1920–1987) Black politician, Barbados, ed. London, law degree 1950, after serving in the Royal Air Force return. Barbados 1950, memb. Barbados Labour Party (BLP), 1951, left it and founded Democratic Labour Party (DLP), 1955, first PM of independent Barbados 1966–1976, defeated 1976 by BLP, second term 1985–1987.

BEN BELLA, MOHAMMED AHMED (1916–1998) Served in French army 1937–1940, joined Allies in Second World War, prepared armed struggle against the French in Algeria, arr. 1950, escaped 1952 and fled to Cairo, supported rebellion of **Front de Libération Nationale (FLN)** in 1954, arr. 1956–1962, Pres. Algeria 1963, overthrown by army 1965.

BEN-GURION, DAVID (1886–1973) Born in Poland, he went to Israel in 1906, joined the British army in the First World War, fighting in Palestine. Co-founder of Mapai (Socialist Party) in 1930, organized Haganah (Jewish Defence Force). Proclaimed independent state of Israel on 14 May 1948. PM 1948–1953 and 1955–1963.

BIRD, VERE CORNWALL (1909–1999) Founder of Antigua Trades and Labour Union, organized canecutters and led their strike in 1951, first PM Antigua 1981, retired 1994.

BOGANDA, BARTHÉLEMY (1910–1959) Ordained as a Catholic priest, memb. French parliament, 1946, founded the **Mouvement d'Évolution Sociale d'Afrique Noire (MESAN)** in 1949, which won all seats in the 1957 elections in the Central African Republic, PM 1958, died in a plane crash 1959 before he could lead his country to independence, succeeded by David **Dacko**.

BOSE, SUBHAS CHANDRA (1897–1945) Ed. Presidency College and Scottish Churches College, Calcutta, passed Indian Civil Service exam 1919 but then joined national movement, arr. 1925–1927, Sec. **Indian National Congress (INC)** 1928, Pres. **INC** 1938 and 1939, arr. 1940–1941, fled to Germany where he hoped to get support from Hitler who only dispatched him to Japan. With Japanese help he formed the **Indian National Army** (Azad Hind Fauj) with Indian prisoners of war in Southeast Asia, died in an aircrash over Taiwan in 1945. Publ. *The Indian Struggle; An Indian Pilgrim*.

BOUMEDIENNE, HOUARI (1927–1978) Ed. Al-Azhar U, Cairo, joined armed rebellion against French in Algeria 1954 and became leader of military operations 1958. Defence minister in **Ben Bella**'s government 1962, overthrew him in 1965.

BOURGUIBA, HABIB (1903–2000) Ed. Paris (law), lawyer in Tunisia, memb. Destour Party, in 1934 he founded the radical **Neo-Destour Party**. Arr. 1938–1943, supported Allies during Second World War, arr. 1952–1954. Became Pres. Constituent Assembly of Tunisia, 1956, Pres. Tunisia 1959–1987. Overthrown in a bloodless coup by PM Ben Ali.

BURNHAM, FORBES (1923–1985) Ed. London, law degree, 1947. Black politician of British Guyana, founded party advocating independence together with Indian leader Cheddi **Jagan**, broke with him in 1955 and established the more moderate People's National Congress (PNC), defeating **Jagan**'s People's Progressive Party (PPP) in 1964; PM 1966 (independence), defeated Jagan again in 1968 and 1973. He was helped by the USA which distrusted the leftist **Jagan**.

BUSTAMANTE, ALEXANDER (1884–1977) Jamaican politician, son of an Irish father and an African mother, worked in Cuba, Panama and New York, return. Jamaica 1934, Pres. Bustamante Industrial Trade Union 1939, arr. 1940–1942. Founded Jamaican Labour Party (JLP), won elections 1944 and 1953, became Chief Minister, but was defeated 1955 by his cousin N. **Manley**. He had campaigned against **West Indies Federation**, which **Manley** had supported. Defeating **Manley**, he became first PM of independent Jamaica 1962–1967.

C

CABRAL, AMILCAR (1924–1973) Ed. U. of Lisbon, worked as an agronomist for the Portuguese colonial administration of Guinea-Bissau, 1952–1954. Founder of **Partido Africano para a Independencia da Guinea e Cabo Verde (PAIGC)**, 1956, also helped Agostinho **Neto** in establishing the **Movimento Popular para a Libertacao Angola (MPLA)**, 1956. Launched military campaign against Portuguese with support of the Soviet Union and Cuba in

1963 and liberated most of Guinea-Bissau. Assassinated in Conakry, 1973, by Portuguese agents.

COMPTON, JOHN GEORGE MELVIN (1925–) Ed. London (law), founded United Labour Party, chief minister, Santa Lucia, 1964, first PM 1964, led country to independence 1979, then resigned, PM again 1982–1996.

D

DAAR, ADEN ABDULLAH OSMAN (1908–) Leader of **Somali Youth League (SYL)**, Pres. Somalia, 1960–1967.

DACKO, DAVID (1930–2003) Related to Barthélemy **Boganda**, succeeded him as party president; PM Central African Republic 1959, Pres. 1960, introduced one-party regime 1962, overthrown 1966 by military dictator Jean-Bedel Bokassa who nominated him as personal adviser; toppled Bokassa with French help in 1979, Pres. Central African Republic 1979–1981, overthrown by military.

DADDAH, MOKTAR OULD (1924–2003) Ed. Paris (law), married daughter of General de Gaulle, elected Pres. of Executive Council, Mauritania, 1958, PM 1959, Pres. of indep. rep., 1961, changed Mauritania to one-party state 1964, ousted 1978 by Lt. Col. Ould Salek, imprisoned, released, established (in French exile) opposition party Alliance pour une Mauretanie Democratique (AMD) in 1980, return. Mauritania 2001.

DANQUAH, JOSEPH (1895–1965) Ed. U London (philosophy, law). Founded United Gold Coast Convention 1947 and asked **K. Nkrumah** to be sec., who then pushed him aside and imprisoned him after Ghana attained independence. Danquah had proposed the ancient name Ghana for the new republic. Publ. *Akan Laws and Customs; The Akan Doctrine of God.*

DIA, MAMADOU (1910–) PM Senegal, 1958–1962, initially an associate of **L. S. Senghor**, he was accused of plotting to overthrow him and imprisoned (1963–1974). Publ. *Memoirs d'un militant du Tiers Monde; Afrique, le prix de la liberté.*

DIORI, HAMANI (1916–1989) Memb. French parliament, 1946–1956, PM Niger, 1958, Pres. 1960–1974.

F

FERRIER, JOHAN (1910–) Ed. Amsterdam, doctorate 1950. Black politician of Suriname (Dutch Guyana). After an administrative career he joined the Nationale Partij Suriname, PM of colonial government 1959–1965. He was appointed the last governor of Suriname in 1968 and became its Pres. in 1975 (independence). Remained Pres. until 1983 when he was ousted by military officers.

G

GAIRY, ERIC MATTHEW (1922–1997) Born and educated in Grenada, went to Dutch Caribbean island Aruba, 1943, worked with Lago Oil Co., organized workers, return. Grenada 1948, organized strike of plantation workers which led to riots in 1951, founded Grenada United Labour Party, PM Grenada 1974, was overthrown by his radical opponent, Maurice Bishop, in 1979. After US military intervention in 1983, Gairy returned to Grenada in 1984.

GANDHI, MOHANDAS KARAMCHAND (1869–1948) Born in Porbandar, Gujarat, India. Ed. London (law), return. India 1891, lawyer and leader of Indian minority in South Africa, 1893–1915, where he developed his method of non-violent resistance to unjust laws which he called **satyagraha** (holding on to the truth). Led Non-cooperation campaign of the **Indian National Congress** in India 1920–1922, arr. 1922–1924. Civil Disobedience movement ('Salt March') 1930, att. Second Round Table Conference, London 1931, arr. 1932–1933. During the Second World War he proposed the 'Quit India Movement' in 1942, arr. 1942–1944. Tried to calm Hindu–Muslim tensions at the time of the partition of India. Assassinated by a radical Hindu, January 30, 1948. Publ. *Hind Swaraj; My Experiments with Truth (Autobiography); Collected Works (90 vols)*.

GARVEY, MARCUS (1887–1940) Born in Jamaica, ed. London, return. Jamaica 1914, organized Jamaica Improvement Society, went to the USA and organized the Universal Negro Improvement Association, campaigned for 'Africa for the Africans' and sponsored the 'Declaration of the Rights of the Negro Peoples of the World' (New York, 1920). Instilled a pride in their African heritage in the American and Caribbean blacks. Landed in jail due to unfortunate business transactions. Deported from the USA to Jamaica in 1927, he participated without success in Jamaican politics. Inspired **Rastafarianism**. Left for Great Britain in 1935 where he died in obscurity.

GIAP, VO NGUYEN (1912–) Ed. Hanoi U (law), organizer of **Vietminh** on behalf of **Ho Chi Minh**. Led victorious battle against French at Dien Bien Phu, 1954, and fought against the USA in the Vietnam War.

GRUNITZKY, NICOLAS (1913–1969) Named after his Polish father, ed. Paris (engineering), return. Togo 1937, joined resistance in Second World War, elected memb. French National Assembly 1951 and 1956. Founded Togolese Progress Party and became the Republic of Togo's first PM 1955, defeated in 1958 by S. **Olympio**, his brother-in-law, exile in Dahomey, return. Togo 1963 to head government after army coup, overthrown 1967.

GUÈYE, LAMINE (1891–1968) Ed. Paris (law), return. Senegal 1922, memb. French Socialist Party, magistrate, Réunion 1931, reorganized Parti Socialiste Sénégalais, 1935, mayor of Dakar, 1945–1961, memb. French parliament, 1946, mentor of L. S. **Senghor** who fell out with him in 1948.

GUSMAO, XANANA (1946–) Ed. Dili (East Timor), joined **FRETILIN** as information officer in 1974. After East Timor was occupied by the Indonesian army, he emerged as guerrilla leader in 1977. Arr. 1992, imprisoned in Indonesia until 1999. His sympathizers called him 'Mandela of Asia'. In 1998 elected Pres. (*in absentia*) by a national convention of East Timorese meeting in Portugal. In 2002 he contested the presidential elections as an independent and won with an overwhelming majority. Publ. *Timor Leste. Uma Povo, Uma Patria (1994); To Resist is to Win* (2000).

H

HADJ, MESSALI (1898–1974) Served in French army, 1918, emigrated from Algeria to France, 1923, co-founder **Étoile Nord-Africaine**, Paris, 1926, founded Parti Populaire Algerienne (PPA) 1937, arr. 1941, deported to Brazzaville, 1945; converted PPA into Mouvement pour La

Triomphe des Libertés Démocratiques (MTLD) 1946. After the prohibition of MTLD he formed Mouvement National Algérien in December 1954, which was opposed to the **Front de Libération Nationale (FLN)**, arr. during war in Algeria, released 1959.

HATTA, MOHAMMAD (1902–1980) Ed. Rotterdam, 1922–1932, formed Perhumpan Indonesia (Indonesian Union), 1926, memb. League against Imperialism, 1927, arr. 1927, return. Indonesia 1932, arr. 1935–1942. Under Japanese occupation headed nationalist mass organization together with **Sukarno** and signed with him the Proclamation of Independence in August 1945. Became vice-president of the republic, PM in 1948. When **Sukarno** turned to a dictatorial style of government, Hatta left politics in 1956.

HO CHI MINH (1890–1969) Worked in France, 1912–21, participated in the founding of the French Communist Party, 1920, went to Canton, China, 1923, organized uprisings in Vietnam from China, sec. **Vietminh** 1941. Proclaimed independence of Democratic Republic of Vietnam, 1945. Pres. of North Vietnam 1954, spearheaded struggle against the South in the Vietnam War.

HOUPHOUET-BOIGNY, FÉLIX (1905–1993) Ed. Dakar (medicine), cocoa planter, founded Agricultural Union of the Ivory Coast, 1944. Memb. French Constituent Assemby, 1945. Established **Rassemblement Démocratique Africain (RDA)**, 1946. Memb. French parliament, holding the post of a minister in the French government, 1956–1958. Participated in the drafting of the **Loi cadre**, 1956. PM and then Pres. Ivory Coast, 1958–1993.

I

IDRIS AL-ZANUSSI (1890–1983), King of Libya, 1951–1969 Succeeded his father as head of the Sufi brotherhood of the Sanusi of the Cyrenaica. Fled to Egypt in 1922 and returned in 1942 when the British had vanquished the Italian colonial rulers of Libya. Idris became king of Libya as a constitutional monarch in December 1951. Returned to Egypt in 1969, after being overthrown in a military coup.

J

JAGAN, CHEDDI (1918–1997) Ed. Northwestern U, Chicago (dentistry), chief minister, British Guyana, 1953, arr. 1954, PM British Guyana, 1961–1964, defeated by former associate Forbes **Burnham**. Leader of the opposition, Pres. of indep. Guyana, 1992–1997.

JINNAH, MOHAMMED ALI (1876–1948) Ed. London (law), 1892–1896, return. India 1896, memb. **Indian National Congress**, 1906–1922, memb. **Muslim League** 1913–1948 f., memb. Imperial Legislative Council, 1911–1930, 1935–1946, Pres. **Muslim League** 1915, att. Round Table Conferences in London 1930, 1931 and practised law in London until 1934. Enunciated 'Two Nations Theory' (Hindus and Muslims) at Lahore session of **Muslim League** 1940, supported demand for Pakistan. First Governor General of Pakistan 1947.

K

KASAVUBU, JOSEPH (1913–1969)
Founded Abako, an association devoted to
the unification of the Bakongo in French and
Belgian Congo and Angola. Belgian ban of
Abako in 1959 led to riots. He negotiated
with Belgians jointly with **P. Lumumba**.
First Pres. of Congo Democratic Republic,
1960, overthrown by General Mobutu 1965.

KAUNDA, KENNETH (1924–) Initially an
associate of **H. Nkumbula** he worked as
an organizer of the **African National
Congress**, but broke with him and founded
Zambia National Congress in 1958, arr.
1954, 1958. First PM then Pres. of Zambia
1964. Continued as Pres. until 1991.
Entered politics again as Pres. United
Independence Party in 1995.

KAYIBANDA, GRÉGOIRE (1924–1976) Ed.
mission school, Rwanda, editor of Catholic
journal *Kinyamateka* (in the local language
Kinyarwanda). Author of 'Hutu Manifesto',
1957. Founder Parti du Mouvement de
l'Emancipation Hutu (PARMEHUTU),
1959, PM Rwanda 1960, Pres. Rwanda
1961.

KEITA, MODIBO (1915–1977) Ed. in
Koran schools, memb. **Rassemblement
Démocratique Africain (RDA)**, associate
of **F. Houphouet-Boigny**, but fell out with
him as he did not share his views on feder-
ating French colonies. Memb. French
parliament 1956 and its vice-president
(i.e. deputy speaker), supported **French
Union** in referendum of 1958. First Pres. of
Federation of Senegal and Mali which broke
up very soon after forming, subsequently
first Pres. Mali. Worked for establishment
of **Organization of African Unity (OAU)**,
1963.

KENYATTA, JOMO (1891–1978) Ed.
Church of Scotland Mission School, Sec.
Kikuyu Central Association, 1928. Visited
England 1929 and studied anthropology
at London School of Economics. Founded
Pan-African Federation with George
Padmore and Kwame **Nkrumah** 1945.
Return. Kenya 1946, Pres. Kenya African
Union. Arr. 1955–1961, accused of sup-
porting **Mau Mau** movement. Pres. **Kenya
African National Union (KANU)** which
won elections in 1963. First PM of Kenya,
then Pres. 1964–1978. Publ. *Facing Mount
Kenya; Suffering without Bitterness.*

KHAMA, SERETSE (1921–1980) Ed. Balliol
College, Oxford, and Inner Temple,
London, kgosi (king) of the Bangwato,
Botswana, under pressure of Union of South
Africa deprived of his kingship because
of his marriage to a white woman, while liv-
ing in exile in Great Britain 1951–1956,
founded Bechuanaland Democratic Party
(BDP) 1961, won elections 1965, PM of
Botswana 1965, Pres. 1966, died in office
1980.

L

LEE KUAN YEW (1923–) Ed. Cambridge,
practised law in Singapore, founded
People's Action Party (PAP), 1954. PM
Singapore, 1959. Achieved merger of
Singapore with Malaya (forming Malaysia)
by winning a referendum in 1962. The
merger was mainly aimed at isolating Lee's
rivals, the leftist Barisan Socialis. In 1965
Singapore seceded from Malaysia and continued as a state dominated by Lee and the
PAP. Resigned as PM 1990, but remained
'senior minister'.

LINI, WALTER (1942–1999) Ed. theology
(Anglican), New Zealand, return. New

Hebrides/Vanuatu 1970, PM indep. Vanuatu 1980, resigned 1991.

LISETTE, GABRIEL (1919–2001) Black French civil servant, born in Panama and posted to Chad in 1946, elected to French parliament from Chad, 1946, founder Chad Progressive Party, Sec. **Rassemblement Démocratique Africain (RDA)** to which his party was affiliated, PM Chad under **Loi cadre**, ousted by his rival F. **Tombalbaye** in 1959. Publ. *Le Combat du Rassemblement Démocratique Africain pour la décolonisation pacifique de l'Afrique noire.*

LUMUMBA, PATRICE (1925–1961) Worked as post office accountant, part-time journalist, Sec. of a local trade union, 1955. Founded Mouvement National Congolais (MNC), 1958, att. **All-African People's Conference**, Accra 1958. Arr. 1959. Released to att. Brussels conference, 1960. MNC won elections, PM Congo June–September 1960. Appealed to Soviet Union for help against secession of Katanga. Pres. **Kasavubu** dismissed Lumumba. Arr. and sent to Katanga where he was killed.

MACHEL, SAMORA (1933–1986) Worked as a male nurse, joined **Frente de Libertacao de Mocambique (FRELIMO)** in 1962, became commander of its guerrilla army, 1970, committed to the establishment of a communist state, Pres. Mozambique 1975, died in a plane crash when his plane was accidentally diverted to South African territory.

MAGA, HUBERT (1916–2000) Trained as a teacher, represented Dahomey in French parliament, 1951–1958, Pres. Dahomey,

1960, overthrown 1963, went into exile, return. Dahomey 1970 and joined triumvirate (national government) with **Apithy** and **Ahomadgebe**, overthrown and imprisoned by the army 1972, released 1981.

MAGSAYSAY, RAMON (1907–1957) Ed. U. of Philippines, fought against invading Japanese in 1942 and continued as underground guerrilla commander. Memb. of parliament 1946–1950. Reformed army as defence minister and put an end to Huk insurgency. Supported land reforms. Pres. Philippines 1953–1957. Died in a plane crash.

MANLEY, NORMAN (1893–1969) Jamaican politician, son of an Irish father and an African mother. Ed. Oxford (law). Pres. People's National Party (PNP), 1938–1967. Chief minister 1955–1959, PM of Jamaica before independence, 1959–1962. Supporter of the **West Indies Federation**, defeated 1962 by his cousin, A. **Bustamante**, who had opposed it.

MARGAI, MILTON (1895–1964) Ed. medicine, Freetown, Sierra Leone and Liverpool School of Tropical Medicine, served as senior medical officer, Sierra Leone, founded Sierra Leone People's Party (SLPP), 1951. Chief minister 1954–1961, PM 1961–1964, succeeded by his brother Albert Margai, PM 1964–1967.

MARSHALL, DAVID (1908–1995) Ed. London (law), first chief minister of Singapore, 1955–1956, resigned when the British refused to transfer power, founded Workers' Party and remained in opposition to the **PAP**. Served as Singapore's ambassador to France, Spain, Portugal and Switzerland, 1978–1993. Publ. *Singapore's Struggle for Nationhood, 1945–1959.*

M'BA, LÉON (1902–1967) PM Gabon

1958, Pres. 1961, survived military coup of 1964 with French help, succeeded in 1967 by Albert-Bernard Bongo (renamed El-Hadj Omar Bongo, 1973) who had been director of his personal office since 1962.

MBOYA, THOMAS JOSEPH (1930–1969) Trade unionist, associate of J. **Kenyatta**, Sec. Kenya Federation of Labour, 1953. Studied in England and India. Return. Kenya 1956. Memb. Kenya Legislative Council, 1957. Pres. **All-African People's Conference**, Accra 1958. Sec. **Kenya African National Union (KANU)**, 1960. After independence minister in government of Kenya, 1963–1969. Assassinated 1969. Publ. *Towards Freedom; Kenya Faces the Future; The Challenge of Nationhood.*

MOHAMMED V, SULTAN OF MOROCCO (1911–1961) Succeeded to the throne in 1927 with French support, but worked with Istiqlal (Independence Party). In Second World War he supported the Free French, but in 1947 he openly advocated the national cause. Deposed by the French, 1953. Exile in Madagascar. Return. Morocco 1955. He had become a national hero. After independence in 1956 he became head of state and adopted the title King of Morocco.

MONDLANE, EDUARDO (1920–1969) Ed. Witwatersrand U, South Africa; Oberlin College, Northwestern U, Harvard U, USA; Research officer, UN Trusteeship Dept, Prof. sociology, Syracuse U, USA; Pres. **Frente de Libertacao de Mocambique (FRELIMO)**, 1962–1969, operating from Tanzania, assassinated 1969 in Dar-es-Salaam.

MUGABE, ROBERT GABRIEL (1924–) Ed. Fort Hare U (South Africa), worked as a teacher in Ghana. Return. Southern Rhodesia 1960, joined J. **Nkomo's**

Zimbabwe African People's Union (ZAPU). Arr. 1964–1974, then left for Mozambique and from there conducted guerrilla warfare. Return. Southern Rhodesia (Zimbabwe) 1979. PM 1980, established virtual one-party rule and has remained in power ever since.

MUTESA II, KABAKA OF BUGANDA (1924–1969) Ed. Makerere College, Uganda, and Cambridge, crowned 1942, opposed **East African Federation**, exiled by British governor 1953. Return. Uganda 1955. Formed alliance with M. **Obote**. Pres. Uganda, 1962–1966, overthrown by Obote. Exile in London, 1966–1969. Publ. *The Desecration of my Kingdom.*

MUZOREWA, ABEL (1925–) Ed. Methodist colleges (USA), Bishop of Methodist Church 1968. Opposed the government of Ian Smith, founded **African National Congress (ANC)** of Rhodesia, which remained the only legal party while the **Zimbabwe African National Union (ZANU)** and the **Zimbabwe African People's Union (ZAPU)** were banned and conducted guerrilla warfare. They considered Muzorewa and his ANC as a convenient front. PM of transitional government 1978 which received no international recognition. When independence was achieved in 1980 Muzorewa lost out to R. **Mugabe**.

N

NAHHAS, MUSTAFA AL- (1876–1965) Ed. Academy of Law, served as a judge, 1904–1919, dismissed because of nationalist activities, joined **Wafd Party** 1919, PM of Egypt 1928, 1930, 1936–1937, 1942–1944, 1950–1952. Pres. Wafd Party 1927 as successor to Saad **Zaghlul.**

Negotiated Anglo-Egyptian treaty 1936, clashed with King Faruq and resigned, imposed by British on Faruq 1942, lost British support 1944 and was dismissed by Faruq. Suggested establishment of **Arab League** 1943. PM once more after **Wafd Party** won elections in 1950.

NASSER, GAMAL ABDEL (1918–1970) Ed. Royal Military Academy, Sandhurst (UK), memb. Free Officers Movement which overthrew King Faruk. PM of Egypt 1954, Pres. 1956–1970. Att. **Bandung Conference** 1955, nationalized Suez Canal 1956, established United Arab Republic (Egypt and Syria) 1958–1961, defeated by Israel in Six Days War of 1967. Publ. *The Philosophy of the Revolution.*

NEHRU, JAWAHARLAL (1889–1964) Ed. Harrow, Cambridge (science), London (law), return. India 1912, joined Mahatma **Gandhi's** Non-cooperation campaign, arr. 1921, Pres. **Indian National Congress (INC)** 1929, participated in Civil Disobedience campaign 1930, arr. several times, Pres. INC 1936 and 1937, led Congress election campaign 1937, spent most of the war in prison, interim PM of British India, August 1946–1947, PM of India 1947–1964, att. **Bandung Conference** 1955 and **Belgrade Conference** 1961. Publ. *Autobiography; The Discovery of India.*

NETO, AGOSTINHO (1922–1979) Ed. Lisbon (medicine), poet and physician, founded **Movimento Popular de Libertacao de Angola (MPLA)**, 1956. Imprisoned in Angola several times, fled to Morocco and directed struggle against Portuguese rule from abroad, relied on Soviet and Cuban support, Pres. Angola 1975–1979; died in Moscow.

NE WIN (1911–2002) Belonged to a group of radical Burmese nationalists in the 1930s and to the 'Thirty Comrades' (**Aung San** *et al.*) who left Burma in 1940 to get military training under the Japanese with whom they returned to Burma in 1942. Served in the Burmese Independence Army. Commander of the Burmese army, 1948. Headed caretaker government at the request of U **Nu**, 1960. Seized power in military coup 1962. President of Burma, 1974, resigned 1988.

NGALA, RONALD (1923–1972) Ed. Makere College, Kampala, a Giriama from coastal Kenya, advocated a federal constitution, Pres. **Kenya African Democratic Union**, 1960. De facto PM (leader of government business), 1961. He later joined **Kenya African National Union** and held various ministerial positions; died in a car accident.

NKOMO, JOSHUA (1917–1999) Ed. South Africa, return. Southern Rhodesia 1948, organized trade union of black railway workers, founded **Zimbabwe African People's Union (ZAPU)**, 1962. R. **Mugabe** was initially associated with him, but became his rival in 1963. Arr. 1964–1974, Nkomo then went to Zambia, conducting guerrilla warfare from there. Defeated by **Mugabe** in the 1980 elections, he joined his government as home minister, was dismissed in 1982, became vice pres. in 1987.

NKRUMAH, KWAME (1909–1972) Ed. Achimota College (Ghana), Lincoln U, U of Pennsylvania (USA), lived in London 1945–47, return. Ghana 1947, Sec. **United Gold Coast Convention** 1946, started **Convention People's Party** 1949, won elections 1951, appointed leader of government business (de facto PM), PM of indep. Ghana 1957, hosted **All-Africa People's Conference**, Accra 1958, att. **Belgrade Conference** 1961, and first conference of the **Organization of African Unity**, Addis Ababa, 1963, overthrown by the army in 1966, spent the rest of his life in Conakry

(Guinea), invited by S. **Touré**. Publ. *Autobiography, I Speak of Freedom. A Statement of African Ideology; Africa Must Unite; Consciencism.*

NKUMBULA, HARRY (1916–1983) Ed. Makerere College, Uganda, London School of Economics. In London associated with J. **Kenyatta** and K. **Nkrumah**. Return. Northern Rhodesia (Zambia), 1950. Pres. Northern Rhodesia African National Congress, 1951. Considered to be too moderate by his younger associate, K. **Kaunda**, he was sidelined and lost elections 1964.

NU, U (1907–1995) Ed. Rangoon U (law), associate of **Aung San** in national movement since the 1930s, foreign minister in Burmese government under Japanese occupation. Vice-pres. **Anti-Fascist People's Freedom League (AFPFL)**, 1946. After **Aung San**'s assassination PM of Burma, 1947–1956, 1957–1958, 1960–1962. Overthrown by General **Ne Win**. Arr. 1962–1966. Exile in Thailand. Return. Burma (Myanmar) 1980, under house arr. 1989–1992. Publ. *The People Win Through; Burma under the Japanese; An Asian Speaks; Autobiography.*

NUJOMA, SAM (1929–) Worker, South African Railways, ed. Trans-Africa Correspondence College, South Africa. Organized resistance to apartheid policy, 1959. In exile (Tanzania) 1960–1989. Founder **South West African People's Organization (SWAPO)** 1960, commander-in-chief of its armed struggle, 1966–1989. Recognized by **OAU** 1968 and by **United Nations** 1973. Signed ceasefire agreement with South Africa 1989, Pres. Namibia 1990, re-elected 1994 and 1999.

NURI AL-SAID (1888–1958) Ed. Military Academy, Istanbul. Iraqi military officer of the Ottoman army, sympathized with Young Turks. In 1930 he became PM of Iraq for the first time then again 1938–1940, 1941–1943, 1946 and several times in subsequent years, assassinated 1958.

NYERERE, JULIUS (1922–1999) Ed. Makerere College, Uganda, and U of Edinburgh. Return. Tanganyika 1952. Pres. Tanganyika African Association, 1953, which became **Tanganyika African National Union (TANU)** in 1954. Chief minister of Tanganyika 1960, resigned to do party work. After independence in 1961 he became Pres. Republic of Tanganyika, survived army mutiny of 1964, united Tanganyika with Zanzibar, 1964. Pres. Tanzania 1964–1985. Publ. *Freedom and Unity; Man and Development.*

O

OBOTE, MILTON (1925–) Ed. Makerere College, Uganda, worked as labourer in Kenya and joined **Kenyatta**'s Kenya African Union. Return. Uganda 1957, memb. Uganda Legislative Council, 1958. Founded Uganda People's Congress, 1960. Formed alliance with Kabaka Yekka, the party of **Mutesa II, Kabaka of Buganda**. After independence 1962 PM with Kabaka as Pres., whom he overthrew in 1966. Pres. Uganda 1966–1971, overthrown by military dictator Idi Amin. Invaded Uganda with Tanzanian army 1979 and deposed Idi Amin. Pres. Uganda 1980–1985.

OLYMPIO, SYLVANUS (1902–1963) Scion of a rich Afro-Brazilian family, ed. U of Vienna, London School of Economics. Return. West Africa 1926, became director of United Africa Company. Leader of Ewe people in Togoland, worked for unification of French and British trust territories. PM pre-indep. Togoland 1958, defeating his rival and brother-in-law, **N. Grunitzky**, secured independence 1960, Pres. Togoland 1962, assassinated in army coup, 1963.

P

PADMORE, GEORGE (1902–1959) Black intellectual born as Malcolm Nurse in Trinidad. Studied in the USA (1924–1929) and joined the US Communist Party. In 1929 he moved to the Soviet Union where he became Sec. of the International Trade Union Committee of Negro Workers. In 1933 he broke with communism and went to London where he established the International African Service Bureau and edited the journal *African Opinion*. He organized the Pan-African Conference in Manchester in 1945 which was attended by **Kenyatta** and **Nkrumah**. In 1957 he settled in Ghana as an advisor to **Nkrumah**.

PATEL VALLABHABAI (1875–1950) Leader of the **Indian National Congress** from Gujarat. Close associate of Mahatma **Ghandi**. Home minister of India, 1946–1950. After his success in integrating the Indian princely states, he was called the 'Bismarck of India'. Being more conservative than **Nehru**, he emerged as his chief political rival.

PENGEL, JOHAN ADOLF (1916–1970) Black politician in Suriname (Dutch Guyana) since 1949, member of colonial legislature for Nationale Partij Suriname (NPS), formed cabinet 1958, PM 1963–1969. Charismatic national leader, cooperated with Indian minority. Pursued an independent foreign policy and was considered to be a threat to the Dutch colonial rulers who were responsible for the fall of his government.

PHETSARAT (PRINCE) (1890–1959) Ed. Paris, the 'Iron Prince', joined French colonial service in Laos in 1914, appointed Viceroy 1941 by the King of Laos, joined **Lao Issara** with his half-brothers **Souvanna Phuma** and **Souphanouvong**. On October 12, 1945, when the King of Laos was forced to abdicate because he wanted to restore French sovereignty, Phetsarat became de facto ruler of the country, proclaimed independence, returning French forced him to flee to Thailand. He appointed **Souphanouvong** as commander of the troops of **Lao Issara**, but remained in exile in Thailand. Return. Laos 1956, helps to establish coalition government of **Souvanna Phuma** and **Souphanouvong**.

PINDLING, LYNDEN (1930–2000) Ed. London, King's College, law degree 1952. Black politician, Bahamas. Elected leader Progressive Liberal Party (1956), PM 1967, led his country to independence in 1973 and remained PM until 1997.

PRICE, GEORGE CADLE (1919–) Ed. theology, Mayor of Belize City (British Honduras), 1958–1962, co-founder of Peoples United Party (PUP), first minister 1961, PM 1964, PM indep. Belize 1981, remained PM until 1984, re-elected PM 1989–1993.

Q

QUEZON, MANUEL LUIS (1878–1944) Ed. U of Santo Tomas, Spain. Return. Philippines 1898, did not participate in the independence movement against Spain but joined the subsequent American–Philippine war. Arr. 1901–1903, but later worked with the Americans as leader of the Nacionalista Party, led negotiations for Philippine independence, fled to the USA at the time of the

Japanese invasion and established a government in exile.

R

RABEMANANJARA, JACQUES (1913–) Ed. Sorbonne, Paris, noted poet (French), edited *Présence Africaine* with L. S. **Senghor**, co-founder of Mouvement Démocratique de la Rénovation Malgache (MDRM), 1946, Member of French parliament, his parliamentary immunity was cancelled in 1947 after the rebellion in Madagascar, imprisonment 1947–1956. Minister in P. **Tsiranana**'s government. In exile after coup of 1972. Publ. *Sur les marches du soir* (poems 1940), *Rites millénaires* (1955), *Nationalisme et problèmes malgaches* (1958), etc.

RAHMAN, TUNKU ABDUL (1903–1990) Ed. Cambridge, London (law), memb. **United Malays National Organization (UMNO)**, campaigned against British proposal of **Malayan Union**, Pres. UMNO 1951. Formed alliance with Malayan Chinese Association in 1952 (National Front). First PM Malaya 1953–1963, and then of Malaysia (1963–1970). Racial clashes between Malays and Chinese (1969) led to his resignation in 1970.

RAMGOOLAM, SEEWOOSAGUR (1900–1985) Ed. London (medicine), Pres. London Branch of **Indian National Congress**, 1924, Return. Mauritius 1935, co-founder, Mauritius Labour Party, nominated memb. legislative council, 1940–1948, then elected memb., chief minister 1961, premier 1965, PM 1968–1982, governor general, 1983–1985.

RASETA, JOSEPH (1886–1979) Ed. medicine, Madagascar, member of militant nationalist movements and co-founder of Parti Communiste Malgache, arr. 1942–1943, elected member of French constitutent assembly and then of French parliament, 1945, 1946. Co-founder **Mouvement Démocratique de la Renovation Malgache (MDRM)**, 1946, parliamentary immunity cancelled after rebellion of 1947, death sentence commuted into imprisonment. Released in 1955 and kept under house arrest, return. Madagascar 1960.

RAVOAHANGY, JOSEPH (1893–1970) Ed. medicine, co-founder **Mouvement Démocratique de la Rénovation Malgache (MDRM)**, 1946, member of French parliament, parliamentary immunity cancelled after rebellion 1947, death sentence commuted to imprisonment.

ROBERTO, JOSÉ HOLDEN (1928–) Born in the Congo, he founded the Union de las Poblaciones de Angola in 1954 and in 1962 the **Frente Nacional para a Liberacion de Angola (FNLA)**. He also established an Angolan government in exile in which J. **Savimbi** served as a minister, before they parted company. In 1975 they joined forces again and started a civil war against the government of A. **Neto**. Roberto was vanquished, withdrew to the forest in 1976 and left Angola for France in 1980 where he lived in exile for some time.

ROXAS, MANUEL (1892–1948) Ed. U of Philippines (law), memb. House of Representatives in the 1930s, captured by the Japanese and forced to collaborate, but covertly supported underground resistance. After independence 1946, first Pres. Philippines.

RWAGASORE, LOUIS (1932–1961) Crown Prince of Burundi, founder of *Unité et Progrès National* (UPRONA), a party of both Tutsi and Hutu, PM Burundi 1961, assassinated October 1961.

S

SAVIMBI, JONAS (1934–2002) Ed. Angola, Portugal and Switzerland, initially associated with José Holden **Roberto** as minister in his Angolan government in exile in 1962. Savimbi left this government in 1964, spent some time in China, then started his own party, **Uniao Nacional para a Independencia Total de Angola (UNITA)**, in 1969. In 1975 he initially joined a coalition government with **Neto** and **Roberto**. But then Savimbi and Roberto conspired with the USA and South Africa against **Neto**. They lost and continued a civil war against **Neto**'s government. Savimbi had a stronghold in his native Ovimbundu country. In 1992 he almost won the Angolan presidential election, but having lost it he continued his fight. He was finally killed in an encounter with government troops.

SAYA SAN (1876–1937) Buddhist monk and Burmese nationalist, conducted agrarian enquiry on behalf of the General Council of Burmese Associations, 1927–1928. Supported the cause of the peasants by petitioning the government for remittance of the poll tax, then led a rebellion starting in the Tharrawaddy District of Lower Burma in December 1930. The rebellion spread, the British deployed 10,000 troops to suppress it, which took them two years. Saya San was arr. 1932, defended by **Ba Maw**, executed 1937.

SENANAYAKE, DON STEPHEN (1884–1952) Ed. St Thomas College, Minister in the State Council of Ceylon (Sri Lanka) since its establishment in 1931, and its head since 1942. First PM 1947, negotiated transfer of power 1948, remained PM until his death.

SENGHOR, LEOPOLD SÉDAR (1906–2001) Ed. Sorbonne, Paris, taught literature and linguistics in France. Memb. French Constituent Assemblies, 1945, 1946. Memb. French parliament, 1946–1958, held various positions in French governments. Noted poet (French); Memb. Académie Française 1983. Pres. Senegal 1960–1985. Publ. *Chants d'Ombre; Hosties Noires; On African Socialism; Selected Poems.*

SIHANOUK, NORODOM (1922–) King of Cambodia, crowned in 1941 as successor to his uncle, forced French to grant independence in 1954. Joined Cambodian politics and abdicated in favour of his father Suramarit who was king until 1960. Subsequently Sihanouk was head of state. He ruled Cambodia from 1955 to 1970 when he was overthrown by Lon Nol. He lived in exile in Beijing until 1976. Return. Cambodia but arr. until 1978. In 1982 he became pres. of a coalition government and in 1993 he was reinstated as king.

SIMMONDS, KENNEDY (1936–) Ed. St Kitts, U of the West Indies, Kingston (medicine), return. St Kitts, 1964, founding member People's Action Movement (PAM) 1965, postgraduate studies, Pittsburgh, 1968–70, elected to the legislative assembly, St Kitts and Nevis, 1979, led coalition of PAM and Nevis Reformation Party, 1980, as premier, led his countrty to independence in 1983 and won subsequent elections in 1984, 1989, 1993. Retired 1995.

SITHOLE, NDABANGINI (1920–2000) Ed. USA, return. Zimbabwe 1958, Methodist clergyman, founder of **Zimbabwe African National Union (ZANU)**, 1963, arr. 1964, spent 10 years in prison; after split of **ZANU** in 1975 he led the moderate ZANU (Ndonga), served in government of Abel **Muzorewa** 1979, was defeated by Robert **Mugabe** in 1980 and spent 1983–1992 in self-imposed exile in USA, arr. 1997 when accused of plot to assassinate **Mugabe**.

SJAHRIR, SUTAN (1909–1966) Ed. Netherlands, joined Partai Nasional Indonesia (PNI) but led a wing of the party opposed to **Sukarno** in 1931, arr. and detained in West Irian, 1934–1942. Liberated by the Japanese, but refused to collaborate with them and went 'underground'. PM, Republic of Indonesia, November 1945 to June 1947, introduced parliamentary democracy. Conducted negotiations with the Dutch, but resigned when he saw that they wanted to destroy the republic. As a democratic socialist he had only a limited following among intellectuals and lost political influence.

SOMARE, MICHAEL (1936–) Ed. school teacher, co-founder of Pangu Party, 1967, chief minister 1972, PM 1975, led Papua New Guinea to independence, in office until 1980, PM again 1982–1985 and from 2002.

SOUPHANOUVONG (PRINCE) (1909–1995) Ed. Hanoi and Paris (civil engineering), half-brother of **Phetsarat** and **Souvanna Phuma**, worked in Vietnam, in 1945 joined **Ho Chi Minh** who supported him in his fight against the returning French, was defeated, fled to Thailand, then joined **Vo Nguyen Giap** and accompanied Vietnamese forces into Laos. At Geneva Conference of 1954 the control of his orgnization **Pathet Lao** over two provinces in Northern Laos was confirmed. Joined **Souvanna Phuma**'s government in 1957. Arr. 1959, escaped 1960, formed new governemt with **Souvanna Phuma** in 1962, new split under impact of Vietnam War. Pres. Democratic Republic of Laos 1975–1986.

SOUVANNA PHUMA (PRINCE) (1901–1984) Half-brother of **Phetsarat** and

Souphanouvong, ed. Paris and Grenoble (civil and electrical engineering), worked as civil engineer in Laos. Joined **Lao Issara** rebel government 1945. PM Laos 1951–1952, sidelined in 1958, PM again 1962, 1970–1975. He then lived in exile in Paris.

SUKARNO (1901–1970) Ed. Bandung Technical College (engineering), founder (1927), **Partai Nasional Indonesia (PNI)**, arr. 1929–1931, 1933–1942. With his associate M. **Hatta** he led a nationalist mass movement under Japanese occupation, proclaimed independence of Republic of Indonesia in 1945. Pres. 1945–1968. After intial experiments with a parliamentary regime introduced by S. **Sjahrir**, Sukarno turned to 'guided democracy' as the 1955 elections had accentuated regional differences. In 1965 he narrowly survived a coup, supposedly attempted by communists. Order was restored and many communists were killed by the army under General Suharto, who then deposed Sukarno in 1968. Publ. *Autobiography as told to Cindy Adams; Nationalism, Islam and Marxism.*

T

TOMBALBAYE, FRANCOIS (NGARTA) (1918–1975) Co-founder of Chad Progressive Party affiliated to the **Rassemblement Démocratique Africain (RDA)**, PM of Chad 1959, Pres. 1960, started movement for 'authentic' culture and changed his first name in this context in 1973, assassinated 1975.

TOURÉ, SEKOU (1922–1984) Trade unionist, worked with GCT (Confédération Générale du Travail), the French communist union, left it in 1957 and became sec. UGTAN, a union of black workers of Africa. Mayor of Conakry, 1955. Memb.

French parliament, 1956–1958. Opposed to French Community, Guinea voted against it in the referendum of 1958. Pres. Guinea 1958–1984.

TSHOMBE, MOISHE KAPENDA (1919–1969) Headed the Confédération des Associations de Katanga, 1959, and opposed **Lumumba**'s plans for a unitary state at the Congo conference in Brussels, 1960. Declared Katanga an independent republic. **UN** troops entered Katanga in 1961, it was reunited with Congo in 1963. Tshombe exiled but recalled in 1964 by Pres. J. **Kasavubu** who made him PM of Congo. After **Kasavubu** sacked him in 1965, General Mobutu took over power in a military coup. Tshombe fled and was detained in Algeria.

TSIRANANA, PHILIBERT (1912–1978) Ed. U of Montpellier (France), memb. Madagascar Representative Assembly, 1952, memb. French parliament 1956. Founded Parti des Désinherités de Madagascar, 1946, Parti Social-Democrate, 1956. Head of provisional government of Madagascar 1958. Pres. 1959, proclaimed independence 1960, re-elected 1965 and 1972. Overthrown by the army in 1972.

WILLIAMS, ERIC (1911–1981) Ed. Trinidad and Oxford U, D.Phil. 1938, taught at Howard U (USA). Return. Trinidad 1955, founded People's National Movement, chief minister 1956. PM 1961–1981, Publ. *Capitalism and Slavery, The Negro in the Caribbean, British Historians and the West Indies, From Columbus to Castro, Inward Hunger* (Autobiography).

YAMÉOGO, MAURICE (1921–1993) Ed. Catholic seminary, deprived of priesthood when he married. Pres. Upper Volta (Burkina Faso) 1960, overthrown by military 1966.

YOULOU, FULBERT (1917–1972) Catholic priest, deprived of priesthood after he had entered politics and founded Union Démocratique pour la Défense des Intérèts Africains. Mayor of Brazzaville, 1956. PM Congo Republic 1958, Pres. 1960. Hosted **Brazzaville Conference (3)** of 12 pro-Western African states, 1960. Overthrown 1963.

Zaghlul, Saad (1859–1927) Ed. al-Azhar U, Cairo (Islamic law, theology), education minister, 1906, law minister 1910, inspired by Woodrow Wilson, he proclaimed Egyptian independence 1918, led delegation (= *wafd*) to conference at Versailles, 1919, founded **Wafd Party** 1919, arr. 1921, after formal independence of Egypt renewed agitation, arr. 1923, PM after Wafd Party won elections 1924, resigned due to clash with King Fuad, 1924.

GLOSSARY

The glossary contains names of conferences, movements, organizations and parties, as well as special political terms, including those derived from African and Asian languages. Some organizations are better know by their acronym or abbreviation (e.g. FRELIMO, POLISARIO, UNITA, etc.). In such cases, the acronym or abbreviation is listed first, followed by the full names in parentheses.

Abbreviations: Att. = attended; Host. = hosted by; Pres. = president; PM = prime minister; Sec. = secretary or secretary general.

ABAKO (ALLIANCE DES BAKONGO) Congolese political party headed by J. **Kasavubu**.

ACTION GROUP Nigerian political party headed by O. **Awolowo**.

AFPFL (ANTI-FASCIST PEOPLE'S FREEDOM LEAGUE) Burmese political party founded by **Aung San** in 1945 after he had turned against the Japanese and supported the British. It contained nationalist and communist elements. It remained in power under PM U **Nu** until 1962, when he was overthrown by General **Ne Win**.

AFRICAN NATIONAL CONGRESS (ANC) Founded in 1912 as South African Native National Congress, adopted its present name in 1923, banned after the Sharpeville Massacre of 1960. The ANC leader, Nelson Mandela, was arrested in 1962. The ban of the ANC was lifted in 1990 and it became the ruling party in the Union of South Africa in 1994. The ANC actively supported national movements in adjacent colonies.

AFRO-ASIAN SOLIDARITY A movement which was inaugurated at the **Bandung Conference**, 1955. Its protagonists met at various subsequent conferences, but interest in it declined due to conflicts among states such as China and India (border war, 1962). It disintegrated when India pleaded for an inclusion of the Soviet Union as a counterweight to China. It was replaced by the **Non-aligned Movement (NAM)** from which China and the Soviet Union were excluded due to their 'aligned' positions.

ALL-AFRICAN PEOPLE'S CONFERENCE, ACCRA, 1958 Host. K. **Nkrumah**, Pres. T. **Mboya**. Att. by many African leaders, e.g. P. **Lumumba**, who played decisive roles in the decolonization of their respective countries. It owed its inspiration to **Pan-Africanism**.

ARAB LEAGUE Founded in March 1945 with headquarters in Cairo and headed by an Egyptian Sec. Abdarrahman Azzam. The inital members of the League were, in addition to Egypt, Saudi Arabia, Lebanon, Iraq, Transjordania and Yemen. The League was supposed to represent a united front in support of Palestine and against Israel but did not achieve much. It was plagued by internal rivalries. After making peace with Israel in 1979, Egypt was expelled from the League and its headquarters were shifted to Tunis.

ARAB LEGION An elite Bedouin force of the Amir of Transjordan, commanded by the British General John Glubb (Glubb Pasha) from 1938 to 1956. During this period the legion grew from 1,200 to 25,000 men. **Nasser** ensured that it was disbanded and Glubb sent home in 1956.

ATLANTIC CHARTER Statement of Allied war aims signed by Pres. Roosevelt and PM Churchill on 14 August 1941 when they met on board the ships 'Augusta' and 'Prince of Wales' in the North Atlantic. It contained a reference to national self-determination which Roosevelt saw as a universal principle, whereas Churchill later on stressed that it was meant to apply only to the nations subjected by Hitler and not to the British Empire.

B

BAATH PARTY (*Harakat al-ba'th al-arabi* = Movement for Arab Rebirth) Founded by M. **Aflaq** in 1943.

BALFOUR DECLARATION In a letter of November 2, 1917 to the Jewish leader, Lord Rothschild, the British Foreign Secretary, A. J. Balfour, pledged British support for a 'national home' for the Jews in Palestine while respecting the rights of non-Jews residing there. This corresponded to the aims of **Zionism** and presupposed British

control of Palestine. The **Sykes-Picot Agreement** of 1916 had assured the British of this control.

BAMAKO CONFERENCE, 1946 Convened by F. **Houphouet-Boigny** in the capital of the French Sudan (Mali). The **Rassemblement Démocratique Africain (RDA)** was established at that time, and it had links with the French Communist Party. Most of the leaders of French African colonies attended the conference, except for L. S. **Senghor** and some of his friends who did not share the political views and party affiliation of the host.

BANDUNG CONFERENCE, 1955 Host. Pres. **Sukarno** of Indonesia and att. by the heads of several African and Asian governments, e.g. Chou En-lai, G.A. **Nasser**, J. **Nehru**. It marked the beginning of the movement for **Afro-Asian Solidarity** and demanded further decolonization.

BELGRADE CONFERENCE, 1961 Host. Pres. Tito of Yugoslavia, first conference of the **Non-aligned Movement (NAM)**. **Nehru**, **Nasser** and Tito had met on the Yugoslavian island of Brioni in 1956 to inaugurate this movement. In addition to these 'founding fathers' the Belgrade Conference was att. by many prominent statesmen, e.g. **Nkrumah** and **Sukarno**.

BERLIN CONFERENCE, 1884 Host. Chancellor Bismarck of Germany. Initially the conference was convened to settle the status and the delimitation of the Belgian Congo. Bismarck had offered to act as 'honest broker'. The conference also took up the claims of various other European powers and contributed to the **Scramble for Africa**.

BRAZZAVILLE CONFERENCE (1), NOVEMBER 1941 General de Gaulle had established the **Free French** government in

Brazzaville in October 1940. In November 1941 he convened a conference of colonial administrators who supported the **Free French**. The conference decided on a new colonial policy. Autonomy but not yet self-government was the guiding principle.

BRAZZAVILLE CONFERENCE (2), FEB-RUARY 1944 The same group met with General de Gaulle to discuss the future of the colonies and to solicit US support. De Gaulle projected a plan for the future **French Union**.

BRAZZAVILLE CONFERENCE (3), DECEMBER 1960 Host. Pres. F. **Youlou**. It was a conference of those former French colonies which showed an interest in further cooperation with France. Guinea and Mali boycotted it and supported the rival **Casablanca Conference**.

BRITISH INDIAN EMPIRE India was conquered by the East India Company operating under a Royal Charter. In 1858 it was taken over by the crown. In 1876 Queen Victoria adopted the title of Empress of India. India was thus in a category of its own among British colonies.

BUGANDA, KABAKA OF The British protectorate of Uganda included several states headed by their respective kings or chiefs. Buganda was the largest of these states. Its king had the title Kabaka (*see* **Mutesa II**).

C

CABINET MISSION (TO INDIA), 1946 When the Labour Party formed a government in 1945, it failed to declare its intentions with regard to Indian decolonization. The Viceroy, Lord Wavell, thus left without a clear policy, drafted a Breakdown Plan

which so alarmed the cabinet that they dispatched three of their members to India: Lord Alexander, Sir Stafford Cripps and Lord Pethick-Lawrence. They discussed constitutional devices with the **Indian National Congress** and the **Muslim League** with a view to avoiding a partition of India. Since they had no mandate to settle the issue, their suggestions remained inconclusive.

CASABLANCA CONFERENCE (1), JANU-ARY 1943 Pres. Roosevelt and PM Churchill met to coordinate warfare. Demand for 'unconditional surrender' of the enemies proclaimed.

CASABLANCA CONFERENCE (2), JANU-ARY 1961 This conference was convened as a reaction to the **Brazzaville Conference (3)**. Att. by Algeria (provisional govt), Ghana, Guinea, Libya, Mali, Morocco, Tunisia, the United Arab Republic, this conference foreshadowed the emergence of the **Organization of African Unity (OAU)** which then also encompassed the rivals.

COMMONWEALTH The British Commonwealth of Nations consisted initially of only those former colonies which had acquired **dominion status** and continued to recognize the British monarch as head of state. When India adopted a republican constitution in 1950 but still wanted to remain a member of the Commonwealth, a compromise formula was found by which republics which acknowledge the monarch as head of the Commonwealth though not as head of their own state could be accommodated.

COMMUNAL REPRESENTATION, *see* **SEPARATE ELECTORATES**.

CONVENTION PEOPLE'S PARTY (CPP) Founded in Ghana in 1949 by K. **Nkrumah** as a radical offshoot of the **United Gold**

Coast Convention, the Sec. of which he had been since 1947. The CPP won the elections of 1951 and Nkrumah formed a government as de facto PM. He later on used the CPP to make Ghana a one-party state.

CROWN COLONY Directly under the control of the British Crown (e.g. Ceylon, Kenya) as distinct from protectorates (e.g. Uganda) or mandate territories (e.g. Tanganyika, Palestine). The British Indian Empire was not a crown colony as it was in a category of its own.

D

DOMINION STATUS A constitutional position which was first achieved by colonies of white settlers (e.g. Australia, Canada). A dominion is fully autonomous and has a government following the Westminster model. It belongs to the British Commonwealth of Nations. Its head of state is the British monarch represented by a Governor General. India and Pakistan acquired dominion status in 1947, before they adopted their republican constitutions.

E

EAST AFRICAN FEDERATION In spite of the different legal positions of Kenya (Crown colony), Tanganyika (mandate territory) and Uganda (protectorate), the British attempted to federate them. A customs union and a common currency were established in 1927, an East African High Commission in 1948 and a Common Court of Appeal for Eastern Africa in 1951. The East African Common Services Organization was added in 1961. J. Nyerere had suggested that the British should grant

independence to all three colonies in 1960. Since this was not feasible, the federation gradually disintegrated. The abandonment of the common currency in 1965 signified the end of a federation which had never been formally inaugurated.

ÉTOILE NORD-AFRICAINE (ENA) Organization devoted to the independence of the French colonies in North Africa, established in Paris, 1926, co-founder Messali Hadj. After ENA was prohibited in 1929 it was reorganized in 1933 but again prohibited in 1937.

F

FEDERATION OF MALAYA Established in 1948 after the Malayan Union had failed due to the opposition of the Malays. It included all Malay states and the Straits Settlements (Penang, Malakka) but excluded Singapore. It preserved the special rights of the Malays and of their sultans, one of whom is head of state (by rotation).

FEDERATION OF MALAYSIA Established in 1963, included Federation of Malaya plus Singapore, Sabah and Sarwak. Singapore was expelled in 1965.

FEDERATION OF RHODESIA AND NYASALAND Established in 1953 and abolished in 1963. It owed its origin to the activities of Roy Welensky, a North Rhodesian labour leader, who served as its PM from 1956 to 1963. It was supposed to preserve the political power of the white minorities in northern and southern Rhodesia. It was challenged by the black majority leaders H. Banda, K. Kaunda, J. Nkomo, et al.

FEDERATION OF THE WEST INDIES, see WEST INDIES FEDERATION.

FLN (FRONT DE LIBÉRATION NATION-ALE) Established in Algeria, November 1954, as a united front of various organizations committed to a violent struggle against French rule. It gave rise to a 'liberation army' (Armée de Libération Nationale). The leader of the **FLN** was M. A. **Ben Bella**.

FNLA (FRENTE NACIONAL PARA A LIBERTACAO DE ANGOLA) Party led by José Holden **Roberto**.

FREE FRENCH After the occupation of France by Germany in 1940, a collaborating French government was established at **Vichy**, France. General de Gaulle then established a French government in exile in Africa, referred to as 'Free French'. Its first convention was the **Brazzaville Conference (1)**.

FRELIMO (FRENTE DA LIBERTACAO DE MOCAMBIQUE) The organization fighting for the liberation of the Portuguese colony Mozambique. Established in Tanganyika in 1962; Pres. Eduardo **Mondlane** (1962–1969); after **Mondlane**'s assassination in 1969 it was led by Samora **Machel**.

FRENCH COMMUNITY (COMMUNAUTÉ FRANÇAISE) Established in 1958 when the Fifth Republic was inaugurated by General de Gaulle. It replaced the **French Union**. A referendum was held in which all African states except for Guinea voted for membership of the French Community in 1958.

FRENCH UNION (UNION FRANÇAISE) According to the constitution of the Fourth Republic, adopted in 1946, France and its colonies would form a union ('une union librement consentie') with common citizenship. However, the representation of the colonies in the national assembly (parlia-

ment) was limited. Many French thought of this as a permanent solution and a completion of the process started at the **Brazzaville Conference (3)**, whereas colonial nationalists looked upon it as a first step towards decolonization. The French Union was replaced by the French Community in 1958.

FRETILIN (FRENTE REVOLUCIONARIA DO TIMOR LESTE INDEPENDENTE) Founded in East Timor in 1974 after the Portuguese revolution. It proclaimed independence in November 1975, but Indonesian troops captured East Timor a few days later. **FRETILIN** continued its freedom struggle against the Indonesians and they withdrew from East Timor in 1998. An interim government, headed by **FRETILIN**,was established under the auspices of the United Nations. The first free elections were held in 2000, followed by presidential elections in 2002: Pres. Xanana Gusmao.

G

GENEVA CONFERENCE, 1954 Att. by representatives of the French and the states of Indo-China as well as the United States and China, it tried to provide a road map for a peaceful future for the region. A dividing line between North and South Vietnam was drawn at the 17th parallel. On the advice of an Indian observer, Krishna Menon, who was sent by J. **Nehru**, an international control commission (Canada, India, Poland) was established which regularly toured all countries of the region in order to prevent further hostilities. Indian hopes were disappointed when the United States sponsored the South East Asia Treaty Organization (SEATO) in 1954 and included the region in the global network of anti-communist military pacts.

GOVERNMENT OF INDIA ACT (1935) The final constitutional reform before independence. It was embodied in the Independence of India Act (1947) and most of it was preserved in the Constitution of the Union of India (1950). It was the longest act ever passed by the British parliament because it had to regulate the administrative details of the devolution of power. It contained a federal part, which did not become operative as it would have required the assent of at least 50 per cent of the Indian princes, and a standard constitution for all provinces of British India.

I

INDIAN NATIONAL ARMY (INA) When the Japanese captured thousands of soldiers of the British Indian Army in Southeast Asia in 1942, they encouraged these prisoners of war to join an Indian National Army which was first led by an Indian officer, Mohan Singh, and then by S. C. **Bose** after he arrived in Southeast Asia in 1943. The INA was used by the Japanese as an auxiliary force when they invaded Burma. After the war the British staged a trial of three INA officers, a Hindu, a Muslim and a Sikh, branding them as traitors. The trial gave added impetus to Indian nationalism. Leaders such as J. **Nehru** acted as lawyers defending the accused.

INDIAN NATIONAL CONGRESS (INC) Founded 1885, initially an annual gathering of politicians, passing resolutions addressed to the Government of India. In 1908 a conference of elected delegates, the All-India Congress Committee (AICC) was established. In 1920 the INC was reorganized by M. K. **Gandhi**. He added a small Working Committee to the organization which could act as an agitational command. While Gandhi conceived of the INC as a national forum which should rival the legislatures introduced by colonial constitutional reforms, the INC actually emerged as a political party participating in elections to those legislatures. In independent India the INC was for a long time the dominant party which won free elections in a multi-party democracy. It was led by J. **Nehru** until his death in 1964.

INDIRECT RULE While conquering India, the British formed alliances with native princes (maharajas, nawabs) who retained some autonomy within their states but had to accept the 'advice' of a British resident or political officer. Nearly one-third of Indian territory was thus ruled 'indirectly'. The Indian princes recognized the **paramountcy** of the British monarch. In dealing with the princes the Viceroy acted as 'crown representative'. Lord Lugard, a British colonial governor born in India, transferred the system of indirect rule to Africa where he first served in Uganda and then in Nigeria and empowered **native authorities**. In his writings he propagated indirect rule as an ideology whereas it had actually been adopted as a convenient method to control territories which were of no direct economic interest for British colonial rulers.

IRGUN (IRGUN ZVAI-LEUMI = MILITARY-NATIONAL ORGANIZATION) This guerrilla group tried to achieve the aims of **Zionism** by violent means. It was founded by Avraham Tehomi in 1931. After 1936 it was secretly supported by the Polish government. In 1943 Menachem Begin, who later became PM of Israel, emerged as its leader. Its most spectacular act was the bomb attack on the King David Hotel, British headquarters in Jerusalem, in July 1946.

ISTIQLAL (MOROCCO) Major political

party founded in 1944. It worked with the sultan, **Mohammed V**, and campaigned for his return when he was forced to flee to Madagascar. It continued to support the sultan after he returned in 1955 and achieved independence from France in 1956. In 1957 the sultan adopted the title of 'king' and reduced democratic rights which led to a split in the Istiqlal party.

K

KENYA AFRICAN DEMOCRATIC UNION (KADU) Founded in 1960 and led by R. **Ngala**, it represented the smaller tribes of Kenya (Masai, Kalenjin, Giriama). In the elections of 1961 it captured only 16 per cent of the vote, but formed a government because **KANU** remained in opposition. Ngala became de facto PM as 'leader of government business'.

KENYA AFRICAN NATIONAL UNION (KANU) Founded by the followers of J. **Kenyatta** when he was still imprisoned in 1960. In addition to the Kikuyu, KANU was also supported by the Luo (T. **Mboya**). In the elections of 1961 KANU got 67 per cent of the vote, but remained in opposition as it insisted on **Kenyatta**'s release. When he was released, KANU joined KADU in a coalition government. In the 1963 elections KANU obtained an absolute majority: PM **Kenyatta**.

KHILAFAT MOVEMENT In 1920, after the Turkish Kalif was deprived of the control of the sacred places of Islam by the victorious British, the Indian Muslims launched a non-cooperation movement together with Mahatma **Gandhi**. Its most prominent leader was Maulana **Abul Kalam Azad**. The movement lost its cause when the Turks abolished the Khilafat in 1924.

KHMER ISSARAK Cambodian national movement against the returning French colonial rulers. Formed in 1945, it was initially based in Thailand and supported by the Indo-Chinese Communist Party. It was finally defeated by the anti-communist forces of Norodom **Sihanouk**.

KIKUYU CENTRAL ORGANIZATION Founded in 1921, Sec. J. **Kenyatta** (since 1929).

KONFRONTASI Militant policy followed by **Sukarno** in the mid-1960s against the consolidation of Malaysia which he saw as a construct of British imperialism.

L

LAO ISSARA (= FREE LAO) A group formed in 1945 after the withdrawal of the Japanese. It formed a short-lived government and tried to arrive at a compromise with the returning French. This compromise led to a split. The more radical wing established the **Pathet Lao**. The French did not abide by the compromise and threw out the Lao Issara which resisted the French under the leadership of Prince **Souvanna Phuma**.

LEAGUE OF NATIONS Established in 1919 with headquarters in Geneva. It owed its origin to the US Pres. Woodrow Wilson who conceived of it as an instrument for the maintenance of a peaceful world order. Isolationism prevented the USA from joining the League. It was dominated by the European colonial powers. They used Article 22 of the League's covenant to distribute **mandate territories** among themselves and interpreted the principle of trusteeship as it suited them. The League of Nations was dissolved in 1946 and replaced by the **United Nations**.

LINGGADJATI AGREEMENT, NOVEMBER 1946 Treaty signed by the Dutch Governor General van Mook and the PM of the Republic of Indonesia, Sutan **Sjahrir**. It contained a de facto recognition of the Republic of Indonesia which would be part of a larger federal union. Several foreign governments recognized the Republic of Indonesia after this treaty was signed.

LOI CADRE, 1956 'Framework' law passed by the French assembly; as an enabling act it empowered the French president to promulgate decrees establishing territorial assemblies in 13 French African colonies. Elections (adult suffrage) were then held in 1957.

M

MALAYAN EMERGENCY After the establishment of the **Federation of Malaya** in 1948, the Malayan Communist Party, which consisted mostly of Chinese and had been supported by the British during the war in their fight against the Japanese, launched a guerrilla struggle against the Malay-dominated government. The British military suppressed the guerrillas and resettled the Chinese so as to isolate the militants in the jungle. The British later used the same strategy to suppress the **Mau Mau** movement.

MALAYAN PEOPLE'S ANTI-JAPANESE ARMY (MPAJA) Established in 1942 after the Japanese had occupied Malaya; supported by the British; consisted mostly of Chinese citizens of Malaya persecuted by the Japanese. Later merged with guerrilla forces in the **Malayan Emergency**.

MALAYAN UNION Established by the British in 1946. It consisted of the nine states of Malaya, but excluded Singapore.

It was resented by the heads (sultans) of those states who feared a more centralized administration, but also by the Malayan population who resented the grant of full citizenship to Chinese and Indians. The **United Malays National Organization (UMNO)** was formed to protest against this union. The British relented and established the **Federation of Malaya** in 1948. It recognized the power of the sultans and satisfied the Malays, but alienated the minorities and gave rise to the **Malayan Emergency**.

MANDATE TERRITORIES During the First World War the Allies made plans about how to distribute the German colonies and the provinces of the Ottoman Empire among themselves after the war. The **League of Nations** was then used as a convenient umbrella for the imposition of a new type of colonialism. General Smuts, who represented South Africa in the British war cabinet, authored a scheme of three classes of (**League of Nations**) mandates (A, B, C). Those in class A were considered to be ready for independence after a period of trusteeship, those in class B were considered to be so immature as to require a longer period of quasi-colonial rule, and those in class C could be annexed by the respective power. German Southwest Africa (Namibia) was in class C and was attached to South Africa, a fact which delayed its decolonization considerably.

MAU MAU Movement of the Kikuyu people of the Kenya highlands against the white settlers who had taken over their land. During the Great Depression of the 1930s, the settlers had accepted black tenants whom they now evicted as 'squatters'. Attacks on the settlers started in the late 1940s. The British attributed them to the influence of J. **Kenyatta** who had returned to Kenya in 1946. They could never establish his complicity. Moreover, Mau Mau reached its climax only after his arrest in 1952 and was then suppressed by the British in military operations along the lines of the preceding **Malayan Emergency**. The term Mau Mau is of uncertain origin, it was used only by those opposed to the movement which referred to itself as 'Land Freedom Army'.

MOUVEMENT DÉMOCRATIQUE DE LA RÉNOVATION MALGACHE (MDRM) Established in 1946 in Paris by J. **Raseta**, J. **Ravoahangy** and J. **Rabemananjara**, prohibited and dissolved by the French after the rebellion in Madagascar of March 1947.

MOUVEMENT D'ÉVOLUTION SOCIALE D'AFRIQUE NOIRE (MESAN) Founded in 1949 by Barthélemy **Boganda** in the Central African Republic, won the elections of 1957 and supported 'yes' in the referendum of 1958. Boganda died in a plane crash in 1959. He was succeeded by David **Dacko**. **MESAN** was later captured and used for his own purposes by the dictator, J. B. Bokassa.

MOUVEMENT NATIONAL CONGOLAIS (MNC) This Congolese national movement was founded in 1958 and headed by P. **Lumumba**.

MOVIMENTO DAS FORCAS ARMADAS (MFA) Movement of young Portuguese officers who led the revolution of April 15, 1974, and supported the independence of Portuguese colonies.

MPLA (MOVIMENTO POPULAR PARA A LIBERTACAO ANGOLA) Founded in 1956 and led by A. **Neto**. It had a Marxist orientation and was supported by Cuban troops against a rival movement, **UNITA**, which was supported by the United States and the Union of South Africa.

MUSLIM LEAGUE Political association of the Muslims of British India, founded in 1906. It demanded the creation of **separate electorates** for Muslims. This was granted by the constitutional reforms of 1909. M. A. **Jinnah** joined the Muslim Legue in 1913 and soon became its most prominent leader. He demanded the creation of Pakistan where the **Muslim League** became the major political party. It soon disintegrated after Jinnah's death in 1948 but was then revived by various political leaders in Pakistan. In independent India the **Muslim League** remained a marginal party, e.g. in Kerala.

N

NATIONAL COUNCIL OF NIGERIA AND THE CAMEROONS (NCNC) Party founded by N. **Azikiwe** in 1942. Originally intended as a party which transcended tribal divisions, it mainly represented the Ibos of eastern Nigeria.

NATIONAL LIBERATION MOVEMENT (NML) Opposition party in Ghana founded in 1954, mainly supported by the Ashanti of central Ghana, as they were affected by the policies of K. **Nkrumah** with respect to fixing the price of cocoa. The NML demanded a federal constitution for Ghana and rejected **Nkrumah**'s centralism. In the elections of 1956 **Nkrumah**'s CPP captured 71 of 104 seats, the NML only 33.

NATIVE AUTHORITIES Under British colonial rule in Africa local government was usually entrusted to indigenous chiefs 'advised' by British residents or political officers (**indirect rule**). The emirates of northern Nigeria were particularly suitable for this system of government. Lord Lugard, who was impressed by the emirs and backed their government, extended government by native authorities to other parts of Nigeria. 'Detribalized', educated African nationalists who did not fit in with this system regarded it as an obstacle to political progress.

NEGRITUDE A term coined by Aimé **Césaire** and then propagated by **Senghor**. It refers to the special quality of black African culture.

NEO-DESTOUR PARTY Tunisian party founded by H. **Bourguiba** in 1934.

NON-ALIGNED MOVEMENT (NAM) Inaugurated at the **Belgrade Conference, 1961**, it encompassed a growing number of African and Asian states not tied by pacts to the superpowers and stressed 'equidistance' in their relations with them. These states also remained 'non-aligned among themselves' as J. **Nehru** had emphasized. The collapse of the Soviet Union terminated this movement.

NON-COOPERATION CAMPAIGN Led by Mahatma **Gandhi** against the British in India in 1920–1922. It included the boycott of institutions such as law courts and colleges and of British textiles.

O

ORGANIZATION OF AFRICAN UNITY (OAU) Established at Addis Ababa, Ethiopia, in 1963. It could be seen as the culmination of K. **Nkrumah**'s endeavours; he had strongly advocated African political unity, even a joint African army, but in fact the OAU put an end to his hopes as it became a 'trade union of African heads of government' (J. **Nyerere**) who jealously protected their sovereignty within the

existing borders of their states. It served as a pressure group, speeding up decolonization, and occasionally helped to settle conflicts. In 2004 it changed its name to 'African Union', obviously in order to emulate the European Union.

P

PAIGC (PARTIDO AFRICANO PARA A INDEPENDENCIA DA GUINEA E CABO VERDE) Party founded in 1956 by Dr Amilcar **Cabral**. It spearheaded the guerrilla warfare against the Portuguese in Guinea-Bissau and declared the independence of that colony in 1973.

PAN-AFRICANISM Movement which owed its origin to black American and Caribbean leaders who looked for their African roots and also advocated the liberation of Africa. The first Pan-African conference was held in London in 1900; the very important fifth one was held in Manchester in 1945. It was organized by George Padmore (1901–1959) who was born in Trinidad, became a communist while living in the USA and then spent some time in Moscow in the 1930s; he later became a critic of communism and a strong advocate of African unity. H. **Banda**, J. **Kenyatta**, K. **Nkrumah** and O. **Awolowo** att. Manchester conference. Padmore was **Nkrumah**'s mentor, settled in Ghana at his invitation in 1957 and died there.

PAN-ARABISM Movement advocating the liberation and unification of an Arab nation from Morocco to Iraq. Initially directed against the Ottoman Empire, but later against the European colonial powers, especially Great Britain which had encouraged Arab nationalism in the First World War but then betrayed it. M. **Aflaq** emerged as its chief ideologist. His **Baath Party** initially collaborated with G. A. **Nasser**, but its more radical ideology then rivalled 'Nasserism', which it considered to be too moderate. The defeat of **Nasser** by Israel in 1967 was a decisive blow for Pan-Arabism.

PARAMOUNTCY This term was used to characterize the relationship between Indian princes and the British Monarch in the system of **indirect rule**. The lapse of paramountcy at the time when India attained independence created a constitutional vacuum. The princes had to come to terms with India or Pakistan, the successor states of British India.

PARMEHUTU (PARTI DU MOUVEMENT DE L'EMANCIPATION HUTU) Founded in 1959 by G. **Kayibanda** in Rwanda.

PARTAI NASIONAL INDONESIA (PNI) Founded by **Sukarno** in 1927. After his arr. the PNI was dissolved and resurrected only in 1931 when two wings emerged, one loyal to **Sukarno** and one led by M. **Hatta** and S. **Sjahrir**. From 1933 to 1942 all leaders were imprisoned; they were then 'liberated' by the Japanese. While **Sukarno** and **Hatta** collaborated with the Japanese, **Sjahrir** refused to do so and went 'underground'. The PNI was revived after Sukarno proclaimed independence in 1945. It later became the dominant party of Indonesia for many years.

PARTAI SOCIALIS INDONESIA (PSI) Founded in 1948 by the followers of Sutan **Sjahrir**. Its precursor was the educational organization Pendidikan Nasional Indonesia, founded by Hatta and Sjahrir in 1931. The PSI was banned by Sukarno in 1960.

PARTI DE REGROUPEMENT AFRICAIN (PRA) Founded by L. S. **Senghor** in 1958.

PATHET LAO (= LAND OF THE LAO) A group which had split off from the **Lao Issara** in 1949. It was led by Prince **Souphanouvong**.

PEOPLE'S ACTION PARTY (PAP) Founded in 1954 by **Lee Kuan Yew** in Singapore.

POLISARIO (FRENTE POPULAR PARA LA LIBERACIÓN DE SAGUIA EL HAMRA Y RIO DE ORO) Established in 1973, started armed struggle against Spanish colonial rule, 1975, and continued it after independence against Mauritania and Morocco which had occupied the territory after the Spanish had left it. Mauritania withdrew after three years of fighting; Morocco then occupied the Mauritanian part, too, and still holds it. **POLISARIO** proclaimed a Democratic Arab Saharawi Republic in 1976 and serves as its government-in-exile in Algeria.

R

RASSEMBLEMENT DÉMOCRATIQUE AFRICAIN (RDA) Founded by F. **Houphouet-Boigny** at a conference held at Bamako in 1946. Initially it was in alliance with the French Communist Party, but in 1950 **Houphouet-Boigny** broke with the communists. Several local political parties in French colonies were affiliated with the **RDA** and some of them retained their alliance with the French communists after 1950.

RASTAFARIANISM Jamaican religious movement initially inspired by Marcus **Garvey**. Since African Christians valued the Ethiopian heritage, **Garvey** had pointed out that a new age would dawn with the coronation of the Ethiopian prince Ras Tafari (Haile Selassi). The Rastafarians stressed their African identity. Generally regarded as a leftist movement, it nevertheless refused to get involved in party politics. Bob Marley, the protagonist of a new style of music, reggae, was their idol.

RENAMO (RESISTENCIA NACIONAL MOCAMBICANA) Initially a guerrilla organization fighting againt the **FRELIMO** government of Mozambique. It was first supported by the secret service of southern Rhodesia and then by South Africa. After its financial support dwindled, it turned to the 'parliamentary path', contested elections and was defeated but became a peaceful opposition party.

RENVILLE AGREEMENT, JANUARY 1948 Treaty signed by Dutch Governor General van Mook and PM Sjarifuddin on behalf of the Republic of Indonesia, which had been greatly reduced due to the Dutch 'police action' of July 1947. The agreement was brokered by the US mediator, Dr Frank Graham. As the Dutch and the Indonesians could not agree on a venue on Indonesian territory, they finally met on board the US ship 'Renville'. The terms of this agreement were much less favourable than the **Linggadjati Agreement**. Since the new agreement practically amounted to a capitulation, Sjarifuddin resigned immediately after signing it.

RESPONSIBLE GOVERNMENT The type of government which follows the **Westminster model**. The executive (cabinet) is responsible to the House of Commons and can hold office only as long as it has a majority in the House. The executive may dissolve the House and hold new elections. This as well as other conventions are part of the unwritten British constitution which has been copied by states which acquired **dominion status** before achieving full independence (e.g. India).

ROUND TABLE CONFERENCES, LONDON, 1930–1932 These conferences were dealing with Indian constitutional reform and were held on the initiative of the Viceroy, Lord Irwin, who wished to associate all political groups in India with the impending reforms which resulted in the **Government of India Act (1935)**. The first conference was held in 1930 but was boycotted by the **Indian National Congress**. The second one (September 1931) was attended by M. K. **Gandhi** as sole representative of the Congress. The third, in 1932, was once again not attended by Congress representatives as most of them were in prison at that time. It dealt mostly with legal details.

S

SATYAGRAHA (= 'holding on to the truth') Sanskrit neologism coined by M. K. **Gandhi** in South Africa in order to highlight the active and non-violent character of his movement of 'passive resistance'.

SCRAMBLE FOR AFRICA The competition of European powers for colonies in Africa culminating in the 1880s. It manifested itself at the Berlin Congo Conference, 1884–1885, convened by German Chancellor Bismarck. This conference settled the boundaries of the Belgian Congo but also defined several other colonial boundaries. By establishing the principle that European states could only stake claims to territories which they had actually occupied, it speeded up the 'scramble'.

SEPARATE ELECTORATES A constitutional device used in several colonies where ethnic or religious divisions (e.g. indigenous people and immigrants as in Fiji, Hindus and Muslims in India, Sinhalese and Tamils in Ceylon) seemed to require such an arrangement. It proved to be incompatible with the evolution of **responsible govern-ment** along the lines of the **Westminster model** as it prevented interest aggregation. As long as the colonial government was 'irresponsible'and would at the most take some notice of the interests of various com-munities, this system served it well.

SOMALI YOUTH LEAGUE (SYL) Party founded in Somalia in 1947; its precursor was the Somali Youth Club, founded in 1943 with the support of the British military administration of the erstwhile Italian colony of Somalia.

SOUTH-WEST AFRICAN PEOPLE'S ORGA-NIZATION (SWAPO) Founded in South-West Africa (Namibia) by S. **Nujoma** in 1960. It remained an underground organi-zation engaged in armed struggle with the Union of South Africa until 1989, and then became the party in power in independent Namibia.

SRI LANKA FREEDOM PARTY (SLFP) Founded in 1951 by Solomon **Bandarana-ike**. The SLFP won the elections of 1956 and introduced Sinhala as the only state lan-guage. In 1965 the SLFP was defeated by the **United National Party (UNP)**.

SWARAJ (= 'self-government, freedom' in Sanskrit and other Indian languages) The slogan of the Indian freedom movement. M. K. **Gandhi** published his political man-ifesto *Hind Swaraj* (India's Freedom) in 1909. He stressed that 'swaraj' could also mean self-control and that national freedom had to be based on the self-control of all citizens.

SYKES-PICOT AGREEMENT In May 1916 the British diplomat Mark Sykes and his French counterpart Picot signed a secret agreement dividing the provinces of the Ottoman Empire into post-war spheres of influence. This foreshadowed the later delineation of **mandate territories**. The agreement violated the promises which the British had made to the Arab nationalists. Sykes may not have seen it this way as he considered it to be a temporary British–French trusteeship only. After the revolu-tion of 1917, the Soviets published the agreement, which alarmed the Arabs.

T

TANGANYIKA AFRICAN NATIONAL UNION (TANU) Founded in 1954 by J. **Nyerere**, it emerged as the party in power in independent Tanganyika/Tanzania after 1962/64.

TRANSFER OF POWER The official termi-nation of colonial rule and the assumption of power by successor states which took over the respective government (including the civil service, the army, etc.) as a going concern. Since decolonization proceeded almost everywhere without a violent revo-lution, the transfer of power was the rule to which the **Unilateral Declaration of Independence** of Southern Rhodesia was the only exception.

TRUSTEESHIP Administration of a territory under the Trusteeship Council of the **United Nations**. The earlier **mandate territories** of the **League of Nations** were converted into trusteeship territories and more territo-ries were added after the Second World War. Whereas the League only had an expert commission receiving and reading reports on the mandate territories, the Trusteeship Council is a political body exercising greater control over the trustee-ship territories so as to assure their advance towards independence.

U

UHURU (= 'freedom' in swahili) Slogan current throughout East Africa.

UJAMAA (= 'mutual aid, community spirit' in Swahili) Slogan introduced by J. Nyerere to justify his particular style of one-party democracy.

UNILATERAL DECLARATION OF INDE-PENDENCE After the dissolution of the *Federation of Rhodesia and Nyasaland* in 1963, Nyasaland and Northern Rhodesia (Zambia) attained independence in 1964. In Southern Rhodesia, Ian Smith had become PM in 1964. His government represented only the white minority and thus did not qualify for a **transfer of power**. Therefore, Smith proclaimed independence unilaterally in November 1965. The British government was not in a position to use armed force to overthrow Smith who held on until 1980 when Southern Rhodesia (Zimbabwe) achieved legal independence.

UNITA (UNIAO NACIONAL PARA A INDE-PENDENCIA TOTAL DE ANGOLA) Originally a faction which broke away from earlier Angolan independence movements in 1966, it established a stronghold in the southeast of Angola, the area of the Ovimbundu tribe. Its leader, Jonas **Savimbi**, projected UNITA as a pro-Western movement and attracted US and South African support. In 1992, after a UN-brokered accord, UNITA participated in elections, but lost and returned to armed struggle. In 1999 UNITA was defeated militarily by the new government of Angola, but resumed guerrilla operations until **Savimbi** was killed in 2002.

UNITED GOLD COAST CONVENTION

Political Party founded in Ghana in 1947 by J. B. **Danquah**. K. **Nkrumah** joined this party as its Sec. but then left it and founded the **Convention People's Party (CPP)**.

UNITED MALAYS NATIONAL ORGANIZA-TION (UMNO) Founded in 1946 in protest against the **Malayan Union** imposed by the British. Led by Tunku Abdul **Rahman** since 1951, it formed the government of Malaya (since 1963, Malaysia) in coalition with the organizations representing the Chinese and Indian minorities.

UNITED NATIONAL PARTY (UNP) Founded in 1946 by Don Stephen **Senanayake**. Formed the government of Sri Lanka from 1947 to 1956 and again from 1965 to 1970 and from 1977 to 1994.

UNITED NATIONS (UN) Established at a conference of 50 states in San Francisco, 1945. It replaced the **League of Nations** and inherited the trusteeship of the **mandate territories**. Under its auspices the supervision of these territories was intensified and this contributed to the process of decolonization.

UPRONA (UNITÉ ET PROGRÈS NATIONAL) Party founded in 1959 by L. **Rwagasore** in Burundi, supported by both Tutsi and Hutu.

V

VICHY REGIME Collaborationist government established at Vichy, France, under German occupation (1940–1944). It was headed by Marshall Pétain. To counteract it, General de Gaulle established the **Free French** government in exile.

VIETMINH (full name: Vietnam Doc Lap

Dang Minh = Vietnam Independence League) Front organization of the Indo-Chinese Communist Party. **Ho Chi Minh** established it in 1941 so as to include non-communist nationalists in the freedom struggle. Later on the name was used to refer to the guerrilla army fighting first against the French and then against the USA.

W

WAFD PARTY Founded in 1919 by Saad **Zaghlul**, who led an Egyptian delegation (= *wafd*) to the Versailles Conference. The party won elections in 1924, PM S. **Zaghlul**, and again in 1928, 1930, 1936, 1942, 1950, PM Mustafa al-**Nahhas.**

WEST INDIES FEDERATION, 1958–1962 A short-lived British creation intended for the decolonization of the colonies in the Caribbean. It was strongly supported by the Jamaican PM N. **Manley**. The first and only PM of the federation was G. H. **Adams** from Barbados. The following ten colonies were included in the federation: Antigua and Barbuda, Barbados, Dominica, Grenada, Jamaica, Montserrat, St Kitts and Nevis, St Lucia, St Vincent and the Grenadines, Trinidad and Tobago. Strong opposition to the federation forced **Manley** to hold a referendum in Jamaica in 1961. Its negative result put an end to the federation whose members either achieved individual independence after some years or reverted to British colonial rule (e.g. Montserrat).

WESTMINSTER MODEL This term refers to the unwritten constitution of Great Britain, i.e. the conventions of **responsible government** as practised in the Houses of Parliament located in the London borough of Westminister.

Z

ZANU (ZIMBABWE AFRICAN NATIONAL UNION) Founded by N. **Sithole** in 1963 and then led by R. **Mugabe** split off from **ZAPU**. It emerged as the most powerful party after Zimbabwe attained legal independence in 1980.

ZAPU (ZIMBABWE AFRICAN PEOPLE'S UNION) Founded in 1961 by J. **Nkomo**. Its support comes mostly from tribes other than the Shona, e.g. Ndebele. The Shona support the rival **ZANU**. **ZAPU** and **ZANU** formed a Patriotic Front to fight Ian Smith and his **Unilateral Declaration of Independence**, but later they became rivals once more.

ZIONISM 'Zion' is originally a Hebrew term for one of the hills of Jerusalem. Later on it came to mean an ideal Jewish state. In 1896 in Vienna Theodor Herzl wrote a book about such a state and then organized the first Zionist conference in Basle in 1897. The persecution of Jews in Europe, especially the Nazi Holocaust, added urgency to this movement which finally led to the establishment of the state of Israel in 1948.

NOTES

Introduction

1 M. J. Bonn, *The Crumbling of Empire. The Disintegration of World Economy*, London: George Allen and Unwin, 1938.
2 K. Hack, 'Theories and Approaches to British Decolonization in Southeast Asia', in: M. Frey *et al.* (eds), *The Transformation of Southeast Asia. International Perspectives on Decolonization*, Armonk, NY: M. E. Sharpe, 2003, p. 113.
3 J. G. Vaillant, *Black, French, and African. A Life of Leopold Sédar Senghor*, Cambridge, MA: Harvard University Press, 1990, p. 309.

Background

1 P. Bairoch, 'Historical Roots of Economic Underdevelopment: Myths and Realities', in: W. Mommsen and J. Osterhammel (eds), *Imperialism and After*, London: Allen and Unwin, 1986, p. 191 ff.
2 D. Rothermund, *Asian Trade and European Expansion in the Age of Mercantilism*, New Delhi: Manohar, 1981.
3 P. J. Cain and A. G. Hopkins, *British Imperialism, 1688–2000* (Second Edn), London: Longman, 2001, p. 92.
4 C. P. Kindleberger, *World Economic Primacy: 1500 to 1990*, New York: Oxford University Press, p. 111.
5 M. Edelstein, 'Foreign Investment and Empire, 1860–1914', in: R. Floud and D. McCloskey (eds), *The Economic History of Britain since 1700*, Vol. II, Cambridge: Cambridge University Press, 1981, p. 74.

Historiography

1 R. von Albertini, *Dekolonisation. Die Diskussion über Verwaltung und Zukunft der Kolonien 1919–1960*, Cologne: Westdeutscher Verlag, 1966; English translation: *Decolonization. The Administration and the Future of the Colonies, 1919–1960*, New York: Doubleday, 1971.
2 H. Grimal, *La Decolonization*, Paris: Armand Colin, 1965; English translation: *Decolonization. The British, French, Dutch and Belgian Empires, 1919–1963*, Boulder, CO: Westview Press, 1978.
3 R. F. Holland, *European Decolonization, 1919–1981. An Introductory Survey*, London: Macmillan, 1985.

4 J. Darwin, *Britain and Decolonization. The Retreat from Empire in the Post-War World*, London: Macmillan, 1988.

5 J. Marseille, *Empire coloniale et capitalisme français. Histoire d'un divorce*, Paris: Albin Michel, 1984.

6 R. Robinson, 'The Excentric Idea of Imperialism with or without Empire', in: W. J. Mommsen and J. Osterhammel (eds), *Imperialism and After. Continuities and Discontinuities*, London: Allen and Unwin, 1986, p. 267 ff.

7 L. Namier, *The Structure of Politics at the Accession of George III*, London: Macmillan, 1929.

8 P. J. Cain and A. G. Hopkins, *British Imperialism, 1688–2000* (Second Edn), London: Longman, 2001, p. 28 f.

9 R. C. Majumdar, *History of the Freedom Movement in India*, Vol. I, Calcutta: K. L. Mukhopadhyay, 1962, Vols II and III, Calcutta: K. L. Mukhopadhyay, 1963.

10 Tara Chand, *History of the Freedom Movement in India*, New Delhi: Government of India, Publications Division, 4 vols, 1961–1972.

11 G. McT. Kahin, *Nationalism and Revolution in Indonesia*, Ithaca, NY: Cornell University Press, 1952.

12 B. Dahm, *History of Indonesia in the Twentieth Century*, London: Pall Mall Press, 1971.

13 B. A. Ogot, *Decolonization and Independence in Kenya, 1940–1993*, Oxford: James Currey, 1995.

14 J. F. Ade Ajayi, *Tradition and Change in Africa. The Essays of J. F. Ade Ajayi* edited by Toyin Falola, Trenton: Africa World Press, 2000.

15 J. Ki-Zerbo, *Histoire de l'Afrique noire, d'hier a demain*, Paris: Hatier, 1978.

16 D. Birmingham, *The Decolonization of Africa*, London: Routledge, 1995.

17 D. Birmingham and P. M. Martin (eds), *History of Central Africa. The Contemporary Years since 1960*, London: Longman, 1998.

18 F. Cooper, *Decolonization and African Society. The Labour Question in French and British Africa*, Cambridge: Cambridge University Press, 1996.

19 T. Ranger, *The African Voice in Southern Rhodesia, 1898–1930*, London: Heinemann, 1970.

20 T. Ranger and E. Hobsbawm (eds), *The Invention of Tradition*, Cambridge: Cambridge University Press, 1983.

21 T. Ranger, *The Invention of Tribalism in Zimbabwe*, Gwelo: Mambo, 1985.

22 W. R. Louis, *Imperialism at Bay. The United States and the Decolonization of the British Empire, 1941–1945*, Oxford: Clarendon Press, 1977 (Repr. 2003).

23 W. R. Louis, *The British Empire in the Middle East, 1945–1951. Arab Nationalism, the United States and Postwar Imperialism*, Oxford: Clarendon Press, 1984.

24 M. Connelly, *A Diplomatic Revolution. Algeria's Fight for Independence and the Origins of the Post-Cold War Era*, Oxford: Oxford University Press, 2002.

25 P. Gleijeses, *Conflicting Missions. Havana, Washington and Africa, 1959–1976*, Chapel Hill: University of North Carolina Press, 2002.

26 K. Fedorowich and M. Thomas (eds), *International Diplomacy and Colonial Retreat*, London: Frank Cass, 2001.

27 M. Frey *et al.* (eds), *The Transformation of Southeast Asia. International Perspectives on Decolonization*, Armonk, NY: M. E. Sharpe, 2003.

28 Ibid., p. 273.

29 J. Darwin, *The End of the British Empire. The Historical Debate*, Oxford: Blackwell, 1991.

30 P. M. Martin, 'Beyond Independence', in: D. Birmingham and P. M. Martin (eds), *History of Central Africa. The Contemporary Years since 1960*, London: Longman, 1998.

31 M. Mamdani, *Citizen and Subject. Contemporary Africa and the Legacy of Late Colonialism*, Princeton, NJ: Princeton University Press, 1996.

32 R. Guha (ed.), *Subaltern Studies, Vol. I*, Delhi: Oxford University Press, 1982. Subsequent volumes II to VI, edited by R. Guha, were published in 1983, 1984, 1985, 1987 and 1989.

33 R. Guha, 'Dominance without Hegemony and its Historiography', in: R. Guha (ed.), *Subaltern Studies, Vol. VI*, Delhi: Oxford University Press, 1989, pp. 210 ff.

34 E. W. Said, *Orientalism*, New York: Vintage, 1979.

35 D. Kennedy, 'Imperial History and Post-Colonial Theory', in: J. D. Le Sueur (ed.), *The Decolonization Reader*, New York: Routledge, 2003, p. 10 ff.

36 B. F. Williams, *Stains on My Name, War in my Veins. Guyana and the Politics of Cultural Struggle*, Durham: Duke University Press, 1991.

The Context of Decolonization

1 M. J. Bonn, *The Crumbling of Empire. The Disintegration of World Economy*, London: Allen and Unwin, 1938, p. 96.

2 B. Eichengreen, *Golden Fetters. The Gold Standard and the Great Depression*, New York: Oxford University Press, 1992.

3 Bonn, *Crumbling of Empire*, p. 324 f.

4 D. Rothermund, *India in the Great Depression, 1929–1939*, New Delhi: Manohar, 1992, p. 33 ff.

5 Bonn, *Crumbling of Empire*, p. 329.

6 Ibid., p. 367.

7 K. W. Deutsch, *Nationalism and Social Communication*, New York: Free Press, 1953.

8 B. Anderson, *Imagined Communities. Reflections on the Spread and Origin of Nationalism*, London: Verso, 1983.

9 E. Gellner, *Nations and Nationalism*, Ithaca, NY: Cornell University Press, 1983.

10 Lord J. Dalberg-Acton, 'Nationality', in: W. McNeill (ed.), *Essays in the Liberal Interpretation of History. Selected Papers of Lord Acton*, Chicago: Chicago University Press, 1967.

11 E. Benner, *Really Existing Nationalisms. A Post-Communist View from Marx and Engels*, Oxford: Clarendon Press, 1995, pp. 144, 154, 199.

12 D. Rothermund, 'Nationalism and the Reconstruction of Tradition in Asia', in: Sri Kuhnt-Saptodewo, Volker Grabowsky, Martin Großheim (eds), *Nationalism and Cultural Revival in Southeast Asia. Perspectives from the Centre and the Periphery*, Wiesbaden: Harrassowitz, 1997, pp. 13–28.

13 D. Rothermund, 'Nehru and Early Indian Socialism', in: S. N. Mukherjee (ed.), *The*

Movement for National Freedom in India (St Antony's Papers No. 18), London: Oxford University Press, 1966, p. 98 ff.

14 A. Mazrui, *Towards a Pax Africana. A Study of Ideology and Ambition*, London: Weidenfeld and Nicolson, 1967.

15 M. Mamdani, *Citizen and Subject. Contemporary Africa and the Legacy of Late Colonialism*, Princeton, NJ: Princeton University Press, 1996, p. 16 ff.

16 H. Kulke and D. Rothermund, *A History of India* (Fourth Edn), London: Routledge, 2004, p. 352.

17 G. Jansen, *Afro-Asia and Non-Alignment*, London: Faber, 1966, p. 51 ff.

18 Ibid., p. 182 ff.

19 Ibid., p. 291 ff., p. 421 (Text of the Resolution).

20 Ibid., p. 363 ff.

21 W. R. Louis, *Imperialism at Bay. The United States and the Decolonization of the British Empire, 1941–1945*, Oxford: Clarendon Press, 1977, p. 4.

22 Ibid., p. 4.

23 Ibid., p. 123.

24 Ibid., p. 200.

25 Ibid, p. 441.

26 Ibid, p. 512 ff.

27 Ibid., p. 486.

28 Ibid., p. 541.

The End of Colonial Empires in Asia

1 H. Kulke and D. Rothermund, *A History of India* (Fourth edn), London: Routledge, 2004, p. 229 f.

2 Ibid., p. 284.

3 Ibid., p. 280 f.

4 D. Rothermund, *Mahatma Gandhi. An Essay in Political Biography*, New Delhi: Manohar, 1991, p. 21 f.

5 Ibid., p. 35.

6 D. Rothermund, *India in the Great Depression, 1929–1939*, New Delhi: Manohar, 1992, p. 79 f.

7 Rothermund, *Mahatma Gandhi*, p. 73.

8 Ibid., p. 77.

9 S. Wolpert, *Jinnah of Pakistan*, New York: Oxford University Press, 1984, p. 150 f.

10 Rothermund, *India in the Great Depression*, p. 214 f.

11 Wolpert, *Jinnah*, p. 145.

12 Kulke and Rothermund, *History of India*, p. 310.

13 R. J. Moore, *Escape from Empire. The Attlee Government and the Indian Problem*, Oxford: Clarendon Press, 1983, p. 15 f.

14 H. Kulke and D. Rothermund, *History of India*, p. 317.

15 Moore, *Escape from Empire*, p. 63.

16 Ibid., p. 189.

17 Wolpert, *Jinnah*, p. 332.

18 Moore, *Escape from Empire*, p. 220 f.

19 Ibid., p. 272 f.
20 Ibid., p. 244.
21 Wolpert, Jinnah, p. 347.
22 D. Rothermund, *An Economic History of India* (Second edn), London: Routledge, 1993, p. 115 ff.
23 Wolpert, *Jinnah*, p. 145.
24 A. Jalal, *The Sole Spokesman. Jinnah, the Muslim League and the Demand for Pakistan*, Cambridge: Cambridge University Press, 1985.
25 A. Jalal, *The State of Martial Rule. The Origins of Pakistan's Political Economy of Defence*, Cambridge: Cambridge University Press, 1991.
26 M. Ahmed, *Bangladesh. Constitutional Quest for Autonomy, 1950–1971*, Wiesbaden: Steiner, 1978.
27 K. M. de Silva, *Managing Tensions in Multi-ethnic Societies. Sri Lanka, 1880–1965*, Lanham, MD: University Press of America, 1986, p. 262 f.
28 B. Dahm, *History of Indonesia in the Twentieth Century*, London: Pall Mall Press, 1971, p. 20 f.
29 Ibid., p. 88.
30 Ibid., p. 108.
31 Ibid., p. 110 f.
32 Ibid., p. 92.
33 J. J. P. De Jong, *Diplomatie of strijd. Het Nederlands beleid tegenover de Indonesische revolutie, 1945–1947*, Amsterdam: Boom Meppel, 1988, p. 138.
34 Ibid., p. 116.
35 Ibid., p. 140.
36 Ibid,, p. 141.
37 Ibid., p. 145 f., 160.
38 Ibid., p. 208 ff.
39 Ibid., p. 275 ff.
40 Ibid., p. 357.
41 Ibid., p. 372 f.
42 Ibid., p. 385.
43 Ibid., p. 400.
44 P. van der Eng, 'Marshall Aid as a Catalyst in the Decolonization of Indonesia, 1947–1949', in: J. D. Le Sueur, *The Decolonization Reader*, London: Routledge, 2003, p. 125.
45 De Jong, *Diplomatie of strijd*, p. 403.
46 A. M. Taylor, *Indonesian Independence and the United Nations*, London: Stevens and Sons, 1960, p. 66 ff.
47 Dahm, *History of Indonesia*, p. 135 f.
48 De Jong, *Diplomatie of strijd*, p. 420 f.
49 Taylor, *Indonesian Independence*, p. 211 ff.
50 Dahm, *History of Indonesia*, p. 141 f.
51 P. van der Eng, 'Marshall Aid', in: Le Sueur, *Decolonization Reader*, p. 136.
52 Dahm, *History of Indonesia*, p. 167 f.
53 H. Feith, *The Decline of Constitutional Democracy in Indonesia*, Ithaca, NY: Cornell University Press, 1962.

54 Dahm, *History of Indonesia*, p. 176 f.

55 Taylor, *Indonesian Independence*, p. 235 ff.

56 D. G. E. Hall, *A History of Southeast Asia*, London: Macmillan, 1961, p. 146 ff., 169 ff.

57 Ibid., p. 647.

58 D. Rothermund, *The Global Impact of the Great Depression*, London: Routledge, 1996, p. 124.

59 P. Brocheux, 'Le Mouvement Indépendantiste Vietnamien pendant la seconde Guerre Mondiale (1939–1945)', in: J. Cantiers and E. Jennings (eds), *L'Empire Colonial sous Vichy*, Paris: Odile Jacob, 2004, p. 265 ff.

60 Ibid., p. 280 f.

61 E. Jennings, 'L'Indochine de l'Admiral Decoux', in: Cantier and Jennings (eds), *L'Empire Colonial*, p. 38 f.

62 Hall, *History of Southeast Asia*, p. 713.

63 Ibid., p. 714.

64 P. Hughes, 'Division and Discord: British Policy, Indo-China, and the Origins of the Vietnam War, 1954–1956', in: K. Fedorowich and M. Thomas (eds), *International Diplomacy and Colonial Retreat*, London: Frank Cass, 2001, p. 99.

65 Kulke and Rothermund, *History of India*, p. 352 f.

66 Nguyen Quang Hung, *Katholizismus in Vietnam, 1954–1975*, Berlin: Logos Verlag, 2003.

67 Hall, *History of Southeast Asia*, p. 117 f., 169 f.

68 M. S. Viravong, *Prinz Phetsarat. Ein Leben für Laos*, Münster: Lit, 2003, p. 82 ff. (Viravong wrote this biography in Lao; he had been the private secretary of Prince Phetsarat. The biography was translated into German and edited by V. Grabowsky).

69 Hall, *History of Southeast Asia*, p. 514 f.

70 M. Adas, *The Burma Delta. Economic Development and Social Change on an Asian Rice Frontier*, Madison, WI: University of Wisconsin Press, 1974.

71 Hall, *History of Southeast Asia*, p. 536 ff.

72 Kulke and Rothermund, *History of India*, p. 351.

73 Rothermund, *Global Impact of the Great Depression*, p. 122 f.

74 Hall, *History of Southeast Asia*, p. 706 ff.

75 Kulke and Rothermund, *History of India*, p. 311.

76 Hall, *History of Southeast Asia*, p. 709.

77 Ibid., p. 710.

78 T. Pires, *Suma Oriental*, trsl. and ed. by A. Cortesao, London: Hakluyt Society, 1944, Vol. II, p. 510.

79 Hall, *History of Southeast Asia*, p. 421 ff.

80 Ibid., p. 482 ff.

81 T. H. Silcock, 'Communal and Party Structure', in: T. H. Silcock and E. K. Fisk (eds), *The Political Economy of Independent Malaya*, Canberra: The Australian National University, 1963, p. 1 ff.

82 Ibid., p. 13 f.

83 K. Ramakrishna, 'Making Malaya Safe for Decolonization: The Rural Chinese Factor in the Counterinsurgency Campaign', in: M. Frey *et al.* (eds), *The Transformation of Southeast Asia*, Armonk, NY: M. E. Sharpe, 2003, p. 161 ff.

84 Hall, *History of Southeast Asia*, p. 703.

85 Silcock, 'Communal and Party Structure', in: Silcock and Fisk (eds), *Independent Malaya*, p. 11.

86 Tan Tai Yong, 'The "Grand Design". British Policy, Local Politics, and the Making of Malaysia, 1955–1961', in: M. Frey *et al.* (eds), *The Transformation of Southeast Asia*, p. 142 ff.

87 E. Sadka, 'Malayasia. The Political Background', in: Silcock and Fisk (eds), *Independent Malaya*, p. 32 ff.

88 J. Subritzky, 'Britain, Konfrontasi, and the End of Empire in Southeast Asia, 1961–1965, in: Fedorowich and Thomas, *International Diplomacy and Colonial Retreat*, p. 209 ff.

89 B. Dahm, *Emanzipationsversuche von kolonialer Herrschaft in Südostasien. Die Philippinen und Indonesien. Ein Vergleich*, Wiesbaden: Harrassowitz, 1974, p. 35 ff.

90 Ibid., p. 44 ff.

91 D. A. Rosenberg, 'Philippines', in: A. T. Embree (ed.), *Encyclopedia of Asian History*, Vol. III, New York: Charles Scribner's Sons, 1988, p. 246 ff.

92 P. W. Stanley, 'Quezon', in: Embree (ed.), *Encylclopedia of Asian History*, Vol. III, p. 312 f.

93 Rothermund, *Global Impact of the Great Depression*, p. 121.

94 D. K. Wyatt, 'Roxas', in: Embree (ed.), *Encylcopedia of Asian History*, Vol. III, p. 350.

95 B. Kerkvliet, 'Huk', in: Embree (ed.), *Encyclopedia of Asian History*, Vol. II, p. 85.

96 S. Simon, 'Taiwan', in: D. Levinson and K. Christensen (eds), *Encyclopedia of Modern Asia*, Vol. V, New York: Charles Scribner's Sons, 2002, p. 378 ff.

97 B. Cumings, 'Colonial Formations and Deformations. Korea, Taiwan and Vietnam', in: P. Duara (ed.), *Decolonization. Perspectives from Now and Then*, London: Routledge, 2004, p. 285 f.

98 D. Kane, 'Korea-History', in: Levinson and Christensen (eds), *Encylclopedia of Modern Asia*, Vol. III, p. 387 ff.

99 Cumings, 'Colonial Formations', in: Duara (ed.), *Decolonization*, p. 280 f.

100 W. R. Louis, *Imperialism at Bay. The United States and the Decolonization of the British Empire, 1941–1945*, Oxford: Clarendon Press, 1977 (Repr. 2003), p. 547.

101 Ibid., p. 556.

102 J. M. Greene, 'Hong Kong', in: Levinson and Christensen (eds), *Encylcopedia of Modern Asia*, Vol. II, p. 547 ff.

103 K. Fedorowich, 'Decolonization Deferred? The Re-establishment of Colonial Rule in Hong Kong, 1942–1945', in: Fedorowich and Thomas (eds), *International Diplomacy and Colonial Retreat*, p. 25 ff.

The Arab World

1 W. R. Louis, *The British Empire in the Middle East, 1945–1951. Arab Nationalism, the United States and Postwar Imperialism*, Oxford: Clarendon Press, 1984, p. 123, 311.

2 B. Maddy-Weitzman, *The Crystallization of the Arab State System, 1945–1954*, Syracuse: Syracuse University Press, 1993, p. 16 ff.

3   Louis, *British Empire*, p. 331.

4   Ibid., p. 334 ff.

5   R. Schulze, *Geschichte der islamischen Welt im 20. Jahrhundert*, München: Beck, 1994, p. 198 f.

6   Louis, *British Empire*, p. 358.

7   Ibid., p. 355.

8   Ibid., p. 362.

9   Schulze, *Geschichte der islamischen Welt*, p. 196.

10 Louis, *British Empire*, p. 165.

11 Ibid., p. 148.

12 Schulze, *Geschichte der islamischen Welt*, p. 195 f.

13 Louis, *British Empire*, p. 397 ff.

14 Ibid., p. 468.

15 Ibid., p. 472.

16 Ibid., p. 474.

17 Maddy-Weitzman, *Arab State System*, p. 55.

18 Louis, *British Empire*, p. 480.

19 Ibid., p. 507.

20 Ibid., p. 514.

21 Ibid., p. 371 f.

22 Ibid., p. 526.

23 Ibid., p. 545.

24 Ibid., p. 546.

25 Ibid., p. 77.

26 Ibid., p. 565.

27 A. Schölch, 'Fremde in der Heimat. Zur Analyse der Situation der Palästinenser in Israel', in: P. Hablützel, H. W. Tobler and A. Wirz (eds), *Dritte Welt. Historische Prägung und politische Herausforderung*, Wiesbaden: Steiner, 1983, p. 135 ff.

28 S. Botman, *Egypt from Independence to Revolution, 1919–1952*, Syracuse: Syracuse University Press, 1991, p. 35 f.

29 R. F. Holland, *European Decolonization, 1918–1981. An Introductory Survey*, New York: St Martin's Press, 1985, p. 123 f.

30 Louis, *British Empire*, p. 716 ff.

31 Ibid., p. 746.

32 Schulze, *Geschichte der islamischen Welt*, p. 190 f.

33 H. S. Sharkey, 'Colonialism, Character-Building and the Culture of Nationalism in the Sudan, 1898–1956', in: J. D. Le Sueur (ed.), *The Decolonization Reader*, London: Routledge, 2003, p. 218 ff.

34 Louis, *British Empire*, p. 703 ff.

35 S. C. Smith, 'Revolution and Reaction. South Arabia in the Aftermath of the Yemeni Revolution', in: Fedorowich and Thomas (eds), *International Diplomacy and Colonial Retreat*, p. 193 ff.

36 Ibid., p. 202.

37 Louis, *British Empire*, p. 287.

38 Holland, *Decolonization*, p. 115.

39 W. R. Louis, 'Libyan Independence, 1951. The Crisis of a Client State', in: P. Gifford and W. R. Louis (eds), *Decolonization and African Independence. The Transfer of Power, 1960–1980*, New Haven, CT: Yale University Press, 1988, p. 167.

40 P. Panther-Brick, 'Independence, French Style', in: Gifford and Louis (eds), *Decolonization*, p. 87.

41 B. Stora, *Algeria, 1830–2000. A Short History*, Ithaca, NY: Cornell University Press, 2004, p. 161 f.

The 'Wind of Change' in Black Africa

1 Lord Hailey, *An African Survey. Revised 1956*, London: Oxford University Press, 1957, p. 651 ff.

2 Ibid., p. 679.

3 Ibid., p. 1311 f.

4 F. Cooper, *Decolonization and African Society. The Labour Question in French and British Africa*, Cambridge: Cambridge University Press, 1996, p. 241 ff.

5 Ibid., p. 305 f.

6 H. Grimal, *Decolonization. The British, French, Dutch and Belgian Empires, 1919–1963*, Boulder, CO: Westview Press, 1978, p. 363 f.

7 Cooper, *Decolonization*, p. 426.

8 Grimal, *Decolonization*, p. 373 f.

9 L. Kaba, 'From Colonialism to Autocracy. Guinea under Sekou Touré', in: P. Gifford and W. R. Louis (eds), *Decolonization and African Independence. The Transfers of Power, 1960–1980*, New Haven, CT: Yale University Press, 1988, p. 225 ff.

10 Grimal, *Decolonization*, p. 378.

11 T. Smith (ed.), *The End of the European Empire. Decolonization after World War II*, Lexington, 1978, p. 96 f.

12 D. A. Mungazi, *The Mind of Black Africa*, Westport, CT: Greenwood, 1996.

13 Hailey, *African Survey*, p. 1179 f.

14 J. M. Allman, *The Quills of the Porcupine. Asante Nationalism in an Emergent Ghana*, Madison, WI: University of Wisconsin Press, 1993, p. 71.

15 Ibid., p. 36 ff.

16 Ibid., p. 119 ff.

17 Hailey, *African Survey*, p. 1179.

18 D. J. R. Scott, 'The Sierra Leone Election, May 1957', in: W. J. M. Mackenzie and K. Robinson (eds), *Five Elections in Africa*, Oxford: Clarendon Press, 1960, p. 168 ff.

19 Ibid., p. 177.

20 Ibid., p. 263 f.

21 Cooper, *Decolonization*, p. 311, 410 f.

22 J. C. Allain, 'L'independance de la Guinée-Conakry à l'ONU (1958)', in: C. R. Ageron et M. Michel (eds), *L'Afrique noire française. L'heure des indépendances*, Paris: CNRS, 1992, p. 551 ff.

23 J. G. Vaillant, *Black, French and African. A Life of Léopold Sédar Senghor*, Cambridge, MA: Harvard University Press, 1990, p. 331.

24 Ibid., p. 224.

25 K. Robinson, 'Senegal. The Elections to the Territorial Assembly, March 1957', in: Mackenzie and Robinson (eds), *Five Elections in Africa*, p. 388.

26 P. Brasseur, 'L'éclatement de la Fédération Mali', in: Ageron and Michel (eds), *L'Afrique noire*, p. 401 ff.

27 Vaillant, *Senghor*, p. 309 ff.

28 T. Weiskel, 'Independence and Long Durée. The Ivory Coast "Miracle" Reconsidered', in: Gifford and Louis (eds), *Decolonization*, p. 347 ff.

29 M. Michel, 'The Independence of Togo', in: Gifford and Louis, *Decolonization*, p. 347 ff.

30 T. Chafer, *The End of Empire in French West Africa*, Oxford: Berg, 2002, p. 62.

31 Ibid., p. 182.

32 Cooper, *Decolonization*, p. 422.

33 Chafer, *End of Empire*, p. 179.

34 R. Buijtenhuijs, 'Chad in the Age of Warlords', in: D. Birmingham and P. M. Martin (eds), *History of Central Africa. The Contemporary Years since 1960*, London: Longman, 1998, p. 21 ff.

35 J. F. Ade Ajayi and A. E. Ekoko, 'Transfer of Power in Nigeria. Its Origins and Consequences', in: Gifford and Louis (eds), *Decolonization*, p. 245 ff.

36 P. Whitaker, 'The Western Region of Nigeria, May 1956', in: Mackenzie and Robinson (eds), *Five Elections in Africa*, p. 94 f.

37 J. H. Price, 'The Eastern Region of Nigeria, March 1957', in: Mackenzie and Robinson (eds), *Five Elections in Africa*, p. 156 f.

38 R. Joseph, 'Radical Nationalism in French Africa. The Case of Cameroon', in: Gifford and Louis, *Decolonization*, p. 321 ff.

39 A. Mehler, 'Cameroun and the Politics of Patronage', in: Birmingham and Martin (eds), *History of Central Africa*, p. 43 ff.

40 E. M'Bokolo, 'Comparisons and Contrasts in Equatorial Africa. Gabon, Congo and the Central African Republic', in: Birmingham and Martin (eds), *History of Central Africa*, p. 67 ff.

41 Ibid., p. 78.

42 Ibid., p. 81.

43 Ibid., p. 83.

44 C. Young, 'Zaire. The Anatomy of a Failed State', in: Birmingham and Martin (eds), *History of Central Africa*, p. 99.

45 A. Wirz, 'Die Entwicklung der kolonialen Zwangswirtschaft in Belgisch Kongo', in: D. Rothermund (ed.), *Die Peripherie in der Weltwirtschaftskrise. Afrika, Asien, Lateinamerika*, Paderborn: Schöningh, 1982, p. 59 ff.

46 Letter to G. Brausch of March 1957, reproduced in Grimal, *Decolonization*, p. 401.

47 I. Kabongo, 'The Catastrophe of Belgian Decolonization', in: Gifford and Louis, *Decolonization*, p. 380 ff.

48 Ibid., p. 388.

49 Young, 'Zaire', in: Birmingham and Martin (eds), *History of Central Africa*, p. 98.

50 J. Listowel, *The Making of Tanganyika*, London: Chatto and Windus, 1965, p. 66.

51 H. Bienen, *Tanzania. Party Transformation and Economic Development*, Princeton, NJ: Princeton University Press, 1967, p. 51 ff.

52 Listowel, *Tanganyika*, p. 380 ff.

53 Nyerere, J., *Freedom and Unity. Selections from Writings and Speeches*, 1952–1965, London: Oxford University Press, 1966, p. 286 f.

54 M. Lofchie, *Zanzibar. Background to Revolution*, Princeton, NJ: Princeton University Press, 1965.

55 Listowel, *Tanganyika*, p. 430 ff.

56 Nyerere, *Freedom*, p. 286 f.

57 D. A. Low and R. C. Pratt, *Buganda and British Overrule, 1900–1955*, London: Oxford University Press, 1960, p. 3 ff., 350 ff.

58 R. Robinson, 'Andrew Cohen and the Transfer of Power in Tropical Africa, 1940–1951', in: W. H. Morris-Jones and G. Fischer (eds), *Decolonization and After*, London: Frank Cass, 1980, p. 50 ff.

59 D. A. Low, *Buganda in Modern History*, London: Faber, 1971, p. 94 ff.

60 Kabaka of Buganda, *Desecration of My Kingdom*, London: Constable, 1967, p. 160 f.

61 H. Strizek, *Zur Lage der Menschenrechte in Ruanda. Leben nach dem Völkermord*, Aachen: Missio, 2003, p. 11 f.

62 Ibid., p. 10, p. 54.

63 Louis, *Imperialism at Bay*, p. 64.

64 Ibid., p. 557.

65 D. Bechtloff, *Madagaskar und die Missionare. Technisch-Zivilisatorische Transfers in der Früh-und Endphase europäischer Expansionsbestrebungen*, Stuttgart: Steiner, 2002, p. 165 ff.

66 M. Shipway, 'Madagascar on the Eve of Insurrection, 1944–1947', in: J. D. Le Sueur (ed.) *The Decolonization Reader*, London: Routledge, 2003, p. 80 ff.

67 Ibid., p. 88 f.

68 Ibid., p. 93.

69 W. Tordoff, *Government and Politics in Africa* (Third Edition), Houndsmill: Macmillan, 1997, p. 319.

White Settlers in Africa

1 J. de Moor and D. Rothermund (eds), *Our Laws, Their Lands. Land Laws and Land Use in Modern Colonial Societies*, Münster: Lit, 1995.

2 B. Stora, *Algeria, 1830–2000. A Short History*, Ithaca, NY: Cornell University Press, 2004, p. 7.

3 O. Le Cour Grandmaison, *Coloniser. Exterminer. Sur la guerre et l'État colonial*, Paris: Fayard, 2005, p. 189.

4 Ibid., p. 100 ff.

5 Stora, *Algeria*, p. 26.

6 Ibid., p. 17 f.

7 Ibid., p. 21.

8 Ibid., p. 22.

9 Ibid., p. 36.

10 Ibid., p. 38.

11 Ibid., p. 46.

12 Ibid., p. 60 f.

13 Ibid., p. 47.
14 M. Connelly, *A Diplomatic Revolution. Algeria's Fight for Independence and the Origins of the Post-Cold War Era*, London: Oxford University Press, 2002, p. 290 ff. (Appendix).
15 Stora, *Algeria*, p. 49 f.
16 Ibid., p. 51.
17 Ibid., p. 65.
18 Ibid., p. 127 f.
19 Connelly, *Diplomatic Revolution*, p. 173 f.
20 Ibid., p. 175.
21 Ibid., p. 4.
22 Stora, *Algeria*, p. 74.
23 Ibid., p. 75.
24 Connelly, *Diplomatic Revolution*, p. 254.
25 Ibid., p. 260.
26 Stora, *Algeria*, p. 126.
27 Connelly, *Diplomatic Revolution*, p. 269.
28 Stora, *Algeria*, p. 141.
29 Ibid., p. 173.
30 Hailey, Lord, *An African Survey. Revised 1956. A Study of Problems Arising in Africa South of the Sahara*, London: Oxford University Press, 1957, p. 1556 f.
31 C. G. Rosberg and J. Nottingham, *The Myth of Mau Mau. Nationalism in Kenya*, New York: Praeger, 1966, p. 249 f.
32 J. Kenyatta, *Facing Mt. Kenya. The Tribal Life of the Gikuyu*, London: Mercury Books, 1961 (First edition, 1938).
33 J. Kenyatta, *Suffering Without Bitterness. The Founding of the Kenya Nation*, Nairobi: East African Publishing House, 1968, p. 56 ff.
34 L. S. B. Leakey, *Defeating Mau Mau*, London: Methuen, 1954, p. 79 f.
35 Ibid., p. 57 ff.
36 Rosberg and Nottingham, *The Myth of Mau Mau*, p. 302 ff.
37 T. Mboya, *Freedom and After*, London: Andre Deutsch, 1963, p. 128 f.
38 Ibid., p. 132 f.
39 D. A. Mungazi, *The Mind of Black Africa*, Westport, CT: Greenwood, 1996, p. 39.
40 Hailey, *African Survey*, p. 275 ff.
41 R. Welensky, *Welensky's 4000 Days. The Life and Death of the Federation of Rhodesia and Nyasaland*, London: Collins, 1964, p. 24 f.
42 Ibid., p. 319.
43 D. Birmingham, *The Decolonization of Africa*, London: Routledge, 1995, p. 75 f.
44 Ibid., p. 77.
45 P. Gleijeses, *Conflicting Missions. Havana, Washington and Africa, 1959–1976*, Chapel Hill: University of North Carolina Press, 2002, p. 273 ff.

Indian Labour and the Sugar Colonies

1 E. Stols, 'The Expansion of the Sugar Market in Western Europe', in: S. B. Schwartz (ed.), *Tropical Babylons. Sugar and the Making of the Atlantic World, 1450–1680*, Chapel Hill, NC: North Carolina Press, 2004, p. 237 ff.

2 A. Vieira, 'Sugar Islands. The Sugar Economy of Madeira and the Canaries, 1450–1650', in: Schwartz (ed.), *Tropical Babylons*, p. 42 ff.

3 G. Rodriguez Morel, 'The Sugar Economy of Espanola in the Sixteenth Century', in: Schwartz (ed.), *Tropical Babylons*, p. 85 ff.

4 J. J. McCusker and R. N. Menard, 'The Sugar Industry in the Seventeenth Century. A New Perspective on the Barbadian "Sugar Revolution"', in: Schwartz (ed.), *Tropical Babylons*, p. 289 ff.

5 Ibid., p. 293.

6 D. Rothermund, *India in the Great Depression, 1929–1939*, New Delhi: Manohar, 1992, p. 179.

7 J. Addison and K. Hazareesingh, *A New History of Mauritius* (Revised edn), London: Macmillan, 1993, p. 45 ff.

8 B. F. Williams, *Stains on My Name, War in My Veins. Guyana and the Politics of Cultural Struggle*, Durham, NC: Duke University Press, 1991, p. 130.

9 J. D. Kelly and M. Kaplan, *Represented Communities. Fiji and World Decolonization*, Chicago, IL: University of Chicago Press, 2001, p. 160.

10 Addison and Hazareesingh, *New History of Mauritius*, p. 3.

11 Ibid., p. 29.

12 Ibid., p. 51.

13 Ibid., p. 52.

14 Ibid., p. 50.

15 Ibid., p. 53.

16 M. D. North-Coombes, 'Struggles in the Cane Fields. Small Growers in Mauritius', in: B. Albert and A. Graves, *The World Sugar Economy in War and Depression, 1914–1940*, London: Routledge, 1988, p. 194 ff.

17 Addison and Hazareesingh, *New History of Mauritius*, p. 83 ff.

18 Ibid., p. 88.

19 Ibid., p. 92.

20 Ibid., p. 95.

21 Ibid., p. 110 ff.

22 G. Standing, 'Contrived Stagnation, Migration and the State in Guyana', in: P. Peek and G. Standing, *State Policies and Migration. Studies in Latin America and the Caribbean*, London: Croom Helm, 1982.

23 Williams, *War in My Veins*, p. 130.

24 Standing, 'Contrived Stagnation', p. 257.

25 Ibid., p. 259.

26 Ibid., p. 281 f.

27 L. M. Potter, 'The Post-Indenture Experience of East Indians in Guyana, 1873–1921', in: B. Brereton and W. Dookeran, *East Indians in the Caribbean. Colonialism and the Struggle for Identity*, Millwood, NY: Kraus, 1982, p. 83.

28 Standing, 'Contrived Stagnation', p. 269.

29 Ibid., p. 312.
30 H. Tinker, 'British Policy Towards a Separate Indian Identity in the Caribbean, 1920–1950', in: Brereton and Dookeran (eds), *East Indians*, p. 40.
31 Standing, 'Contrived Stagnation', p. 290.
32 Williams, *War in My Veins*, p. 131.
33 G. Danns, 'Decolonization and Militarization in the Caribbean. The Case of Guyana', in: P. Henry and C. Stone (eds), *The Newer Caribbean. Decolonization, Democracy, Development*, Philadelphia, PA: Institute of Human Issues, 1983, p. 63 ff.
34 J. R. Mandle, *Patterns of Caribbean Development. An Interpretative Essay on Economic Change*, New York: Gordon and Breach, 1982, p. 112 ff.
35 G. Oostindie and I. Klinkers, *Decolonising the Caribbean. Dutch Policies in a Comparative Perspective*, Amsterdam: Amsterdam University Press, 2003, p. 177.
36 Ibid., p. 94 ff.
37 Ibid., p. 84 ff.
38 Ibid., p. 96.
39 Ibid., p. 99.
40 Ibid., p. 177 ff.
41 Ibid., p. 108.
42 Ibid., p. 113.
43 Ibid., p. 154 f.
44 J. D. Kelly and M. Kaplan, *Represented Communities*, p. 84.
45 Ibid., p. 160 ff.
46 Ibid., p. 156.
47 Ibid., p. 174 f.
48 Ibid., p. 178 f.
49 Ibid., p. 180 f.
50 Ibid., p. 189.

The Commonwealth Caribbean

1 F. W. Knight, *The Caribbean. The Genesis of a Fragmented Nationalism* (Second edn), New York: Oxford University Press, 1990, p. 33.
2 Ibid., p. 76.
3 Ibid., p. 282 f.
4 Ibid., p. 186.
5 Ibid., p. 289.
6 Ibid., p. 300.
7 P. Henry, 'Decolonization and Cultural Underdevelopment in the Commonwealth Caribbean', in: P. Henry and C. Stone (eds), *The New Caribbean. Decolonization, Democracy and Development*, Philadelphia, PA: Institute for the Study of Human Issues, 1983, p. 106.
8 Knight, *The Caribbean*, p. 289, 300.
9 Henry, 'Decolonization and Cultural Underdevelopment', in: Henry and Stone (eds), *The New Caribbean*, p. 111.
10 *Report of Mission to Africa*, Kingston: The Government Printer, 1961.
11 W. Zips, 'Mama Africa, lange nicht mehr gesehen . . . ', in: B. Hausberger and

G. Pfeisinger (eds), *Die Karibik. Geschichte und Gesellschaft, 1942–2000*, Wien: Promedia, 2005, p. 289 ff.

12 Knight, *The Caribbean*, p. 301.

13 M. Figueroa, 'W. Arthur Lewis versus the Lewis Model. Agricultural or Industrial Development?', in: *The Manchester School*, Vol. 72, No. 6, December 2004, pp. 736–750.

14 P. W. Ashley, 'The Commonwealth Caribbean and the Contemporary World Order', in: Henry and Stone (eds), *The New Carribean*, p. 160 ff.

15 C. D. Parris, 'Resource Ownership and the Prospects for Democracy. The Case of Trinidad and Tobago', in: Henry and Stone (eds), *The New Caribbean*, p. 318.

16 J. R. Mandle, *Patterns of Caribbean Development. An Interpretative Eassy on Economic Change*, New York: Gordon and Breach, 1982, p. 126 ff.

17 Oostindie and Klinkers, *Decolonising the Caribbean*, p. 154.

18 Mandle, *Patterns of Caribbean Development*, p. 94 ff.

19 Ibid., p. 100.

20 Ibid., p. 128.

21 P. Henry, 'Decolonization and the Authoritarian Context of Democracy in Antigua', in: Henry and Stone (eds), *The New Caribbean*, p. 300.

22 Knight, *The Caribbean*, p. 303.

23 Henry, 'Decolonization', in: Henry and Stone (eds), *The New Caribbean*, p. 297 f.

24 C. Stone, 'Decolonization and the Caribbean State System', in: Henry and Stone (eds), *The New Caribbean*, p. 41 ff.

A Diehard Empire

1 G. B. Souza, *The Survival of Empire. Portuguese Trade and Society in China and the South China Sea 1630–1754*, Cambridge: Cambridge University Press, 1986, p. 14.

2 N. McQueen, *The Decolonization of Portuguese Africa. Metropolitan Revolution and the Dissolution of Empire*, London: Longman, 1997, p. 67.

3 Ibid., p. 70.

4 Ibid., p. 76.

5 T. Gurr, *Why Men Rebel*, Princeton, NJ: Princeton University Press, 1970.

6 McQueen, *Portuguese Africa*, p. 73.

7 Ibid., p. 88 f.

8 Ibid., p. 166 ff.

9 H. Kulke and D. Rothermund, *A History of India* (Fourth edn), London: Routledge, 2004, p. 356.

10 P. Chabal with D. Birmingham, J. Forrest, M. Newitt, G. Seibert, E. S. Andrade, *A History of Postcolonial Lusophone Africa*, London: Hurst, 2002, p. 81.

11 McQueen, *Portuguese Africa*, p. 20 f.

12 Ibid., p. 38.

13 P. Gleijeses, *Conflicting Missions. Havana, Washington, and Africa, 1959–1976*, Chapel Hill, NC: University of North Carolina Press, 2002, p. 187.

14 Ibid., p. 190.

15 Ibid., p. 88 f.

16 McQueen, *Portuguese Africa*, p. 21.

17 Ibid., p. 33.
18 Ibid., p. 30.
19 Ibid., p. 33.
20 Ibid., p. 164.
21 Ibid., p. 175.
22 Ibid., p. 181.
23 Ibid., p. 196.
24 Gleijeses, *Conflicting Missions*, p. 261 f.
25 Ibid., p. 307.
26 Ibid., p. 309.
27 Ibid., p. 317.
28 Ibid., p. 344.
29 D. Birmingham, 'Angola', in: Chabal *et al.* (eds) *Lusophone Africa*, p. 153.
30 Gleijeses, *Conflicting Missions*, p. 87.
31 McQueen, *Portuguese Africa*, p. 133 f.
32 Ibid., p. 145 ff.
33 Ibid., p. 152.
34 M. Newitt, 'Mozambique', in: Chabal *et al.* (eds), *Lusophone Africa*, p. 196.
35 Ibid., p. 211.
36 Ibid., p. 222 f.
37 Ibid., p. 216.

The Pacific Islands

1 CIA World Fact Book, Palau (http://www.cia.gov/cia/publications/factbook/geos/ps.html).
2 CIA World Fact Book, Micronesia (http://www.cia.gov/cia/publications/factbook/geos/fm.html).
3 CIA World Fact Book, Marshall Islands (http://www.cia.gov/cia/publications/factbook/geos/rm.html).
4 J. Springhall, *Decolonization since 1945*, London: Palgrave, 2001, p. 195 ff.
5 CIA World Fact Book, Tonga (http://www.cia.gov/cia/publications/factbook/geos/tn.htm).

The Legacy of Colonial Rule

1 M. Mamdani, *Citizen and Subject*, Princeton, NJ: Princeton University Press, 1996, p. 16 ff.
2 W. Wallace, 'Rescue or Retreat? The Nation State in Western Europe, 1945–1993', in: J. Dunn (ed.), *Contemporary Crisis of the Nation State?*, Oxford: Blackwell, 1995, pp. 52–76.
3 H. Kulke and D. Rothermund, *A History of India* (Fourth edn), London: Routledge, 2004, p. 327.
4 M. W. Mathews (ed.), *A Dictionary of Americanisms*, Chicago, IL: University of Chicago Press, 1951, p. 692 f. (article: gerrymander).

5 D. Rothermund, *Mahatma Gandhi. An Essay in Political Biography*, New Delhi: Manohar, 1991, p. 8 f.

6 Ibid., p. 33.

7 D. Rothermund, 'The Legacy of the British-Indian Empire', in: W. Mommsen and J. Osterhammel (eds), *Imperialism and After*, London: Allen and Unwin, 1986, p. 143.

8 Ibid., p. 142.

9 W. Tordoff, *Government and Politics in Africa* (Third edn), London: Macmillan, 1997, p. 189.

10 Ibid. p. 188.

11 Ibid., p. 190 f.

12 Ibid., p. 197 f.

13 P. M. Martin, 'Beyond Independence', in: D. Birmingham and P. M. Martin, *History of Central Africa*, London: Longman, 1998, p. 14 f.

14 P. Darby, 'Football, Colonial Doctrine and Indigenous Resistance', in: J. D. Le Sueur, *The Decolonization Reader*, London: Routledge, 2003, p. 358 ff.

15 Ibid., p. 370.

From Colonialism to Neocolonialism?

1 R. P. T. Davenport-Hines and G. Jones (eds), *British Business in Asia since 1860*, Cambridge: Cambridge University Press, 1989.

2 K. T. Telang, *Selected Writings and Speeches*, Bombay: Manoranjan Press, 1916, p. 179.

3 R. M. Lala, *The Creation of Wealth. A Tata Story*, Bombay: Popular Prakshan, 1981.

4 D. Rothermund, *India in the Great Depression, 1929–1939*, New Delhi: Manohar, 1992, p. 142 ff.

5 D. Rothermund, 'Die Anfänge der indischen Wirtschaftsplanung im Zweiten Weltkrieg', in: P. Hablützel, H. Werner Tobler and A. Wirz (eds), *Dritte Welt. Historische Prägung und politische Herausforderung*, Wiesbaden: Steiner, 1983, p. 81 ff.

6 D. Rothermund, *Mahatma Gandhi. An Essay in Political Biography*, New Delhi: Manohar, 1991, p. 129.

7 H. Sieberg, *Colonial Development. Die Grundlegung moderner Entwicklungspolitik durch Großbritannien, 1919–1945*, Stuttgart: Steiner, 1985, p. 503 ff.

8 M. Havinden and D. Meredith, *Colonialism and Development. Britain and its Tropical Colonies, 1850–1960*, London: Routledge, 1993, p. 229 ff., p. 276 ff.

9 Sieberg, *Colonial Development*, p. 557 ff.

10 Rothermund, 'Die Anfänge' in: Hablützel *et al.* (eds), *Dritte Welt*, p. 83 f.

11 P. Thakurdas, G. D. Birla, J. R. D. Tata, A. Dalal, J. Mathai, *A Brief Memorandum Outlining a Plan of Economic Development*, Bombay, 1944.

12 A. Hanson, *The Process of Planning. A Study of India's Five Year Plans, 1950–1964*, London: Macmillan, 1966.

13 D. Rothermund, *An Economic History of India*, London: Routledge (Second edn), 1993, p. 138 ff.

14 W. W. Rostow, *The Stages of Economic Growth*, Cambridge: Cambridge University

Press, 1960; see also W. W. Rostow (ed.), *The Economics of Take-Off into Sustained Growth*, New York: St Martin's Press, 1963.

15 J. Nyerere, *Freedom and Unity. Selections from Writings and Speeches*, 1952–1963, London: Oxford University Press, 1967, p. 254.

16 Government of Kenya, *Development Plan 1964–1970*, Nairobi, 1964, p. i ff. (Introduction by the Prime Minister).

17 A. Cairncross, 'Marshall Plan', in: P. Newman, M. Milgate, J. Eatwell (eds), *The New Palgrave Dictionary of Money and Finance*, Vol. II, London: Macmillan, 1992, p. 673 ff.

18 H. Chenery, 'Foreign Aid', in: Newman *et al.* (eds), *Dictionary of Money and Finance*, Vol .II, p. 144 ff.

19 C. Bell, 'Development Economics', in: J. Eatwell, M. Milgate, P. Newman (eds), *The New Palgrave Dictionary of Economics*, Vol. I, London: Macmillan, 1987, p. 818 ff.

20 A. Hirschman, *The Strategy of Economic Development*, New Haven: Yale University Press, 1958.

21 C. Leys, *The Rise and Fall of Development Theory*, Nairobi: East African Educational Publishers, 1996, p. 108 ff.

22 H. W. Singer, 'Terms of Trade and Economic Development', in: Eatwell *et al.* (eds), *Dictionary of Economics*, Vol. IV, p. 626 ff.

23 Leys, *Development Theory*, p. 185 ff.

24 Rothermund, *Economic History of India*, p. 170 ff.

25 K. Nkrumah, *Consciencism. Philosophy and Ideology for Decolonization and Development with particular reference to the African Revolution*, London: Heinemann, 1964, p. 100.

26 Leys, *Development Theory*, p. 22 f.

Guide to Sources and Secondary Reading

1 M. E. Chamberlain, *The Longman Companion to European Decolonisation in the Twentieth Century*, London: Longman, 1998.

2 J. Springhall, *Decolonization since 1945*, London: Palgrave, 2001.

3 R. F. Betts, *Decolonization*, New York: Routledge (Second edn), 2004.

4 C. Coquery-Vidrovitch, *Afrique noire. Permanences et ruptures*, Paris: L'Harmattan, 1993.

5 E. Luard, *A History of the United Nations, Vol. II. The Age of Decolonization, 1955–1965*, London: Macmillan, 1989.

6 P. Duara (ed.), *Decolonization. Perspectives from Now and Then*, London: Routledge, 2003.

7 J. D. Le Sueur (ed.), *The Decolonization Reader*, New York: Routledge, 2003.

8 S. R. Ashton and S. E. Stockwell (eds), *Imperial Policy and Colonial Practice, 1925–1945 (British Documents on the End of Empire*, Series A, Vol. I), London: HMSO, 1996. Part I: Metropolitan Reorganisation, Defence and International Relations, Political Change and Constitutional Reform, Part II: Economic Policy, Social Policies and Colonial Research.

9 R. Hyam (ed.), *The Labour Government and the End of Empire, 1945–1951 (British*

Documents on the End of Empire, Series A, Vol. II), London: HMSO, 1992. Part I: High Policy and Administration, Part II: Economics and International Relations, Part III: Strategy, Politics and Constitutional Change, Part IV: Race Relations and the Commonwealth.

10 D. Goldsworthy (ed.), *The Conservative Government and the End of Empire, 1951–1957* (*British Documents on the End of Empire*, Series A, Vol. III), London: HMSO, 1994. Part I: International Relations, Part II: Politics and Administration, Part III: Economics and Social Policies.

11 R. Hyam and W. R. Louis (eds), *The Conservative Government and the End of Empire, 1957–1964* (*British Documents on the End of Empire*, Vol. IV), London: HMSO, 2000. Part I: High Policy, Political and Constitutional Change, Part II: Economics, International Relations, and the Commonwealth.

12 S. R. Ashton and W. R. Louis (eds), *East of Suez and the Commonwealth, 1964–1971* (*British Documents on the End of Empire*, Series A, Vol. V), London: HMSO, 2004. Part I: East of Suez, Defence Reviews etc., Part II: Rhodesia Policy, Commonwealth Relations Office, Europe, Part III: Dependent Territories, Relations with Postcolonial Africa, Economic Affairs, etc.

13 A. Thurston and S. R. Ashton (eds), *Sources for Colonial Studies in the Public Records Office* (*British Documents on the End of Empire*, Series C, Vol. I and II), Vol. I, London: HMSO, 1995, Vol. II, London: HMSO, 1998.

14 A. J. Stockwell (ed.), *British Imperial Policy and Decolonization, 1938–1964*, 2 vols, New York: St Martin's Press, 1987, 1989.

15 F. Heinlein, *British Government Policy and Decolonisation, 1945–1963*, London: Frank Cass, 2002.

16 N. Mansergh (ed.), *The Transfer of Power, 1942–1947. Constitutional Relations between Britain and India*, 12 vols, London: HMSO, 1971–1983.

17 *The Collected Works of Mahatma Gandhi*, New Delhi: Government of India, Publications Division, 1958–1984.

18 P. N. Chopra (ed.), *Towards Freedom. Documents on the Movement for Independence in India, 1937*, Delhi: Oxford University Press, 1986.

19 B. Chatterjee (ed.), *Towards Freedom. Documents on the Movement for Independence in India, 1938*, 3 vols, Delhi: Oxford University Press, 1999.

20 P. S. Gupta (ed.), *Towards Freedom. Documents on the Movement for Independence in India, 1942–1944*, 3 vols, Delhi: Oxford University Press, 1997.

21 H. Kulke and D. Rothermund, *A History of India* (Fourth edn), London: Routledge, 2004.

22 J. M. Brown, *Modern India. The Origins of an Asian Democracy*, London: Oxford University Press, 1985.

23 S. S. Pirzada (ed.), *Foundations of Pakistan. All-Indian Muslim League Documents, 1906–1947*, 2 vols, Karachi: National Publishing House, 1970. Vol. I: 1906–1924, Vol. II: 1924–1947.

24 M. M. Sadullah (ed.), *The Partition of the Punjab, 1947*, 4 vols, Lahore: National Documentation Centre, 1983.

25 C. H. Philipps and D. H. Wainwright (eds), *The Partition of India. Policies and Perspectives, 1935–1947*, London: Allen and Unwin, 1970.

26 K. M. De Silva (ed.), *Sri Lanka* (*British Documents on the End of Empire*, Series B,

Vol. II), London: HMSO, 1997. Part I: The Second World War and the Soulbury Commission, 1939–1945, Part II: Towards Independence, 1945–1948.

27 K. M. De Silva, *A History of Sri Lanka*, London: Oxford University Press, 1981.

28 S. L. van der Wal/ P. J. Drooglever and M. J. B. Schouten (eds), *Officielle bescheiden betreffende de Nederlands-Indonesische betrekkeningen, 1945–1950*, The Hague: Rijks Geschiedkundige Publikatien (Kleine Serie), Vols 36–39, 41, 45, 48, 50, 52, 54, 58, 61, 63, 66, 70, 71, 75, 77, 80, 1971–1996 (S. L. van der Wal edited the first eight volumes, the rest were edited by the other editors).

29 B. Dahm, *History of Indonesia in the Twentieth Century*, London: Pall Mall Press, 1971.

30 G. Bodinier (ed.), *La Guerre d'Indochine, 1945–1954. Textes et Documents, Vol. I: Le retour de la France en Indochine, 1945–1946, Vol II: Indochine 1947, Règlement politique ou solution militaire? Textes es documents Français et Vietminh*, Vincennes: Service Historique de l'Armée de Terre, 1987, 1989.

31 L. Bodard, *La Guerre d'Indochine*, 4 vols, Paris: Gallimard, 1963–1973; abridged English translation of the first two volumes: *The Quicksand War*, London: Faber, 1967.

32 B. Fall, *Street without Joy*, Mechanicsburg, PA: Stackpole Books (latest edition), 1994.

33 J. Buttinger, *Vietnam. A Dragon Embattled, Vol. I: From Colonialism to Vietminh*, New York: Praeger, 1967.

34 J. Dalloz, *La Guerre d'Indochine, 1945–1954*, Paris: Editions du Seuil, 1987.

35 H. Tinker (ed.), *Burma. The Struggle for Independence*, London: HMSO, 1983–1984.

36 J. F. Cady, *A History of Modern Burma*, Ithaca, NY: Cornell University Press, 1958.

37 A. J. Stockwell and S. R. Ashton (eds), *Malaya (British Documents on the End of Empire*, Series B, Vol. III), London: HMSO, 1995. Part I: The Malayan Union Experiment, 1942–1948, Part II: The Communist Insurrection, 1948–1953, Part III: The Alliance Route to Independence, 1953–1957.

38 A. J. Stockwell (ed.), *Malaysia (British Documents on the End of Empire*, Series B, Vol. VIII), London: HMSO, 2004.

39 A. Short, *The Communist Insurrection in Malaya, 1948–1960*, London: Frederick Muller, 1975.

40 E. C. T. Chew and E. Lee (eds), *A History of Singapore*, Singapore: Oxford University Press, 1991.

41 T. Friend, *Between Two Empires. The Ordeal of the Philippines, 1929–1946*, New Haven, CT: Yale University Press, 1965.

42 B. J. Kerkvliet, *The Huk Rebellion. A Study of Peasant Revolt in the Philippines*, Berkeley, CA: University of California Press, 1977.

43 M. Rubinstein, *Taiwan. A New History*, Armonk, NY: M. E. Sharpe, 1999.

44 B. Cumings, *Korea's Place in the Sun. A Modern History*, New York: W. W. Norton, 1998.

45 D. L. McNamara, *The Colonial Origins of Korean Enterprise*, 1910–1945, New York: Cambridge University Press, 1990.

46 C. Chang, *Politics of Hong Kong's Reversion to China*, New York: St Martin's Press, 1998.

47 Y. P. Ghai, *Hong Kong's New Constitutional Order. The Resumption of Chinese Sovereignty and the Basic Law*, Hong Kong: Hong Kong University Press, 1998.

48 S. Tsang, *Modern History of Hong Kong, 1841–1998*, Hong Kong: I. B. Tauris, 1998.

49 P. K. Hitti, *Syria. A Short History*, London: Macmillan, 1959.

50 P. S. Khoury, *Syria and the French Mandate. The Politics of Arab Nationalism*, Princeton, NJ: Princeton University Press, 1987.

51 S. H. Longrigg, *Syria and Lebanon under French Mandate*, London: Oxford University Press, 1958.

52 J. F. Devlin, *The Ba'th Party. A History from its Origins to 1966*, Stanford, CA: Hoover Institution Press, 1976.

53 M. Zamir, *The Formation of Modern Lebanon*, London: Croom Helm, 1985.

54 M. Elliot, *Independent Iraq. The Monarchy and British Influence*, London: I. B. Tauris, 1996.

55 C. Tripp, *A History of Iraq*, Cambridge: Cambridge University Press, 2002.

56 M. C. Wilson, *King Abdullah, Britain and the Making of Jordan*, Cambridge: Cambridge University Press, 1995.

57 M. J. Cohen, *Palestine. Retreat from the Mandate*, London/New York: Paul Elek, 1978.

58 M. J. Cohen, *Palestine and the Great Powers, 1945–1948*, Princeton, NJ: Princeton University Press, 1982.

59 R. Ovendale, *Britain, the United States and the End of the Palestine Mandate, 1942–1948*, Woodbridge, Suffolk: Boydele Press, 1989.

60 J. Kent (ed.), *Egypt and the Defence of the Middle East* (*British Documents on the End of Empire*, Series B, Vol. IV), London: HMSO, 1998. Part I: 1945–1949, Part II: 1949–1963, Part III: 1953–1956.

61 P. J. Vatikiotis, *The History of Modern Egypt*, Baltimore, MD: Johns Hopkins University Press, 1991.

62 M. F. Holland, *America and Egypt. From Roosevelt to Eisenhower*, New York: Praeger, 1996.

63 S. R. Ashton and J. Kent, *Egypt and the Defence of the Middle East*, London: The Stationery Office Books, 1999.

64 D. Johnson (ed.), *Sudan* (*British Documents on the End of Empire*, Series B, Vol. V), London: HMSO, 1998. Part I: 1942–1950, Part II: 1951–1956.

65 M. W. Daly, *Imperial Sudan. The Anglo-Egyptian Condominium, 1934–1956*, Cambridge: Cambridge University Press, 1991.

66 M. O. Beshir, *Revolution and Nationalism in the Sudan*, New York: Barnes and Noble, 1974.

67 A. M. Lesch, *The Sudan. Contested National Identities*, Oxford: James Currey, 1999.

68 R. J. Gavin, *Aden under British Rule, 1839–1967*, New York: Harper and Row, 1975.

69 A. Pelt, *Libyan Independence and the United Nations. A Case of Planned Decolonization*, New Haven, CT: Yale University Press, 1970.

70 M. Khadduri, *Modern Libya. A Study in Political Development*, Baltimore, MD: Johns Hopkins University Press, 1963.

71 K. J. Perkins, *History of Modern Tunisia*, Cambridge: Cambridge University Press, 2004.

72 C. R. Pennell, *Morocco since 1830. A History*, London: Hurst, 2000.

73 R. Adloff, *The Western Saharans. Background to Conflict*, London: Croom Helm, 1980.

74 T. Hodges, *The Western Sahara. The Roots of a Desert War*, Westport, CT: Lawrence Hill, 1984.

75 T. Shelley, *Endgame in Western Sahara. What Future for Africa's Last Colony?*, London: Zed Books, 2004.

76 G. Diallo, *Mauritania. The Other Apartheid?*, Uppsala: Nordic Africa Institute, 1993.

77 G. Gerteiny, *Mauritania*, London: Pall Mall Press, 1967.

78 R. Rathbone, *Ghana* (*British Documents on the End of Empire*, Series B, Vol. I), London: HMSO, 1992. Part I: 1941–1952, Part II: 1953–1957.

79 R. Rathbone, *Nkrumah and the Chiefs. The Politics of Chieftaincy in Ghana, 1951–1960*, Oxford: James Currey, 2000.

80 J. A. D. Alie, *A New History of Sierra Leone*, New York: St Martin's Press, 1990.

81 V. Du Bois, *The Decline of the Guinean Revolution*, New York: Columbia University Press, 1965.

82 A. Ly, *Les regroupements politiques au Sénégal, 1956–1970*, Dakar: CODESRIA/Karthala, 1992.

83 G. P. Pfefferman, *Industrial Labour in the Republic of Senegal*, New York: Praeger, 1968.

84 A. R. Zolberg, *One-Party Government in the Ivory Coast*, Princeton, NJ: Princeton University Press, 1969.

85 R. Cornevin, *Le Togo. Des origines à nos jours*, Paris: Academie des sciences d'outre-mer, 1988.

86 R. Cornevin, *La republique populaire du Bénin. Des origines dahoméennes à nos jours*, Paris: Académie des sciences d'outre-mer, 1981.

87 P. Manning, *Slavery, Colonialism and Economic Growth in Dahomey*, Cambridge: Cambridge University Press, 1982.

88 F. Fugelstad, *A History of Niger*, Cambridge: Cambridge University Press, 1984.

89 M. J. Azevedo, *Roots of Violence. A History of War in Chad*, Williston, VT: Gordon and Breach Science Publishers, 1998.

90 M. Azevedo and E. Nnandozie, *Chad. A Nation in Search of its Future*, Boulder, CO: Westview Press, 1998.

91 M. Lynn, *Nigeria* (*British Documents on the End of Empire*, Series B, Vol. VII), London, HMSO, 2001. Part I: Managing Political Reform, 1943–1953, Part II: Moving Towards Independence, 1953–1960.

92 M. Crowder, *The Story of Nigeria*, London: Faber, 1978.

93 R. Joseph, *Radical Nationalism in Cameroon: Social Origins of the UPC Rebellion*, London: Oxford University Press, 1977.

94 R. Joseph, *Gaullist Africa. Africa under Ahmadu Ahidjo*, Enugu, Nigeria: Fourth Dimension Publications, 2002.

95 M. A. de Saint-Paul, *Gabon. Development of a Nation*, London: Routledge, 1989.

96 G. Nzongola-Ntalaja, *Congo. From Leopold to Kabila*, London: Zed Books, 2002.

97 L. De Witte, *The Assassination of Lumumba*, London: Verso, 2001.

98 C. D. Gondola, *The History of the Congo*, Westport, CT: Greenwood Publ., 2002.

99 J. Iliffe, *A Modern History of Tanganyika*, Cambridge: Cambridge University Press, 1979.

100 S. R. Karugire, *A Political History of Uganda*, Exeter: Heinemann, 1980.

101 K. Ingham, *The Making of Modern Uganda*, Westport, CT: Greenwood Press, 1983.

102 G. Prunier, *The Rwanda Crisis. History of a Genocide*, London: Hurst, 1997.

103 R. Lemarchand, *Burundi. Ethnic Conflict and Genocide*, Cambridge: Cambridge University Press, 1994.

104 I. M. Lewis, *A Modern History of the Somali. Nation and State in the Horn of Africa*, Oxford: James Currey, 2002.

105 D. Connell, *Against all Odds. A Chronicle of the Eritrean Revolution*, Asmara, Eritrea: Red Sea Press, 1997.

106 R. Iyob, *The Eritrean Struggle for Independence. Domination, Resistance, Nationalism, 1941–1993*, Cambridge: Cambridge University Press, 1995.

107 M. Covell, *Madagascar. Politics, Economics and Society*, New York: Francis Pinter, 1987.

108 J. Tronchon, *L'insurrection malegache de 1947. Essai d'interprétation historique*, Paris: Maspero, 1974.

109 A. Sillery, *Botswana. A Short History*, London: Methuen, 1974.

110 S. Gill, *A Short History of Lesotho*, Morija: Morija Museum and Archives, 1993.

111 J. C. Jauffret (ed.), *La Guerre d'Algérie par les documents*, Vol. I: Les Avertissements, 1943–1946, Vincennes: Service Historique de l'Armée de Terre, 1990, Vol. II: Les portes de la guerre, 1946–1954, 1998.

112 B. Stora, *Algeria, 1830–2000. A Short History*, Ithaca, NY: Cornell University Press, 2001.

113 M. Connelly, *A Diplomatic Revolution. Algeria's Fight for Independence and the Origins of the Post-Cold War Era*, London: Oxford University Press, 2002.

114 G. Bennett, *Kenya. A Political History*, London: Oxford University Press, 1963.

115 G. Bennett and C. Rosberg, *The Kenyatta Elections, 1960–1961*, London: Oxford University Press, 1961.

116 B. Ogot and W. R. Ochieng (eds), *Decolonization and Independence in Kenya, 1940–1993*, Oxford: James Currey, 1995.

117 A. Sardanis, *Africa, Another Side of the Coin. Northern Rhodesia's Final Years and Zambia's Nationhood*, London: I. B. Tauris, 2003.

118 R. Blake, *A History of Rhodesia*, London: Eyre Methuen, 1977.

119 W. H. Morris-Jones (ed.), *From Rhodesia to Zimbabwe. Behind and Beyond Lancaster House*, London: Frank Cass, 1980.

120 R. I. Rotberg, *The Rise of Nationalism in Central Africa. The Making of Malawi and Zambia*, Bloomington, IN: Indiana University Press, 1965.

121 P. K. Katjavivi, *A History of Resistance in Namibia*, Oxford: James Currey, 2004.

122 C. Leys and S. Brown, *Histories of Namibia. Living Through the Liberation Struggle*, London: The Merlin Press, 2005.

123 R. Allen, *Slaves, Freedmen and Indentured Labourers in Colonial Mauritius*, Cambridge: Cambridge University Press, 1999.

124 L. A. Despres, *Cultural Pluralism and Nationalist Politics in Guyana*, Chicago: Rand McNally, 1967.

125 R. R. Premdas, *Party Politics and Racial Division in Guyana*, Denver, CO: University of Colorado Press, 1973.

126 G. Oostindie and I. Klinkers, *Decolonising the Caribbean. Dutch Policies in a Comparative Perspective*, Amsterdam: Amsterdam University Press, 2003.

127 J. D. Kelly and M. Kaplan, *Represented Communities. Fiji and World Decolonization*, Chicago, IL: University of Chicago Press, 2001.

128 B. V. Lal, *Broken Waves. A History of the Fiji Islands in the Twentieth Century*, Honolulu: University of Hawaii Press, 1992.

129 S. R. Ashton and D. Killingray (eds), *The West Indies* (*British Documents on the End of Empire*, Series B, Vol. VI), London: HMSO, 1999.

130 F. W. Knight, *The Caribbean. The Genesis of a Fragmented Nationalism*, New York: Oxford University Press, 1990.

131 Commissao para o Estudo das Campanhas de Africa, *Resenha Histórico-Militar das Campanhas de Africa, 1961–1974*, Lisboa: Estado-Maior do Exército, 1988–1998, Vol. I (1988), Vols II and III (1989), Vol. IV (1990), Vol. V, Part 1 and 2 (1991), Vol. V, Part 3 and 4 (1992), Vol. V, Part 7 (1995), Vol. V, Part 8 (1997), Vol. VI (1998).

132 N. McQueen, *The Decolonization of Portuguese Africa. Metropolitan Revolution and the Dissolution of Empire*, London: Longman, 1997.

133 P. Chabal with D. Birmingham, J. Forrest, M. Newitt, G. Seibert, E. S. Andrade (eds), *A History of Postcolonial Lusophone Africa*, London: Hurst, 2002.

134 A. Rubinoff, *India's Use of Force in Goa*, Bombay: Popular Prakashan, 1971.

135 B. Lal and K. Fortune (eds), *The Pacific Islands. An Encyclopedia*, Honolulu: University of Hawaii Press, 2000.

136 J. D. Waiko, *A Short History of Papua New Guinea*, Melbourne: Oxford University Press, 1993.

137 Kalkot Matas Kele-Kele (ed.), *New Hebrides. The Road to Independence*, Suva, Fiji: Institute of Pacific Studies, University of the South Pacific, 1977.

138 I. C. Campbell, *Island Kingdom. Tonga, Ancient and Modern*, Christchurch, New Zealand: Canterbury University Press, 2001.

BIBLIOGRAPHY

Note: For a bibliography of the source publications in the series *British Documents on the End of Empire* and source publications by the Dutch, French and Portuguese governments, see the 'Guide to Sources and Secondary Reading'.

Addison, J. and Hazareesingh, K., *A New History of Mauritius* (Revised edn), Stanley: Édition de l'Océan Indien, 1996.

Ageron, C. R., *La décolonisation française*, Paris: Armand Colin, 1991.

Ageron, C. R. et Michel, M. (eds), *L'Afrique noire française. L'heure des Indépendances*, Paris: CNRS, 1992.

Albertini, R. von, *Decolonization. The Administration and the Future of the Colonies, 1919–1960*, New York: Doubleday, 1971.

Allman, J. M. , *The Quills of the Porcupine. Asante Nationalism in an Emergent Ghana*, Madison, WI: University of Wisconsin Press, 1993.

Andaya, L. and B., *Malaysia*, London: Macmillan, 1981.

Anderson, B., *Imagined Communities. Reflections on the Spread and Origin of Nationalism*, New York: Verso, 1983.

Barnett, D. L., *Mau Mau From Within. The Autobiography of Karari Njama*, Letchworth: MacGibbon and Kee, 1966.

Benner, E., *Really Existing Nationalisms. A Post-Communist View from Marx and Engels*, Oxford: Clarendon Press, 1995.

Betts, R. F., *Decolonization* (Second edn), New York: Routledge, 2004.

Bienen, H., *Tanzania. Party Transformation and Economic Development*, Princeton, NJ: Princeton University Press, 1967.

Birmingham, D., *The Decolonization of Africa*, London: Routledge, 1995.

Birmingham, D. and Martin, P. M. (eds), *History of Central Africa. The Contemporary Years since 1960*, London: Longman, 1998.

Bonn, M. J., *The Crumbling of Empire. The Disintegration of World Economy*, London: George Allen and Unwin, 1938.

Botman, S., *Egypt from Independence to Revolution, 1919–1952*, Syracuse, NY: Syracuse University Press, 1991.

Brecher, M., *Nehru. A Political Biography*, London: Oxford University Press, 1959.

Brereton, B. and Dookeran, W. (eds), *East Indians in the Caribbean. Colonisation and the Struggle for Identity*, Millwood, NY: Kraus, 1982.

Cain, P. J. and Hopkins, A. G., *British Imperialism 1688–2000*, Harlow: Longman/Pearson, 2002.

Cantier, J. et Jennings, E. (eds), *L'Empire Colonial sous Vichy*, Paris: Odile Jacob, 2004.

Carter, G. (ed.), *African One-Party States*, Ithaca, NY: Cornell University Press, 1962.

Chabal, P. with D. Birmingham, J. Forrest, M. Newitt, G. Seibert, E. S. Andrade (eds), *A History of Postcolonial Lusophone Africa*, London: Hurst, 2002.

Chafer, T., *The End of Empire in French*

West Africa. France's Successful Decolonization?, Oxford: Berg, 2002.

Chamberlain, M., *The Longman Companion to European Decolonisation in the Twentieth Century*, London: Longman, 1998.

Chatterji, R., *Working Class and the Nationalist Movement in India. The Critical Years*, New Delhi: South Asian Publishers, 1984.

Chidzero, B. T. G., *Tanganyika and International Trusteeship*, London: Oxford University Press, 1961.

Connelly, M., *A Diplomatic Revolution. Algeria's Fight for Independence and the Origins of the Post-Cold War Era*, New York: Oxford University Press, 2002.

Cooper, F., *Decolonization and African Society. The Labour Question in French and British Africa*, Cambridge: Cambridge University Press, 1996.

Le Cour Grandmaison, O., *Coloniser. Exterminer. Sur la guerre et l'État colonial*, Paris: Fayard, 2005.

Dahm, B., *History of Indonesia in the Twentieth Century*, London: Pall Mall Press, 1971.

Darwin, J., *Britain and Decolonization. The Retreat from Empire in the Post-War World*, London: Macmillan, 1988.

Darwin, J., *The End of the British Empire. The Historical Debate*, Oxford: Blackwell, 1991.

De Jong, J. J. P., *Diplomatie of Strijd. Het Nederlands beleid tegenover de Indonesische revolutie, 1945–1947*, Amsterdam: Boom Meppel, 1988.

De Silva, K. M., *A History of Sri Lanka*, London: Oxford University Press, 1981.

De Silva, K. M., *Managing Ethnic Tensions in Multi-Ethnic Societies. Sri Lanka, 1880–1985*, Lanham, MD: University Press of America, 1986.

Deutsch, K. W., *Nationalism and Social Communication. An Inquiry into the Foundations of Nationality*, New York: Free Press, 1953.

Duara, P. (ed.), *Decolonization. Perspectives from Now and Then*, London: Routledge, 2003.

Dumbuya, P. A., *Tanganyika under International Mandate, 1919–1946*, Lanham, MD: University Press of America, 1995.

Dunn, J. (ed.), *Contemporary Crisis of the Nation State?*, Oxford: Blackwell, 1995.

El-Ayouty, Yassin, *The United Nations and Decolonization. The Role of Afro-Asia*, The Hague: Martinus Nijhoff, 1971.

Emerson, R., *From Empire to Nation. The Rise of Self-Assertion of Asian and African Peoples*, Cambridge, MA: Harvard University Press, 1960.

Fedorowich, K. and Thomas, M. (eds), *International Diplomacy and Colonial Retreat*, London: Frank Cass, 2001.

Frey, M., Pruessen, R. W. and Tan, T. Y. (eds), *The Transformation of Southeast Asia. International Perspectives on Decolonization*, Armonk, NY: M. E. Sharpe, 2003.

Friend, T., *Between Two Empires: The Ordeal of the Philippines, 1929–1946*, New Haven, CT: Yale University Press, 1965.

Gallagher, J., *The Decline, Revival and Fall of the British Empire*, Cambridge: Cambridge University Press, 1982.

Gellner, E., *Nations and Nationalism*, Ithaca, NY: Cornell University Press, 1983.

Gifford, P. and Louis, W. R. (eds), *Decolonization and African Independence. The Transfers of Power, 1960–1980*, New Haven, CT: Yale University Press, 1988.

Gleijeses, P., *Conflicting Missions. Havana, Washington and Africa, 1959–1976*, Chapel Hill, NC: University of North Carolina Press, 2002.

Grimal, H., *Decolonization. The British, French, Dutch and Belgian Empires, 1919–1963*, Boulder, CO: Westview Press, 1978.

Gupta, P. S., *Imperialism and the British Labour Movement, 1914–1964*, Basingstoke: Macmillan, 1975.

Hack, K., *Defence and Decolonisation in Southeast Asia. Britain, Malaya and Singapore, 1941–1968*, London: Curzon, 2001.

Hailey, Lord, *An African Survey. Revised 1956. A Study of Problems Arising in Africa South of the Sahara*, London: Oxford University Press, 1957.

Hall, D. G. E, *A History of South-East Asia*, London: Macmillan, 1961.

Hargreaves, J. R., *Decolonization in Africa*, Basingstoke: Macmillan, 1988.

Harper, T., *The End of Empire and the Making of Malaya*, Cambridge: Cambridge University Press, 1999.

Havinden, M. and Meredith, D., *Colonialism and Development. Britain and its Tropical Colonies, 1850–1960*, London: Routledge, 1993.

Heinlein, F., *British Government Policy and Decolonisation, 1945–1963*, London: Frank Cass, 2002.

Henry, P. and Stone, C., *The Newer Caribbean. Decolonization, Democracy and Development*, Philadelphia, PA: Institute for the Study of Human Issues, 1983.

Holland, R. F., *European Decolonization, 1919–1981. An Introductory Survey*, London: Macmillan, 1985.

Huxley, E. and Perham, M., *Race and Politics in Kenya*, London: Faber, 1955.

Jalal, A., *The Sole Spokesman. Jinnah, the Muslim League and the Demand for Pakistan*, Cambridge: Cambridge University Press, 1985.

Jansen, G. H., *Afro-Asia and Non-Alignment*, London: Faber, 1966.

Kabaka of Buganda, *Desecration of My Kingdom*, London: Constable, 1967.

Kahin, G. McT., *Nationalism and Revolution in Indonesia*, Ithaca, NY: Cornell University Press, 1952.

Kelly, J. D. and Kaplan, M., *Represented Communities. Fiji and World Decolonization*, Chicago, IL: University of Chicago Press, 2001.

Kenyatta, Y., *Facing Mount Kenya. The Tribal Life of the Gikuyu*, London: Mercury Books, 1961 (First edn 1938).

Kenyatta, Y., *Suffering without Bitterness. The Founding of the Kenya Nation*, Nairobi: East African Publishing House, 1968.

Kerkvliet, B. J., *The Huk Rebellion. A Study of Peasant Revolt in the Philippines*, Berkeley, CA: University of California Press, 1977.

Knight, F. W., *The Caribbean. The Genesis of a Fragmented Nationalism*, New York: Oxford University Press, 1990.

Kratoska, P., *The Japanese Occupation of Malaya, 1941–1945*, London: Allen and Unwin, 1998.

Kulke, H. and Rothermund, D., *A History of India* (Fourth edn), London: Routledge, 2004.

Leakey, L. S. B., *Defeating Mau Mau*, London: Methuen, 1954.

Leys, C., *The Rise and Fall of Development Theory*, Nairobi/London: East African Educational Publishers/ James Currey, 1996.

Listowel, J., *The Making of Tanganyika*, London: Chatto and Windus, 1965.

Lofchie, M., *Zanzibar. Background to Revolution*, Princeton, NJ: Princeton University Press, 1965.

Louis, W. R., *Imperialism at Bay. The United States and the Decolonization of the British Empire, 1941–1945*, Oxford: Clarendon Press, 1977 (Repr. 2003).

Louis, W. R., *The British Empire in the*

Middle East, 1945–1951. Arab Nationalism, the United States and Postwar Imperialism, Oxford: Clarendon Press, 1984.

Low, D. A., *Buganda in Modern History*, London: Faber, 1971.

Low, D. A., *The Eclipse of Empire*, Cambridge: Cambridge University Press, 1991.

Low, D. A. and Pratt, R. C., *Buganda and British Overrule, 1900–1955*, London: Oxford University Press, 1960.

Mackenzie, W. J. M. and Robinson, K., *Five Elections in Africa*, Oxford: Clarendon Press, 1960.

McMahon, R. J., *Colonialism and Cold War. The United States and the Struggle for Indonesian Independence*, Ithaca, NY: Cornell University Press, 1981.

McMahon, R. J., *The Limits of Empire. The United States and Southeast Asia since World War II*, New York: Columbia University Press, 1999.

McQueen, N., *The Decolonization of Portuguese Africa. Metropolitan Revolution and the Dissolution of Empire*, London: Longman, 1997.

Maddy-Weizman, B., *The Crystalization of the Arab State System, 1945–1954*, Syracuse, NY: Syracuse University Press, 1993.

Marshall, D., *Singapore's Struggle for Nationhood, 1945–1959*, Singapore: University Education Press, 1971.

Mamdani, M., *Citizen and Subject. Contemporary Africa and the Legacy of Late Colonialism*, Princeton, NJ: Princeton University Press, 1996.

Mandle, J. R., *Patterns of Caribbean Development. An Interpretative Essay on Economic Change*, New York: Gordon and Breach, 1982.

Mazrui, A. A., *Towards a Pax Africana. A Study of Ideology and Ambition*, London: Weidenfeld and Nicolson, 1967.

Mboya, T., *Freedom and After*, London: Andre Deutsch, 1963.

Meek, C. K, *Land Law and Custom in the Colonies*, London: Frank Cass, 1968.

Michel, M., *Décolonisations et émergence du tiers monde*, Paris: Hachette, 1993.

Mommsen, W. and Osterhammel, J. (eds), *Imperialism and After. Continuities and Discontinuities*, London: Allen and Unwin, 1986.

Moore, R. J., *Escape from Empire. The Attlee Government and the Indian Problem*, Oxford: Clarendon Press, 1983.

Morris, H. F. and Read, J. A., *Uganda. The Devolopment of its Laws and Constitution*, London: Stevens and Sons, 1966.

Morris-Jones, W. H. and Fischer, G., *Decolonisation and After*, London: Frank Cass, 1980.

Mungazi, D., *The Mind of Black Africa*, Westport, CT: Greenwood, 1996.

Nyerere, J., *Freedom and Unity. Selections from Writings and Speeches, 1952–1965*, London: Oxford University Press, 1966.

Ogot, B. A., *Decolonization and Independence in Kenya, 1940–1993*, Oxford: James Currey, 1995.

Oostindie, G. and Klinkers, I., *Decolonising the Caribbean. Dutch Policies in a Comparative Perspective*, Amsterdam: Amsterdam University Press, 2003.

Peek, P. and Standing, G. (eds), *State Policies and Migration in Latin America and the Caribbean*, London: Croom Helm, 1982.

Porath, Y., *In Search of Arab Unity, 1930–1945*, London: Frank Cass, 1965.

Poulgrain, G., *The Genesis of Konfrontasi. Malaysia, Brunei, Indonesia, 1945–1965*, London: Hurst, 1998.

Ramakrishna, K., *Emergency Propaganda. The Winning of Malayan Heart and*

Minds, 1948–1958, Richmond, Surrey: Curzon, 2002.

Roff, W. R., *The Origins of Malay Nationalism*, New Haven, CT: Yale University Press, 1967.

Rossberg, C. G. Jr and Nottingham, J., *The Myth of Mau Mau. Nationalism in Kenya*, New York: Praeger, 1966.

Rothermund, D., *Die politische Willensbildung in Indien, 1900–1960*, Wiesbaden: Harrassowitz, 1965.

Rothermund, D., *The Phases of Indian Nationalism*, Bombay: Nachiketa, 1971.

Rothermund, D., *Government, Landlord and Peasant in India. Agrarian Relations under British Rule, 1865–1935*, Wiesbaden: Steiner, 1978.

Rothermund, D., *Mahatma Gandhi. Der Revolutionär der Gewaltlosigkeit. Eine politische Biographie*, München: Piper, 1989.

Rothermund, D., *India in the Great Depression, 1929–1939*, New Delhi: Manohar, 1992.

Rothermund, D., *The Global Impact of the Great Depression*, London: Routledge, 1996.

Rothermund, D., *The Role of the State in South Asia and Other Essays*, New Delhi: Manohar, 2000.

Ryan, D. and Pungong, V. (eds), *The United States and Decolonization. Power and Freedom*, Basingstoke: Macmillan, 2000.

Sanger, C., *Malcolm Macdonald. Bringing an End to Empire*, Montreal: McGill University Press, 1995.

Schwartz, S. B. (ed.), *Tropical Babylons. Sugar and the Making of the Atlantic World, 1450–1680*, Chapel Hill, NC: University of North Carolina Press, 2004.

Shipway, M., *The Road to War. France and Vietnam, 1944–1947*, Providence, RI: Berghahn, 1996.

Sieberg, H., *Colonial Development. Die Grundlagen moderner Entwicklungspolitik durch Großbritannien, 1919–1949*, Stuttgart: Steiner, 1985.

Silcock, T. H. and Fisk, E. K. (eds), *The Political Economy of Independent Malaya*, Canberra: The Australian National University, 1963.

Slater, M., *The Trial of Yomo Kenyatta*, London: Mercury Books, 1965.

Sopiee, M. N., *From Malayan Union to Singapore Separation*, Kuala Lumpur: Penerbit Universiti Malaya, 1974.

Springhall, J., *Decolonization since 1945*, London: Palgrave, 2001.

Stora, B., *Algeria, 1830–2000. A Short History*, Ithaca, NY: Cornell University Press, 2001.

Stubbs, R., *Hearts and Minds in Guerrilla Warfare. The Malayan Emergency, 1948–1960*, Singapore: Oxford University Press, 1993.

Le Sueur, J. D. (ed.), *The Decolonization Reader*, New York: Routledge, 2003.

Tarling, N., *The Fall of Imperial Britain in Southeast Asia*, London: Oxford University Press, 1995.

Tarling, N., *Britain, Southeast Asia and the Onset of the Cold War, 1945–1950*, Cambridge: Cambridge University Press, 1998.

Tarling, N., (ed.), *The Cambridge History of Southeast Asia*, 4 vols, Cambridge: Cambridge University Press, 2000 (Vol. IV deals with the period from the Second World War to the present).

Taylor, A. M., *Indonesian Independence and the United Nations*, London: Stevens and Sons, 1960.

Tertrais, H., *La Piastre et le Fusil. Le Coût de la guerre d'Indochine*, Paris: Ministère de L'Économie, 2002.

Tordoff, W., *Government and Politics in Tanzania*, Nairobi: East African Publishing House, 1967.

Tordoff, W., *Government and Politics in*

Africa (Third edn), Basingstoke: Macmillan, 1997.

Vaillant, J. G., *Black, French and African. A Life of Léopold Sédar Senghor*, Cambridge, MA: Harvard University Press, 1990.

Welensky, R., *Welensky's 4000 Days. The Life and Death of the Federation of Rhodesia and Nyasaland*, London: Collins, 1964.

Williams, B. F., *Stains on My Name, War in my Veins. Guyana and the Politics of Cultural Struggle*, Durham, NC: Duke University Press, 1991.

Wolpert, S., *Jinnah of Pakistan*, New York: Oxford University Press, 1984.

Zips, W., *Black Rebels. African Caribbean Freedom Fighters in Jamaica*, Kingston: Ian Randle, 1999.

INDEX

Note: The index does not cover the NOTES and the BIBLIOGRAPHY. Only authors whose work has been discussed in the text have been listed here. General terms such as "colonialism, decolonization, nation, nationalism, transfer of power" are not included in the index. Organizations which are better known by their abbreviated names (e.g. POLISARIO, UNITA etc.) are listed accordingly. The full names have been added in parentheses.

Routledge History

The Decolonization Reader
Edited by James Le Sueur

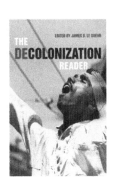

The process of decolonization transformed colonial and European metropolitan societies culturally, politically and economically. Its legacy continues to affect postcolonial politics as well as cultural and intellectual life in Europe and its former colonies and overseas territories. Grouped around the most salient themes, this compilation includes discussions of metropolitan politics, gender, sexuality, race, culture, nationalism and economy, and thereby offers a comparative and interdisciplinary assessment of decolonization.

The Decolonization Reader will provide scholars and students with a thorough understanding of the impact of decolonization on world history and cross-cultural encounters worldwide.

Hb 0-415-23116-7 Pb 0-415-23117-5

Routledge History
Decolonization, 2ⁿᵈ Edition
Raymond F. Betts

The mid-twentieth century saw the end of colonial empires, a global phenomenon that brought about profound changes and created enormous problems. Decolonization played a major part in shaping the contemporary world order and the domestic development of newly emerging states in the 'Third World'.

In the second edition of this concise introduction to the phenomenon, Raymond Betts brings the discussion up to date and looks at contemporary concerns such as the growth of Islamic Fundamentalism, 9/11, globalization and the AIDS pandemic.

Hb 0-415-31820-3 Pb 0-415-31821-1

Available at all good bookshops
For ordering and further information please visit:
www.routledge.com

A History of India, 4th Edition
Hermann Kulke and Dietmar Rothermund

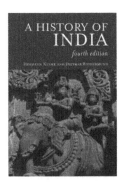

Reviews of the previous editions:
'India produced an amazing succession of inter-esting cultures across five millennia and *A History of India* covers that in eight serious, balanced and readable chapters' – *Times Higher Educational Supplement*

'The most comprehensive history of India today' – *Journal Asiatique*

A History of India presents the grand sweep of Indian history from antiquity to the present in a compact and readable survey. The authors examine the major political, economic, social and cultural forces which have shaped the history of the subcontinent. Providing an authoritative and detailed account Hermann Kulke and Dietmar Rothermund emphasise and analyse the structural pattern of Indian history.

Hb 0-415-32919-1 Pb 0-415-32920-5

A History of the World from the 20th to the 21st Century
J.A.S Grenville

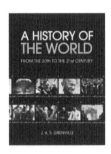

Reviews of previous editions:
'A sweeping synopsis for the history buff' –
Philadelphia Inquirer

'This book by the masterful international relations historian, Grenville, already finds primacy of place in the reading lists of most university courses as the single definitive history of this century' – *The Journal of the United Service Institution in India*

With the onset of decolonisation, the rise and fall of fascism and communism, the technological revolution and the rapidly increasing power of the US, the world since 1900 has witnessed global change on an immense scale. Providing a comprehensive survey of the key events and personalities of this period through the world, this acclaimed history has been updated throughout to take account of events including 9/11, the second Gulf War and the enlargement of the European Union.

Hb 0-41528954-8 Pb 0-415-28955-6

Available at all good bookshops
For ordering and further information please visit:
www.routledge.com

Lightning Source UK Ltd.
Milton Keynes UK
UKOW07f1134130115

244403UK00005B/136/P